STYLE IN FICTION

ENGLISH LANGUAGE SERIES

General Editor:
RANDOLPH QUIRK

STYLE IN FICTION

A Linguistic Introduction to English Fictional Prose

Second edition

GEOFFREY LEECH
Emeritus Professor of Linguistics and English Language,
Lancaster University

MICK SHORT
Professor of English Language and Literature,
Lancaster University

PEARSON
Longman

Harlow, England • London • New York • Boston • San Francisco • Toronto
Sydney • Tokyo • Singapore • Hong Kong • Seoul • Taipei • New Delhi
Cape Town • Madrid • Mexico City • Amsterdam • Munich • Paris • Milan

PEARSON EDUCATION LIMITED

Edinburgh Gate
Harlow CM20 2JE
United Kingdom
Tel: +44 (0)1279 623623
Fax: +44 (0)1279 431059
Website: www.pearsoned.co.uk

First edition 1981
Second edition published in Great Britain in 2007

© Pearson Education Limited 2007

The right of Geoffrey Leech and Mick Short to be identified as authors of this
work has been asserted by them in accordance with the
Copyright, Designs and Patents Act 1998.

ISBN: 978-0-582-78409-3

British Library Cataloguing in Publication Data
A CIP catalogue record for this book can be obtained from the British Library

Library of Congress Cataloging in Publication Data
A CIP catalog record for this book can be obtained from the Library of
Congress

10 9 8 7 6 5 4 3 2 1
10 09 08 07

Set by 35 in 9/11.5pt Palatino
Printed in Malaysia (CTP-VVP)

The Publisher's policy is to use paper manufactured from sustainable forests.

Contents

Contents

Contents

Foreword

Since the first volumes of the *English Language Series* appeared there has been something like a revolution in the relation between linguistic and literary studies, in part through the mediation of the anthropological 'structuralists'. Numerous critics have turned to the work of professional linguists and equipped themselves with a far sharper knowledge of language. At the same time (and again in part through the same mediating influences), linguists have come to take a far more sophisticated interest in literature. Where the goal was once little more than the assembly of linguistic 'facts' that might (just might) be used by literary critics, we now find linguists confidently making critical analyses that contribute directly to literary interpretation and evaluation.

In this revolution, Geoffrey Leech has played a leading part – testified, for example, by an earlier volume in this series, *A Linguistic Guide to English Poetry*. In the present book, in which he is joined by his colleague Mick Short, a still closer approximation is achieved between the role of linguist and critic. The field – prose fiction – is one in which, as the authors explain in their Introduction, the linguist's contribution has hitherto been relatively slight, because the small-scale structures on which linguists have in the past most successfully focused are more amenable to discussion in the context of analysing poetry. But in recent years, more and more linguists have extended their scope 'beyond the sentence', and studies of discourse have now become sufficiently developed to give promise of far more insightful linguistic work on extensive prose texts than was conceivable a generation ago.

These convergences of interest have produced a new 'stylistics' in which linguist and critic can alike work without their ultimately differing union cards being visible and hence, increasingly, without aridly raising demarcation disputes. *Style in Fiction* is a book of precisely this genre. Though written by scholars who are undoubtedly (but certainly not solely) linguists, a quarter-century has shown that it is read with equal pleasure and profit by other linguists and by those whose predominant interest lies in the critical study of literature. Small wonder that in 2005 it was awarded the 25th Anniversary Prize by the Poetics and Linguistics Association.

Now, in its new edition, the book's value has been radically enhanced. A great deal has been written in the field of stylistics in the past 25 years, not least by the authors themselves and the scholars worldwide that they have inspired. In consequence, many revisions have been made to the book and many references added. Moreover, the authors have enlarged their work by the addition of the substantial, new Chapters 11 and 12.

Style in Fiction has long held a distinguished place in the *English Language Series*: I am proud to greet so splendid a second edition.

RANDOLPH QUIRK
General Editor
University College London
August 2006

Preface to the second edition

Over the last 25 years we have been asked on a number of occasions to produce a second edition of *Style in Fiction*. Until now we have resisted this urge because (a) we have always been involved in other, new, projects which have excited our interest and (b) for some considerable time there would not have been that much that we would have wanted to change. There were plenty of things we would have wanted to *add*, but as the English edition of '*SIF*', as we came to call it, was already some 400 pages long, we were rather hesitant at the thought of taxing our poor long-suffering readers even further. Even in 1979 (when the manuscript was finished) we had resisted a strong urge to add a chapter on the structural analysis of plot and its relation to the interpretation of fiction, on the grounds that the manuscript was already over-long.

But then in 2001 we were asked to add an extra chapter for a Japanese translation of our book (eventually published in 2003) and twenty years after the original publication of the book seemed a good time to take stock. This extra chapter took the form of a review of what had happened in stylistics since *Style in Fiction* (1981) was published.

Soon after the Japanese translation appeared, our British publishers re-approached us about a second edition of *Style in Fiction*, and although it would have been too big an undertaking to go through the whole manuscript, updating it in detail in the light of the large amount of work that has taken place since then, the fact that we already had an extra chapter which we could use as a draft gave us the idea of adding two chapters to the original, which is what we have now done for this second edition. The first of these two chapters, Chapter 11, is based on the extra chapter for the 2003 Japanese translation, but updated further. It reviews what has happened in stylistics, in particular prose stylistics, since 1981, and indicates in general terms how we think the book would be different if we were writing it now, by indicating what we would want to add and what we would want to change. We hope that this review will help those new to the field to understand the developments in stylistics of the last 25 years, and in particular developments relating to prose fiction. The second added chapter is an analysis of a short story by T.F. Powys in the light of those new developments in the stylistic treatment of narrative.

When we wrote *Style in Fiction* we had no idea how well-received it was going to be. Indeed, we did not know how our academic peers would react to it. But the book has now been continuously in print from 1981 to 2006, the date of this preface, and has been translated into Malay as well as Japanese, suggesting that it has been of some use to others. A Chinese edition (in English) has also been produced. *SIF* has become a course reader for advanced stylistics courses worldwide and has been used not just by those working on prose fiction in English but also by scholars and students of the literature of other modern languages (e.g. German and French).

In July 2005 the members of the Poetics and Linguistics Association (PALA) awarded to *Style in Fiction* the PALA 25th Anniversary Prize for being the most influential book in stylistics since the association was established in 1980. A one-day symposium on style in fiction was organised at Lancaster University on 11 March 2006 to celebrate the prize, and digital video-recordings of the talks given at the symposium were made. They are available until May 2111 (in the first instance) from the members-only parts of the PALA website (http://www.pala.ac.uk/).

So, with this renewal of interest, we felt somewhat obliged to provide the two extra chapters for this second edition of *Style in Fiction*. Other changes to the second edition are an updating of the Acknowledgements, the list of Contents, the Further Reading section, and the Bibliography, particularly incorporating the many references to publications since 1980 cited in Chapters 11 and 12. Other changes are matters of correction to the first edition, as well as a few necessary changes to the notes to the earlier Chapters 1–10, for example, where bibliographical references have had to be changed.

GEOFFREY LEECH
MICK SHORT
Lancaster University
July 2006

Acknowledgements

We thank all those friends who have helped to make this a better book than it would otherwise have been. Among them, we are particularly grateful to Joan Lord Hall, Roger Fowler and Randolph Quirk, who were generous enough to send us valuable and detailed comments on the whole book in manuscript. We are also indebted to a number of colleagues in the School of English, especially to Richard Dutton, James Hurford and Willy van Peer, who gave us their constructive criticisms of certain sections of the book. We thank Hilary Short for help throughout, especially with proof-reading, and Valerie Lomas has earned our gratitude for being our excellent and long-suffering typist.

GL, MS
Lancaster University
September 1979

Acknowledgements to the second edition

We would like to thank Derek Bousfield, Beatrix Busse, Lesley Jeffries and Dan McIntyre for reading and commenting on one or both of the two extra chapters in the second edition. Brian Walker deserves our sincere thanks for reading and commenting on material for us, and also for helping in the annotation of the story in Chapter 12 with speech and thought presentation analysis. We would also like to give very special thanks to Yufang Ho for proof-reading the scanned version of the first edition for errors, and for her sterling work on the bibliography to the second edition.

GL, MS
Lancaster University
July 2006

Publisher's acknowledgements

The publishers are grateful to the following for permission to reproduce copyright material:

David Higham Associates for an extract from *The Great Gatsby* by F. Scott Fitzgerald from *The Bodley Head Scott Fitzgerald* (The Bodley Head Ltd, 1963); The Random House Group Ltd and Random House, Inc. for an extract from *Requiem for a Nun* by William Faulkner Ruth Ford, adapter, copyright 1950, 1951 by William Faulkner and Ruth Ford, published by Chatto & Windus. Reprinted by permission of The Random House Group Ltd and Random House, Inc.; Penguin Group (USA) Inc. for extracts from *A Portrait of the Artist as a Young Man* by James Joyce, copyright 1916 by B. W. Huebsch, copyright 1944 by Nora Joyce, copyright © 1964 by the Estate of James Joyce. Used by permission of Viking Penguin, a division of Penguin Group (USA) Inc.; Penguin Group (USA) Inc. for extracts from *One Flew Over the Cuckoo's Nest* by Ken Kesey, copyright © 1962, renewed © 1990 by Ken Kesey. Used by permission of Viking Penguin, a division of Penguin Group (USA) Inc.; The Wylie Agency for an extract from *The Armies of the Night* by Norman Mailer, © Norman Mailer. Reproduced by permission of the Wylie Agency (UK) Ltd; Pollinger Limited for the short story *The Bucket and the Rope* by T. F. Powys, originally printed in *No Painted Plumage* (Chatto and Windus, 1941). Reproduced by permission of Pollinger Limited and the proprietor; Penguin Group (USA) Inc., Penguin Books Ltd and Curtis Brown Group Ltd for extracts from *Of Mice and Men* by John Steinbeck, copyright 1937, renewed © 1965 by John Steinbeck. Used by permission of Viking Penguin, a division of Penguin Group (USA) Inc., Penguin Books Ltd and Curtis Brown Group Ltd.

In some instances we have been unable to trace the owners of copyright material, and we would appreciate any information that would enable us to do so.

Introduction

Aim

An earlier book in this series (*A Linguistic Guide to English Poetry*)[1] was written with the aim of showing the student of English that examining the language of a literary text can be a means to a fuller understanding and appreciation of the writer's artistic achievement. The present book is written with the same aim in mind, this time taking prose fiction, not poetry, as the object of study.

The book takes its direction from the 'new stylistics' which has applied techniques and concepts of modern linguistics to the study of literature.[2] This does not mean that we expect our readers to know a great deal about linguistics: we shall aim to interpret the principles and methods of linguistic study in a way that demands relatively little technical knowledge. Readers who are familiar with some basic concepts and traditional terms in grammar, phonetics and rhetoric will, we hope, find themselves at home in this book, and even readers new to language study should have little difficulty if they follow up occasional explanations and references given in the notes (see especially section 3.2). The main thing is that the reader should approach the subject of style with appreciative curiosity, and should take a sympathetic view of our guiding maxim, which is that to make progress in understanding style one has to make use of an explicit understanding of language – not just language in a literary context.

This means that we propose not to dissect the flower of beauty (for that is a misleading metaphor), but at least to scrutinise it carefully, even, from time to time, under a microscope. For those who are reluctant to do this, we can do no better than to quote the eminent linguist-critic Leo Spitzer:

> I would maintain that to formulate observation by means of words is not to cause the artistic beauty to evaporate in vain intellectualities; rather, it makes for a widening and deepening of the aesthetic taste. It is only

a frivolous love that cannot survive intellectual definition; great love prospers with understanding.[3]

Spitzer's insistence that the smallest detail of language can unlock the 'soul' of a literary work is an extreme expression of the philosophy to which we subscribe: by making ourselves explain *how* a particular effect or meaning is achieved we not only understand better how it is achieved (which in itself is essential to the critical task of explanation) but also gain a greater appreciation of what the writer has created.

Language in prose and poetry

The student of literature is, perhaps, more likely to accept the usefulness of linguistic analysis in the study of poetry than prose. The poet, more obviously than the prose writer, does 'interesting things' with language. And if one wanted to find a definition of poetry that went deeper than the run-of-the-mill dictionary definition, it might be that whereas in poetry, aesthetic effect cannot be separated from the creative manipulation of the linguistic code, in prose, it tends to reside more in other factors (such as character, theme, argument) which are expressed through, rather than inherent in, language. Yet the great novelists of the English language have been, arguably without exception, also great artists in the use of words, and the challenge remains of trying to explain the nature of that artistry, and how it integrates with the larger artistic achievement of the writer.

The twelve-year gap which separates this volume from its companion volume on poetry is perhaps symbolic of the more problematic nature of the task. The challenge is greater because the effects of prose style, and their sources in the language, are often more unobtrusive than those of poetic language. While a condensed poetic metaphor, or a metrical pattern, will jump to the attention as something which distinguishes the language of poetry from everyday language, the distinguishing features of a prose style tend to become detectable over longer stretches of text, and to be demonstrable ultimately only in quantitative terms. And the sheer bulk of prose writing is intimidating; linguistic techniques are more readily adapted to the miniature exegesis of a lyric poem, than to the examination of a full-scale novel. In prose, the problem of how to select – what sample passages, what features to study – is more acute, and the incompleteness of even the most detailed analysis more apparent.

Because of these difficulties of scale and concentration, it is understandable that the study of prose style has tended to suffer from 'bittiness'. A writer's style has all too frequently been reduced to one feature, or a handful of features. Some aspects of style, such as methods of speech presentation (see Chapter 10), have been recognised as 'interesting', and have been

intensively studied, whereas others have been neglected. And where the
data are so vast and varied, there is the inevitable temptation to retreat into
vague generalisation. Although the 'new stylistics' has brought illuminating studies of this or that stylistic feature of this or that work or writer, no
adequate theory of prose style has emerged. Again, no one seems to have provided a satisfactory and reliable methodology for prose style analysis. Even Spitzer confided to his readers:

> How often, with all the theoretical experience of method accumulated
> in me over the years, have I stared blankly, quite similar to one of my
> beginning students, at a page that would not yield its magic. The only
> way out of this state of unproductivity is to read and reread.[4]

The critic Ian Watt began his notable explication of Henry James's style
in the first paragraph of *The Ambassadors* with a similar confession that he
was 'virtually helpless ... as far as any fully developed and acceptable
technique of explicating prose is concerned'.[5] Yet another writer on prose
style, Edward Corbett,[6] recommended the laborious practice of copying out
the whole text, as a preliminary to style analysis – a means of focusing the
mind which is not to be underrated, but would have been less practical had
Corbett chosen *Clarissa* rather than *A Modest Proposal* for his text! Coming
to terms with prose style has seemed a hit-and-miss matter even to its more
successful practitioners.

Where linguistics comes in

These cautionary remarks will, we hope, gently deter readers from expecting too much from this book. We shall try to give the breadth of coverage
which previous studies have lacked, and this means putting forward, in
informal terms, an overall 'theory' or 'model' of prose style (see especially
sections 1.6–1.7, 4.5–4.7). We shall also propose a general informal classification of features of style as a tool of analysis which can be applied to any
text (see section 3.1). But these are attempts to give shape and system to a
field of study in which much remains unclear, and hidden beneath the
threshold of observation. As we argue in Chapter 2, stylistics, as the study
of the relation between linguistic form and literary function, cannot be
reduced to mechanical objectivity. In both the literary and the linguistic
spheres much rests on the intuition and personal judgment of the reader,
for which a system, however good, is an aid rather than a substitute. There
will always remain, as Dylan Thomas says, 'the mystery of having been
moved by words'.

But let us now turn to a more positive viewpoint. In the twenty or more
years since Spitzer and Watt wrote the articles already cited, there have

been important developments in the linguistic study of prose style. Just as important, linguistics itself has developed from a discipline with narrowly defined formal concerns to a more comprehensive, if more inchoate discipline, in which the role of language in relation to the conceptualisation and communication of meaning has been fruitfully investigated. There have been new ways of looking at language in psychological, sociological and philosophical terms, and their application to literature has been tentatively explored. The time seems right, then, for a book which aims to synthesise such viewpoints in the practical study of literary language.

We speak of 'viewpoints' in the plural, because there is no single body of theory to which one can appeal in applying the results of linguistic research. The model of Transformational Grammar (see section 1.3.2), which dominated linguistic thinking fifteen years ago, sees language primarily as a capability of the human mind, and therefore highlights the formal and cognitive aspects of language. But Transformational Grammar has been challenged by various other models, particularly those which emphasise the social role of language. Halliday's functional model (see section 1.5) for example sees language as a 'social semiotic', and so directs attention particularly to the communicative and socially expressive functions of language. The same shift of focus has resulted, in a different way, from the influence on linguistics of work by 'ordinary language' philosophers such as Searle (on speech acts, see section 9.1.1) and Grice (on conversational implicature, see section 9.1.2). Yet another set of linguistic traditions, which we may assemble under the name of 'European structuralism', sees the same structural principles of contrast and pattern as underlying varied forms of human activity, and so as equally manifested in language, art and other cultural forms.

If there is a single characteristic which unites these diverse enterprises in linguistics today, it is a tendency to explore for pattern and system below the surface forms of language; to search for the principles of meaning and language use which activate and control the code. In this, the linguist's concerns have moved in directions which are likely to bring them closer to those of the critic. If a text is regarded in objective simplicity as a sequence of symbols on paper, then the modern linguist's scrutiny is not just a matter of looking *at* the text, but of looking *through* the text to its significance.

This is why it would be wrong to expect linguistics to provide an objective, mechanical technique of stylistic analysis. One major concern of stylistics is to check or validate intuitions by detailed analysis, but stylistics is also a dialogue between literary reader and linguistic observer, in which insight, not mere objectivity, is the goal. Linguistic analysis does not replace the reader's intuition, what Spitzer calls the 'click' in the mind; but it may prompt, direct, and shape it into an understanding.

Linguistics places literary uses of language against the background of more 'ordinary' uses of language, so that we see the poet or novelist making use of the same code, the same set of communicative resources, as the journalist, the scientist, or the garden-wall gossip. This is a weakness to the extent that it leads us to trivialise our subject by seeking the common denominator which it shares with banal linguistic transactions. But it is also a strength, for linguistics has taught us that even in its more mundane uses, language is an immensely complex, rich and variable instrument. To call language an 'instrument' in fact devalues it: it is virtually the medium in which human beings, as 'speaking animals', exist, defining for them their relation to their fellow human beings, their culture, even their own identity. It is unthinkable that the literary artist should cut himself adrift from the all-embracing role that language has in our everyday lives. So literary expression is an enhancement, or a creative liberation of the resources of language which we use from day to day. Correspondingly, stylistics builds on linguistics, and in return, stylistics challenges our linguistic frameworks, reveals their deficiencies, and urges us to refine them. In this sense, stylistics is an adventure of discovery for both the critic and the linguist.

The scope and design of this book

Because prose style is such a large subject, we have restricted the material of this book in various ways. First, we have concentrated on *fictional* prose: this is a natural way of limiting our field and permits a more cohesive relation to be established between a writer's style and his subject matter, that is to say the fictional world he portrays (see sections 4.2–4.3, 5.1–5.2, 5.5). At the same time, much of what we say (especially in Part I) can be easily adapted to non-fictional prose. Second, our illustrations are largely taken from the eighteenth to the twentieth centuries, so that we cover the period of the rise and development of the novel as a major literary form. This again gives a certain homogeneity, and releases us from the need to take more than incidental notice of the diachronic perspectives of literary and linguistic history. Thirdly, we concentrate on the practical examination of texts and text extracts: this means that we leave in the background the larger issues of authorial, genre and period style, preferring to focus on the most tangible domain of style, where the reader's response is most immediate, and where the techniques of stylistics can be most demonstrably applied. It will be noted, incidentally, that the *English Language Series* contains several volumes which are complementary to the present book in their coverage of the language of prose.

In Part One, 'Approaches and Methods', we examine first of all (in Chapters 1 and 2) differing views of what style means and how it should be studied. Then, in Chapter 3, we present an informal technique of stylistic analysis, which is illustrated by a comparison of three passages, by Joseph

Conrad, D.H. Lawrence and Henry James. In Chapter 4 we show how style can be studied in terms of forms which are linguistically equivalent at some level (stylistic variants), and the literary or communicative function associated with the choice of one variant or another (stylistic values).

This concept of style is the main basis for Part Two, 'Aspects of Style', in which we investigate different kinds of stylistic value more closely. Chapter 5, 'Language and the fictional world', is the backdrop against which we consider first (Chapter 6) 'mind style' – the way in which language conceptualises the fiction; then (Chapter 7) – the way in which language presents the fiction in linear, textual form; and finally (Chapters 11 and 12)[7] the ways in which language represents the fiction through the social dimension of language use: through the relation between author and reader, and more indirectly, through the participation in literary discourse of fictional speakers and hearers.

Since the purpose of the book is more practical than theoretical, we shall place emphasis throughout on looking at textual illustrations, and the book concludes with a set of exercises and passages for further study. By this means we hope to lead students towards a more active engagement with the study of prose style, so that after working through these passages they can go on to apply similar methods to passages and works of their choice.

Notes

1. G.N. LEECH (1969).
2. 'The new stylistics' is a convenient term used by Roger Fowler for a rather loosely knit body of research which, over the past twenty years, has used the methods and concepts of linguistics in the study of literary style. See his essay of that title in R. FOWLER (1975).
3. Quoted before the Preface to G. HOUGH (1969). The source of this quotation from Spitzer is unknown.
4. L. SPITZER (1948), 27.
5. I. WATT (1960/1969), 269.
6. E.P.J. CORBETT (1969), 86.
7. In this new edition, two further chapters have been added, as explained in the *Preface to the Second Edition*, pp. xii–xiii.

PART ONE

Approaches and Methods

CHAPTER 1

Style and choice

The task of this chapter is to investigate the phenomenon of style in general terms, and so to prepare the ground for the analysis of its various aspects and manifestations in later chapters. We must take account of the various ways in which the word 'style' has been used in the past; but we should be wary of becoming slaves to verbal definition. Definitions are useful only in so far as they encapsulate a particular conception or theory of the phenomena one wishes to study. They can broaden or narrow, illuminate or inhibit the understanding of verbal artistry. So we shall aim to work *through* definitions towards a richer appreciation of what literary style is and how it can best be analysed.

1.1 The domain of style

In its most general interpretation, the word 'STYLE' has a fairly uncontroversial meaning: it refers to the way in which language is used in a given context, by a given person, for a given purpose, and so on. To clarify this, we may adopt the Swiss linguist Saussure's distinction between *langue* and *parole*,[1] *langue* being the code or system of rules common to speakers of a language (such as English), and *parole* being the particular uses of this system, or selections from this system, that speakers or writers make on this or that occasion. One may say, for example, that certain English expressions belong to the official style of weather forecasting ('bright intervals', 'scattered showers', etc.), while other expressions ('lovely day', 'a bit chilly', etc.) belong to the style of everyday conversational remarks about the weather. Style, then, pertains to *parole*: it is selection from a total linguistic repertoire that constitutes a style. This definition does not take us very far, however. In what follows, we shall narrow the scope of the term to something more adapted to the present purpose.

In practice, writers on style have differed a great deal in their understanding of the subject,[2] and one source of disagreement has been the question 'To what or whom do we attribute style?' In the broadest sense, style can be applied to both spoken and written, both 'literary' and 'everyday' varieties of language; but by tradition, it is particularly associated with written literary texts, and this is the sense of the term which will concern us.

Within the field of literary writing, there is again scope for varying definition and emphasis. Sometimes the term has been applied to the linguistic habits of a particular writer ('the style of Dickens, of Proust', etc.); at other times it has been applied to the way language is used in a particular genre, period, school of writing or some combination of these: 'epistolary style', 'early eighteenth-century style', 'euphuistic style', 'the style of Victorian novels', etc. All these uses seem natural and serviceable. It would be artificial to limit our understanding of style to one of them, let us say authorial style, and exclude the others. The only assumption one makes in using such expressions is that in the corpus of writings referred to there are some characteristic uses of language, which are capable of abstraction as a style.

Style is a relational term: we talk about 'the style of *x*', referring through 'style' to characteristics of language use, and correlating these with some extralinguistic *x*, which we may call the stylistic DOMAIN. The *x* (writer, period, etc.) defines some corpus of writings in which the characteristics of language use are to be found. But the more extensive and varied the corpus of writings, the more difficult it is to identify a common set of linguistic habits. This applies even to the concept of authorial style. Traditionally, an intimate connection has been seen between style and an author's personality. This is urged by the Latin tag *Stilus virum arguit* ('The style proclaims the man') and by many later studies and definitions.[3] For that matter, all of us are familiar with the experience of trying, and perhaps managing, to guess the author of a piece of writing simply on the evidence of his language. Sometimes the author's identity is given away by some small detail reflecting a habit of expression or thought, and this seems to confirm that each writer has a linguistic 'thumbprint', an individual combination of linguistic habits which somehow betrays him in all that he writes. But the distinctiveness of personal style can be overemphasised. Even with a writer like Samuel Johnson, who seems to stamp his personality on all that he writes, there is a vast difference between the didactic and expository prose of the essays in *The Rambler*, the simpler narrative prose of much of *Rasselas*, and the more informal discursiveness of his private letters.[4] If it is difficult to generalise about the style of an author, how much more difficult may it be to generalise about the style of a genre or an epoch? The more general the domain, the more general, selective and tentative are the statements about its style.

This brings us to the most specific domain of style, and the one which will be the main focus of this book: we shall be concerned primarily with the style of TEXTS. A text, whether considered as a whole work or as an extract from a work, is the nearest we can get to a homogeneous and specific use of language. It is therefore the natural starting place for the study of style. In a text we can study style in more detail, and with more systematic attention to what words or structures are chosen in preference to others. We can exhibit our material on the page, and examine the interrelations between one choice of language and another. We can thus put our study on a firmer basis of observation and evidence than if we took a broader domain. Of course, it is natural to examine a text in the light of what we know of ambient domains – its author, the period in which it was written, and so on – and to regard it as exemplifying or representing something of more general interest. But it is arguable that the soundness of statements about wider matters such as authorial style relies ultimately on the statements we can make about particular texts. So if we think of style as 'the linguistic characteristics of a particular text', we shall be on the safest ground.

1.2 Stylistics

There is another reason why texts are the natural focus for our study: within a text it is possible to be more specific about how language serves a particular artistic function. Here we touch on the purpose of studying style, and hence on the nature of stylistics.

STYLISTICS, simply defined as the (linguistic) study of style, is rarely undertaken for its own sake, simply as an exercise in describing *what* use is made of language. We normally study style because we want to explain something, and in general, literary stylistics has, implicitly or explicitly, the goal of explaining the relation between language and artistic function. The motivating questions are not so much *what* as *why* and *how*. From the linguist's angle, it is '*Why* does the author here choose this form of expression?' From the literary critic's viewpoint, it is '*How* is such-and-such an aesthetic effect achieved through language?' We should scarcely find the style of Henry James worth studying unless we assumed it could tell us something about James as a literary artist. Style being a relational concept, the aim of literary stylistics is to be relational in a more interesting sense than that already mentioned: to relate the critic's concern of aesthetic appreciation with the linguist's concern of linguistic description. (We use the term 'appreciation' to comprehend both critical evaluation and

11

interpretation, although it is with interpretation that stylistics is more directly concerned.)

A question which is often asked in this connection is, 'At which end do we start, the aesthetic or the linguistic?' But this question assumes that the task of stylistics is to provide a hard-and-fast technology of analysis, which is not the case. The image used by Spitzer of the 'philological circle', the circle of understanding, is more appropriate.[5] Spitzer argued that the task of linguistic–literary explanation proceeded by the movement to and fro from linguistic details to the literary 'centre' of a work or a writer's art. There is a cyclic motion whereby linguistic observation stimulates or modifies literary insight, and whereby literary insight in its turn stimulates further linguistic observation. This motion is something like the cycle of theory formulation and theory testing which underlies scientific method.[6] There is no logical starting point, since we bring to a literary text simultaneously two faculties, however imperfectly developed: our ability to respond to it as a literary work and our ability to observe its language. The cycle is represented in Figure 1.1.

Figure 1.1

For completeness, it must be mentioned that stylistics can have other goals than this. Some of the more rigorous statistical studies of style have had the purpose of discovering the author of works of doubtful attribution.[7] Such investigations have tended to concentrate on linguistic traits which may not necessarily be artistically relevant, such as range of vocabulary, sentence length or frequency of certain conjunctions, on the principle that a writer's genuine 'thumbprint' is more likely to be found in unobtrusive habits beyond conscious artistic control.

This forewarns us of the issue of SELECTION which will be taken up in Chapter 2. In studying style, we have to select what aspects of language matter, and the principle of selection depends on the purpose we have in mind. The authorship 'detective' will try to identify features of text which remain constant whatever the artistic or other motives of the writer, whereas in literary stylistics, features determined by artistic motivation are of primary interest. Not surprisingly, then, literary stylistics and attributional stylistics have tended to move in different orbits.

1.3 Style and content

We have so far limited our interpretation of 'style' and 'stylistics' to match the kind of activity in which we wish to engage: the study of language as used in literary texts, with the aim of relating it to its artistic functions. This does not deny the legitimacy of using these terms differently for other purposes. But there is still one further narrowing of the meaning of STYLE to consider, and this brings us on to more controversial ground, where different definitions of style involve conflicting views of the use of language in literature. Such conflicting views or theories of style will concern us for the remainder of this chapter, but rather than argue that one view is wholly superior to another, we shall try to harmonise the apparent conflicts, so that at the end of the chapter, we shall have worked through to a balanced view of what stylistics is about.

There is a strong tradition of thought which restricts style to those choices which are choices of MANNER rather than MATTER, of EXPRESSION rather than CONTENT. Some such separation is implied in the common definition of style as a 'way of writing' or a 'mode of expression'. This approach may be called DUALIST, because it rests on an assumed dualism, in language, between form and meaning. There is an equally strong academic and literary tradition which assumes the opposite; in Flaubert's words: 'It is like body and soul: form and content to me are one.'[8] Let us call this the MONIST view. Controversy on this issue takes us back to the beginnings of literary theory, to Aristotle and Plato. The controversy has not yet been settled.

1.3.1 Style as the 'dress of thought': one kind of dualism

The distinction between what a writer has to say, and how it is presented to the reader, underlies one of the earliest and most persistent concepts of style: that of style as the 'dress of thought'. Although this metaphor of style as some kind of 'adornment' or 'covering' of thought or meaning is no longer widely current, it frequently appears in Renaissance and rationalist pronouncements on style, and is implicit, for example, in Pope's well-known definition of wit:

> True wit is nature to advantage dressed,
> What oft was thought but ne'er so well expressed.
> > *An Essay on Criticism*

The fact that the 'adornment' theory was entertained for so long deserves some explanation, and its appropriateness cannot be altogether dismissed in the case of 'artificial' styles cultivated by such Renaissance mannerists as Sidney and Lyly. Take part of Lyly's description of his hero at the beginning of *Euphues*, which deserves our attention as 'the first novel in English':

```
This young gallant,
 ⎡ of  ⎡ more wit
 ⎢     ⎣ than wrath      and yet
 ⎣ of  ⎡ more wrath⁹
       ⎣ than wisdom,  ⎡ seeing himself
          ⎡ inferior to ⎢ none in pleasant conceits
          ⎢             ⎣ THOUGHT himself
          ⎣ superior to all in honest conditions,    in so much that
    ⎡ he deemed himself so apt in all things   that
    ⎣ he gave himself almost to nothing   but
       practising of those things commonly which
          are incident to these sharp wits –
 ⎡ fine phrases,
 ⎢ smooth     ⎡ quipping,
 ⎢ merry      ⎢ taunting,
 ⎣ using      ⎢ jesting    ⎡ without mean      and
             ⎣ abusing    ⎣ without measure.
```

As therefore

```
    ⎡ the sweetest rose hath his prickle,
    ⎢ the finest velvet his brack,
    ⎢ the fairest flour his bran,        so
 ⎡  ⎡ the sharpest wit    HATH
 ⎢  ⎢ his wanton will     and
 ⎢  ⎢ the holiest head
 ⎣  ⎣ his wicked way.
```

The elaborate parallelistic structure of these two sentences has been displayed above by placing the parallelisms, or structural equivalences, in brackets. The parallelisms are reinforced by frequent alliteration, indicated by italics. The architecture of parallelism is to some extent in conflict or in counterpoint with the grammatical structure of each sentence, so that the main verb (shown in capitals) occurs in mid-parallelism, and forms (continuing the architectural simile) a concealed centre of gravity, balancing subject against predicate.

It is obviously the aesthetics of form which tends to attract the reader's attention here, rather than the meaning. We might almost go so far as to say that Lyly has embroidered an elaborate garment round the simple idea 'Euphues was a young coxcomb'. If 'adornment' is to be identified in linguistic patterns which have no semantic utility, we can point to the alliterations clustered in the last few lines. We can also point to grammatical parallelisms which, although not devoid of content, seem merely to have an elaborative function, providing further examples of a concept already expressed: 'The sweetest rose hath his prickle' already conveys, by proverbial extension, the meaning 'even the best things are alloyed with bad', and to that extent, the repetition of the pattern in 'the finest velvet his brack, the fairest flour his bran', is redundant. Lyly might not, one imagines, have added his last piece of pattern, the similitude of sanctity, unless he had hit on the alliteration of 'holiest head' and 'wicked way'.

But however plausible the concept of stylistic embellishment appears, even in a favourable case like this there are difficulties. The elaboration of form inevitably brings an elaboration of meaning. Even the repetition in parallel of examples from different spheres of experience ('rose . . . velvet . . . flour . . . wit . . . head') enforces the generality of a didactic principle which is otherwise seen to be particular. The repetition in 'wit . . . wrath . . . wisdom' is not mere repetition, but a progression implying an increasing weightiness of the qualities listed. The parallelism of 'inferior to none in pleasant conceits' and 'superior to all in honest conditions' gives a schematic balance to the image of something light ('pleasant conceits') being weighed against something heavy ('honest conditions'), underlining the faulty logic of Euphues's youthful mind. So the schematism of form cannot be divorced from the schematic relation between the ideas being presented. The 'dress of thought' metaphor retains some appropriacy, but only by virtue of an impression, difficult to justify, that the formal tail is wagging the semantic dog.

A converse implication of the 'dress of thought' view is that it is possible to write in a style which is the nadir of plainness and neutrality. As Wesley put it in an age stylistically more austere than that of Lyly:

Style is the dress of thought; a modest dress,
Neat, but not gaudy, will true critics please.

Pursuing the image further than the modesty of Wesley would permit, we could in theory have a manner of writing in which there is no style, in which content is presented in its nakedness. A more recent variant of this view is that of French stylisticians such as Bally and Riffaterre, that style is that expressive or emotive element of language which is added to the neutral presentation of the message itself.[10] So style need not occur in all texts: for example, Eliza's 'Not bloody likely' in *Pygmalion* by Shaw has an expressiveness, and therefore a style; while the otherwise equivalent monosyllable 'No' does not. More recently, another French writer, Roland Barthes, has referred to the 'transparency' of classical writing, and has postulated a mode of 'writing at degree zero', which, 'initiated by Camus's *Outsider*, achieves a style of absence which is almost an ideal absence of style'.[11]

15

If we take these views literally, we arrive at the notion of style as an optional additive, and there is an obvious problem: how can we judge when the factor of style is absent? Surely every word or expression has *some* associations – emotive, moral, ideological – in addition to its brute sense. It is true that in grammar some linguistic choices may be designated 'unmarked' and 'neutral' in contrast to others: for example, the choice of third-person pronouns (*he, she, they,* etc.) may be regarded as neutral in narration as compared with *I* and *you*. Yet the choice of such a neutral form is as much a linguistic choice as any other, and may have implications which may be fruitfully examined in stylistics: the third-person pronoun, for example, distances the author and the reader from the character it denotes. So at least it is wiser, as a matter of terminological decision, to say that style is a property of *all* texts. In theory, this still allows one to postulate a completely 'neutral' style, although in practice this postulate is difficult to sustain.

Once again, we can recognise a certain truth in what is otherwise a misleading conception of style. It is hard to deny, from a common-sense reader's point of view, that texts differ greatly in their degree of stylistic interest or markedness; or that some texts are more 'transparent', in the sense of showing forth their meaning directly, than others. In section 1.4, we shall try to give more substance to the metaphor of 'transparency' and 'opacity' in style. But for all practical purposes, the idea of style as an 'optional extra' must be firmly rejected.

1.3.2 Style as manner of expression: another kind of dualism

Thus we come to a more general and tenable version of dualism: that every writer necessarily makes choices of expression, and that it is in these choices, in a particular 'way of putting things', that style resides. So understood, dualism can be contrasted with monism in simple diagrammatic terms as presented in Figure 1.2.

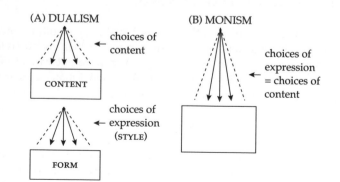

Figure 1.2

Figures 1.2(A) and (B) show the contrast between dualism and monism from an author's point of view. The dualist holds that there can be different ways of conveying the same content. The monist holds that this is a mistake, and that any alteration of form entails a change of content.

The dualist gains credence from the everyday use of the word 'style' as a 'manner of doing something', as reflected in dictionary definitions, and as applied, outside language, to other art forms such as music, painting and architecture, and to varied activities such as playing the piano or playing tennis. In such activities, there are assumed to be some INVARIANT elements which have to be performed (e.g. conforming to the rules of tennis), but that there are VARIANT ways in which the individual may perform them (e.g. in choice of backhands, forehands, volleys). Such an analogy is used by Richard Ohmann, a modern apostle of dualism:

> A style is a way of writing – that is what the word means. . . . In general, [style] applies to human action that is partly invariant and partly variable. . . . Now this picture leads to few complications if the action is playing the piano or playing tennis. . . . But the relevant division between fixed and variable components in literature is by no means so obvious. What *is* content, and what is form, or style? The attack on a dichotomy of form and content has been persistent in modern criticism; to change so much as a word, the argument runs, is to change the meaning as well. This austere doctrine has a certain theoretical appeal. . . . Yet at the same time this doctrine leads to the altogether counterintuitive conclusion that there can be no such thing as style, or that style is simply a part of content.
>
> To put the problem more concretely, the idea of style implies that the words on the page might have been different, or differently arranged, without a corresponding difference in substance.[12]

To back up the intuitive sense that there are 'different ways of saying the same thing', Ohmann (in the article quoted) enlists the authority of linguistics. He offers the following among paraphrases of 'After dinner, the senator made a speech':

[1] When dinner was over, the senator made a speech.*
[2] A speech was made by the senator after dinner.
[3] The senator made a postprandial oration.

and points out that these are variants of the original in a sense which is not true, for example, of 'Columbus was brave' or 'Columbus was nautical'.

---

* In this, as in subsequent chapters, we number examples and extracts only where we need to refer to them in the text.

Apart from the Johnsonian 'postprandial oration', the differences among [1]–[3] are chiefly grammatical rather than lexical; and the grammatical aspect of style is the one on which Ohmann concentrates. He appeals to transformational grammar, which postulates two main kinds of rules, phrase structure rules and transformational rules, and argues that optional transformational rules are the ones which determine style. Informally, these are rules which change the form of a basic sentence type without changing its lexical content. Thus one rule changes an active construction to a passive:

[4] Columbus discovered America → America was discovered by Columbus.

Other transformational rules have the effect of combining two or more simple sentence structures into a single more complex unit:

[5] Night fell
    The wind freshened } → Night fell and the wind freshened.
[6] We visited the house
    The house was still empty } → We visited the house, which was still empty.

Still other rules cause the deletion of elements from the structure:

[7] The house was empty and the house was neglected
    → The house was empty and neglected.

Since such rules can be optionally applied to the same basic sentence structures, they provide a linguistic basis for the notion of paraphrase, and hence (according to Ohmann) for the grammar of style. We can study in these terms what an author *has* written against the background of what he *might have* written, had he failed to apply certain transformations, or chosen to apply others instead. For illustration, Ohmann hits on the device of reversing the effects of transformations, and pointing out the effect this artificial operation has on style. He takes as an example a 'typically Faulknerian' passage from *The Bear*, part of a labyrinthine sentence extending over nearly two pages. Here we give only the first part of Ohmann's illustration:

[8] . . . the desk and the shelf above it on which rested the ledgers in which McCaslin recorded the slow outward trickle of food and supplies and equipment which returned each fall as cotton made and ginned and sold . . .

This is then 'destransformed' as follows:

[9] ... the desk. The shelf was above it. The ledgers rested on the shelf. The ledgers were old. McCaslin recorded the trickle of food in the ledgers. McCaslin recorded the trickle of supplies in the ledgers. McCaslin recorded the trickle of equipment in the ledgers. The trickle was slow. The trickle was outward. The trickle returned each fall as cotton. The cotton was made. The cotton was ginned. The cotton was sold ...

The resulting 'Ohmannised' Faulkner consists of a sequence of short, atomic sentences, not far removed from the most elementary sentences, or KERNEL sentences,[13] postulated by the theory of transformational grammar that Ohmann uses. Yet to arrive at this version, Ohmann has nullified the effect of only a few transformations: those transformations used to form coordinated sentences (*cf* [5]), relative clauses (*cf* [6]), and comparative clauses, together with certain deletion rules. His point is that the eliminationof these transformations also eliminates the Faulknerian quality of the passage, and that therefore Faulkner's style is distinguished by a heavy use of these transformations, which, in general terms, happen to be rules which introduce and condense syntactic complexity.

Ohmann goes on to apply this technique to passages regarded as characteristic of other authors: Hemingway, James and Lawrence. Predictably, the terse prose of Hemingway is found to lack the transformational complexities typical of Faulkner: which is not to say that Hemingway is innocent of transformations, only that he tends to use transformations of a different kind.

Although we cannot go into the technicalities of Ohmann's method, it is worth mentioning that the apparatus he used was that of an earlier version of transformational grammar, one which subsequently underwent profound modifications.[14] The assumption that transformations represent paraphrase relations has been undermined, for example, by consideration of cases in which the passive and deletion transformations illustrated in [4] and [7] do not preserve the same 'logical content':

Many arrows did not hit the target ≠ The target was not hit by
                                                    many arrows.
Some girls are tall and some girls are short ≠ Some girls are tall
                                                    and short.

Such cases have led linguists to argue that transformations have a more complex interrelation with meaning than was assumed by Ohmann.

At the same time, the basic insight of Ohmann's approach continues to have linguistic validity: it is widely held that the basic logical content of a sentence can be represented as a (set of) elementary propositions, which, together with their interrelations, constitute its 'deep structure' or 'semantic representation'.[15] The principle of paraphrase (or 'same meaning in different form') is one which many schools of linguistic thought continue to take for granted as a basic fact of language.

But paraphrase, as the concept on which stylistic dualism is founded, itself depends on an agreed conception of 'meaning' or 'content', two terms often used loosely and interchangeably. It is useful here to replace these terms by terms whose use we can control more carefully. Let us use SENSE to refer to the basic logical, conceptual, paraphrasable meaning, and SIGNIFICANCE to refer to the total of what is communicated to the world by a given sentence or text. Dualism assumes that one can paraphrase the SENSE of a text, and that there is a valid separation of sense from significance. Dualists do not in general treat stylistic choices as devoid of significance: if they did, they would scarcely find style worth studying. Rather, an enlightened dualist will search for some significance, which we may call STYLISTIC VALUE, in a writer's choice to express a certain 'sense' in *this* rather than *that* way. This view may be formalised in the equation: SENSE + STYLISTIC VALUE = (total) SIGNIFICANCE.

Ohmann's detransforming technique seems to provide some linguistic basis for the idea of stylistic 'neutrality' mentioned in section 1.3.1. If a passage can be reduced to a set of elementary propositions of the kind approximately represented in [9], can we not regard this as the neutral, 'styleless' version against which all other paraphrases, such as [8], are stylistically marked in varying degrees? Such a claim would clearly be limited to the grammatical aspect of style, and even here, to say that a text has a 'neutral style' is to mislead: the choice of expressing one's sense in elemental, disconnected sentences has its stylistic value as much as any other choice (see section 7.4.2). Nevertheless, the degree to which a writer complicates his style by applying syntactic transformations might be one linguistic measure of markedness; we shall consider another such measure in the next section.

1.3.3 The inseparability of style and content: monism

The dualist's notion of paraphrase rests on the assumption that there is some basic sense that can be preserved in different renderings. This possibility is not likely to be challenged in workaday uses of language. But in literature, particularly in poetry, paraphrase becomes problematic. Every metaphor, for instance, confronts us with a paraphrase problem:

> Come, seeling night,
> Scarf up the tender eye of pitiful day.
>
> [*Macbeth*, III. ii. 46]

If asked to paraphrase this, do we try to expound the hidden, metaphorical meanings, or the surface literal meanings? Can we even identify, for paraphrase purposes, what the underlying meaning is? As Terence Hawkes says, 'Metaphor . . . is not fanciful embroidery of the facts. It is a way of experiencing the facts'.[16] Poetic metaphor denies us a literal sense, and so induces us to *make* sense, i.e., to find interpretations beyond the truth-functional meaning captured by paraphrase.

Hence stylistic monism finds its strongest ground in poetry, where through such devices as metaphor, irony and ambiguity, meaning becomes multivalued, and sense loses its primacy. Monism, with its rejection of the form-meaning dichotomy, was a tenet of the New Critics,[17] who rejected the idea that a poem conveys a message, preferring to see it as an autonomous verbal artefact. 'A poem should not mean but be' was Archibald MacLeish's extreme statement of this position, and the strength of monism in the 1940s and 1950s can be gauged from Wimsatt's pronouncement:

It is hardly necessary to adduce proof that the doctrine of identity of style and meaning is today firmly established. The doctrine is, I take it, one from which a modern theorist can hardly escape, or hardly wishes to.[18]

It was against the New Critics that Ohmann argued for the reinstatement of dualism in the passage already quoted. But monism has had many other manifestations: in the philosophy of Croce, in the one-form-one-meaning postulate of pretransformational linguistics,[19] and not least, in some authors' own sense of the artistic integrity and inviolability of their work; in Tolstoy's words: 'This indeed is one of the significant facts about a true work of art – that its content in its entirety can be expressed only by itself.'[20] It is to be noted that this sentiment comes from a great prose writer. The features that make poetry difficult for the dualist are not found exclusively in poetry: metaphor, for example, is found in the most prosaic of prose, not to mention everyday speech. So it is not surprising that efforts have been made to apply New Critical methods to prose fiction. The novelist and critic David Lodge, in *Language of Fiction*, adopts a monist stance, arguing that there is no essential difference between poetry and prose, in so far as the following tenets apply to both:

(i) It is impossible to paraphrase literary writing;
(ii) It is impossible to translate a literary work;
(iii) It is impossible to divorce the general appreciation of a literary work from the appreciation of its style.[21]

It is easy to see that both (i) paraphrase and (ii) translation, if understood as the expression of the same content in different words, presuppose a dualist philosophy. As to tenet (iii), Lodge cites the case of Hardy, who has figured in criticism as 'a great novelist "in spite of" gross defects', including the 'capacity to write badly'.[22] He opposes this view by arguing that Hardy's so-called lapses of style cannot be considered apart from a more general consideration of his strengths and weaknesses as a novelist.

For fictional prose, as for poetry, New Criticism urges the view that criticism is, in essence, language criticism. If a novel is no more and no less than a verbal artefact, there can be no separation of the author's creation of a fiction of plot, character, social and moral life from the language in which it is portrayed. As Lodge puts it: 'The novelist's medium is language: whatever he does, *qua* novelist, he does in and through language.'[23] In keeping with this thesis, Lodge is prepared to see no difference between the kind of choice a writer makes in deciding to call a character *dark* or *fair*, and the choice between synonyms such as *dark* and *swarthy*. All the choices the author makes are equally matters of language.

1.4 Comparing dualism and monism

We can see the justice of Lodge's claim that there is no discontinuity between the way language is used in prose and in poetry. But this conclusion should lead us to an accommodation between dualism and monism rather than the rejection of one in favour of the other. The monist can be as easily floored by awkward questions as the dualist. We can challenge the monist by simply asking 'How is it possible to translate a novel?' Everyone seems to agree that it is easier to translate a novel than a poem: that one may appreciate the greatness of Dostoevsky in translation in a way that is not possible (say) of Pushkin. It is admittedly relatively easy for a monist to show (as Lodge does) that even the best translation of a prose work loses something of the original. But this is not sufficient: the monist must show how translation is possible *at all*. He must also show how it is possible to translate a novel into the visual medium, as a film.

To put it most simply, dualism is happier with prose, and monism with poetry. But this oversimplifies a more complex situation. If the difference between prose and poetry is defined at its most banal level, by the absence or presence of verse form, then some types of poetry are more 'prosaic' than others, and some types of prose are more 'poetic' than others. Here we may confront Lodge with his fellow critic–novelist, Anthony Burgess, who in *Joysprick: an introduction to the language of James Joyce*, proposes a division of novelists into 'Class 1' and 'Class 2'. A Class 1 novelist is one 'in whose work language is a zero quality, transparent, unseductive, the overtones of connotation and ambiguity totally damped'.[24] The Class 2 novelist is one for whom 'ambiguities, puns and centrifugal connotations are to be enjoyed rather than regretted, and whose books, made out of words as much as characters and incidents, lose a great deal when adapted to a visual medium'.

James Joyce is a pre-eminently Class 2 novelist, and so for comparative purposes, Burgess offers us (tongue-in-cheek) a translation into Class 1 language of the opening of *A Portrait of the Artist as a Young Man*. We give here a brief sample both of the original [10] and of Burgess's Class 1 version [11]:

[10] Once upon a time and a very good time it was there was a moocow coming down along the road and this moocow that was coming down along the road met a nicens little boy named baby tuckoo . . .
    His father told him that story: his father looked at him through a glass: he had a hairy face.
    He was baby tuckoo. The moocow came down the road where Betty Byrne lived: she sold lemon platt.

[11] My earliest recollections are of my father and my mother bending over my cot and of the difference in personal odour that subsisted between my two parents. My father, certainly, did not have so pleasant an odour as my mother. I remember I would be told infantile stories, altogether appropriate to my infantile station. One of them, I seem to recall, was concerned with a cow coming down the lane – which lane was never specified – and meeting a child who was called (I am embarrassed, inevitably, to recollect this in maturity) some such name as Baby Tuckoo. I myself, apparently, was to be thought of as Baby Tuckoo. Or was it Cuckoo? It is, of course, so long ago . . .[25]

We need not take Burgess's parody too seriously, nor need we accept the absoluteness of his Class 1 and Class 2 categories, since he himself acknowledges that the two classes overlap. The main point is that prose varies a great deal in the amount of aesthetic interest which attaches to linguistic form. This does not have to correspond with the aesthetic merit of the work as a whole: the opening of *David Copperfield* is in many respects more like the Class 1 sample than the Class 2 sample above. But one can reasonably envisage a spectrum extending between two extremes of 'language use' and 'language exploitation'; that is, between prose which conforms to the code (Saussure's *langue*) and normal expectations of communication, and prose which deviates from the code in exploring new frontiers of communication.

The Prague School of poetics[26] has distinguished the 'poetic function' of language by its FOREGROUNDING or DEAUTOMATISATION of the linguistic code. This means that the aesthetic exploitation of language takes the form of surprising a reader into a fresh awareness of, and sensitivity to, the linguistic medium which is normally taken for granted as an 'automatised' background of communication. As the Joyce example shows, this foregrounding is not limited to the more obvious poetic devices, such as metaphor and alliteration. It may take the form of denying the normally expected clues of context and coherence (see sections 6.3 and 7.8). Joyce confronts us with a piece of apparently inept, uncontextualised, childish language lacking normal 'prosaic' logical transitions, and so shocks us into a *re-experience* (rather than a reminiscence) of the childhood consciousness from which the 'young man's portrait' will gradually evolve in his novel.

The aesthetic theory of foregrounding or deautomatisation enables us to see the references to TRANSPARENT and OPAQUE qualities of prose style (see section 1.3.1) as more than vague metaphors. Burgess's Class 1 prose is transparent in the sense that the reader need not become consciously aware of the medium through which sense is conveyed to him. Class 2 prose is opaque in the sense that the medium attracts attention in its own right; and indeed, the interpretation of sense may be frustrated and obstructed by abnormalities in the use of the lexical and grammatical features of the medium. It will be enough to quote, in illustration of opacity, a few lines from the beginning of a novel noted for its linguistic singularity:

> Titus is seven. His confines, Gormenghast. Suckled on shadows; weaned, as it were, on webs of ritual: for his ears, echoes, for his eyes, a labyrinth of stone: and yet within his body something other – other than this umbrageous legacy. For first and ever foremost he is *child*.
>
> [Mervyn Peake, *Gormenghast*, Chapter 1]

It is a justifiable paradox in language, as well as in other spheres, that to be truly creative, an artist must be destructive: destructive of rules, conventions and expectations. But in this sense, creativity of the writer also requires creativity from the reader, who must fill in the gaps of sense with an associative logic of his own. So opacity can be equated with the extent to which the *reader* is required to be creative.

Opacity is also a useful metaphor because it correctly suggests there are many degrees of translucency of style between the extremes of (let us say) *The Forsyte Saga* and *Finnegans Wake*. For most novels of literary merit, neither the dualist nor the monist doctrine will be entirely satisfactory. There is need for an approach which avoids the weaknesses of both.

1.5 Pluralism: analysing style in terms of functions

An alternative to both monism and dualism which is in some ways more enlightening than either is the approach which may fittingly be called stylistic PLURALISM. According to the pluralist, language performs a number of different functions, and any piece of language is likely to be the result of choices made on different functional levels. Hence the pluralist is not content with the dualist's division between 'expression' and 'content': he wants to distinguish various strands of meaning according to the various functions.

That language can perform varied functions or communicative roles is a commonplace of linguistic thought. The popular assumption that language simply serves to communicate 'thoughts' or 'ideas' is too simplistic. Some kinds of language have a referential function (e.g., newspaper reports); others have a directive or persuasive function (e.g., advertising); others have an emotive function or a social function (e.g., casual conversation). To this general appreciation of functional variety in language, the pluralist adds the idea that language is intrinsically multifunctional, so that even the simplest utterance conveys more than one kind of meaning. For example, 'Is your father feeling better?' may be simultaneously referential (referring to a person and his illness), directive (demanding a reply from the hearer), and social (maintaining a bond of sympathy between speaker and hearer). From this point of view, the dualist is wrong in assuming that there is some unitary conceptual 'content' in every piece of language.

Of the many functional classifications of language that have been proposed, three have had some currency in literary studies. The oldest of the three is that of I.A. Richards, who in *Practical Criticism* (1929) distinguishes four types of function, and four kinds of meaning: sense, feeling, tone, and intention.[27] Jakobson's (1961) scheme is based on a more systematic theory of language, and distinguishes six functions (referential, emotive, conative, phatic, poetic, metalinguistic), each corresponding to one essential aspect of the discourse situation.[28] More recently still, Halliday's functional model of language acknowledges three major functions, which he calls 'ideational', 'interpersonal' and 'textual'.[29]

It can be seen that pluralists tend to disagree on what the functions are, and even on their number. They also disagree on how functions are manifested in literary language. Richards holds that in poetry the function of 'feeling' tends to dominate that of 'sense', while Jakobson identifies a special 'poetic' function, which can be found in many uses of language, but which dominates over other functions in poetry.

Although Halliday does not commit himself to a functional definition of literary language, he does recognise that different kinds of literary writing may foreground different functions. We shall take a part of his analysis of the language of William Golding's novel *The Inheritors* to illustrate the relation of pluralism to dualism and monism.[30] (We shall also take Halliday's model as our example of pluralism, because its application to language, and in particular to grammar, has been worked out in considerable detail.)

The passage below illustrates the stylistic interest of Golding's novel: it deals with the prehistoric struggle for survival between *homo sapiens* and Neanderthal man, resulting in the latter's extinction. The major part of the book presents events through the limited Neanderthal outlook of Lok. The special Lok-style which Golding devises for this purpose differs considerably from the style he uses towards the end of the novel, when the point of view shifts to *homo sapiens*. It is important to notice that the contrast lies primarily in the function of language which Halliday calls IDEATIONAL: that is, the way in which language conveys and organises the cognitive realities of experience, roughly corresponding to what we have earlier called 'sense':

[12] The bushes twitched again. Lok steadied by the tree and gazed. A head and a chest faced him, half-hidden. There were white bone things behind the leaves and hair. The man had white bone things above his eyes and under the mouth so that his face was longer than a face should be. The man turned sideways in the bushes and looked at Lok along his shoulder. A stick rose upright and there was a lump of bone in the middle. Lok peered at the stick and the lump of bone and the small eyes in the bone things over the face. Suddenly Lok understood that the man was holding the stick out to him but neither he nor Lok could reach across the river. He would have laughed if it were not for the echo of the screaming in his head. The stick began to grow shorter at both ends. Then it shot out to full length again.   ʹ

The dead tree by Lok's ear acquired a voice.

'Clop!'

His ears twitched and he turned to the tree.

[William Golding, *The Inheritors*]

It requires careful attention to realise that here we are seeing, through the uncomprehending mind of Lok, a man's attempt to shoot him with an arrow. Lok's view of things lacks the sense of cause and effect, of mind controlling matter, which we, as descendants of his vanquishers, take for granted. A linguistic clue of this is the limited grammar of Lok's language, particularly its paucity of clauses with a direct object or clauses with a human subject. Such clauses are the chief means by which we describe events in which human beings are involved: 'Lok saw the man', 'The man raised his bow and arrow'. Instead, Lok's language is full of clauses with inanimate subjects or intransitive verbs or both: 'The bushes twitched again', 'Lok steadied by the tree', 'A stick arose upright'. Further, there are no adverbs or adverbial phrases except those of time and place. To represent the limited universe of Lok, Golding uses a limited language, particularly in the area of 'transitivity' (a term which, for Halliday, comprehends relations between verbs, noun phrases, and adverbials in the clause).

Halliday goes on to claim that the theme of the whole novel, in a way, is 'transitivity': the linguistic pattern of choices realises a primitive pattern of cognition, which in turn is the key to the tragic vision of the novel.

Halliday's analysis is revealing in the way it relates precise linguistic observation to literary effect. But for our present purposes, its interest is that it locates stylistic significance in the ideational function of language; that is, in the cognitive meaning or sense which for the dualist is the invariant factor of content rather than the variable factor of style. The choice, for example, between 'A stick rose upright' and 'He raised his bow' is not something which Ohmann could regard as a matter of style. These sentences contrast grammatically in terms of phrase structure, and could not, in any logical sense, be regarded as paraphrases of one another.

There is thus an incompatibility between the pluralist and the dualist. Comparing Ohmann and Halliday as representatives of these two schools of thought, we can establish approximate correspondences as follows:

OHMANN (1964)	HALLIDAY (1973)
(A) 'content' (phrase structure)	(A) Ideational function
(B) 'expression'	(B) Textual function
(optional transformations)	
(C) –	(C) Interpersonal function

(The equivalences here are *very* approximate, and are based on what Ohmann and Halliday actually do in their analyses, rather than their theoretical positions. In particular, Halliday does not accept that his three functions form a hierarchy.) For Ohmann, style belongs only to level (B), whereas for Halliday style can be located in (A), (B) and (C). (The interpersonal function is something extra to which we shall return in Chapter 8. It concerns the relation between language and its users, and combines two categories which are often kept separate in functional models: the affective or emotive function (communicating the speaker's attitudes), and the directive function (influencing the behaviour and attitudes of the hearer). Although in his work using transformational grammar, Ohmann neglected this function, he concentrated on it in subsequent work.)[31]

Halliday's view is that all linguistic choices are meaningful, and all linguistic choices are stylistic. In this respect, his pluralism can be regarded as a more sophisticated version of monism. The flaw of monism is that it tends to view a text as an undifferentiated whole, so that examination of linguistic choices cannot be made except on some *ad hoc* principle. One might even argue that the monist, if he followed the logic of his position, would not be able to discuss language at all: if meaning is inseparable from form, one cannot discuss meaning except by repeating the very words in which it is expressed, and one cannot discuss form except by saying that it appropriately expresses its own meaning. But the pluralist is in a happier position. He can show how choices of language are interrelated within a network of functional choices. What choices a writer makes can be seen against the background of relations of contrast and dependence between one choice and another; for example (to take a simple case) the choice between transitive and intransitive verbs. Perhaps this is merely to say that the pluralist has a theory of language, whereas the monist does not.

1.6 A multilevel approach to style

If Halliday's pluralism is superior to monism, it also has some advantages over dualism. Dualism, as we have seen, can say nothing about how language creates a particular cognitive view of things, what Fowler calls MINDSTYLE,[32] as illustrated in the Golding passage. This is a pity, since it thereby excludes much that is worthy of attention in modern fiction writing (see Chapter 6).

But in section 1.4 we argued that monism is more suited to opaque than transparent styles of writing, and the same point may be made about pluralism. It is significant that Halliday discusses *The Inheritors* against the background of the theory of foregrounding, and that Golding's Lok-language in its opacity bears some resemblance to the language of the child Stephen in Joyce's portrait, as quoted in [10]. In both cases, the author shocks us into an unfamiliar mode of experience, by using language suggestive of a primitive state of consciousness.

Let us think again about what is good in the dualist position: it captures the insight that two pieces of language can be seen as alternative ways of saying the same thing: that is, that there can be STYLISTIC VARIANTS with different STYLISTIC VALUES. This is not an unproblematic statement (as we saw in section 1.4), but is sufficiently true of a wide enough range of cases not to be cast aside lightly. By comparing a writer's choices against other choices with the same sense, 'what the writer might have said but didn't', one has a greater control over the notion of stylistic value.

Halliday's approach is one that is hard to reconcile with this everyday insight about 'style'. For him, even choices that are clearly dictated by subject matter are part of style: it is part of the style of a particular cookery book that it contains words like *butter, flour, boil* and *bake*; and it is part of the style of *Animal Farm* that it contains many occurrences of *pigs, farm* and *Napoleon*. Even choice of proper names, or of whether to call a character fair or dark-haired, is a matter of style – in this Halliday the pluralist must agree with Lodge the monist.

Applied to non-fictional language, this position fails to make an important discrimination. In a medical textbook, the choice between *clavicle* and *collar-bone* can justly be called a matter of stylistic variation. But if the author replaced *clavicle* by *thigh-bone*, this would no longer be a matter of stylistic variation, but a matter of fact, and of potential disaster to the patient! There is no reason to treat fictional language in a totally different way. The referential, truth-functional nature of language is not in abeyance in fiction: rather it is exploited in referring to, and thereby creating, a fictional universe, a mock-reality (see Chapter 5). So, from *The Inheritors*, we understand that certain things are going on in the fictional world. These could have been described in other language, just as in Burgess's Class 1 version of Joyce's *Portrait* [11]. At the referential level, Golding's sentences:

[13] The stick began to grow shorter at both ends.
[14] Then it shot out to full length again.

tell the same story as:

[15] Lok saw the man draw the bow and release it.

Although these are not paraphrases, they can be regarded as stylistic variants in a more liberal sense: as alternative conceptualisations, or ways of 'making sense' of the same event. To see this is to recognise the stylistic value of Golding's choice: that his version of the event is of movements perceived in space and time, from which the reader has to work out a normal understanding of what is happening.

It is important to understand that language is used, in fiction, to project a world 'beyond language', in that we use not only our knowledge of language, the meanings of words, etc., but also our general knowledge of the real world, to furnish it. It is important in this case, because only on this assumption can one explain the experience a reader gets from *The Inheritors* of 'looking round the sides' of Lok's world-view, to see a more substantial reality behind it. It is as if we have two pairs of eyes, one pair inside and another outside the blinkers: without this, Golding's technique would not produce its ironic effect of dual vision.

It is reasonable to say, therefore, that some aspects of language have to do with the referential function of language, and that these must be distinguished from those which have to do with stylistic variation. If Golding had replaced *bushes* by *reeds*, or *river* by *pond*, these would not have been stylistic variants, but would have brought about a change in the fictional world.

Returning now to the dualist's notion of invariant content and variable style, we can retain what is good in this distinction by refining it to allo for more than one level of stylistic variation. The traditional term 'content' fails to discriminate between the philosopher's concepts of SENSE and REFERENCE:[33] what a linguistic form means, and what it refers to. Once we take account of this distinction, we recognise that there can be alternative CONCEPTUALISATIONS of the same event (illustrated in the Golding passage), as well as alternative syntactic expressions of the same sense (as in Ohmann's treatment of Faulkner). The dualist's diagram (Figure 1.3) therefore splits into two.

The fiction remains the invariant element: the element which, from the point of view of stylistic variation, must be taken for granted. But of course it is only invariant in a special sense: the author is free to order his universe as he wants, but for the purposes of stylistic variation we are only interested in those choices of language which do not involve changes in the fictional universe.

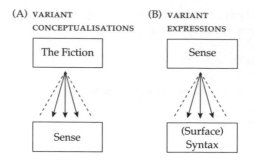

(A) VARIANT
    CONCEPTUALISATIONS

(B) VARIANT
    EXPRESSIONS

| The Fiction | | Sense |

| Sense | | (Surface) Syntax |

Figure 1.3

In this light, the view of Lodge, that whatever the novelist 'does, *qua* novelist, he does in and through language', is an attractive but slightly misleading truism. It is undeniable that a novel, as a text, consists entirely of language, and that we gain access to the fictional world only through language. But as a work of fiction, a novel has a more abstract level of existence, which in principle is partly independent of the language through which it is represented, and may be realised, for example, through the visual medium of film. In support of this, it has been pointed out that two distinct kinds of descriptive statement can be made about a verbal work of art.[34] On the one hand, it can be described as a linguistic text:

X contains simple words, more abstract than concrete nouns, etc.
X is written in ornate/lucid/vigorous/colloquial language, etc.

Or it can be described as we might describe other fictional forms, such as an opera, a play, a film, or even a mime, where there is no linguistic dimension at all:

X contains several Neanderthal characters.
X is about a woman who kills her husband.
X is about events which take place in nineteenth-century Africa.

These are all descriptive statements; that is, they are statements of a kind about which readers can readily agree, without appeal to critical judgment. The way we acquire 'knowledge' of a fictional world has much in common with the way we acquire indirect knowledge, through language, of the real world (see section 5.2). A novel has therefore these two interrelated modes of existence – as a fiction, and as a text; and, to adapt Lodge's statement to our own purpose, it is as *text-maker* that the novelist works *in* language, and it is as *fiction-maker* that the novelist works *through* language. It is in this more general context that the distinction between 'what one has to say' and 'how one says it' can ultimately be upheld.

We have arrived at a multilevel view of style, which is composed of elements of dualism and pluralism. So far we have distinguished two levels of stylistic variation: that of sense reference, and that of syntax sense, but a further level will be added when we consider the multilevel coding of language in more detail in Chapter 4.

1.7 Conclusion: meanings of style

Monism, dualism, pluralism, although apparently in conflict with one another, all have something to contribute to a comprehensive view of style. It will be our object in this book to combine the insights from these approaches in a multilevel, multifunctional view of style which will be applicable to the practical study of texts.

We shall not be dogmatic on the use of the term 'style' itself. Like many semi-technical terms, it has suffered from overdefinition, and the history of literary and linguistic thought is littered with unsuccessful attempts to attach a precise meaning to it. All too often these attempts have resulted in an impoverishment of the subject. We may conclude, however, with a list of points which have been made in this chapter, and which form the basis of the use of the term 'style' in this book.

   (i) Style is a way in which language is *used*: i.e., it belongs to *parole* rather than to *langue*.
  (ii) Therefore style consists in *choices* made from the repertoire of the language.
 (iii) A style is defined in terms of a *domain* of language use (e.g., what choices are made by a particular author, in a particular genre, or in a particular text).
  (iv) Stylistics (or the study of style) has typically (as in this book) been concerned with *literary* language.
   (v) Literary stylistics is typically (again, as in this book) concerned with *explaining the relation between* style and literary or aesthetic function.
  (vi) Style is relatively *transparent* or *opaque*: transparency implies paraphrasability; opacity implies that a text cannot be adequately paraphrased, and that interpretation of the text depends greatly on the creative imagination of the reader.

We come finally to a statement which is controversial, and about which much of this chapter has been concerned:

 (vii) Stylistic choice is limited to those aspects of linguistic choice which concern *alternative ways of rendering the same subject matter*.

This defines a more restricted concept of style, which may be called STYLE₂, to distinguish it from the notion of style as linguistic choice in general, STYLE₁.

We have argued in favour of the tenet that underlies (vii), namely that it is possible to distinguish between what the writer chooses to talk about, and how he chooses to talk about it. This means that the study of the literary function of language can be directed towards the STYLISTIC VALUES associated with STYLISTIC VARIANTS; that is, with forms of language which can be seen as equivalent in terms of the 'referential reality' they describe. This principle is questionable when it comes to more opaque varieties of literary language, where the writer tends towards the innovative techniques of poetry. Here, the study of foregrounding and its interpretation[35] is likely to be a better guide to the aesthetic function of language than the study of stylistic variants. In other words, there is no one model of prose style which is applicable to all texts.

This is one reason why we do not restrict the use of 'style' to what we have called stylistic variation, i.e., 'style₂'. It is best to acknowledge that 'style', like 'meaning', is a word which can be used either in a broader or a narrower sense.[36] In practice, little danger lies in this ambiguity. Style₂ is the concept we shall use in exploring the nature of stylistic value, as a basis for understanding the detailed workings of stylistic effect (see Chapter 4). Style₁, the more general concept, lies at the back of more large-scale studies of style, when for example we try to give a stylistic characterisation of a whole text. In such studies, to which we turn in the next chapter, it will be necessary to consider yet other components which have frequently entered into the definition of style.

Notes

1. See F. DE SAUSSURE (1959), 13.
2. For various approaches to, and definitions of, style, see N.E. ENKVIST (1964, 1973), and S. CHATMAN (1971a).
3. On authorial style, see for example, S. ULLMANN (1973).
4. Variations in Johnson's style are studied in W.K. WIMSATT (1941).
5. L. SPITZER (1948), 19, 27 *ff*.
6. On the analogy between science and stylistics, see G. LEECH (1977b). This article expands on the methodology of stylistics as presented here.
7. A historical review of attribution studies is given in R.W. BAILEY (1969).
8. From a letter of 12 December 1857, to Mlle Leroyer de Chantepie.
9. The /w/ could have been pronounced in Lyly's English.
10. See C. BALLY (1951), 12–16, and M. RIFFATERRE (1971), 30.
11. R. BARTHES (1967), 82–83.
12. R. OHMANN (1964), 423 *ff*. A succinct definition of style along these lines is that of C.F. HOCKETT (1958), 556: 'two utterances in the same language which convey approximately the same information, but which are different in their linguistic structure, can be said to differ in style'.

13. On the notion of 'kernel sentence', see N. CHOMSKY (1957). A useful introduction to transformational grammar is given in J. LYONS (1970). Ohmann uses Chomsky's earlier model of transformational grammar, that of *Syntactic Structures*, in his article 'Generative grammar and the concept of literary style'. In a later article, 'Literature as sentences', he draws on a later model put forward in CHOMSKY's *Aspects of the Theory of Syntax*. Both articles by Ohmann are reprinted in G.A. LOVE and M. PAYNE (1969).

14. For later developments in transformational grammar, see a brief survey in D. BOLINGER (1975), Chapter 15. At a more abstract level; consult CHOMSKY (1972, 1976).

15. On the notion of semantic representation (and the related notion of deep structure) see, for example, G. LEECH (1974), esp Chapter 14.

16. T. HAWKES (1972), 69.

17. On new criticism and style, see B. LEE (1966), and R. FOWLER and P. MERCER (1971).

18. W.K. WIMSATT (1941), 2.

19. See, for example, L. BLOOMFIELD (1935), 145. A recent reaffirmation of the 'one-meaning-one-form' principle is to be found in D. BOLINGER (1977).

20. From A.B. GOLDENVEIZER (1923).

21. These tenets are argued (although they are not stated in quite this form) in D. LODGE (1966), 18–34.

22. *Ibid*, 164.

23. *Ibid*, ix.

24. A. BURGESS (1973), 15.

25. *Ibid*, 63.

26. See P.L. GARVIN (1958), esp. J. Mukařovský, 'Standard Language and Poetic Language', 18 *ff* (also reprinted in D.C. FREEMAN (1970)).

27. I.A. RICHARDS (1929), 181.

28. R. JAKOBSON (1961).

29. See M.A.K. HALLIDAY (1973), (esp. Chapter 2) and many other publications by the same author since 1970.

30. M.A.K. HALLIDAY (1971).

31. See esp. R. OHMANN (1971a, 1971b, 1972).

32. See R. FOWLER (1977), 103–113.

33. On the distinction between sense and reference, see for example J. LYONS (1977), 174.

34. See J.F. IHWE (1976).

35. On the application of the notion of foregrounding to the practical interpretation of poetry, see G. LEECH (1965) and (1969), Chapter 4.

36. The two meanings of style (style$_1$ and style$_2$) are perhaps not so distinct as this discussion suggests. Both are ultimately concerned with the 'how' rather than the 'what' of language phenomena. Style$_1$ is 'how language is used in a given context' (language use against the background of the language code), and style$_2$ is 'how language renders some subject matter' (language use against the background of referential reality). In this connection, it is illuminating to read Chapter 1 of E.L. EPSTEIN (1978). Epstein makes a bold attempt to interrelate various concepts of style (not only in language) through the notion of style as a perceptive strategy, whereby we pick out from an identified background secondary phenomena which attract attention as individualising elements. He recognises, as we do, the multilayered nature of style.

CHAPTER 2

Style, text and frequency

In talking about USE and CHOICE in Chapter 1 we were implicitly looking at language from the author's point of view. Now, in turning to style as recurrence, pattern, frequency, we find ourselves taking the reader's point of view. The question we consider in this chapter is: How, as readers, do we investigate the style of a text?

Once again, we take as a starting point the ordinary use of the word 'style'. Generally, in looking at style in a text, one is not interested in choices in isolation, but rather at a pattern of choices: something that belongs to the text as a whole. Suppose we choose between active and passive sentences, saying '*Persuasion* was written by Jane Austen' in preference to 'Jane Austen wrote *Persuasion*'. This is a choice (whether conscious or unconscious is a different matter), but could scarcely be called a style. On the other hand, if a text shows a pattern of unusual preference for passives over actives, it is natural to consider this preference a feature of style. It is not that stylistics is uninterested in this or that local feature of a text, but rather that local or specific features have to be seen in relation to other features, against the background of the pervasive tendency of preferences in the text. The recognition of cohesion and consistency in preference is important: without it, one would scarcely acknowledge a style. To go one stage further, 'consistency' and 'tendency' are most naturally reduced to 'frequency', and so, it appears, the stylistician becomes a statistician.

2.1 The problem of 'measuring' style

If style is regarded as a function of frequency, it seems reasonable to suppose that style can be measured. Some definitions of style have been based on this assumption. An example often quoted is that of Bernard Bloch, who defined the style of a text as 'the message carried by the frequency distributions and transitional probabilities of its linguistic features, especially as they differ from those of the same features in the language as a whole'.[1] Such definitions appeal to the empiricist, who would like to reduce a subjectively perceived phenomenon to something objective, but they tend to alarm the student of literature. We hope to reassure the latter by showing that quantification is a less essential part of stylistics than this definition suggests.

The principle underlying Bloch's formulation is simple enough. To find out what is distinctive about the style of a certain corpus or text we work out the frequencies of the features it contains and then measure these figures against equivalent figures which are 'normal' for the language in question. The style is then to be measured in terms of deviations – either higher frequencies or lower frequencies – from the norm.

Many impressionistic statements about style would gain meaning from such a comparison. We often read statements or suggestions that writer X 'favours', 'is fond of', 'tends to use' language feature Y: for example, that Hemingway tends to use short sentences, or that Johnson favours abstract vocabulary. Such statements may be based on strong conviction and close observation, and may even be felt to be self-evident, but they appear to have no empirical status – are merely, we might say, guesses – unless supported by frequency data. Under Bloch's type of analysis, the statement that Hemingway uses 'short sentences' amounts to a claim that the average length of a Hemingway sentence is shorter (to a significant extent) than the average length of an English sentence; something which can in principle be verified or falsified.

But even this simple illustration exposes the difficulties of the quantitative definition of style. How does one determine the average length of an English sentence? Does one use conversation, written prose, modern novels, etc., as one's standard for determining the norm of 'the language as a whole'? None of these could individually be regarded as representative. To arrive at the average length of an English sentence, one should ideally amass a complete corpus of the language at a given period. Leaving aside the problem of what time period to specify, we should have to ransack the libraries of the world to find a complete list of published works written during the period. This would still leave out manuscript compositions (e.g. private letters) and spoken language (e.g. private conversations). The operation would be totally impracticable. Even if it were not, there would be other problems, such as whether a book read by millions would count equally, in the corpus, with a private letter; whether some publications (e.g. literary magazines) would be weightier, in determining the norm for the language, than others. In this situation the obvious resort is to sampling; but without some clear-cut notion, for statistical purposes, of what is meant by 'the language as a whole', any sampling procedure is bound to involve subjective decisions.[2] The norm of 'the language as a whole' is not the objective reality that it seems to be in Bloch's definition, and some less absolute standard of comparison has to be found (see section 2.4).

Not to overdo the argument against objectivity, we should mention that there *are* fairly reliable statements to be made about the statistical properties of language, particularly about categories of great frequency.[3] For example, the frequencies of vowels and consonants (in speech) or of letters (in writing) are relatively constant from one variety of English to another. Such categories, however, do not take us very deeply into the study of style. In general, we must find our statistical bearings through more specific standards of comparison, written English having a different set of norms from spoken English, and so on.

A second and more serious objection to this definition concerns the impossibility of completeness in another direction. How is it possible to list exhaustively all linguistic features that may be found in a text? For this, as a first condition, we should require a completely exhaustive description of the language: its lexicon, its syntax, its semantics and other characteristics. Languages are such complicated systems, and so open-ended, that no complete descriptions have been produced, even for a well-studied language such as English. Many linguists would place the conception of 'an agreed complete description of English' in the realms of fancy. Even if there were such a description, it would be difficult to imagine the number of working years it would take to arrive at a complete frequency description of a novel, let alone 'the language as a whole'.

Bloch includes in the measurement of style 'transitional probability', the probability that some form X will be followed by another form Y; this opens the door to an infinity of combinations of stylistic factors that might reasonably enter into a definition of a style. Frequencies of word occurrences could be augmented, for example, by frequencies of word *co*-occurrences, or COLLOCATIONS. This means that in addition to the separate frequencies of the words *silver* and *moon*, we should determine the frequency of their combination (*silver moon*). But why stop at juxtaposition? Why not extend the study to co-occurrence within the same phrase (*moon* in a *silver* sky) or within the same sentence (the *moon* stared down with its *silver* eye)? There would also be combinatory frequencies of a different kind, where two categories are simultaneously present in a single item. Examples of such coincident categories are monosyllabic verbs (combining the phonological category of syllable with the syntactic category of verb), and colour adjectives (combining the syntactic category of adjective with the semantic category of colour). The study of combinatory frequencies is open-ended.

This would seem an over-subtle argument, were it not that studies of style often indicate the importance of such combinatory features in the creation of literary effect. Onomatopoeic effects are generally of this kind, as we see from the opening sentence of D.H. Lawrence's *Odour of Chrysanthemums* (see section 3.4):

The small locomotive engine, Number 4, came clanking, stumbling down from Selston with seven full wagons.

The sense of listening to and 'feeling' the motion of the locomotive is created by a combination of rhythm (the trochaic regularity of 'clánking, stúmbling, dówn from Sélston'), the dragging effect of consonant clusters (/kl/, /nk/, /mbl/, /lst/), and the actual qualities of the consonants themselves (e.g., the hard effect of the stop consonants /k/, /k/, /t/, /b/). In the past, the study of onomatopoeia, and of imitative effects generally, has been vitiated by a tendency to assume that there is a direct evocative connection between a particular sound and a particular reference, say between an /s/ sound and the sighing of the wind or (here) the hiss of a steam-engine. But onomatopoeia is on stronger ground if it is appreciated that the effect is generally a result of phonological features acting in combination with one another, and in combination with meaning.

Similarly on the syntactic level, individual features are likely to have a less significant effect than features in combination. The frequency of a particular kind of syntactic structure (say a relative clause) will probably be less important than the fact that that structure tends to occur in a particular position in the sentence (e.g. at the end, or at the middle). Traditional stylistic terms (e.g. that of the periodic sentence – see section 7.5.3), although often ill-defined, seem to refer to such configurations of categories. Stylistics, that is, often uses not categories of the language as such, but special stylistic categories, derived, by abstraction and combination, from more basic linguistic categories.

It seems, then, that the list of linguistic features to be counted is indefinitely large, if we want a quantitative description of a text to have a fine enough mesh to catch the linguistic details which contribute to readers' feeling for differences of style. The quest for a completely objective measurement of style must be abandoned on this score, as well as on that of determining frequencies for the language as a whole.

2.2 The uses of arithmetic

In rejecting the 'fallacy of objectivity' in stylistics, we may have seemed to be labouring the obvious. But it is important to be aware of the limitations of the statistical concept of style before going on to a more realistic assessment of its value. If some studies of style are of doubtful value because of their emphasis on quantitative methods, the opposite tendency to rely entirely on what we may call stylistic intuition has, if anything, been even more prevalent.

Aesthetic terms[4] used in the discussion of style (urbane, curt, exuberant, florid, lucid, plain, vigorous, etc.) are not directly referable to any observable linguistic features of texts, and one of the long-term aims of stylistics must be to see how far such descriptions can be justified in terms of descriptions of a more linguistic kind. The more I, as a critic, wish to substantiate what I say about style, the more I will need to point to the linguistic evidence of texts; and linguistic evidence, to be firm, must be couched in terms of numerical frequency. I may 'observe', from close familiarity with her novels, that Jane Austen favours abstract nouns of a particular kind (nouns referring to moral qualities such as *right, vice, propriety, injustice*). Perhaps no one will doubt the correctness of my observation. But what if another person has 'observed' that Jane Austen has no such stylistic propensity? If challenged, I ought to be, and can be, in a position to support my claim with quantitative evidence. 'Observation' here misleadingly refers to something it would be safer to call an intuition or a hunch (even if it may be a sensitive reader's well-informed hunch) that such-and-such is the case. I shall only be able to convince another person that such-and-such is the case if I take the trouble to present evidence which is available to both my challenger and myself.

So let us see quantitative stylistics as serving a role in the 'circle of explanation' (see Figure 1.1) as follows. On the one hand, it may provide confirmation for the 'hunches' or insights we have about style. On the other, it may bring to light significant features of style which would otherwise have been overlooked, and so lead to further insights; but only in a limited sense does it provide an objective measurement of style. Moreover, the role of quantification depends on how necessary it is to prove one's point. The escape from intuition in the study of style leads inevitably in the direction of quantification. But intuition has a respectable place both in linguistics and criticism, and the work of the stylo-statistician too often makes him seem, in Dr Johnson's words, 'the stately son of demonstration, who proves with mathematical formality what no man has yet pretended to doubt'. Style is such a complicated phenomenon that it would be impractical to demand hard evidence for every observation made. It may be sufficient for many purposes just to enumerate textual examples of the feature under discussion. In many other cases, one may agree with Halliday that 'a rough indication of frequencies is often just what is needed: enough to suggest why we should accept the analyst's assertion that some feature is prominent in the text, and allow us to check his statements'.[5] Others would go further, and insist on more rigorous methods.[6] The essential point is that the use of numerical data should be adapted to the need.

2.3 Deviance, prominence and literary relevance

The role of quantitative evidence can be understood more clearly if we look at the interrelation of the three concepts of DEVIANCE, PROMINENCE and LITERARY RELEVANCE. Leaving aside for the moment the problem of determining a norm, we may define deviance as a purely statistical notion: as the difference between the normal frequency of a feature, and its frequency in the text or corpus. Prominence is the related psychological notion: Halliday defines it simply as 'the general name for the phenomenon of linguistic highlighting, whereby some linguistic feature stands out in some way'.[7] We assume that prominence of various degrees and kinds provides the basis for a reader's subjective recognition of a style. Halliday distinguishes prominence from literary 'relevance', which he calls 'value in the game'. Like Halliday, we associate literary relevance with the Prague School notion of FOREGROUNDING, or artistically motivated deviation, as discussed in section 1.4. Foregrounding may be QUALITATIVE, i.e. deviation from the language code itself – a breach of some rule or convention of English – or it may simply be QUANTITATIVE, i.e. deviance from some expected frequency. The question stylistics must consider is: how are these three concepts of deviance, prominence and foregrounding interrelated?

First, let us consider the relation between prominence and deviance. Prominence must obviously be understood in relative terms: if features can register on a reader's mind in his recognition of style, the degree to which they are salient will vary, and the degree to which the reader responds in a given reading will also vary according to a number of factors, such as his attentiveness, sensitivity to style and previous reading experience. But this ability to react to what is 'noticeable' in style must underlie our ability to recognise one passage as Dickensian, another as Jamesian, and so on. We may go so far as to suggest that each reader has a 'stylistic competence', analogous to and additional to the 'linguistic competence' shared (according to Chomsky) by all native speakers of a language. The analogy holds in so far as stylistic competence, like linguistic competence, is a capacity that we possess and exercise unconsciously and intuitively: only with special training can it be turned into explicit knowledge. But unlike Chomsky's ideal linguistic competence, stylistic competence is an ability which different people possess in different measure, so that although there may be a great deal in common between different English speakers' responsiveness to style, allowance must be made for differences of degree and kind.

We presume a fairly direct relation between prominence (psychological saliency) and deviance (a function of textual frequency). It is reasonable to suppose that a sense of what is usual or unusual or noticeable in language is built up from a lifelong experience of linguistic use, so that we are able to affirm with reasonable confidence and without resort to a pocket calculator (to take a simple case already mentioned) that Hemingway favours short sentences. It is in this sense that statistics may be an elaborate way of demonstrating the obvious. But it would be hazardous to assume that prominence and deviance are simply subjective and objective aspects of the same phenomenon. This is first because of the individual differences in stylistic competence already noted; second because our sense of style is essentially vague and indeterminate, not reducible to quantities; and third because it is likely that certain deviances (below a certain level of significance) do not reach the threshold of response, even for the most experienced, alert and sensitive reader.

Both prominence and deviance have a negative, as well as a positive, side: a feature which occurs more rarely than usual is just as much a part of the statistical pattern as one which occurs more often than usual; and it may also be a significant aspect of our sense of style. Recall that in Halliday's analysis of Lok's language, the rarity of certain categories (e.g. transitive verbs) was just as important as the high frequency of others: the most striking features of Lok's language were its limitations.

Like the relation between prominence and deviance, that between prominence and literary relevance or foregrounding is not a one-to-one match. Prominence, which is the basis for our sense of the particularity of a style, also provides the condition for recognition that a style is being used for a particular literary end: that it has a 'value in the game'. But there is an additional condition: we should be able to see a prominent feature of style as forming a significant relationship with other features of style, in an artistically coherent pattern of choice. According to Mukařovský, it is the 'consistency and systematic character of foregrounding',[8] not just the isolated occurrence of this or that prominent feature, that is the distinguishing mark of literary language. Instances can be cited where this appears not to be the case: where prominence is due to other than literary considerations. Swift's dislike of monosyllables and Dryden's avoidance of final prepositions[9] are cases of a writer's preferences being guided by a general sense of linguistic propriety, of what is 'good English'. Lesser writers could provide many examples of idiosyncrasies of style which have no discernible literary function. In other cases, there is room for disagreement. It may be a relevant feature of the later style of Henry James that he favours manner adverbs, and avoids adjectives. James himself seems to have felt an aesthetic reason for these propensities, for he is reported to have said: 'Adjectives are the sugar of literature and adverbs the salt.'[10] Whatever the force of this cryptic remark, it is up to us as readers to find a value for these preferences, or else to dismiss them as the outcome of prejudice or eccentricity. The dividing line between foregrounding and unmotivated prominence must be drawn in principle: where it is drawn in practice depends on a coherent literary interpretation of style.

To conclude, we can place the three notions of saliency in an ordered relation as follows:

literary   psychological   statistical
RELEVANCE - - - - - - - - - - ➤ PROMINENCE - - - - - - - - - - ➤ DEVIANCE
(foregrounding)

Figure 2.1

We interpret the arrow in 'X - - - - - → Y' to mean 'all instances of X are instances of Y'.[11] But in the opposite direction, the relation does not hold. In other words, deviance can be used to suggest and support hypotheses about style; but nothing can be adduced from, or proved by, statistics alone.

2.4 Relative norms

It is time to return to the question of 'norm' on which the notion of deviance depends. Given that the ideal of a completely objective description of style is a myth, we can only aim at RELATIVELY reliable statements about what is frequent or infrequent in a text.

Some kind of comparison outside the text or corpus is necessary, otherwise statements of frequency are vacuous. For example, discovering that x per cent of Gibbon's nouns are concrete, and only y per cent abstract, is of little use by itself. This might be treated as evidence that Gibbon uses an abnormally large number of abstract nouns, but of course it cannot, for we might then discover that a preponderance of abstract nouns is quite normal in the prose of Gibbon's contemporaries, and that Gibbon's language in this respect is not exceptional. We might even discover that he uses a lower number of abstract nouns than other writers of his time. Thus what at first appeared to be evidence in favour of one hypothesis might turn out to be evidence against it. This example teaches us that a statement 'x is frequent in A' is only meaningful if it acts as a shorthand for 'x is more frequent in A than in B'.

This object lesson leads to the use of a RELATIVE NORM of comparison (B in the above formula). Where an absolute norm for English cannot be relied on, the next best thing is to compare the corpus whose style is under scrutiny with one or more comparable corpuses, thus establishing a relative norm. For example, Milic, in his study of Swift's prose style, confirms Swift's predilection for clause connectives by comparing his results for a sample of Swift with those for equivalent samples of Addison, Johnson and Macaulay:[12]

Table 2.1   PERCENTAGE OF INITIAL CONNECTIVES IN 2000-SENTENCE
SAMPLES OF ADDISON, JOHNSON, MACAULAY AND SWIFT

Connective	Addison	Johnson	Macaulay	Swift
C	5.5	5.8	7.4	20.2
S	7.1	6.2	4.1	5.4
SC	3.3	1.4	1.5	8.3
Total	15.9	13.4	13.0	33.9

[C = coordinating conjunctions; S = subordinating conjunctions; SC = sentence-connectors]

Swift's habit of reinforcing connections between clauses sometimes reaches the extreme of sequences such as *and therefore if notwithstanding* . . . Milic sees this habit as having a role in Swift's persuasive rhetoric: as helping to create an impression of consummate logical clarity. Table 2.1 is fairly convincing,[13] since there is a strong supposition that the markedly lower figures for other writers come closer to an absolute norm than those for Swift. The more comparable writers we study, the less likely it is that *they* are out of step with the norm of the language rather than Swift. The same technique may be used within the canon of a single author. For instance, Corbett, in support of the observation that Swift uses abnormally long sentences in *A Modest Proposal*, cites a much lower sentence length from a sample from *A Tale of a Tub*. The long sentences in Swift's ironic essay in support of cannibalism are explicable as a stylistic expression of the persona he adopts in order to intensify the impact of his outrageous proposal: in Corbett's words, we seem to be 'listening to a man who is so filled with his subject, so careful about qualifying his statements and computations, so infatuated with the sound of his own words, that he rambles on at inordinate length'.[14] The greater the range and size of the corpus which acts as a relative norm, the more valid the statement of relative frequency. But a small sample for comparison is better than nothing at all.

There are manifest dangers in the way a relative norm is chosen, but once it is accepted that relative validity is all we can aim at these need not worry us unduly. It is obvious that a suitable norm of comparison should be what Enkvist calls 'a contextually related norm'.[15] There would be little point in comparing Jane Austen's style with that of contemporary legal writs or twentieth-century parliamentary reports. What counts as 'the same category of writing', however, can be defined to different degrees of narrowness. The books of Jane Austen could be compared (a) with other prose writings of the period, (b) with other novels of the period, (c) with other novels with similar subject matter, and so on. The narrower the range of comparison, the surer we are that the stylistic features we are attributing to Jane Austen are peculiar to her style, rather than to the style of a larger category of writings which includes hers.

In adopting the necessary expedient of a relative norm, quantitative stylistics abandons the idea that there is a single way of measuring deviance in a text. There are as many measures as there are relative norms. This conclusion is not a bad thing, for it leads to a better match between deviance and prominence. What was overlooked in our discussion of stylistic competence is that our intuitive 'placing' of a text depends not on an undifferentiated capacity to compare a text with *the* norm of the language, but rather on a responsiveness to a *set* of norms: a norm for spoken conversation, a norm for news reporting, a norm for writing diaries, a norm for historical novels, etc. However inchoate the norms may be, they collectively give us our bearings for responding to a style. They account for our general sense of the appropriateness and inappropriateness of language as reflected in impromptu observations about style, varying from Queen Victoria's remark on Mr Gladstone that 'he speaks to Me as if I were a public meeting', to more everyday comments like 'No one would ever speak like that', and to attributions like colloquial, journalistic, biblical, childlike, pedantic. Thus prominence, like deviance, is best understood in terms of relative norms: the set of expectancies we have acquired as speakers, hearers, readers and writers, varies from one kind of language situation to another. At the same time it must be borne in mind that in literature, prominence and deviance frequently take a more extreme form (for example in the *Gormenghast* passage on p. 112) which would show up against practically any norm we should choose; this more general deviance can be demonstrated by taking one's relative norms from as broad a range as possible.

The concept of relative norm also explains a more wholesale kind of deviance: the adoption, in literature, of a style borrowed from some 'foreign' norm. This phenomenon of STYLE BORROWING has many manifestations in prose: the child language at the beginning of Joyce's *Portrait* is an example we have already noted; others are the style of private correspondence used in epistolary novels such as *Pamela*; the racy colloquialism of first-person novels such as *The Catcher in the Rye*; the use of stylistic parody and pastiche as exemplified in *Ulysses*. In such cases the recognition of style involves awareness of deviation from one norm (the norm of a particular writer, genre, period, register to which the text owes its provenance), and approximation to another contrasting norm. The adopted norm may of course (as in the case of the epistolary novel) become a literary norm or a convention in itself. But the mimetic, borrowed origin of the norm is still relevant.

2.5 Primary and secondary norms

Style borrowing is thus a telling illustration of a principle on which Halliday insists: that prominence is not only 'departure from a norm' but 'attainment of a norm'.[16] In one case 'attainment of a norm' will mean style borrowing: the approximation to some external norm as a 'disguise' or at least as a point of reference. In another case it will mean that the writer creates his own special kind of language, and it is in this sense that Halliday applies it to the Neanderthal language of *The Inheritors*. In this novel, he argues, the particular pattern of frequencies sets up its own expectancies, and the consequence is that we can generalise beyond the text, and judge whether a particular non-occurring sentence would be appropriate to its 'language' or not. He shows, for instance, that 'A branch curved downwards over the water' could have easily occurred in the language of Lok, while 'He had very quickly broken off the lowest branches' would be highly deviant.[17]

The norm which is 'attained' by stylistic consistency in a text might be called a SECONDARY NORM, since it is established by deviance from the PRIMARY (relative) NORMS which determine our more general expectations of language. Golding's novel is to some degree experimental in style, and when we read it, we sense there is something 'odd' about Lok's language. This we do by reference to primary norms. But when we consider what might be deviant in terms of Lok's own 'dialect', we refer to the secondary norm.

2.6 Internal deviation

The recognition that a text may set up its own secondary norms leads to a further conclusion, that features of language within that text may depart from the norms of the text itself: that is, they may 'stand out' against the background of what the text has led us to expect. This is the phenomenon of INTERNAL DEVIATION,[18] which, although it is most striking in poetry, may equally well be observed in prose style. Internal deviation explains the prominence, not uncommon in prose fiction, of an ordinary, even banal piece of language which seems to gain its impact from the context in which it is found. A sudden variation in sentence complexity may help to give this effect: Norman Page[19] points out that at the beginning of Jane Austen's *Emma*, the three-word sentence 'Miss Taylor married' stands out momentously against a background of longer sentences (the average sentence length for the first five paragraphs of the novel being 26.5 words). A similar case is the sentence (7) which ends the opening paragraph of *The Secret Sharer* (see section 3.3, example 1) where the brevity of the sentence

'And then I was left alone with my ship, anchored at the head of the Gulf of Siam' contrasts with the complexities of the preceding scene-setting sentences, as if to emphasise the insignificance of the lonely narrator against his background, the sea. The opposite case, where the departure from the norm is in the direction of sentence complexity rather than simplicity, is illustrated in Hemingway's *The Old Man and the Sea*: the culmination of the Old Man's battle with the fish is related in (for Hemingway) unusually complex sentences, conveying a climactic frenzy of movement against the background of Hemingway's more usual simplicity of style. The contrast can only be appreciated if we first quote a more characteristic passage from the same episode:

[1] That way nothing is accomplished, he thought. His mouth was too dry to speak but he could not reach for the water now. I must get him alongside this time, he thought. I am not good for many more turns. Yes you are, he told himself. You're good for ever.

On the next turn he nearly had him. But again the fish righted himself and swam slowly away.

[2] He took all his pain and what was left of his strength and his long-gone pride and he put it against the fish's agony and the fish came over onto his side and swam gently on his side, his bill almost touching the planking of the skiff, and started to pass the boat, long, deep, wide, silver and barred with purple and interminable in the water.

The old man dropped the line and put his foot on it and lifted the harpoon as high as he could and drove it down with all his strength, and more strength he had just summoned, into the fish's side just behind the great chest fin that rose high in the air to the altitude of the man's chest. He felt the iron go in and he leaned on it and drove it further and then pushed all his weight after it.

[Ernest Hemingway, *The Old Man and the Sea*, illus. edn 1953, pp. 84–87]

2.7 Pervasive and local characteristics of style

Internal deviation draws attention to a limitation of the view of style with which this chapter started. It was assumed that when we talk of 'a style' or 'the style of X' we refer to what is pervasive or recurrent in a text. This is true as a matter of general usage, but there is no reason why stylistics should not cover local and individual, as well as general and pervasive aspects of linguistic choice. It may be less important to examine the 'lowest common denominator' of linguistic usage throughout a work than to study style as a dynamic phenomenon: as something which develops through peaks and valleys of dramatic tension, which not only establishes expectancies, but which frustrates and modifies them as a work progresses. In this dynamic perspective, pervasive and local features of style are equally parts of the pattern. The concepts of deviation, prominence and foregrounding may be given an individual, as well as a frequential interpretation. At the same time the pervasive features are an essential background, against which local features become contrastively salient.

2.8 Variations in style

But the 'pervasive' view of style also has to confront the fact that there may be a multiplicity of styles within the same work. Such stylistic variation can follow various patterns. An evolutionary pattern is one. In his *Portrait*, Joyce offers a development of style corresponding to his hero's development from the dawning of linguistic consciousness, in childhood, to maturity. More ambitiously, in the Scylla and Charybdis episode of *Ulysses*, he offers a recapitulation, through parody, of English literary history.

Another kind of pattern is alternation. In *Bleak House*, the impersonal ironic voice of the author is interspersed with the more humanly involved voice of Esther. In Faulkner's *The Sound and the Fury*, four 'narrators' take it in turn to present their vision of events to the reader. A quantitative method can still be applied to these cases, if stylistically homogeneous sections can be separated out as different 'texts' within the same work. This can lead to revealing internal comparisons: Halliday, for example, compares the Neanderthal style in *The Inheritors* with the '*homo sapiens* style' and a third, transitional style in the same novel.

It is less easy to reconcile the 'pervasive' approach with a more general and subtle type of stylistic shift which must be found, to some extent, in every novel. This is the adaptation of style, sometimes abrupt, sometimes gradual, to the ongoing narrative focus, with its changes of tone, mood and subject.

The variation of style with tone (see section 8.5) is supremely exemplified in Dickens; and we may take, for illustration, four passages from the earlier part of *Dombey and Son*, in which style variation is intrinsic to the novel's satiric-epic picture of Victorian urban society, concentrating on the capitalist house of Dombey. The book begins with the description of father and son at the latter's birth; the following paragraph is so formal in its rhetorical design, balancing each element of Mr Dombey's description against a similar element of the description of Paul, that we may set it out in tabular form (reading the columns from left to right):

[3]	Dombey was about eight-and-forty years of age.	Son about eight-and-forty minutes.
	Dombey was rather bald, rather red, and though a handsome well-made man, too stern and pompous in appearance, to be prepossessing.	Son was very bald, and very red, and though (of course) an undeniably fine infant, somewhat crushed and spotty in his general effect, as yet.
	On the brow of Dombey, Time and his brother Care had set some marks, as on a tree that was to come down in good time – remorseless twins they are for striding through their human forests, notching as they go –	while the countenance of Son was crossed with a thousand little creases, which the same deceitful Time would take delight in smoothing out and wearing away with the flat part of his scythe, as a preparation of the surface for his deeper operations.

This is a brief glimpse of one kind of language which recurs at intervals throughout the book, especially at symbolic and ceremonial points in the fortunes of the Dombey family: births, funerals and marriages. It is poised between comedy and moral seriousness, and the dominant note of irony is struck in the balancing of father and son, and in the reiterated unmodified nouns *Dombey* and *Son* – appropriate references to individuals whose lives are respectively dedicated and mortgaged to the gods of family pride and commerce. The tone is maintained by an armoury of traditional rhetorical devices: anaphora, parallelism (with antithesis), personification. At the same time, the formalism is broken up (particularly in the last and longest sentence) by elements which will ease transition to a lighter tone of comedy: for example, the bantering irony signalled by the parenthesis of 'though (of course) an undeniably fine infant' (directed against a general human frailty, partiality of parents for their offspring, rather than against the more repellant form that partiality takes in Mr Dombey); also, the fanciful extensions of the well-worn personifications of Time and Care, again expressed through parenthetical elaboration of the syntax.

A different kind of style, and a different kind of rhetoric, is employed in passages where Dickens wants to move us with compassion: notably in Paul's death scene, where he can afford to use simple syntax and vocabulary (expressing the simple images of the child's mind) in the assurance that understatement will merely intensify the reader's sympathy:

[4] Paul had never risen from his little bed (1). He lay there, listening to the noises in the street, quite tranquilly; not caring much how the time

went, but watching it and watching everything about him with observing eyes (2).

When the sunbeams struck into his room through the rustling blinds, and quivered on the opposite wall like golden water, he knew that evening was coming on, and that the sky was red and beautiful (3). As the reflection died away, and a gloom went creeping up the wall, he watched it deepen, deepen, deepen into night (4). Then he thought how the long streets were dotted with lamps, and how the peaceful stars were shining overhead (5). His fancy had a strange tendency to wander to the river, which he knew was flowing through the great city; and now he thought how black it was, and how deep it would look, reflecting the hosts of stars – and more than all, how steadily it rolled away to meet the sea (6).

[Dombey and Son, Chapter 16]

The artlessness of the child's mind is reflected partly in the repetitions 'watching it and watching everything' and 'deepen, deepen, deepen'; in the use of common words, especially those with monosyllabic stems: 'he thought how the long streets were dotted with lamps', 'and now he thought how black it was'; and in the way the cohesion of the passage rests on the subject pronoun *he* and the conjunction *and*. There is a lack of the bold artifice of the preceding passage; and yet it is there in a less noticeable form: in the manner in which throughout the passage constructions are matched in pairs. Sentences (2) and (3) illustrate the point:

```
(2)  He  ⎡lay        │there
         ⎣listening   │to the noises

         ⎡not caring how time went
         ⎣but  ⎡watching │it and
               ⎣watching │everything ...

(3)  When the sunbeams ⎡struck    │into his room
                   and ⎣quivered  │on the opposite wall
         │through the rustling blinds
         │like golden water
       he knew
         ⎡that │evening │was coming on, and
         ⎣that │the sky │was red and beautiful.
```

The pattern of duality is broken, significantly, in two places: at the very beginning, in the poignantly simple opening sentence; and at the very end, where there is the unexpected addition of a third, and longer, member to the parallelism of *how* clauses: 'and more than all, how steadily it rolled away to meet the sea'. This is a good example of how internal deviation can give prominence (here with an effect of resolving finality) to a piece of language which carries special significance. The sea is both the end-point of the movement from near to far running through the second paragraph, and Dickens's often-iterated symbol of the 'great beyond'. The syntactic coupling, the balancing of one construction against another parallel construction of similar form or similar length, seems to bring to the passage a feeling that all is well: Paul is following the destiny which is ordained for him, and no agonising will disturb the peace of his passing.

Later in the same chapter, at the point of death, Dickens breaks into a further kind of rhetoric, the declamatory rhetoric he reserves for moments of high drama:

[5] The golden ripple on the wall came back again, and nothing else stirred in the room (1). The old, old fashion! (2) The fashion that came in with our first garments, and will last unchanged until our race has run its course, and the wide firmament is rolled up like a scroll (3). The old, old fashion – Death! (4)

Oh thank GOD, all who see it, for that older fashion yet, of immortality! (5) And look upon us, angels of young children, with regards not quite estranged, when the swift river bears us to the ocean! (6)

At such points Dickens has a way of enlarging his theme beyond the narrative pretext, addressing his readers directly as sharers of a common human lot with himself and his characters. We note his use in (3) of the inclusive first-person pronoun *our*, and the change from the narrative past tense to the perfective (*has run*) and the future (*will last*). The syntax is that of direct histrionic appeal: disjunctive, verbless sentences, exclamations, apostrophes and imperatives. The more schematic rhetoric of passages [3] and [4] is found here too, especially in the parallelisms of sentences (3), (5) and (6), and in the repetition of the leitmotiv *the old, old fashion*. The musical term 'leitmotiv' is not inappropriate for the way in which Dickens repeats an idiom or expression, under various modifications and transformations, through episodes of a novel, allowing it to accumulate thematic significance as it goes, an illustration on a small scale of his use of dynamic variation in style. 'The old, old fashion' and 'the older fashion yet' are the culmination of a chain of verbal echoes which begin, in Chapter 8, with the mention of Paul's having 'a strange, old-fashioned, thoughtful way', and which develop from a whimsical sign of his premature aging to a portent of his premature death.

From this high point of religiosity we descend to an ironic concluding sentence, recalling another leitmotiv which makes its first appearance in passage [3]:

[6] 'Dear me, dear me! To think,' said Miss Tox, bursting out afresh that night, as if her heart were broken, 'that Dombey and Son should be a Daughter after all!'[20]

And directly after this, at the beginning of Chapter 17, there is another abrupt change of tone:

[7] Captain Cuttle, in the *exercise* of that surprising *talent* for deep-laid and unfathomable *scheming*, with *which* (as is not unusual in men of transparent *simplicity*) he sincerely believed himself to be endowed by nature, had gone to Mr Dombey's house on the eventful Sunday, *winking* all the way as a *vent* for his superfluous *sagacity*, and had presented himself in the full *lustre* of the ankle-jacks before the eyes of Towlinson (1). *Hearing* from that individual, to his great *concern*, of the impending *calamity*, Captain Cuttle, in his *delicacy*, sheered off again confounded; merely *handing* in the nosegay as a small mark of his *solicitude*, and *leaving* his respectful *compliments* for the family in general, *which* he accompanied with an *expression* of his *hope* that they would lay their heads well to the wind under existing *circumstances*, and a friendly *intimation* that he would 'look up again' tomorrow (2).

Here is an example of Dickens's mock-elevated style, his comic version of the 'Big Bow-wow strain'[21] cultivated by many eighteenth-century and early nineteenth-century authors. The markers of this style are Latin wordiness and complex syntax: the former especially evident in the frequency of abstract nouns (usually polysyllabic and often accompanied by a polysyllabic adjective), and the latter in the use of relative clauses and *-ing* participial constructions. (Abstract nouns, participles, and relative pronouns are italicised in the above passage.) Grandiloquence was the besetting linguistic vice of Dickens's era, and it is clear from many burlesque treatments of it in his novels (notably in the language of Mr Micawber), that he himself regarded it as a vice. The occurrence of it in Dickens's own narrative is thus a sure sign of non-seriousness, a linguistic game-playing which is a prose counterpart of the mock-heroic style in poetry. The burlesque is most apparent where learned words keep company with the homely and seafaring vocabulary associated with the Captain: 'in his delicacy, sheered off again confounded', 'in the full lustre of the ankle-jacks'. One reaction to this style is that it is *merely* game-playing, and rather tedious at that. But the elevation of style functions as a distancing device, especially needful when, as in the passage quoted, Paul's death scene is still fresh in the mind. Classical polysyllables such as *solitude* and *calamity* keep feelings at bay, so that the reader is led into a frame of mind where the farcical aspects of the good Captain's behaviour can innocently rub shoulders with tragedy.

Dickens varies his style like a virtuoso who can grade and colour the tone of his instrument as the mood requires. Yet this variation takes place within the encompassing medium of a pervasive Dickensian style. For example, Dickens is fond of parenthetical constructions which allow the generalising authorial voice to interrupt the narrative flow. This trait is not restricted to one variety of style, for we can observe it both in passage [3] ('though (of course) an undeniably fine infant'; 'remorseless twins they are for striding through their human forests, notching as they go'); and in passage [7] ('as is not unusual in men of transparent simplicity'). Even in *Bleak House*, where the two narrators – Esther and the impersonal author – are quite distinct, the unifying factors of authorial style are still striking. One irrepressible Dickensian feature is the far-fetched quasi-simile, introduced by *as if* or by some equivalent make-believe construction. Esther says of Mrs Jellyby:

> her voice impressed my fancy as if it had a sort of spectacles on too
> [Chapter 8]

and of Mr Turveydrop:

> As he bowed to me in that tight state, I almost believe I saw creases come into the white of his eyes.
> [Chapter 14]

It is with a more elaborate example of this type of fanciful similitude that the impersonal 'Dickens' introduces Mrs Rouncewell:

> She is a fine old lady, handsome, stately, wonderfully neat, and has such a back, and such a stomacher that if her stays should turn out when she dies to have been a broad old-fashioned family fire-grate, nobody who knows her would have cause to be surprised.
> [Chapter 7]

As a further example, we may observe that the formal rhetoric of parallelism, anaphora, and so on is characteristic of Dickens in many of his moods: it is illustrated in passages [3], [4] and [5].

This excursion into Dickens's style has indicated that the pervasive approach to style has its proper place, even where style variation attracts the attention more than stylistic consistency. But it also shows that a writer's verbal art can often be more profitably examined within the narrower scope of a chapter, a page, or even a paragraph, where the stylistic values can be more closely related to their function within a particular context. This again implies some limitation on the quantitative measurement of style, for within the limited compass of a few hundred words, little statistical significance can be attached to the frequency of this or that feature.

In the following chapter, we use relatively short passages for exemplifying the analysis of prose style. This, it will now be seen, can be justified not only by necessary limitations of space, but by the advantage that can be gained in many respects from sacrificing generality in favour of contextual particularity. For our purposes, a 'text' can happily be defined as a fairly short extract.

2.9 Features of style

The term 'feature' has occurred many times in this chapter. We define it simply as the occurrence in a text of a linguistic or stylistic category (see section 2.1). Examples of linguistic categories are 'nasal consonant', 'noun', 'transitive verb', 'question', 'negative', 'future', 'colour term'. Examples of stylistic categories are 'balanced sentence', 'alliteration', 'personification'. Stylistic categories are more complex phenomena which are often difficult to define, but which are assumed to be describable in terms of linguistic categories, although they are not a necessary part of the description of a language. We need to refer to them because they are a significant element of style, but we do not in general distinguish them formally from linguistic categories.

Linguistic categories are essentially contrastive, and therefore their occurrence entails the non-occurrence of other categories: for example, the occurrence of a nasal consonant (say, /n/ or /m/) entails the non-occurrence of a fricative consonant, a stop consonant, or (more distantly) a vowel. The contrastive nature of linguistic categories is clear in cases where the category label contains two words: for example, a transitive verb obviously contrasts with other types of verb (intransitive verbs, linking verbs, etc.). In cases where there is only one term (e.g. 'noun'), there is always an omitted generic term: a noun would be explicitly labelled a 'noun word'; a question, a 'question sentence', and so on. It is part of the function of a linguistic theory, and of its linguistic description of the English language, to specify what linguistic categories there are and what are the contrastive relations between them. We do not attempt a detailed account of linguistic categories in this book, but use as far as possible those which are well enough known not to need explanation in terms of some linguistic theory.[22]

Categories contrast with one another either directly or indirectly: the indirectness of contrast can be shown hierarchically, in terms of a tree diagram. We now show this in an uncomplicated way in Figure 2.2, which illustrates the classification of words.

In terms of this diagram, nouns, for example, contrast directly with adjectives, but only indirectly with prepositions. Similarly, transitive verbs contrast directly with intransitive verbs, but only indirectly with adjectives. A word is not a category at all in the sense used: since a text may be decomposed entirely into a sequence of words, there is no linguistic sense in which one could choose to use something else instead of a word. This is why counting the number of words in a text cannot give any indication of its style. A word, like a sentence, a letter, and a phoneme, is a UNIT, not a category.

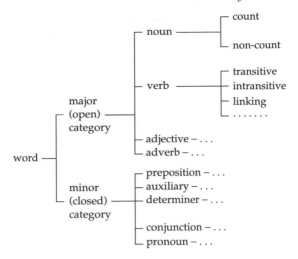

Figure 2.2

When determining the frequency of a particular feature or category, we work out the number of times it occurs per X, where X is some standard measure. For example, frequency of nouns can be expressed as a percentage of the number of words in a text: X should normally be a more general, superordinate category including the feature being counted. It would be rather pointless, for example, to count the number of nouns per sentence, or the number of intransitive verbs per noun: these frequencies would be difficult to interpret, because the result would be affected by independent variables, namely the length of sentences, and the frequency of nouns respectively. The ideal standard of measurement is provided by the *immediately* superordinate category: i.e., according to Figure 2.2, we should count the number of nouns against major category words, rather than words. This is because the noun-per-word frequency again involves an independent variable: the frequency of major-category words, as compared with minor-category words. However, we do not adhere too pedantically to this principle, since the details of diagrams such as that of Figure 2.2 are matters of disagreement among linguists. For most purposes, where 'a rough indication of frequency' is all that is required, it is often convenient to use the most general term (e.g. the word unit) as a convenient standard of comparison.

An alternative method, useful in some cases, is to express frequency in terms of the ratio of occurrences of one category to occurrences of another; for example, the ratio of nouns to adjectives. The most relevant categories to compare in such cases are ones which are immediately in contrast to one another.

Some stylistic features are themselves variable, for example sentence complexity. A rough but convenient measure of sentence complexity is the average number of words per sentence: that is, we have first to determine the complexity of each sentence by counting the words, and then to derive from this an overall measure of complexity. If desired, further measurement can be obtained from this; for example, we can measure the dispersion of a frequency distribution of sentence length, and so determine how far complexity tends to vary from one sentence to another. Other, similar, measures can be made for phonemes per syllable, morphemes per word, etc.

Here we touch on another type of linguistic hierarchy, which interacts with the one already mentioned. Linguistic units tend to form a hierarchy of extent. For example, in grammar, sentences are not directly composed of words, but rather sentences are composed of clauses, which in turn are composed of phrases or further (subordinate) clauses, the phrases in turn being composed of words. Words themselves can be broken down into the minimal grammatical units known as MORPHEMES (stems and affixes). Complexity of structure can be located at any of these points. For example, the following two sentences of Ruskin's contain the same number of words, but [8] consists of just one main clause, whereas [9] contains two subordinate clauses (which are italicised):

[8] *Mountains* are *the beginning and the end of all natural scenery.*
[9] *When we build*, let us think *that we build for ever.*

The complexity of [8] lies not in clause structure, but in noun phrase structure (in this case it is the noun phrases that are italicised). These examples also show how the word-per-sentence measure fails to deal with the internal complexity of words: [8] on this level is more complex than [9], which contains no words with more than one morpheme. Grammatical complexity is in reality not a simple quantitative measure, but a multiplicity of different measures, not only different in terms of hierarchical level, but varying according to the positions and the categories in which complexity is found (see section 7.5). It is for this reason that averaging words per sentence is a crude and undifferentiated, albeit very convenient, measure.

In phonology and grammar, there is a broad area of agreement about linguistic categories and the contrasts into which they enter, even though different linguistic theories will formalise them in different ways. In semantics, on the other hand, there is much less agreement. When we deal with semantic categories, we find that occurrences cut across grammatical categories: for example, the concept of 'negation' can include not only the negative particle *not*, but other word classes such as pronouns (*nothing, nobody*) and adverbs (*nowhere, never*), and even items which have no morphological resemblance to these, such as *unfinished, impossible, false, hardly*. Even with negation, a fairly well understood category, the limits are difficult to define. And in other cases, for example if we want to count the occurrence of notions of visual perception, morality, causation, kinship, etc., the boundaries are even more vague. Contrastiveness is much less clear-cut in semantics, and in practice we have to rely on fairly intuitive identification of the category in question. It is also difficult to hit on an appropriate standard of measurement: it is clear that 'past', 'present' and 'future' all belong to the category of time reference; but to what higher generic category (say) do moral attributes belong? Studying the semantic features of texts is inevitably rather an intuitive business, and in so far as we can quantify such features at all, it often seems best to attach them to grammatical labels (e.g. 'colour adjectives', 'adverbials of place'), and to use some arbitrary standard of measurement, such as number of words.

This discussion has exposed yet another severe problem for quantitative stylistics. The measurement of frequency depends on the existence of a clearly articulated set of linguistic and stylistic categories. We may say, in fact, that a stylo-statistician is only as good as the linguistic theory on which he relies. On the one hand, this is an argument for preferring an analysis of style which has a sound linguistic basis over one which merely uses *ad hoc* categories. On the other hand, it leads to the admission that in so far as all linguistic theories are provisional and incomplete (particularly in the sphere of semantics), even the best-informed linguistic analysis leaves a great deal to be desired. Once again, comfort can be found in the principle of approximation: 'a rough indication of frequencies is often just what is needed'.

2.10 Style markers and the principle of selection

We have seen in sections 2.1–2.3 that any practicable method of stylistic analysis must select some features for analysis and ignore others. It is clear, in fact, that stylistic analysis must be very selective indeed: some studies concentrate on just one feature, and others on a mere handful of features. For example, Ian Watt bases his analysis of the first paragraph of Henry James's *The Ambassadors*[23] on five features: (1) non-transitive verbs; (2) abstract nouns; (3) the word *that*; (4) elegant variation; and (5) delayed specification of referents. His categories are not well-defined, and yet his essay is an admirable example of how, even with a limited analysis of limited material, it is possible to give an illuminating account of a writer's style.

How are the features for analysis to be selected? We have assumed that stylistics investigates the relation between the writer's artistic achievement, and how it is achieved through language. That is, it studies the relation between the significances of a text, and the linguistic characteristics in which they are manifest. This implies two criteria of relevance for the selection of stylistic features: a literary criterion and a linguistic criterion. We have suggested that these two criteria converge in the concept of foregrounding (section 2.3).

By combining literary discrimination and linguistic discrimination in this way, we should become alert to those particular features of style which call for more careful investigation. Such salient features of style may be called STYLE MARKERS.[24]

The heuristic notion of 'style marker' is the key to the method. If we can identify style markers, we rule out, simply by ignoring them, whole areas of the English language which do not seem to be exploited in any unusual way in a particular text. This is in keeping with a reasonable assumption that even the most ingenious writer will not use every part of the linguistic code for particular artistic purposes. But of course there is no way of knowing in advance for a particular author or text which parts of the code will be exploited in a stylistically interesting way and which will not.

The reliance on 'intuitive observation' in selection means that a heavy burden falls on the reader's training in the art of alert reading, and of responding to linguistic and other cues. You may miss out significant features of style that you happen not to have been looking for, or you may have an inadequate understanding of how language works and lack a terminology for talking about it. This is where a linguistic method comes in. We find it valuable to have a checklist of potential style markers (even though this list itself is necessarily selective) so that a reader may carry out a linguistic survey of the text, searching for significant features. The checklist is rather like a map which leaves out a lot of detail, but shows what is likely to be most relevant for the traveller. We present the list in the following chapter and follow it with analyses of three specimen passages of prose.

2.11 Conclusion

This chapter has argued that just as the study of style cannot entirely rely on quantitative data, neither can it ultimately do without them. We have presented five arguments against the view that style can be defined objectively in terms of the frequencies of the linguistic properties of a text or corpus.

(i) There is no purely objective way of determining a statistical norm: as a matter of both convenience and practical necessity we have to rely in general on relative norms.

(ii) There is no complete list of the linguistic properties of a text; therefore, we have to select the features to study.

(iii) There is no direct relation between statistical deviance and stylistic significance: literary considerations must therefore guide us in selecting what features to examine.

(iv) There is no absolute consistency of style with a given domain, and therefore, in measuring the overall statistical properties of texts, we may fail to capture significant variations of style.

(v) There is no agreement on the set of descriptive categories required for an adequate account of a language such as English; consequently, different investigators are likely to differ in the way they identify linguistic features in a text.

Together, these arguments may seem to leave very little foothold for quantitative methods in the study of literary style. But on the other hand there still remains the basic fact that without quantitative confirmation, statements on style lack the support of concrete evidence. Thus, although we are wary of claiming too much for statistical analysis, we would regard it as an essential and important tool in stylistic description. In the next chapter, we aim to demonstrate, on a limited scale, how frequency counts can be an important aid in practical analyses.

Notes

1. B. BLOCH (1953), 40–44.
2. For practical purposes, it is possible to set up as a norm a corpus consisting of a broad cross-section of texts of a particular period. For modern American English, there is a wide range of text corpora including the Brown University Corpus, compiled in the early 1960s, officially known as 'A Standard Sample of Present-Day English for use with Digital Computers' (see H. KUČERA and W.N. FRANCIS, 1967). A parallel corpus (the Lancaster–Oslo/Bergen Corpus) exists for British English. A much larger and more up-to-date corpus of British English is the British National Corpus, compiled in the early 1990s and containing both spoken and written textual material (G. ASTON and L. BURNARD, 1998). But even in such cases there is an arbitrary element in the sampling: the general composition of the Brown Corpus, for example, was determined by subjective decisions on the importance of this or that kind of text. It cannot claim, in spite of its considerable size (over a million words) to be representative of 'the language as a whole'.
3. See A. ELLEGÅRD (1978), for frequencies of various grammatical categories in part of the Brown Corpus. Ellegård's conclusion (pp. 76–79) is that grammatical frequencies are relatively consistent between different varieties of English in some areas (e.g. frequency of clause-types), but that in other areas (e.g. length of phrases) they vary considerably. A detailed study of grammatical frequency based on a very large corpus of spoken and written English is provided by D. BIBER *et al.* (1999).
4. On aesthetic terms, see F. SIBLEY (1968). Sibley's analysis of the relation between aesthetic and non-aesthetic terms is instructive for stylistics, since much of the vocabulary of criticism is aesthetic, whereas that of linguistics is largely non-aesthetic or descriptive. The relevant point is that non-aesthetic terms cannot

be used to define aesthetic terms, but that they may be used, in a reasoned way, to provide evidence for the appropriate use of aesthetic terms.

5. M.A.K. HALLIDAY (1971), 344.

6. The journal *Poetics* (7.1 (1978) 1–2) has adopted 'Guidelines for Statistical Papers' drawn up by the Statistics Workshop of the Third International Conference on Computers and the Humanities. These guidelines commit researchers to doing statistics properly if they do it at all; for example: 'When sample means (averages) are obtained, the sample size and standard deviation should be routinely included'; 'Comparison between sample means from a common normal population should present the *t* statistic'. But the editor of *Poetics*, T.A. Van Dijk, pertinently comments: 'statistical sophistication . . . may not be substituted for the main goals of scholarly inquiry. . . . In this respect the humanities should learn from the bad examples of statistical smoke-screens in so many papers in the social sciences'.

7. HALLIDAY (1971), 340. Halliday assumes (343) that what we call 'prominence' and 'deviance' are aspects of the same phenomenon: i.e. that prominence can be expressed statistically.

8. J. MUKAŘOVSKÝ (1958), 44.

9. See A.C. BAUGH and T. CABLE (2002), 311–314, and G.L. BROOK (1958), 148.

10. Reported by James's secretary, Miss Bosanquet, and discussed in S. CHATMAN (1972), 50.

11. In one respect, Figure 2.1 overdetermines the relation between the three factors: prominence is an immeasurable subjective sense of 'what is special' in a piece of language; and while one may reasonably assume that such an impression must have some basis in the text, it is not inconceivable that it may be distorted by other factors, such as the reader's attention span.

12. L.T. MILIC (1967), 125.

13. The significance of the results in Milic's table is confirmed by statistical test. In this, they are particularly convincing, showing that what strikes the investigator as subjectively significant is also significant from a statistical point of view. But we should not assume a requirement that stylistic significance should be automatically corroborated by statistical significance: this follows from the distinction we draw between prominence and deviance.

14. E.P.J. CORBETT (1966), repr. in G.A. LOVE and M. PAYNE (1969), 89.

15. *Cf* N.E. ENKVIST (1964), 28.

16. HALLIDAY (1971), 340.

17. *Ibid*, 353. The latter of these sentences 'breaks four rules: it has a human actor with a transitive verb, a tense other than simple past, a defining modifier, and a non-spatial adjunct'. Halliday's specification of the 'grammar' of a prose text can be compared with a similar approach to the grammar of poetry taken by J.P. THORNE (1965). In both cases, the idea is that a special 'counter-grammar' can be written to account for the phenomenon of deviation in a literary text. But needless to say this only works where the consistency of foregrounding in the text is particularly regular.

18. *Cf* S.R. LEVIN (1965).

19. N. PAGE (1972), 104–105.

20. This sentence was omitted from all editions of *Dombey and Son* after 1858 (except for reprints of the first edition).

21. Sir WALTER SCOTT, *Journal*, 14 March 1826.

22. 'Standard' textbooks and works of reference may be used for this purpose; for example, for phonetics, A.C. GIMSON (1980) and D. JONES (1977); also, for a brief introduction to English phonology, see A.C. GIMSON, Supp. II, in R. QUIRK (1968). For grammar, reference can be made to R. QUIRK *et al.* (1985) and to the shorter textbook S. GREENBAUM and R. QUIRK, *A Student's Grammar of the English Language* (1990). See also the Introduction to Chapter 3.

23. I. WATT (1969).

24. On style markers, *cf* ENKVIST (1964), 34: 'We may now define style markers as those linguistic items that only appear, or are most or least frequent, in one group of contexts.'

CHAPTER 3

A method of analysis and some examples

This chapter has the practical purpose of showing how the apparatus of linguistic description can be used in analysing the style of a prose text. We take for granted the principles that have been argued in Chapters 1 and 2. We also take for granted a set of linguistic categories which will be more or less common knowledge to those who have a basic familiarity with the workings of the English language, whether in literary or non-literary contexts. One particular area in which technical terms are likely to cause some problems is that of grammar, and here we follow the terminology and general view of grammar presented in Greenbaum and Quirk's *A Student's Grammar of the English Language* and many other grammars using a similar framework.[1] Another area is that of foregrounding, where we draw on the terminology of traditional poetics ('metaphor', 'metonymy', 'onomatopoeia', etc.). Although many of these terms are widely current in literary scholarship, we presuppose a linguistic account of these phenomena, and for this purpose, it is convenient to refer the reader to Leech's *A Linguistic Guide to English Poetry*.[2] Following the list of categories in section 3.1, explanations of selected points will be added in section 3.2.

Every analysis of style, in our terms, is an attempt to find the artistic principles underlying a writer's choice of language. All writers, and for that matter, all texts, have individual qualities. Therefore the features which call themselves to our attention in one text will not necessarily be important in another text by the same or a different author. There is no infallible technique for selecting what is significant. We have to make ourselves newly aware, for each text, of the artistic effect of the whole, and the way linguistic details fit into this whole.

Nevertheless, it is useful to have a checklist of features which may or may not be significant in a given text. For this reason, the following list of questions has been prepared. The answers to these questions will give a range of data which may be examined in relation to the literary effect of each passage. We stress that the list serves a heuristic purpose: it enables us to collect data on a fairly systematic basis. It is not exhaustive, of course, but is rather a list of 'good bets': categories which, in our experience, are likely to yield stylistically relevant information. The stylistic values associated with the linguistic data must be largely taken on trust at present; in subsequent chapters, we endeavour to show how these values, too, can be studied systematically.

3.1 A checklist of linguistic and stylistic categories

The categories are placed under four general headings: lexical categories, grammatical categories, figures of speech, and cohesion and context. Semantic categories are not listed separately, since, as suggested in section 2.9, it is easier to arrive at these through other categories; for example, we use our lexical categories to find out how choice of words involves various types of meaning. Since the purpose of the list is heuristic, there is no harm in mixing categories in this way. It is also in the nature of things that categories will overlap, so that the same feature may well be noted under different headings.

A: Lexical categories

[For notes (i–xiv) on the categories see pp. 66–7]

1 GENERAL. Is the vocabulary simple or complex[(i)]? formal or colloquial? descriptive or evaluative? general or specific? How far does the writer make use of the emotive and other associations of words, as opposed to their referential meaning? Does the text contain idiomatic phrases or notable collocations[(ii)], and if so, with what kind of dialect or register[(iii)] are these idioms or collocations associated? Is there any use of rare or specialised vocabulary? Are any particular morphological categories noteworthy (e.g. compound words, words with particular suffixes)? To what semantic fields do words belong?

2 NOUNS. Are the nouns abstract or concrete? What kinds of abstract nouns occur (e.g. nouns referring to events, perceptions, processes, moral qualities, social qualities)? What use is made of proper names? Collective nouns?

3 ADJECTIVES. Are the adjectives frequent? To what kinds of attribute do adjectives refer? Physical? Psychological? Visual? Auditory? Colour? Referential? Emotive? Evaluative? etc. Are adjectives restrictive or non-restrictive? Gradable or non-gradable? Attributive or predicative?

4 VERBS. Do the verbs carry an important part of the meaning? Are they stative (referring to states) or dynamic (referring to actions, events, etc.)? Do they 'refer' to movements, physical acts, speech acts, psychological states or activities, perceptions, etc.? Are they transitive, intransitive, linking (intensive), etc.? Are they factive or non-factive[iv]?

5 ADVERBS. Are adverbs frequent? What semantic functions do they perform (manner, place, direction, time, degree, etc.)? Is there any significant use of sentence adverbs (conjuncts such as *so, therefore, however*; disjuncts such as *certainly, obviously, frankly*)[v]?

B: Grammatical categories

1 SENTENCE TYPES. Does the author use only statements (declarative sentences), or do questions, commands, exclamations or minor sentence types (such as sentences with no verb) also occur in the text? If these other types appear, what is their function?

2 SENTENCE COMPLEXITY. Do sentences on the whole have a simple or a complex structure? What is the average sentence length (in number of words)? What is the ratio of dependent to independent clauses? Does complexity vary strikingly from one sentence to another? Is complexity mainly due to (i) coordination, (ii) subordination, or (iii) parataxis (juxtaposition of clauses or other equivalent structures)? In what parts of a sentence does complexity tend to occur? For instance, is there any notable occurrence of anticipatory structure (e.g. of complex subjects preceding the verbs, of dependent clauses preceding the subject of a main clause)[vi]?

3 CLAUSE TYPES. What types of dependent clause are favoured: relative clauses, adverbial clauses, different types of nominal clauses (*that*-clauses, *wh*-clauses, etc.)? Are reduced or non-finite clauses commonly used and, if so, of what type are they (infinitive clauses, *-ing* clauses, *-ed* clauses, verbless clauses)[vii]?

4 CLAUSE STRUCTURE. Is there anything significant about clause elements (e.g. frequency of objects, complements, adverbials; of transitive or intransitive verb constructions)[viii]? Are there any unusual orderings (initial adverbials, fronting of object or complement, etc.)? Do special kinds of clause construction occur (such as those with preparatory *it* or *there*)?

5 NOUN PHRASES. Are they relatively simple or complex? Where does the complexity lie (in premodification by adjectives, nouns, etc., or in postmodification by prepositional phrases, relative clauses, etc.)? Note occurrence of listings (e.g. sequences of adjectives), coordination or apposition.

6 VERB PHRASES. Are there any significant departures from the use of the simple past tense? For example, notice occurrences and functions of the present tense; of the progressive aspect (e.g. *was lying*); of the perfective

aspect (e.g. *has/had appeared*); of modal auxiliaries (e.g. *can, must, would,* etc.). Look out for phrasal verbs and how they are used.

7 OTHER PHRASE TYPES. Is there anything to be said about other phrase types: prepositional phrases, adverb phrases, adjective phrases?

8 WORD CLASSES. Having already considered major or lexical word classes, we may here consider minor word classes ('function words'): prepositions, conjunctions, pronouns, determiners, auxiliaries, interjections. Are particular words of these types used for particular effect (e.g. the definite or indefinite article; first person pronouns *I, we,* etc.; demonstratives such as *this* and *that*; negative words such as *not, nothing, no*)[ix]?

9 GENERAL. Note here whether any general types of grammatical construction are used to special effect; e.g. comparative or superlative constructions; coordinative or listing constructions; parenthetical constructions; appended or interpolated structures such as occur in casual speech. Do lists and coordinations (e.g. lists of nouns) tend to occur with two, three or more than three members? Do the coordinations, unlike the standard construction with one conjunction (*sun, moon and stars*), tend to omit conjunctions (*sun, moon, stars*) or have more than one conjunction (*sun and moon and stars*)?

C: Figures of speech, etc.

Here we consider the incidence of features which are foregrounded (see section 1.4) by virtue of departing in some way from general norms of communication by means of the language code; for example, exploitation of regularities of formal patterning, or of deviations from the linguistic code. For identifying such features, the traditional figures of speech (schemes and tropes) are often useful categories.

1 GRAMMATICAL AND LEXICAL. Are there any cases of formal and structural repetition (anaphora, parallelism, etc.) or of mirror-image patterns (chiasmus)? Is the rhetorical effect of these one of antithesis, reinforcement, climax, anticlimax, etc.[x]?

2 PHONOLOGICAL SCHEMES. Are there any phonological patterns of rhyme, alliteration, assonance, etc.? Are there any salient rhythmical patterns? Do vowel and consonant sounds pattern or cluster in particular ways? How do these phonological features interact with meaning[xi]?

3 TROPES. Are there any obvious violations of, or departures from, the linguistic code? For example, are there any neologisms (such as *Americanly*)? Deviant lexical collocations (such as *portentous infants*)? Semantic, syntactic, phonological, or graphological deviations? Such deviations (although they can occur in everyday speech and writing) will often be the clue to special interpretations associated with traditional poetic figures of speech such as metaphor, metonymy, synecdoche,

paradox and irony[xii]. If such tropes occur, what kind of special interpretation is involved (e.g. metaphors can be classified as personifying,
animising, concretising, synaesthetic, etc.)? Because of its close connection with metaphor, simile may also be considered here. Does the text
contain any similes, or similar constructions (e.g. 'as if' constructions)?
What dissimilar semantic fields are related through simile?

D: Context and cohesion

Finally, we take a preliminary look at features which will be more fully
dealt with in Chapters 7 to 10. Under COHESION, ways in which one part of
a text is linked to another are considered: for example, the ways in which
sentences are connected. This is the internal organisation of the text. Under
CONTEXT (see the discussion of discourse situation in section 8.1) we
consider the external relations of a text or a part of a text, seeing it as a
discourse presupposing a social relation between its participants (author
and reader; character and character, etc.), and a sharing by participants of
knowledge and assumptions.

1 COHESION[xiii]. Does the text contain logical or other links between sentences (e.g. coordinating conjunctions, or linking adverbials)? Or does it
tend to rely on implicit connections of meaning?
   What sort of use is made of cross-reference by pronouns (*she, it, they,*
etc.)? by substitute forms (*do, so,* etc.), or ellipsis? Alternatively, is any
use made of elegant variation – the avoidance of repetition by the substitution of a descriptive phrase (as, for example, 'the old lawyer' or 'her
uncle' may substitute for the repetition of an earlier 'Mr Jones')?
   Are meaning connections reinforced by repetition of words and phrases,
or by repeatedly using words from the same semantic field?
2 CONTEXT. Does the writer address the reader directly, or through the
words or thoughts of some fictional character? What linguistic clues (e.g.
first-person pronouns *I, me, my, mine*) are there of the addresser–addressee
relationship? What attitude does the author imply towards his or her
subject? If a character's words or thoughts are represented, is this done
by direct quotation (direct speech), or by some other method (e.g. indirect speech, free indirect speech)[xiv]? Are there significant changes of
style according to who is supposedly speaking or thinking the words on
the page?

3.2 Notes on the categories

(i) In a formal sense, word complexity should be measured by counting
morphemes. For example, *un-friend-li-ness* contains four morphemes,

and *war* only one. But determining the number of morphemes in a word can be a problem, especially with words of foreign or classical origin, such as *signification*. For this reason, counting the number of syllables per word is a more convenient measure of complexity. Morphemic complexity and syllabic complexity are in gross terms reasonably equivalent; but they are not necessarily equivalent for individual words; for example, *six-th-s* contains three morphemes, but only one syllable; *establish*, on the other hand, contains only one morpheme, but three syllables.

(ii) An idiom may be roughly defined as a sequence of two or more words, the meaning of which is not predictable from the meanings of the constituent words; e.g. *get by, as it were, under the weather.* A collocation is a combination of words, which may be habitual (e.g. *blue sea*) or contrary to expectation (e.g. *mad sea*).

(iii) REGISTER is the term commonly used for language variation of a non-dialectal type; e.g. differences between polite and familiar language; spoken and written language; scientific, religious, legal language, etc.

(iv) On the classification of verbs in terms of their relation to other elements in the clause, see Greenbaum and Quirk (1990), sections 10.1–10.18 and 16.11–16.37. This aspect of lexical choice is closely bound up with semantic relations between noun phrases in the clause: these have been investigated by Fillmore[3] under the heading of 'case', and by Halliday[4] under the heading of 'transitivity'. Their role in style is discussed in section 6.1. Factive verbs presuppose the truth of what is being asserted (e.g. 'Mary *liked* the show'). Counterfactives presuppose the negation of what is asserted (e.g. 'Mary *pretended* to like the show') and nonfactives leave the question of truth open (e.g. 'I *believe* that Mary liked the show').

(v) The traditional classification of adverbs and adverbials into adverbs of time, place, manner, frequency, etc. is serviceable enough; a more thorough and systematic classification of adverbs is given in Greenbaum and Quirk (1990) Chapters 7 and 8, where a major distinction is made between adjuncts, disjuncts and conjuncts.

(vi) The delaying of the main 'information point' of a sentence by anticipatory and parenthetic structure is discussed further in section 7.5. This is the defining feature of the traditional rhetorical category of 'periodic' sentence, often contrasted with the 'loose' sentence.

(vii) We follow a common practice in treating as clauses what are traditionally called participial, gerund and infinitive constructions; for example '*Eating people* is wrong', 'a woman *destined for greatness*', 'I'm sorry *to hear it*'. These are all regarded as non-finite clauses (see Greenbaum and Quirk (1990) especially sections 14.3–14.5).

(viii) See note (iv) above, and Greenbaum and Quirk (1990) sections 10.1–10.18, on clause elements.

(ix) Of course, the same word form may occur in more than one word class. For example, *that* is a determiner (specifically, a demonstrative determiner) in 'That day nothing happened', a pronoun in 'I know *that*', and a conjunction in 'I know *that* he's wrong'. In English, the overlap between the pronoun and determiner classes, for instance, is very striking. (See Greenbaum and Quirk (1990), sections 5.3–5.10 and Chapter 6.)

(x) A linguistic reinterpretation of the traditional distinction between schemes and tropes is given in Leech (1969), section 5.1. Schemes are defined as 'foregrounded repetitions of expression', and tropes as 'foregrounded irregularities of content'. Various kinds of scheme, corresponding to traditional figures of speech such as 'anaphora' and 'antithesis' are discussed in Leech (1969), Chapters 4 and 5.

(xi) The auditory aspect of prose writing should not be neglected, and forms part of the larger topic of iconicity or mimesis in language (see section 7.7). For an introductory classification and discussion of auditory effects in poetry, see Leech (1969), Chapter 6.

(xii) Once again, reference may conveniently be made to the treatment of these figures of speech (paradox, metaphor, irony, etc.) in Leech (1969), Chapters 8–10.

(xiii) Some aspects of cohesion are discussed and illustrated in section 7.8. Sentence connection is treated in Greenbaum and Quirk (1990), Chapter 19. For a more extended analysis of cohesion in English, see Halliday and Hasan (1976).

(xiv) The topic of speech and thought presentation is developed in Chapter 10.

3.3 Joseph Conrad: example 1

In the remainder of this chapter we apply the categories in section 3.1 selectively to three texts which are comparable both in length and in that each is the opening passage of a short story. Our three authors are Conrad, Lawrence and James. The procedure in each case will be to begin with some general first impression of the passage, and then to make selective use of the checklist in order to bring to readers' attention what appear to be the most significant style markers of each. These style markers, in turn, will be related to other style markers within the context of the passage's literary function. In section 3.7, we give a table of quantitative data (Table 3.1) from these three passages, so that our analysis can be seen to be based on 'hard evidence'. Cross-references to this appendix are given by *italic* numbers (e.g. *16*).

From Joseph Conrad, *The Secret Sharer*:

On my right hand there were lines of fishing-stakes resembling a mysterious system of half-submerged bamboo fences, incomprehensible in its division of the domain of tropical fishes, and crazy of aspect as if abandoned forever by some nomad tribe of fishermen now gone to the other end of the ocean; for there was no sign of human habitation as far as the eye could reach (1). To the left a group of barren islets, suggesting ruins of stone walls, towers and block houses, had its foundations set in a blue sea that itself looked solid, so still and stable did it lie below my feet; even the track of light from the westering sun shone smoothly, without that animated glitter which tells of an imperceptible ripple (2). And when I turned my head to take a parting glance at the tug which had just left us anchored outside the bar, I saw the straight line of the flat shore joined to the stable sea, edge to edge, with a perfect and unmarked closeness, in one levelled floor half brown, half blue under the enormous dome of the sky (3). Corresponding in their insignificance to the islets of the sea, two small clumps of trees, one on each side of the only fault in the impeccable joint, marked the mouth of the river Meinam we had just left on the first preparatory stage of our homeward journey; and, far back on the inland level, a larger and loftier mass, the grove surrounding the great Paknam pagoda, was the only thing on which the eye could rest from the vain task of exploring the monotonous sweep of the horizon (4). Here and there gleams as of a few scattered pieces of silver marked the windings of the great river; and on the nearest of them, just within the bar, the tug steaming right into the land became lost to my sight, hull and funnel and masts, as though the impassive earth had swallowed her up without an effort, without a tremor (5). My eye followed the light cloud of her smoke, now here, now there, above the plain, according to the devious curves of the stream, but always fainter and farther away, till I lost it at last behind the mitre-shaped hill of the great pagoda (6). And then I was left alone with my ship, anchored at the head of the Gulf of Siam (7).

Our first impression of this passage is of a meticulously detailed setting of the scene for the story. The description is clearly etched, so that we can reconstruct, in our mind's eye, the whole topography. But more than this, we have a vivid sense of the loneliness of the human observer, set apart from his surroundings, and of 'a mind energetically stretching to subdue a dazzling experience *outside* the self, in a way that has innumerable counterparts elsewhere in Conrad'.[5]

A: Lexical features

Nouns
As a physical description, we expect the passage to contain a large number of physical, concrete nouns (*stakes, bamboo, fences, fishermen, ruins,* etc.) but what is more striking is that these concrete nouns are matched by nouns

67

which are more abstract in one way or another. Significantly, these tend to occur as heads of major noun phrases (*'lines* of ... stakes', *'system* of ... fences'), so that concreteness is subordinated to abstraction (20, 21).

First, we may notice that almost half the concrete nouns refer to general topographical features which, as it were, divide the field of vision into geographical areas and points of focus: *domain, ocean, islets, sea, shore, sky, river, earth, cloud, gulf*, etc. Also contributing to this effect are what may be called 'abstract locative' nouns, indicating geometrical features: *lines, division, end, track, head, line, edge, joint, sweep, curves*, etc. All these nouns refer to objects of vision: the other senses are excluded. Perhaps this is one reason why the observer seems to stand apart from the scene he experiences.

General

Other comments on lexis cut across word class divisions.

It is important to note that we are given not simply a description of a scene, but an account of the relation between the visual world and its observer, who strives to comprehend and interpret it. This relational emphasis is found in the repetition of the word *eye* itself, in abstract nouns implying perception (*aspect, sign, glitter, ripple, glance*, etc.), and in verbs such as *see, mark*, and *look*. The passage is concerned not only with objects of perception, but with the process of perceiving them; the occurrence of first-person pronouns (over half of the personal pronouns are of this type) is a symptom of this (37).

On the other hand, Conrad avoids using verbs with a human agent. The 'eye', as if with a will of its own, becomes the subject-agent in 'as far as *the eye could reach*' (1), *'My eye followed* the light cloud' (6), 'the only thing on which *the eye could rest*' (4). The only example of an agentive verb with a human subject is 'I turned my head' (3). Other verbs which could involve agency are deprived of their active meaning by being used in the passive participle form: *abandoned, anchored* (55); whereas stative verbs are quite frequent: *resembling, looked, lie, shone, marked*, etc. (22). The general feeling is that the narrator, although acutely alive to his environment, is detached and powerless in the face of its immensity.

Another, related, tendency is in the occurrence of adjectives which express strangeness or lack of definition, often by the use of negatives: *half-submerged, mysterious, incomprehensible, unmarked, devious*. To these may be added other negative expressions such as *insignificance, no sign, without a tremor*. Other adjectives, such as *still, monotonous, stable*, also have a negative element of meaning ('not moving', 'not varied', 'not easily moved') stressing the uncanny featurelessness of the scene. These contrast with a few words which suggest a faint potential disturbance of the underlying calmness: *animated, glitter, gleams, ripple*. There is a congruity between the eye to which things are 'imperceptible' and the mind to which things are 'incomprehensible'.

B: Grammatical features

Sentence length
It is perhaps significant, in this opening paragraph, that the sentences move to a peak of length in sentence (4), and thence slope down to the final brevity of (7). (The progression of sentence lengths in words is: 66 – 59 – 61 – 88 – 61 – 44 – 18.) The effect of placing the short sentence at the end is powerful: whereas other sentences relate the setting to the observer, this one relates the observer to his setting, and thereby summarises what has been implied in the rest of the paragraph. Since this sentence explains the context for what precedes, we might think it more natural to place it (deprived of the connecting words 'And then') at the beginning of the paragraph. But in that case the expression 'I was alone' would have been banal: it is only after we have *felt* the isolation of the speaker in all its particularity, and have seen the last vestige of human life disappear over the horizon, that we can understand the force of the simple statement.

Sentence structure
Sentences (1)–(6) are all quite complex, and have a certain similarity of structure. All except (6) have an introductory adverbial clause or phrase providing a point of orientation before we launch into a main clause. From here, each sentence is elaborated by coordination and subordination – by progressive elaboration of 'trailing constituents' (see sections 7.5.3–7.5.4), as if to imitate the movement from the observer's eye towards the distance. Sentence (1) illustrates this characteristic 'reaching out' effect. 'On my right hand' establishes the observer as the point of reference. This sentence structure then develops as set out in Figure 3.1.

On my right hand there were lines . . . (independent clause)

A resembling a . . . system . . . (participial clause modifying *lines*)

{ B₁ incomprehensible . . . } (verbless clauses modifying *system*)
{ B₂ and crazy of aspect . . . }

C as if abandoned forever by some . . . tribe . . . (adverbial clause embedded in B₂)

D now gone to the other end of the ocean (participial clause modifying *tribe*)

E for there was no sign . . . (adverbial clause embedded in D)

F as far as the eye could reach . . . (adverbial clause embedded in E)

Figure 3.1
Note: The sentence is structurally ambiguous in certain respects, but the above analysis is the one which appears to match the sense. For instance, E is shown as subordinate to D, because 'for there was no sign . . .' provides a reason for imagining that the tribe of fishermen have 'gone to the other end of the ocean'.

Figure 3.1 shows six degrees of subordination (*A–F*), each representing, as it were, a further step away from the starting point towards the remotest horizon, and even beyond (for the observer's imagination takes him 'to the other end of the ocean'). Accompanying this progressive distancing, there is a distancing from graspable reality, an increasing emphasis on what cannot be known or explained: 'resembling . . . mysterious . . . incomprehensible . . . crazy of aspect as if abandoned . . . no sign . . .'. Other sentences have a similar type of structure, and tend to end in a similar evocation of vastness and remoteness, as the eye reaches its limit of vision: 'under the enormous dome of the sky'; 'the monotonous sweep of the horizon'; 'as if the impassive earth had swallowed her up without an effort, without a tremor'; 'till I lost it at last behind the mitre-shaped hill of the great pagoda'.

Prepositions
The passage has an unusually large number of prepositions (9), particularly prepositions of place and direction, such as *on* and *to*, and the preposition *of* (40). In fact, a large part of the syntactic complexity of the sentence comes from the use of prepositional phrases. The role of *of*, in particular, is to relate two noun-expressions together, and the former of these expressions is always an abstract noun – if we include as 'abstract' geometrical and topographical nouns like 'the straight *line* of the flat shore', 'the devious *curves* of the stream' – and collective nouns such as 'a *group* of barren islets', 'two small *clumps* of trees'. What this suggests is that perception and cognition go hand in hand (as indeed they do in modern psychological theories): the eye does not passively record objects in the raw, but structures and schematises them in cognitively coded groupings. For Conrad, this is as it should be: that *see* means both to perceive and to comprehend is more than an accident of metaphor. In his struggle with the alien and threatening 'beyondness', a man must faithfully use his full sensibility, in which his senses and his understanding are indissolubly joined.

C: Figures of speech etc.

Quasi-simile
Although Conrad does not use conventional similes of the kind 'X is like Y', he uses a range of constructions which express or imply similitude: '*resembling* some mysterious system . . .' (1), '*as if* abandoned for ever.' (1), '*suggesting* ruins of stone walls . . .' (2), '*looked* solid . . .' (2), '*Corresponding* in their insignificance' (4), '*as of* a few scattered pieces of silver . . .' (5), '*as though* the impassive earth had swallowed her up . . .' (5), 'mitre-shaped' (6). Unlike orthodox similes, a number of these constructions suggest an 'explanation' which we know is not true. These, coupled with the element

of mystery and unfathomability, strengthen the impression of a mind stretched to explore and understand. Again, the eye's exploration of the panorama is not inert, but active and imaginative: 'looking *at*' something means grasping what it 'looks *like*'.

Metaphor

This analogising faculty is also revealed through metaphor. The feeling that the vista, for all its peacefulness, is disquieting, comes to us partly through two diverse types of metaphor: the 'civilising' metaphor which allows islands (already compared to man-made buildings) to have *foundations* (2), the sea to be *stable* (3), the sea and land to constitute a *floor* (3), and the sky a *dome* (3). Such metaphors indicate an unreal calm, because they render the immensities of nature in terms of things which are familiar, solid and manmade. In contrast, other metaphors make reference to an animacy which seems to threaten by its very absence. Except for that of the tug being 'swallowed up', these metaphors are expressed through modifying adjectives. They are therefore subdued, and scarcely noticeable to a casual reader: the '*animated* glitter' (2), the '*impassive* earth' (5), the '*devious* curves' (6) (the fact that the earth is impassive, or devoid of feeling, suggests that it has capabilities in that direction). These small hints of life give an uneasy impression that what is apparently so lifeless may have undisclosed resources of power and activity.

Other metaphors are associated with the observer's eye: unlike the observer himself, his eye behaves like an independent agent: it 'reaches' (1), it seeks 'rest' from the 'vain task of exploring' (4), and it 'follows' the cloud of smoke of the tug (6). Although the metaphor whereby perception is equated with movement towards the object perceived is commonplace, the effect of making the eye, rather than the observer himself, the subject of these verbs is to disassociate the observer, as if in contemplative detachment, from the eye, which is restless and energetic. We sense the alienation of the man who experiences his surroundings without participation: even his observations seem to come from some extrinsic impulse.

Schemes

The passage somehow communicates its visual experience not only with intense realisation, but with a sense of wonder. This comes in part from patterns which have an emotively reinforcing effect, particularly pairings of like-sounding words and phrases: '*larger* and *loftier*' (4), '*without* an *effort*, *without* a *tremor*' (5), '*fainter* and *farther*' (6). Rhythmic parallelism accompanies the parallelism of grammar. These couplings stress the dominant dimensions of the experience: immensity, stillness, distance. Occasionally consonant and vowel repetitions are employed in a way which lends force to semantic connections: 'solid, so still and stable' (2), 'sun shone smoothly' (2). There is onomatopoeia in the alliteration, assonance, and quickening rhythm of 'animated glitter'(/ x x x / x) and '*imperceptible* ripple' (x x / x x / x). The speeding-up effect is caused partly by the number of unstressed syllables, partly by short vowels, and partly by the brevity of the stop consonants /p/ and /t/. We may contrast these with the broadening, expansive effect of the long vowels and monosyllables in 'enormous dome of the sky' (3). These are not gratuitous embellishments: they integrate into the sound texture of the language the extremes of infinite space and microscopic detail between which the description so remarkably ranges.

D: Cohesion and context

Cohesion

The passage does not make conspicuous use of logical and referential links between sentences: for example, there are no cross-referring demonstratives or linking adverbials, and few third-person pronouns (38). The definite article is sometimes a mark of co-reference: for instance, '*the* islets of the sea' (4) refers back to 'a group of barren islets' (2) and '*the* great river' (5) refers back to 'the river Meinam' (4). But continuity between the parts of the description depends largely on the observer, whose vantage point is the pivot around which the cycloramic picture unfolds. Thus most sentences begin with a reference, actual or implied, to the first-person narrator: 'On my right hand . . .' (1), 'To the left . . .' (2), 'And when I turned my head . . .' (3), 'My eye followed . . .' (6), 'And then I was left alone . . .' (7). Through this progression, we build up a vista in the round, the lone figure of the narrator at its centre; then, in (4) and (5), the eye focuses on a particular point: the distant river and vanishing tug, whose disappearance from the scene reinforces the narrator's isolation. In the final sentence our attention is abruptly brought back from the remote horizon to the observer himself.

3.4 D.H. Lawrence: example 2

At the beginning of *Odour of Chrysanthemums*, Lawrence's general plan is similar to that of Conrad in *The Secret Sharer*: he presents a setting, following a path of unfolding detail until the scene is evoked in all its particularity, and then moves our attention to focus on the predicament of humanity within that setting. In both cases, humanity – however dissimilar may be the lot of the lonely sea captain from that of the woman who comes 'stooping out of the . . . fowl-house' – seems dwarfed and overwhelmed by the environment. But in other respects these descriptions are strikingly different.

From D.H. Lawrence, *Odour of Chrysanthemums*:

The small locomotive engine, Number 4, came clanking, stumbling down from Selston with seven full waggons (1). It appeared round the corner with loud threats of speed, but the colt that it startled from among the gorse, which still flickered indistinctly in the raw afternoon, outdistanced it at a canter (2). A woman, walking up the railway line to Underwood, drew back into the hedge, held her basket aside, and watched the foot-plate of the engine advancing (3). The trucks thumped heavily past, one by one, with slow inevitable movement, as she stood insignificantly trapped between the jolting black waggons and the hedge; then they curved away towards the coppice where the withered oak leaves dropped noiselessly, while the birds, pulling at the scarlet hips beside the track, made off into the dusk that had already crept into the spinney (4). In the open, the smoke from the engine sank and cleaved to the rough grass (5). The fields were dreary and forsaken, and in the marshy strip that led to the whimsey, a reedy pit-pond, the fowls had already abandoned their run among the alders, to roost in the tarred fowl-house (6). The pit-bank loomed up beyond the pond, flames like red sores licking its ashy sides, in the afternoon's stagnant light (7). Just beyond rose the tapering chimneys and the clumsy black headstocks of Brinsley Colliery (8). The two wheels were spinning fast up against the sky, and the winding-engine rapped out its little spasms (9). The miners were being turned up (10).

The engine whistled as it came into the wide bay of railway lines beside the colliery, where rows of trucks stood in harbour (11).

Miners, single, trailing and in groups, passed like shadows diverging home (12). At the edge of the ribbed level of sidings squat a low cottage, three steps down from the cinder track (13). A large bony vine clutched at the house, as if to claw down the tiled roof (14). Round the bricked yard grew a few wintry primroses (15). Beyond, the long garden sloped down to a bush-covered brook course (16). There were some twiggy apple trees, winter-crack trees, and ragged cabbages (17). Beside the path hung dishevelled pink chrysanthemums, like pink cloths hung on bushes (18). A woman came stooping out of the felt-covered fowl-house, half-way down the garden (19).

A: Lexical features

Nouns

In comparison with the Conrad passage, purely concrete nouns (*engine*, *wagons*, *colt*, *gorse*, *railway*, *hedge*, *basket*, etc.) are here more frequent, and indeed account for more than two-thirds of all nouns. The description is direct and concrete, rather than being abstracted and intellectualised through the act of perception. Abstract nouns, when they occur, often refer to movement and action: *threats*, *speed*, *canter*, *movement*, *winding*, *spasms* (20).

Verbs

Verbs are far more frequent in this passage (5). Most verbs are dynamic, and many indicate movement: *came, clanking, flickered, licking, trailing, claw, grew,* etc. (24). Even static elements of the landscape have implications of movement: the pit bank 'looms up', the chimneys 'taper', the vine 'clutches'. Verbs which are stative generally have implications of movement, indicating physical position or posture: *held, stood, cleaved, squat, hung,* etc. Auditory verbs are used for mechanical activities: *clanking, thumped, rapped, whistled.*

The number of intransitive verbs is very striking (28). Since intransitive verbs do not specify, as transitive verbs usually do, a cause–effect relationship, the impression we get is that movement is divorced from purpose: all the strident activity of the industrial scene seems to be self-generating and uncontrolled.

Adjectives

To accompany the auditory imagery of verbs, the adjectives bring visual imagery, particularly of colour (30): *red, scarlet* and *pink* contrast vividly with *black, tarred* and *ashy,* bringing into relief small signs of light or life against the drab and blighted background. Another notable grouping of adjectives, this time morphologically defined, consists of adjectives ending in -*y*: *marshy, reedy, ashy, dreary, clumsy, wintry, twiggy.* Such adjectives belong to the popular, rather than learned, stratum of English vocabulary and tend to have emotive connotations, here largely pejorative. They tie in with the large number of adjectives which emphasise ugliness and torpor: *raw, rough, ragged, forsaken, stagnant, dishevelled,* etc. Adjectives underline the theme of lifelessness: *wintry, bony, ashy* and *stagnant* all connote death in their various spheres of meaning.

Adverbs

The largest group of adverbs is that of place, and especially direction (32): *down, back, aside, away, up, behind.* These tend to combine with verbs to emphasise movement and activity ('stumbling down', 'walking up', 'drew back', etc.). There are also four manner adverbs in -*ly*: *indistinctly, heavily, insignificantly* and *noiselessly.* Other adverbs, especially *still* and *already,* refer to time, emphasising the premature nightfall, which, with its increase of gloom, colours the passage with despondency.

General

In comparison with Conrad, Lawrence uses relatively simple, homely, common-core Anglo-Saxon vocabulary. Rare words like *whimsey* and *winter-crack* do occur, but they are of the kind one may suppose to have local dialect currency. In this respect, they may be linked with other 'local' words like *coppice* and *spinney.* In addition, Lawrence exploits emotive associations, not only in his choice of words, but in the way he combines them.

In juxtapositions such as *large bony vine, clumsy black headstocks, dishevelled pink chrysanthemums*, the associations of adjectives seem to interact, so that, for example, *pink* is given a tawdry overtone by its neighbour *dishevelled*.

B: Grammatical features

Sentence complexity
The average sentence lengths of the two passages are fifty-seven words for Conrad, and only twenty for Lawrence (3); in Conrad the ratio of independent clauses to dependent clauses is 1:2.8, and in Lawrence 1:1 (46). Lawrence, then, uses much simpler sentences than Conrad, especially in his third paragraph. Much of what complexity there is occurs in the adverbials specifying place, direction, etc. (32, 40, 63), and in the noun phrases, descriptively loaded with pre-modifying adjectives (57). (Contrast Conrad's heavily post-modified noun phrases.) We may note an almost obligatory use of adjective modifiers in the third paragraph: 'Round the *bricked* yard grew a few *wintry* primroses. . . . Beyond, the *long* garden sloped down to a *bush-covered* brook course. There were some *twiggy* apple trees, *winter-crack* trees, and *ragged* cabbages.'

At the end of the first paragraph, the sudden brevity of the sentence 'The miners were being turned up' has an effect comparable to that of Conrad's final sentence. The sentence summarises and interprets a setting which up to now we have seen more or less as detached onlookers: by using the language which the locals themselves might use ('being turned up'), it invites us to become humanly involved, to see ourselves as insiders.

Word classes
It is noteworthy that major word classes ('content words') account for a high percentage of the total number of words (58 per cent, as compared with 52 per cent in the Conrad passage, and 47 per cent in the James passage). For example, Lawrence makes little use of pronouns, conjunctions, and auxiliaries; and whereas in the Conrad passage the preposition *of* occurs twenty-nine times (out of 397 words in all), in this one it occurs only seven times (out of 377 words). Perhaps these are symptoms of the greater concreteness of Lawrence's description: he makes his nouns, adjectives, verbs and adverbs work for him without weaving them into an abstract web of relationships. Thus where Conrad talks of 'a clump of trees', separating the shape from the substance, Lawrence simply talks of 'coppices' and 'spinneys'; where Conrad refers to a 'tribe of fishermen', Lawrence is content to refer to 'miners'. This is undoubtedly one of the factors that make Lawrence's style seem easier and more accessible than Conrad's.

C: Figures of speech etc.

Schemes

Lawrence does not neglect sound effects in impressing on us the harsh sensory qualities of the industrial scene. He makes use of verbs which are intrinsically onomatopoeic, such as *clanking*, *thumped* and *rapped*, as well as words which are phonaesthetic in a less direct sense, such as *stumbling* and *clumsy, clutch* and *claw*, in which the similarities of sound connote similarities of meaning.[6] In the description of the train, regularities of rhythm ('clánkĭng, stúmblĭng dówn frŏm Sélstŏn', 'óne bў óne, wĭth slów ĭnévĭtáble móvemĕnt') are interspersed with the clogging effect of juxtaposed heavily stressed syllables ('lóud thréats of spéed', 'The trúcks thúmped héavily pást'), to which consonant clusters add vehement emphasis: /θrets/, /spiːd/, /trʌks/, /θʌmpt/, /paːst/. Elsewhere, the short vowel /æ/ combines with repeated stop consonants to intensify hard, uncompromising features of the landscape: 'jolting *black wag*gons', '*black* hea*dstocks*', '*rapped* out its spasms'. 'twiggy *app*le trees', '*ragged cabb*ages'.

Metaphor and simile

Metaphor and simile serve to animate and humanise what is inanimate: the engine 'stumbles', the headstocks are 'clumsy', the winding engine has 'spasms', the cottage 'squats'. The humanoid vigour of manmade things, as suggested by these metaphors, is at the same time ungainly and unnatural. It is also charged, like the 'looming' pit bank, with menace: 'loud *threats* of speed', 'flames like red *sores licking* its ashy sides'. In the third paragraph, these same qualities are transferred to nature, as if it has been contaminated: the '*bony* vine' 'claws and clutches' at the house. At the same time, nature is given the lifeless and blighted quality of man's world: 'ragged cabbages' and 'dishevelled chrysanthemums' are odd collocations because *ragged* normally applies to clothes, and *dishevelled* to hair. Actions are as if self-initiated by inanimates: this is seen in the large number of inanimate subjects of verbs of motion and activity. Industry seems to have become a driving force of strident activity, against which background human beings, the miners, are 'like shadows'. The dominant effects of the animation of the lifeless, and the dehumanisation of man, combine with the more obvious symbolism of the woman 'insignificantly trapped' by the train, and the woman 'stooping out of' the fowl house.

D: Cohesion and context

Lexical repetition

Perhaps the most notable feature of cohesion in the passage is lexical repetition of various kinds (65). Typically, Lawrence makes use of the reinforcing effect of repetition in cases like '*pink* chrysanthemums like *pink* cloths' (18).

Definite article

We have noticed that Lawrence uses few pronouns, and to some extent the definite article may be seen as an alternative device of cross-reference, less ambiguous, because it is accompanied by a noun identifying a previous reference. Thus '*the* engine' in (3), (5) and (11) refers back to the engine introduced in (1); '*the* house' in (14) refers back to the low cottage introduced in (13). But this alone does not account for the remarkable frequency of *the* in the extract (fifty-one instances, (42)), because even on their first mention, features of the scene are generally introduced by *the*. The passage begins, for instance, with '*the* small locomotive engine' rather than '*a* small locomotive engine'. Since the function of *the* is to identify something which is contextually known to be unique, it tends to signal continuity on a contextual, rather than textual, level: Lawrence makes a pretence of shared knowledge with the reader, who by implication is already familiar with the surroundings, is already an inhabitant of the fictional world. There is nothing unusual about this in itself: using *the* as an aspect of *in medias res* technique (see section 5.5.2) is commonplace, and we find one or two examples in the Conrad passage (e.g. 'the tug', (5)). But Lawrence's pervasive use of *the* is exceptional, extending even to '*the* colt', and to insignificant topographical details such as '*the* marshy strip that led to *the* whimsey' (6). But it is noticeable that on all three occasions when human beings are brought on the scene, they are introduced by indefinite noun phrases: '*a* woman' (3), 'miners' (12), and '*a* woman' (19). This makes them stand out as new and unfamiliar against the industrial background, as if they are somehow out of place.

Other contextual features

This use of the definite article is part of a more general strategy of sympathetically involving the reader. We have seen other examples in the local flavour of words like *whimsey*, and phrases like 'being turned up'. Yet another is the use of numbers and names: the locomotive in the very first sentence is named as 'Number 4', it comes 'from Selston', and it draws '*seven* full waggons'. No one but a native would consider such details, uninformative to the outsider, as worthy of note. So, by suggestion, Lawrence invites us to become members of the mining community, and to share the lot of the shadowy miners and the stooping housewife. The third-person narration of Lawrence is paradoxically more humanly subjective than the first-person narration of Conrad. In *The Secret Sharer*, the narrator–reader relationship is objectified by the use of 'I', so that we feel the observer as being a separate identity from ourselves, however much we may be invited to share his vision. But in the Lawrence passage, there is no such intermediary to deflect us from direct participation in the fictional world.

3.5 Henry James: example 3

The opening passage of Henry James's *The Pupil* resembles the preceding extract in its *in medias res* technique, but in other respects one could scarcely find two more dissimilar beginnings to a story. James raises the curtain on his tragi-comedy of social relations in the middle of a conversation – in fact, in the middle of a rather uncomfortable interview between two strangers. Many differences of language between this and the other passages can be attributed to different subject matter: James is concerned with a world of human values and relationships, and the external universe of nature has no part to play in it. At the same time, we are able to identify features of style which belong not so much to the subject as to James's characteristic way of handling it.

From Henry James, *The Pupil*:

The poor young man hesitated and procrastinated: it cost him such an effort to broach the subject of terms, to speak of money to a person who spoke only of feelings and, as it were, of the aristocracy (1). Yet he was unwilling to take leave, treating his engagement as settled, without some more conventional glance in that direction than he could find an opening for in the manner of the large, affable lady who sat there drawing a pair of soiled *gants de Suède* through a fat, jewelled hand and, at once pressing and gliding, repeated over and over everything but the thing he would have liked to hear (2). He would have liked to hear the figure of his salary; but just as he was nervously about to sound that note the little boy came back – the little boy Mrs Moreen had sent out of the room to fetch her fan (3). He came back without the fan, only with the casual observation that he couldn't find it (4). As he dropped this cynical confession he looked straight and hard at the candidate for the honour of taking his education in hand (5). This personage reflected, somewhat grimly, that the first thing he should have to teach his little charge would be to appear to address himself to his mother when he spoke to her – especially not to make her such an improper answer as that (6).

When Mrs Moreen bethought herself of this pretext for getting rid of their companion, Pemberton supposed it was precisely to approach the delicate subject of his remuneration (7). But it had been only to say some things about her son which it was better that a boy of eleven shouldn't catch (8). They were extravagantly to his advantage, save when she lowered her voice to sigh, tapping her left side familiarly: 'And all over-clouded by *this*, you know – all at the mercy of a weakness – !' (9) Pemberton gathered that the weakness was in the region of the heart (10). He had known the poor child was not robust: this was the basis on which he had been invited to treat, through an English lady, an Oxford acquaintance, then at Nice, who happened to know both his needs and those of the amiable American family looking out for something really superior in the way of a resident tutor (11).

A: Lexical features

Nouns
In comparison with the other two passages, this one has a rather low frequency of nouns (4); moreover, over half of these nouns are abstract (20), referring to entities which exist on a social or psychological plane: *effort, subject, terms, money, feelings* and *aristocracy* all occur in the first sentence.

Adjectives
Similarly, James makes sparse use of adjectives (6), and, of those that occur, many have nothing to do with physical attributes: *unwilling, conventional, affable, casual, cynical*, etc.

Verbs
In contrast, verbs are particularly frequent in the passage (5); but this does not mean that it is full of action. The copula occurs as frequently as twelve times (out of sixty-five main verbs), and other categories of verb which are prominent include those denoting attitudes (*hesitated, liked, treating*, etc.), cognitions (*known, supposed, reflected*, etc.), speech acts (*speak, repeated, address, invited*, etc.), and perceptions (*hear, looked, appear*, etc.).

Adverbs
The most notable classes of adverb are those of manner (*straight, nervously, familiarly*, etc.) and of degree (*somewhat, precisely, extravagantly*, etc.), together with focusing adverbs such as *only* and *even* (34–36).

General
In contrast to Lawrence's simpler and more homely vocabulary, James seems to prefer rather more formal Latinate terms: *procrastinated, reflected, remuneration, observation, confession*, etc. It is easy to find more simple language in which the same ideas might have been expressed in a more humdrum context: *delay* for *procrastinate*, for example, or *pay* for *remuneration*. The loftier tone of these words blends with a certain tendency to affectation (the gallicism *gants de Suède*), and to euphemism (payment is referred to by *terms* and *remuneration*, the child's ill-health is glossed over in the noun *weakness* and the negative phrase 'not robust'). There is also a tendency towards circumlocution, particularly in combinations of a verb with an abstract object, as in 'take leave', 'sound that note', and 'dropped the cynical confession'. But mingled with these linguistic mannerisms are colloquial turns of phrase like 'getting rid of' and 'shouldn't catch'.

James exploits the associative meaning of words, but in a different way from Lawrence. In his choice of words such as *aristocracy, cynical, honour, improper* and *acquaintance,* it is the social connotations which are important. For example, the adjectives *affable* and *amiable* which describe Mrs Moreen and her family refer to a superficial benignity of manner, rather than to the more solid social qualities which would be suggested by such Anglo-Saxon equivalents as *friendly* and *kind-hearted.*

B: Grammatical features

Sentence structure
James's sentences in this passage are on the average much shorter than those of Conrad (35 words per sentence). At the same time, the impression is that James's syntax is more involved. This may be caused to some extent by the general abstractness of the language, but it is also a matter of the kinds of syntactic presentation and complexity that James favours:

(i) Just as he seems to avoid calling a spade a spade, so James seems to avoid putting first things first. He tends to mention antecedent events after subsequent ones, and causes after effects. The two longest sentences in the passage, (2) and (11), show this clearly. In (2), the independent clause begins 'He was unwilling to *take leave* . . .', the phrase 'take leave' indicating the end of a meeting with another person: but neither the identity of the other person nor the nature of the meeting has yet been revealed. Only later in the sentence is his interlocutor described; even here, though, the description is limited to her outward appearance and behaviour: 'the large affable lady . . . to hear'. Further enlightenment is delayed until (11), which at last explains how the interview came to take place at all; but again, this information is postponed to the end of the main clause, in the relative clause 'on which he had been invited . . .' which in turn contains a further relative clause 'who happened to know . . . resident tutor'. Here we are told for the first time such details as that the Moreens are American, that they require a resident tutor for their sickly child, and that Pemberton is looking for the tutor's job; or rather, we are not told, but are led to infer these facts, for James avoids a direct statement of them.

(ii) The sequence in which pieces of information are released is only part of what is odd about this way of putting things. It is also to be noted that the factual antecedent information is backgrounded by being placed in a subordinate positions in these sentences (see section 7.5.1). The following is a skeleton diagram of the clause structure of (11), and we note that the progressive embedding of one clause in another follows the *retro*gressive path of Pemberton's mind reconstructing the sources of his present predicament:

INDEPENDENT CL.　→　INDEPENDENT CL.

He had known . . .　　this was the basis . . .

↘

NOUN CL.　　　　　RELATIVE CL.

the poor child . . .　　on which . . .　at Nice . . .

　　　　　　　　　↘　　　　　↘

　　　　　　　　INFIN. CL.　　RELATIVE CL.

　　　　　　　　to treat　　　who happened . . .

　　　　　　　　　　　　　　↘

　　　　　　　　　　　　　INFIN. CL.

　　　　　　　　　　　　　to know . . .

　　　　　　　　　　　　　↘

　　　　　　　　　　　　　　-ING CL.

　　　　　　　　　　　　　　looking out . . . tutor

(iii) The occurrence of anticipatory structure (see section 7.5.4) is another source of difficulty in James's syntax. This sometimes takes the form of one or more anticipatory subordinate clauses before the verb of the main (superordinate) clause, as in this section of (2): 'and, *at once pressing and gliding,* repeated over and over . . .' The common occurrence of parenthetic structures can also be noted: 'somewhat grimly' (6); 'tapping her left side familiarly' (9); 'then at Nice' (11). Anticipatory and parenthetical structures increase difficulty because they require the reader's mind to store up syntactic information which it will use later on (see sections 7.5.3–7.5.4). A similar processing difficulty is caused by relative and comparative clauses in which the introductory word (*who, which, than,* etc.) has an embedded syntactic function; for example in (8): 'some things about her son [which it was better that a boy of eleven shouldn't catch]'. Although *which* occurs at the head of the relative clause, its syntactic function is actually as object of the verb (*catch*) of the *that* clause which is *subordinate* to the relative clause. Therefore we cannot make syntactic sense of *which* until we get to the end of the sentence.

These apparent perversities of James's syntax become meaningful in the light of an appraisal of his particular concern with psychological realism: his unremitting endeavour to pin down the psychological moment 'in the full complexity of its circumambient conditions'.[7] The passage has virtually no narrative progression: indeed, it begins more or less at the end of the interview. We are introduced to Pemberton at the point where he is screwing up the courage to say something about money, and all that happens in the subsequent two paragraphs is that the boy returns and his effort is frustrated. In between times, a whole psychological scenario is elaborated, in which we piece together the flavour of his anxiety about the pay, his disappointment at not getting the information out of the lady, his interpretation of what she is like (inferred from her appearance, actions and conversation), his assessment of her son, his misunderstanding of the son's errand, and his recollection of how he came to be involved in the interview. In the vague reference to 'his needs' in the last sentence we even get a glimpse of why the question of money is so important for him. The progression is determined largely not by time sequence, but by other connections. James grapples with this insuperable problem: that whereas for the human sensibility one moment holds a myriad of simultaneous conditions and possibilities, for the writer and reader one thing must come after another. Although he cannot escape from the linearity of language (see sections 7.2 and 7.5.3), James does the next best thing, which is to fasten our attention initially on the most immediate feature of Pemberton's predicament: his uncomfortable sense of indecision, and then to expatiate on it so that by the time we have threaded our way through two paragraphs, we have built up a sensitive grasp of the coexisting intricacies and ironies of that predicament (the ironies will concern us in section C below). Thus progression means not so much going from before to after, as from the more immediate to the more remote circumstances which impinge on the central character's consciousness.

It is for this reason that James's style here is more expository than narrative. An important part of the technique is delay of clarification, for immediate clarification, in the nature of things, cannot be supplied without oversimplification. When James begins with the simple statement 'The poor young man hesitated and procrastinated', he begs such questions as: Who was the young man? Why was he hesitating and procrastinating? Where was he? And the answers to those questions will in turn beg further questions, as we apprehend more and more of the situation (see sections 5.2 and 5.5.2). It is necessary for the reader's initiation into James's world for us to hold our convictions in suspense, i.e. we should be aware that more things are hidden than have yet been shown. In this, the role of delaying syntax is to postpone the interpretation of one structure until another has been taken in, so that they ultimately make sense as a whole rather than in sequence.

Subordinate clauses

By one measure, James's syntax is more complex than Conrad's: his ratio of dependent clauses to independent clauses is over 3:1 (*46*). A large proportion of his dependent clauses are in fact noun clauses which complement verbs (*49, 53*); such clauses are entirely absent from the Conrad and Lawrence passages. They are either finite *that* clauses (although the conjunction *that* may be omitted: 'He had known [that] *the poor child was not robust*' (11)); or else infinitive clauses ('He would have liked *to hear the figure of his salary*' (3)). The frequency of such clauses is not surprising, since they express some proposition or thought which is related, by the main clause, to the person experiencing it. These constructions are the stuff of James's psychological elaboration, since he is concerned not so much with the relation between persons and persons, or between persons and things, as between persons and psychological states and events. The use of infinitive clauses is particularly remarkable: James has thirteen of these, whereas Conrad and Lawrence have only three between them. Since infinitive clauses are generally non-factive, this indicates how much of James's psychological web is woven out of possibilities and hypotheses, rather than known facts.

Verb phrases
A factor related to the above is the relatively high incidence of complex verbs phrases in the extract (59–62): unlike the other two writers, James makes substantial use of modal and aspectual auxiliaries in such phrases as 'would be', 'shouldn't catch', 'could find', 'Would have liked', 'had been invited', 'had been'. These involve awareness not only of a narrative point of time, but of circumstances which, in relation to that point, are past, future or hypothetical. Such auxiliaries are rare in the Conrad and Lawrence passages. In James they are a further indication of the ramifications of consciousness: past memories, future expectations and hypothetical suppositions are as much implicated in the would-be tutor's predicament as what is happening at the time.

Negatives
In commenting on James's use of negation, Watt raises the philosophical point that 'there are no negatives in nature, but only in the human consciousness'.[8] We may go further, and affirm that a negative is used, generally speaking, when there is a need to deny some expectation (in the mind of author, reader, character) that the positive is true. In other words, a negative cancels the expectation of its positive. Hence negation can be a device for irony and comedy, as is amply shown in this passage. The negative particle *not* occurs four times (twice in its suffixed form *n't*), but more important are instances of implied negation: *only* ('no more than, nothing else than') occurs three times, *without* twice, and there are in addition the negative prefixes of *unwilling, improper,* and the words *but* (2), *save* (9) expressing exception.

From one point of view, this passage portrays a comedy of disappointed expectations, and the subtlety of it comes from the fact that not only Pemberton's expectations are in question, but those of Mrs Moreen and her son, as interpreted predominantly through the mind of Pemberton. It is partly by following the intimations of the negatives that we feel the pressure of his own expectations and of the expectations that Mrs Moreen seems to have with regard to him.

C: Figures of speech etc.

Irony

We look in vain for strikingly deviant or schematic uses of language in James. His method is rather to suggest ambivalences of meaning by subtle deviations from expectation. There are one or two mild metaphors and parellelisms, but these tend to serve the purpose of irony (see 8.4–8.5), which is the overarching figure of speech in this passage. For example, Mrs Moreen's remark 'And all overclouded by this, you know – all at the mercy of a weakness' (9) has the anaphoric repetition of *all* at the beginning of successive clauses, and has two banal colloquial metaphors in the expressions 'overclouded' and 'at the mercy of'. These rhetorical features seem, however, to suffer from being at odds with the rest of the passage, as if James wants us to catch in them a certain false emotionalism in the tone of the speaker. This impression is backed up by the following sentence, which stands out as being the shortest and most straightforward sentence in the extract:

Pemberton gathered that the weakness was in the region of the heart (10).

We must assume that this sentence is meant ironically because it says nothing other than what can be inferred from the preceding sentence: Pemberton registers this completely obvious fact, the location of the illness, from Mrs Moreen's somewhat overdramatised confidentiality.

The irony is primarily at the expense of Mrs Moreen (a lady less refined than she would like to appear), and secondarily at the expense of Pemberton (whom we smile at and with over his impotence to get at the information he wants). Irony is perhaps too harsh a word for an incongruous and humorous awareness that things are not as they seem, for either of these characters. But whatever we call it, this sense that words do not just have their face-value meaning, but are to be critically interpreted as indicators of tone and attitude, is an essential part of James's technique.

Other ironic signals are:

 (i) *negation*: The double negative '*unwilling . . . without . . .*' (2), for example, suggests a contrast between the willingness that seems to be expected of Pemberton and the reluctance that his own circumstances force upon him.
(ii) *collocations*: There is an associative incongruity in the way words are combined in such phrases as: 'fat jewelled hand' and 'soiled *gants de Suède*'. The unappealing qualities *fat* and *soiled* influence their more agreeable neighbours *jewelled* and *gants de Suède*, which by contamination come to seem pretentious. This kind of incongruous juxtaposition is one technique which James shares with Lawrence.

(iii) *disparities of register and tone*: We have already noted euphemisms, genteelisms and circumlocutions, where the choice of locution seems too inflated for the occasion. Subtle mixing of tone points to an ironic interpretation of these phrases: for instance, the preciosity of *bethought herself* contrasts oddly with the colloquial bluntness of *getting rid of* in 'When Mrs Moreen *bethought herself* of this pretext for *getting rid of* their companion' (7); and in the final clause of the passage, the colloquial 'looking out for' foregrounds the specious gentility of 'something really superior in the way of a resident tutor'.

D: Cohesion and context

Elegant variation

James's partiality for elegant variation (*69*) is well illustrated in the passage, particularly in the way he varies the manner of referring to the three characters. In the first paragraph, Pemberton is referred to as 'the poor young man' (1), 'the candidate for the honour of taking his education in hand' (5) and 'this personage' (6), as well as by the standard devices of name and pronoun. Similarly, Mrs Moreen is called 'a person who spoke only of feeling and, as it were, of the aristocracy' (1), 'the large, affable lady who sat there . . . liked to hear' (2), and 'his mother' (6). Moreen Junior becomes 'the little boy' (3), 'his little charge' (6), 'their companion' (7), 'her son' (8), 'the poor child' (11). Clearly such references are not merely long-winded substitutes for a name: they draw attention now to this, now to that, aspect of the same person, and so build up a many-sided picture of each character. Thus the boy is seen at one point in relation to Pemberton ('his little charge'), at another in relation to Mrs Moreen ('her son'), and at another in relation to both ('their companion'). These viewpoints are complementary, and form part of the multidimensional awareness which James's style fosters. In this context, elegant variation lends itself to irony. The rather pompous periphrasis 'the candidate for the honour of taking his education in hand' doubtless represents the boy's self-centred view of Pemberton, but in language quite above the boy's apparently limited powers of expression: what it seems to express is Pemberton's image of himself as he sees it reflected through the mind of the child. Similarly, 'this personage', a mock-dignified label for Pemberton himself, perhaps fits the rather forbidding image he presents to the child, as well as reflecting sadly on Pemberton's own lack of dignity in the situation in which he finds himself.

Co-reference generally

James is careful in making co-referential links between one sentence and another, as he unravels step by step the complications of the situation. The types of sentence connection used are various. Sentence (3) takes up the content of its predecessor by repeating the whole phrase 'he would have liked to hear'; (10) repeats the word *weakness* from (9); in (5), 'this cynical confession' refers, in different words, to the 'casual observation' just mentioned in (4). The demonstratives *this* and *that* occur eight times in a connective function ('sounds *that* note' (3), '*this* pretext' (7), etc.), and personal pronouns are also heavily used (66–68). Prominent, too, is the use of adversative connections: *yet* in (2), *but* in (3) and (8). These, like the negative forms, indicate the conflict between expectation and fact.

All these features of cohesion indicate the author's concern with the interrelatedness of individual circumstances within a complex psychological whole. But here, too, he employs the strategy of delaying clarification. Sentence (2) leaves us in mid-air, guessing what the 'thing' may be that Pemberton 'would like to hear'; (3) provides the answer, but only in part. Sentence (10) tells us of a 'weakness' of the 'heart', but not until (11), where this matter is taken up again in the expression 'the poor child was not robust', do we learn that it provided a reason for the present interview: it was for this reason (we surmise) that the Moreens wished to engage a resident tutor.

The same strategy is at work in elegant variation. The introduction of characters' names is strangely delayed – but this is accountable if we consider that names have a low priority in the elaboration of psychological reality: if James had begun his first sentence: 'Pemberton hesitated and procrastinated', he would have succeeded in giving his main character a label, and nothing else. The son is introduced first, uninformatively, as 'the little boy', as if that is the only appellation that characterises Pemberton's immediate awareness. This is immediately expanded to 'the little boy Mrs Moreen had sent out of the room to fetch her fan' – again, a point of immediate situational relevance, but involving a step from the present into the recent past. Later we find Pemberton speculating about his future role with respect to 'his little charge', but at that stage we can only guess what this role will be. Later still, the boy is acknowledged to be Mrs Moreen's 'son', but that he is the prospective 'pupil' in the story's title is a fact that James does not bring into the open until the end of the passage. Thus throughout a reading of the passage, we are learning some things, and surmising others. The task the reader is set is rather like that of completing a jigsaw puzzle, where we are given a few pieces at a time, and have to keep guessing what the rest of the picture will be like. The technique may be a taxing one for us as readers, but it ensures that in seizing on details, we do not lose sight of the ramifications of the whole.

Context

The passage is almost entirely in third-person narration. There is a little direct speech ('And all overclouded by this, you know . . .') and indirect speech ('the casual observation that he couldn't find it'), but otherwise there are no clear signals to countermand the assumption that we are reading an impersonal narrator's version of events. On the other hand, it is intuitively obvious that at least for most of the passage we are inside Pemberton's consciousness. This comes in part from the use of indirect thought (see section 10.2) constructions (with *that* clauses or infinitive clauses as complements). These express the content of Pemberton's inner consciousness: 'Pemberton gathered that the weakness was in the region of the heart' (10): 'he would have liked to hear the figure of his salary' (3). Elsewhere Pemberton's status as 'reflector' (see pp. 139–40) is evident in the assertion of statements which no one but he would be in a position to verify: 'it cost him such an effort to broach the subject of terms'. But there are occasions when this is not so clear. For example, the opening clause, without further context, could be seen as another person's view of Pemberton, derived from observation of his behaviour: 'The poor young man hesitated and procrastinated', but from what follows this is less likely. More obviously, in (7), we appear to have an inside view of Mrs Moreen: 'When Mrs Moreen bethought herself of this pretext . . .'. With subsequent context, however, even this can be interpreted as mediated through the mind of Pemberton, who after all is able to draw his own conclusions from Mrs Moreen's fairly obvious strategy of ridding them of the boy's company. So all in all, since most of the passage is told from Pemberton's point of view, we are led in the absence of contrary evidence into taking the whole passage in that light. This demonstration illustrates a characteristic ambivalence of point of view in James's writing: although one character is evidently the 'centre of consciousness', there are times when we seem to have an outside view of him, or an inside view of another character. But, to add a further twist, even these shifts of point of view are reconcilable with a unitary consciousness, for they may be interpreted as the main character's sense of what others are thinking and feeling.

Such ambivalence makes shifts of register suggestive, for they tend to imply that we are listening to this or that person's manner of speaking, and to shift point of view accordingly. Colloquialism is a useful clue. The qualification 'as it were' in (1) suggests Pemberton's own inner voice; 'that he couldn't find it' in (4) suggests the boy's peremptory style of speech; 'something really superior in the way of a resident tutor' (11) suggests the Moreens' way of expressing their requirements in the style of genteel private advertisements. On other occasions we detect language which can only be that of James, the third-person narrator. The opening phrase 'The poor young man' is significant in this respect: since it can hardly be treated as Pemberton's own self-pitying assessment of himself, it must be taken as the author's narrative voice; and thus establishes, from the beginning, a relation between the author and the main character which is at the same time sympathetic and distanced.

Shifts of register therefore work with other indications of point of view to give a multidimensional sense of situation. There are insights into different characters, but one character has the privileged position of 'centre of consciousness', and the author does not relinquish his controlling position as third-person narrator.

3.6 Conclusion

In analysing these three passages in terms of a selection of their stylistic features, we have no doubt lost a great deal by isolating them from their literary context. We have also, by dividing our observations into different linguistic categories, separated things which from the literary point of view should be brought together. But through cross-connections between one section and another, there has emerged a common literary focus on which linguistic features of widely differing kinds seem to converge. In Conrad, for example, the focus lies in the sense of individual man vividly exploring and seeking to comprehend the elusive data of his alien environment. In Lawrence, it is natural man that we see threatened by the meretricious energy of his industrial environment, which renders nature lifeless and artificial. In James, it is civilised, social man negotiating and experiencing a world of irreducible ambivalence and complexity. All three writers deal with a haunting problem which humanity faces in coming to terms with its lot. But these abstract generalisations are facile and reductive, as are all such abstractions. The discovery that varied aspects of a writer's style point towards a common literary purpose is something that can only be demonstrated through the details of stylistic analysis. And this discovery of unity in diversity, by which stylistic analysis is ultimately justified, cannot be abstracted or summarised.

3.7 Quantitative appendix

Our final task in this chapter is to bring together, for reference, a selection of the quantitative data by which the stylistic analysis of our three passages is supported. In Table 3.1 the figures for the three extracts by Conrad, Lawrence and James are set side by side, so that there is some standard of comparison, some 'relative norm', however limited (see section 2.4), for judging the significant properties of each text. For external comparison, we give in the right-hand column of the table a comparable figure (where available) derived from a fairly representative sample of modern English.[9]

Of course the table, like the preceding stylistic analyses, has to be selective. Since the passages are of approximately the same length, it has not been felt necessary to give percentages in those parts of the table where numbers are small. Moreover, we have included only three of the four sections of our checklist presented in section 3.1 (see pp. 61–4). The section on figures of speech, in the nature of things, deals with stylistic features which cannot be precisely quantified. The same is true, to a lesser extent, of many of the categories included in the table, particularly categories such as 'Verbs of motion' and 'Evaluative/Emotive adjectives' which involve judgments of meaning. Although the criteria may be unclear, they have been applied impartially to the three extracts and, to this extent, the figures may be taken as a reliable guide.

The letters (a), (b), (c) etc. in the table refer to the explanatory notes preceding the table. The asterisked entries are those which show significant differences between the passages according to the chi-square test of statistical significance.[10]

Explanatory notes (Table 3.1)

(a) (18) There is some discrepancy between the number of orthographic words (see 1) and the number of syntactic words: for example, we count *couldn't* as two syntactic words (modal auxiliary + negative particle), but *a few* as one syntactic word (determiner).

(b) (19–43) This part of the table breaks down word classes into subclasses such as 'human nouns'. The subclasses are not exhaustive, and their incidence should be compared with that of the general word classes (4–16) to which they belong. The categories selected are, in the main, those which illustrate obvious contrasts between the extracts.

(c) (25) We include under 'psychological verbs' verbs of feeling (*liked*), thought (*supposed*), and perception (*hear*).

(d) (32) Adverbs of location include those referring to position (*here*) and direction (*home*).

(e) (33) Adverbs of time include not only adverbs of 'time when' such as *then*, but adverbs of duration and frequency such as *always*.

(f) (45) Dependent clauses include both finite clauses (48–52) and non-finite clauses (53–56). We break down finite clauses into functional categories (adverbial clause, relative clause, etc.), and non-finite clauses into formal categories (infinitive, verbless, etc.).

(g) (57–58) These figures are percentages of the total nouns in each sample (4). They thus indicate the frequency with which nouns are pre- and post-modified, which is a rough measure of complexity in noun phrases.

(h) (62) Under 'passive voice' we include instances of the passive (or *-ed*) participle (*anchored*, *abandoned*, etc.).

(j) (65) Our count of 'lexical repetition' registers second and subsequent occurrences of words of major word classes.

Table 3.1

	CONRAD		LAWRENCE		JAMES		(general English)
	(000) : 55 (per 100 wds)		(000) : 79 (per 100 wds)		(000) : 42 (per 100 wds)		(1.4 per 100 wds)
1 No. of (graphological) words in extract	397		377		386		
2 No. of (graphological) sentences	7		19		11		
3 No. of words per sentence	56.7*		19.8		35.1		(17.8)
(A) LEXICAL DATA							
Major word classes		(per 100 wds)		(per 100 wds)		(per 100 wds)	(per 100 wds)
4 Nouns	97	24.6	100	26.9	68*	17.6	(25.1)
5 (Main) verbs	35	8.9	48	12.9	65*	16.8	(13.4)
6 Adjectives	48	12.2	42	11.3	25*	6.5	(7.5)
7 Adverbs	27	6.8	27	7.3	25	6.5	(6.1)
TOTAL	(207)	(52.4)	(217)	(58.3)	(183)	(47.4)	(52.1)
Minor word classes							
9 Prepositions	64	16.2	52	14.0	44	11.4	(12.0)
10 Pronouns	27	6.8	14	3.8	52*	13.5	(10.2)
11 Determiners	62	15.7	60	16.1	44	11.4	(10.0)
12 Conjunctions (coordinating)	14	3.5	10	2.7	11	2.8	(3.6)
13 Conjunctions (subordinating)	7	1.8	6	1.6	13	3.4	(2.0)
14 Auxiliaries	7	1.8	5	1.3	14	3.6	(4.4)
15 Negative (*not/n't*)	–		–		4	1.0	(1.2)
16 Others	7	1.8	8	2.2	21*	5.4	(4.5)
17 TOTAL	(188)	(47.6)	(155)	(41.7)	(203)	(52.6)	(47.9)
18 TOTAL NO. OF WORDS[a]	(395)		(372)		(386)		

(both pronouns and determiners)

Selected categories[b] *of words*

Nouns:			
19 Human	1	4	20*
20 Abstract: concrete	42 : 55	21 : 79*	36 : 32
21 'Abstract locative'	20	14	2
(Main) Verbs:			
22 Stative: dynamic	18 : 17	12 : 36	26 : 42
23 Copula (*BE*)	3	2	12*
24 Verbs of motion	10	22*	5
25 Psychological verbs[c]	7	1	15*
26 Speech act verbs	–	–	13
27 Transitive verbs	20	12	34*
28 Intransitive verbs	7	28*	12
Adjectives:			
29 Physical adjectives	28	32	9*
30 Colour adjectives	3	8	–
31 Evaluative/emotive adjectives	2	3	9
Adverbs:			
32 Adverbs of location[d]	8	15	3
33 Adverbs of time[e]	9	4	3
34 Adverbs of manner	1	4	5
35 Adverbs of degree	6	1	4
36 Focusing adverbs (*even, only*, etc.)	1	–	5
37 Pronouns: 1st person personal pronouns	13	–	–
38 Pronouns: 3rd person personal pronouns	9	10	38*
39 Demonstratives (*this, that, those*) (both pronouns and determiners)	1	–	9

Table 3.1 (cont'd)

	CONRAD	LAWRENCE	JAMES	(general English)
Prepositions:				
40 Locative	20	34*	6*	
41 Other	44	18*	38	
Determiners:				
42 Definite article	44	51	24*	
43 Indefinite article	12	7	11	
(B) GRAMMATICAL DATA				
Clauses				
44 Independent clauses	10	26*	15	
45 Dependent clauses[f]	28	25	48	
46 Ratio of dependent clauses to independent clauses	2.8	0.96*	3.2	(1.63)
47 No. of clause coordinations	3	4	3	
Dependent clauses[f]				
(*a*) **Finite clauses**				
48 Adverbial clauses	5	3	7	
49 Noun clauses	–	–	5	
50 Relative clauses	5	6	9	
51 Comparative clauses	1	–	1	
52 TOTAL	(11)	(9)	(22)	

						(1.4 per 100 wds)
(b) Non-finite clauses						
53 Infinitive clauses	1		2		13*	
54 Participle clauses (*-ing*)	6		9		8	
55 Participle clauses (*-ed*)	7		2		2	
56 Verbless clauses	3		3		3	
TOTAL	(17)		(16)		(26)	
Noun phrases						
57 Premodification	38	39.2[g]	41	41.0	19*	27.9
58 Postmodification	34*	35.1	17	17.0	19	27.9
Verb phrase constructions						
59 Modal auxiliaries	2		–		7	
60 Progressive aspect	–		2		–	
61 Perfective aspect	3		2		6	
62 Passive voice[h]	8		3		3	
Prepositional phrases						
63 as adverbials	28		33		17	
64 as postmodifiers	30		15		19	
(C) COHESION DATA						
65 Lexical repetitions[j]	25		33		26	
Cross reference by						
66 (i) personal pronouns	9		10		35*	
67 (ii) definite article	11		16		5	
68 (iii) demonstratives	–		–		8	
69 (iv) 'elegant' variation	4		3		11*	

Notes

1. s. GREENBAUM and R. QUIRK (1990). Alternatively, the reader may consult G. LEECH and J. SVARTVIK (1975, 3rd edn, 2002), especially Part 3, 'Grammatical Compendium'.
2. G.N. LEECH (1969).
3. See, for example, C.J. FILLMORE (1968).
4. See M.A.K. HALLIDAY (1967).
5. R. OHMANN (1966), 152.
6. On the symbolic value of such phonaesthetic series in English see H. MARCHAND (1969), 397–428.
7. I. WATT (1960), 275.
8. *Ibid*, 274.
9. For this purpose, we used Ellegård's statistical study of part of the Brown Corpus (see notes 2 and 3, p. 59). These have been updated for the second edition with figures from a quantitative study of the Lancaster–Oslo/Bergen corpus by Nicholas Smith and Geoffrey Leech and from the British National Corpus. However, the difference between frequencies extracted from these British corpora and those of the American Brown Corpus are relatively minor, and make little difference in practice.
10. We applied the chi-square test to all rows of the table in which the total number of occurrences in the three passages was fifteen or more (with two degrees of freedom and a significance level of 0.05). The asterisk marks the column in which the value with the greatest mean deviation occurs; i.e., for a given stylistic feature, the asterisk indicates the author who (in these chosen passages) is most notable for using that feature either more or less frequently than the other two authors.

CHAPTER 4

Levels of style

At the conclusion to Chapter 1 we provisionally adopted a multilevel concept of style, whereby more or less equivalent choices at a particular linguistic level could be seen as STYLISTIC VARIANTS, and in which these variants could be associated with STYLISTIC VALUES, or special significances associated with one variant rather than another. We shall now take this conception of style further, in order to lay the groundwork for examining communicative effects of style in more detail in Part Two. But to do this, it will be necessary to take a closer look at language as a system of communication, and at the way in which it operates in non-fictional as well as fictional contexts.

4.1 Language as a cognitive code

Language is often compared to a code, and we have also used this analogy in earlier chapters. The analogy has its limitations, but is a valuable starting point. The first observation to make is that as a code, language is multilevelled. The dualist position, as we saw in Chapter 1, distinguishes only between the two levels of 'expression' and 'content'. But even if we restrict ourselves to the ideational or cognitive function of language (see pp. 24–7), it is necessary to distinguish three levels of organisation in language. In addition to the level of SEMANTICS (meaning), there are the levels of SYNTAX (also called 'lexigrammar') and PHONOLOGY, which together form the expression plane of language. These two levels constitute what is often referred to as the 'double articulation' of linguistic form: phonology being the 'sound pattern' of the language (phonemes, stress, rhythm, intonation), and syntax being, roughly speaking, the more abstract grammatical and lexical form of language.

The distinction between grammar and lexis which we used in the last chapter cuts across this distinction between levels. Syntax (in the broad sense in which it is commonly used today) is the level of lexico-grammatical form that mediates between the levels of sound and meaning. Thus it includes both lexical choice – choice of words and multi-word expressions from the vocabulary of the language – and the grammatical choices involved in combining these into sentences.

Considered primarily as a means of spoken communication, language has been regarded, both traditionally and in modern linguistics,[1] as a system for translating meanings in the speaker's mind into sounds or, conversely, for translating sounds into meanings in the hearer's mind. Whether we think of the ENCODING (meaning-to-sound) or the DECODING (sound-to-meaning) process, syntax is the formal code which mediates between structures of meaning and structures of sound.

Since literature is normally encountered in the written medium, a fourth level of organisation and analysis must be given its place: that of GRAPHOLOGY, the writing system. The syntactic form of a sentence must be rendered either in speech or in writing, so graphology is an alternative system of realisation to phonology. But it would be a mistake to suppose that a written sentence has no phonology. When we read a poem silently, we are still aware of its phonological structure of rhythm, rhyme, etc. In prose reading, this unvocalised realisation is normally less obvious, and no doubt varies in strength from writer to writer, from reader to reader, and from one situation to another. But the phonological potential is always there, and the exploitation of rhythmic, onomatopoeic and other auditory effects in prose bears witness to it. Some people, when they read a novel, claim to 'hear' it as well. Whether or not this is true of all of us, it is clear that we have the ability to react, when the situation demands it, to the unspoken sound of a written text.

Thus a very simple view of the operation of language as a coding system can be represented as follows:

Figure 4.1

The broken line in this diagram indicates that although phonology is not actually realised in a written text, it is there 'by implication'. In English, in fact, graphology is largely derived from phonology: our alphabetic writing system represents, however imperfectly, the sounds of speech; and punctuation, at least in part, duplicates the roles of stress and intonation in spoken discourse.

Before we go on to illustrate and extend this model, there are one or two disclaimers to be made. First, the description of language as a code is too limiting if it conjures up analogies with signalling systems such as Morse code, or more widely with such systems of rules as the highway code or a legal code. Such comparisons suggest a fixed set of symbols or rules which operate in a fixed way, whereas this is only partially true of language. Language is open-ended in that it permits the generation of new meanings and new forms (for example, metaphorical meanings and neologisms). And it also has no clearly defined boundaries as to what is in the code and what is an infringement of it. There is no clear boundary, for instance, between a metaphorical meaning which is an institutionalised part of language, such as 'to steal a kiss', and one which is not, such as 'a euphemistic shingle' (John Updike). It is this creative extendability of the linguistic code that we had in mind in the earlier discussion of deviation and foregrounding (see section 1.4) and to which we shall return in section 4.6; but it is now time to recognise that these are relative, not absolute, concepts. If language is a code, it is a complexly variable code, adaptable to the innovative skill of its users.

We must also avoid taking too simple a view of the encoding and decoding processes. Both writing and reading are enormously complex skills, involving the coordination of sensory and cognitive processes; and although psycholinguistic research supports the structuring of these activities in terms of multilevel coding,[2] the coding takes place simultaneously on different levels, and many other factors, such as memory span and general extralinguistic knowledge, play a part. We cannot entertain the simplistic notion of reading as a process which proceeds by decoding the message, in real time, from one level to another. If reading is complex, so also is writing; and when we come to the mystery of literary composition, we can scarcely begin to explain the operations of the creative mind which result in a sequence of words on the written page.[3]

There is a further limitation of the view of language as a code. The meanings, in this view, are part of the code, for each language organises its view of reality, in terms of contrasts and structures, in its own way. It is well known in linguistics, for example, that languages vary in the way they encode perceptual phenomena such as colour; and this variation is probably greater still in the conceptualisation of abstract and cultural phenomena.[4] Speakers of English, as of any other language, are constrained to interpret the realities of their experience – whether perceptual, physical, mental, emotive or social – in ways that their language permits. At the semantic level, as at other levels, a writer exercises choice in terms of 'a grammar of possibilities'. But this codification, or structuring of meaning, applies only to meaning narrowly, though centrally, defined as conceptual or logical meaning – what we earlier called SENSE. There is a whole range of language communication, particularly that which involves the interrelation between speaker and hearer, which cannot be fitted into this conceptual view of semantics (see sections 9.1–9.1.2). The distinction we made in section 1.3.2 between SENSE (meaning in the narrow sense) and SIGNIFICANCE (meaning in the broad sense) still stands, and if two sentences are equivalent in terms of the message encoded, this certainly does not mean that they are equivalent in terms of their significance. In studying stylistic values, we are precisely trying to determine the significances which are not part of the code itself, but are generated in its use of the code. The aim of Part Two is to explain and illustrate the main aspects of stylistic significance.

Although these considerations make us wary of interpreting Figure 4.1 too literally, they do not undermine its value as a representation of the essential core of language, and as a starting point for stylistics. For if we can identify what features of language are equivalent in terms of the code, we shall be in a better position to study the effects of stylistic choice.

'Equivalent in terms of the code': this needs explanation. Linguistic phenomena may be equivalent in the sense that at one level of coding they may be different, but at another level they may be the same. It is the possibility of such many–one codings that justifies a multilevel model of language in the first place. To take some simple lexical examples: *judgment* and *judgment* are two orthographic encodings, or variants, of the same (syntactic-level) word; *often* and *frequently* are two syntactic-level encodings of the same meaning (which is what we mean when we say they are 'synonyms'). In the decoding direction, *hard* has at least two senses: one which is the opposite of 'easy', and another which is the opposite of 'soft' – in other words, *hard* is ambiguous or polysemous. Again, the sequence of letters *s*, *a* and *w* represents two different words, one a noun and the other a verb which is the past tense form of *see*. Although stylistics is chiefly interested in encoding variants, it is in the nature of language, as a multicoding system, that the many–one mappings go in both directions:

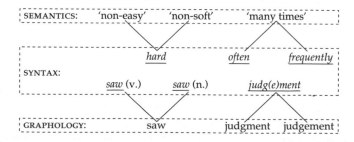

Figure 4.2[5]

4.2 Messages and models of reality

To complete the analogy between language and a code, we must talk about MESSAGES. A code is a means of conveying messages, a vehicle of communication. How shall we understand the term 'message' as applied to language? It is necessary, first, to go back to the distinction between SENSE and REFERENCE. The need for this distinction is traditionally argued, by philosophers, through examples such as 'the morning star' and 'the evening star'. Although these two expressions have the same referent (they both refer to the same celestial object, Venus), they differ in sense, as *the evening star* means 'the star which appears in the evening', and *the morning star* means 'the star which appears in the morning'. Here again, there are many–one mappings in both directions: just as there are expressions which are different in sense, but equivalent in reference, so there are expressions which are equivalent in sense, but can differ in reference. *Yesterday*, for example, means 'the day before today' on every occasion of its use. However, if uttered on 25th June, it refers to 24th June, but if uttered on 30th June, it refers to 29th June. It belongs to the class of items (deictics, see section 10.1.1) which vary systematically, in their reference, according to the situation in which they are uttered. Consider the two sentences:

[1] John Smith's birthday was on the twenty-fourth of June.
[2] Yesterday was my birthday.

Although these sentences differ in sense, it is quite possible for them to have the same reference, and the same truth value. This would be the case if [2] were uttered on 25th June by the John Smith referred to in [1]. On the basis of this identity of reference, they can be said to convey the SAME MESSAGE. That is, we may take the 'message' of an utterance to be what it conveys about 'the real world'.

In prose writing, the discrepancy between identity of meaning and identity of sense is well exemplified in the device of so-called elegant variation: we have already noted, for instance (see p. 85), Henry James's use of non-synonymous expressions: 'the poor young man', 'this personage', etc., as ways of referring to the same person. But by bringing in such literary examples, we are confronted with the question of whether the notions of 'truth value' and 'reference' can be applied to the mock realities of fiction. From the linguistic point of view (and this is one way in which linguistics differs from philosophy) it is more profitable to apply terms like 'truth' and 'reference' to psychological realities: one is not interested in what is really the case, but what particular individuals *know* or *believe* to be the case. Communication, in these terms, has to do with some general UNIVERSE OF REFERENCE or MODEL OF REALITY which we as human beings carry inside our heads, and which consists of all the things we know, believe, judge or

99

understand to be the case in the world in which we live. How we have acquired this model of reality need not concern us, nor need the complexities of its structure. It will be sufficient to regard it as the starting point and finishing point of communication in an informational sense. That is, when we inform someone by means of language we retrieve a message from our model of reality and by means of the encoding and decoding of language transfer it to the addressee, who then fits it into his own model of reality. From this it is easy to go one step further and to say that the same thing happens in fictional discourse, except that it is a postulated or imagined model of reality – in short, a fiction – that is transferred to the addressee.

A crucial difference, of course, between the 'real' model of reality and the 'mock reality' of fiction is that the mock reality does not exist apart from the message by which it is conveyed: this is the case, at least, if we regard a fictional work in its entirety as constituting a single message. But we shall later (in sections 4.3 and 5.2.3) have occasion to develop the view that the mock reality depends a great deal, for its understanding, on our knowledge of the real world. Now, however, we elaborate the left-hand part of Figure 4.1, in order to include this more complete picture of the communication process (restricting the diagram to written language), and to illustrate how Figure 4.3 can be applied to the study of style, concentrating on stylistic variation as choice of equivalent encodings at each of the three linguistic levels:

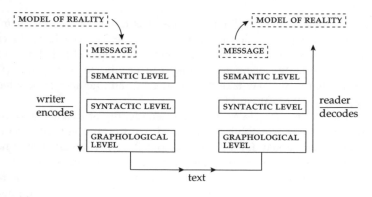

Figure 4.3

4.3 An example: Katherine Mansfield

As an illustration, we shall take a simple seven-word sentence from Katherine Mansfield's story *A Cup of Tea*:

[3] The discreet door shut with a click.

It fits into the following part of the story, where the author describes her rich and rather spoilt heroine's exit from a high-class antique shop in London's West End:

[4] 'Charming!' Rosemary admired the flowers. But what was the price? For a moment the shopman did not seem to hear. Then a murmur reached her. 'Twenty-eight guineas, madam.'
'Twenty-eight guineas.' Rosemary gave no sign. She laid the little box down; she buttoned her gloves again. Twenty-eight guineas. Even if one is rich . . . She looked vague. She stared at a plump tea-kettle like a plump hen above the shopman's head, and her voice was dreamy as she answered: 'Well, keep it for me – will you? I'll. . . .'
But the shopman had already bowed as though keeping it for her was all any human being could ask. He would be willing, of course, to keep it for her for ever.

The discreet door shut with a click. She was outside on the step, gazing at the winter afternoon.

As a means of placing this sentence stylistically, let us consider what other sentences, in some sense equivalent to this one, the author could have used in its place. In a general sense, of course, she could have chosen any other sentence from the English language:

[5] The discreet door shut with a bang.
[6] She rushed from the shop, hat in hand.

or even:

[7] As the clock struck twelve, Cinderella remembered what her fairy god-mother had told her.

But the vast majority of such sentences would either not fit into the story (message) meaningfully, or would alter the story to a greater or lesser degree. It would no longer be, in this particular, the same 'mock reality'. *Opened* is not a stylistic alternative to *shut*, nor *bang* to *click*, because they describe a different event from that which the author chose to describe.

4.3.1 The semantic level

But she could also have written one of the following, which can more readily be considered variants of the original:

[8] The discreet door closed with a click.
[9] There was a click as the discreet door shut.

[10] The discreet door was shut with a click.
[11] The door discreetly shut with a click.

The difference between these sentences and [5] and [6] is that they can be interpreted as descriptions of the event portrayed in [3]. This is not to say that they convey the same sense, nor that they *necessarily* refer to the same event; but, given what we know, both about the real world and the fictional world, it is reasonable to *infer* from each the same event.

Inference has an important role in comprehension. From the statement 'It has been raining for an hour in Chicago', for example, we are able to infer, using our knowledge of the real world, that the streets of Chicago are wet. Such inferences are also available to the reader of fiction. The mock reality of fiction has its points of overlap with our model of the real world, and indeed it can be argued that readers will assume isomorphism between the two unless given indications to the contrary. The overlap is great in the case of realistic fiction, and smaller in the case of fantasy. But in general, the things which furnish the mock reality belong to classes of things which do exist. The door referred to in Katherine Mansfield's sentence may not have existed, but plenty of other doors, of which we have real experience, do. So from our knowledge of entities and goings-on in the real world, as well as from our knowledge, acquired from the text, of the fictional world, we are able to postulate the nature of the fictional world, drawing inferences about matters not directly communicated by the text. Katherine Mansfield describes the noise made by the door as a *click*. From the fact that a *click* (as opposed to a *bang*, for example) is a soft, unresonant (though abrupt) noise, we are able to conclude that the door was shut without great force. From this again, if we read with an eye to the preceding context, we can draw further conclusions of a social nature. We are not told so, but surely we must surmise that the door was shut unobtrusively, and therefore gently, by the shopkeeper. In this shrine of opulence, deference to one's customer requires that a shopkeeper should not appear to talk of price ('a murmur reached her'), nor treat his goods as merchandise ('He would be willing ... to keep it ... for ever'), nor should he appear to shut the door on his customer. The adjective *discreet* (which, notice, is applied to the door rather than to the man) strengthens this inference from the 'click'.

Although [8]–[11] are broadly referentially equivalent, in the sense that they 'tell the same story', there are subtle differences which invest them with different stylistic values. In [8], *closed* is used instead of *shut*. These verbs are very similar in sense, but it can be maintained that they are not quite synonyms, because *shut* focuses on the completion of the event, and so suggests an abrupt momentariness which chimes with *click*.[6] In [9], the separation of the 'shutting' and 'clicking' into two clauses means that they are conceived of as separate, though simultaneous, events. It would be possible to interpret this sentence as referring to causally unconnected events

– say, a gunman clicking the safety-catch of his gun at the moment when the door shut. But inference from context would rule out such an interpretation in this story. Nevertheless, this sentence has the effect of making the click come before the shutting, thus reversing the normal precedence of cause to effect. Because of this, and because of its greater length, it would be more obtrusive in the context than Katherine Mansfield's sentence, and would attach greater importance to the door-shutting than seems to be required.

In [10], the intransitive verb *shut* is replaced by the passive *was shut*, which tells us that there is an implicit agent, a doer of the action. This sentence is therefore more specific than [3], and cannot be regarded as entirely equivalent in sense. It excludes the interpretation that the door shut of its own accord, and so leads more explicitly to the conclusion that the door was shut by the shopman. But in any case, this is a likely inference from [3], so again the sentences are referentially virtually equivalent. It seems that the author has deliberately left things vague by choosing the intransitive verb construction; that she wants us to have the delicately ironic impression of a deferential, high-class shop in which doors, as it were, open and shut almost of their own accord. This is the world of self-effacing service in which the heroine moves with assurance: even if servitors are visible, it is not for her to notice them. That this is a likely interpretation is supported by the negative evidence of another variant:

[11] The door discreetly shut with a click.

By changing the adjective *discreet* into an adverb, this would have lost some of the force of the original, which attributes the behavioural quality of discretion metonymically to the door, an inanimate object which cannot, in literal actuality, possess it. The author makes it seem as if in this euphemistic world, tradesmen, dealers men of the flesh – have refined themselves out of existence, and have imparted their qualities to the shop itself, its furniture and fittings, in a general ambience of discretion.

The equivalences we have noted in these examples are not absolute, since the inferences the reader draws are a matter of high likelihood, rather than necessity. It is often part of an author's technique to leave us in some doubt as to what precisely is going on in the fictional world, as Katherine Mansfield does here. At the same time, the identification of such equivalence or near-equivalence is a tool of analysis which sharpens one's awareness of the consequences of the author's choice of language.

4.3.2 The syntactic level

The above examples are termed 'semantic variants' or 'variant conceptualisations' because they involve differences of meaning, however slight. It goes without saying that semantic variants also involve differences of expression – of syntax and graphology/phonology – since codings at the more abstract level of meaning have consequences of expression. But now we turn to sentences which, though differing in syntactic form, are equivalent in sense; that is, they are paraphrases, or syntactic variants of [3]:

[3] The discreet door shut with a click.
[12] With a click the discreet door shut.
[13] The discreet door clicked shut.

Unlike [9], these sentences do not treat the two events of shutting and clicking as separate things: in this respect, as in other respects, [12] and [13] are just different ways of expressing the same sense as [3]. But again there are differences of effect. In [12], the adverbial *with a click* is placed before the rest of the sentence, perversely making us aware of the 'click' before the 'shutting' which caused it (see section 7.7.1). In [13], the change of syntactic form, although it makes the sentence more concise, has phonological consequences which appear to be undesirable. To see this, we first have to note that the original sentence [3] has a phonological aptness to its meaning. The word *click* is onomatopoeic in itself, and the neat, abrupt quality of the sound it signifies is echoed in the final /t/ consonance of *discreet* and *shut*, and by the initial /d/ alliteration of *discreet* and *door*. In [13] this effect is accentuated because of the succession of stressed syllables ('-créet dóor clícked shút'), and because of the accompanying clattering of consonants, especially the stops /k/, /t/ and /d/. We may say, in fact, that the onomatopoeic effect is here overdone, resulting in a sentence which is so cluttered with consonants that it is difficult to say aloud. This awkwardness, which might be successfully exploited by a writer in a different context, forces itself on the reader's attention, detracting from the force of *discreet*.

4.3.3 The graphological level

The lowest level of style in Figure 4.3 is the choice of graphological realisations of a given syntactic form. For example, [3] might have been divided into two separate units of information by punctuation:

[14] The discreet door shut – with a click.

Or a similar division might have been made by a comma in [12]:

[15] With a click, the discreet door shut.

This punctuation would have made some difference to the reader's processing of the sentence; [14] in particular would have made the 'click' seem a matter of importance and surprise in its own right, dividing the reader's attention between the two events, instead of making him see them as integral parts of a whole.

Graphological variation is a relatively minor and superficial part of style (see sections 7.4–7.4.1), concerning such matters as spelling, capitalisation, hyphenation, italicisation and paragraphing. Such matters are to a great extent determined conventionally by syntax, and become noticeably expressive only when a writer makes a graphological choice which is to some degree marked or unconventional, such as a deliberate misspelling. This is why graphology was not given a separate heading in our checklist of stylistic features in section 3.1; it was understood that such features, where of stylistic interest, would be noted under the heading of foregrounding. Examples of unconventional graphology are found in the work of writers such as Sterne, Dickens and Joyce, who, although widely separated in age and style, share an interest in the expressive power of the written symbol. We may mention Joyce's habit of running words together in unbroken compounds (*coffinlid, petticoatbodice*), and Dickens's talking clock in *Dombey and Son* (Chapter 11), which overawes young Paul by its repetition of: 'How, is, my, lit, tle, friend? How, is, my, lit, tle, friend?'.

4.3.4 Phonological effects

Although a written text has no phonological level of style as such, we cannot ignore, in a treatment of levels of language, the phonological potentials of the written word. Phonological choices form a distinct level of style in oral literature, and in written literature the implicit sound pattern can always be made explicit in reading aloud. To a large extent, this implicit phonology is determined by choices of words and structures at the syntactic level, where it can be regarded as an important ingredient of stylistic value (see section 7.6). This has already been seen in the discussion of example [13] above.

However, since the writing system is in many respects a system for representing the sound pattern of speech, a further source of phonological effects is graphology, particularly in the evocation of a character's style of speech in dialogue. Dickens is a rich source of examples:[7]

[16] Mlud, no – variety of points – feel it my duty tsubmit – ludship . . .
    Begludship's pardon – boy . . .

So speaks the perfunctory lawyer in *Bleak House* (Chapter 1). Mr Podsnap, in *Our Mutual Friend*, speaks in capital letters when addressing foreigners:

'How Do You Like London?' Such mimicry, of course, often extends to the use of unorthodox spelling to suggest a character's accent, as when in *Bleak House* the debilitated cousin's favourite word *fellow* gets reduced to the monosyllable *fler*: "normously rich fler', 'Far better hang wrong fler than no fler'. There is apparently no graphological device, whether of spelling, punctuation, capitalisation, etc. that cannot be exploited for such purposes. But because the correspondence between graphological and phonological features is far from precise, it cannot be said that a writer has actually represented the speech style of a character. Graphological conventions are exploited impressionistically, in a way which suggests what sort of pronunciation a reader should adopt in reading aloud. For example, the capital letters of 'How Do You Like London?' might suggest a number of phonetic factors – abnormal loudness, slow-motion delivery, stressing of every syllable – all expressive of the proverbial Englishman's assumption that those who cannot speak his language as a native are deaf, or stupid, or both. The significant point is that an initial capital is a form of emphasis or highlighting in writing, and therefore can be used as a visual correlative of emphasis in speech (see also section 5.4.2).

4.4 A justification for studying stylistic variants

Our examination of one unremarkable sentence from Katherine Mansfield's *A Cup of Tea* shows how it is possible to focus on the stylistic value of a piece of language by comparing with unwritten alternatives: 'what might have been written, but wasn't'. The comparison was only partial, since we considered only a selection of possible stylistic variants. Even so, this kind of exercise probably goes against the grain for a large number of readers, who will ask 'What is the point?' In considering variant realisations of the same message, we pointed out what seemed to be the stylistic values of the original and of the alternatives, and in passing gave reasons why none of the variants were quite so satisfactory as the original. This gives some substance, then, to the intuition (which we hope other readers share with us) that those seven words 'The discreet door shut with a click' are 'just right' for their purpose. No one would claim, of course, that they constitute a literary *tour de force*. This, if anything, strengthens the claim for the analysis; for one of the problems of prose style (as contrasted with poetry) is that the ingredients of effective writing frequently seem invisible even to an attentive reader. It is a common experience to feel that an author writes well, without being able to lay one's finger on the reasons. Looking at the might-have-beens of stylistic variation is a way of laying the elusive quality of good writing open to inspection.

Against this, two voices of protest may be heard. The first asks: 'Is it not artistic sacrilege to disturb the text? What is written is written, and no might-have-beens enter into it.' In reply to this we may claim that only by considering unrealised possibilities can we define the nature of a writer's achievement. Definitions have both a positive and a negative element: what occurs is only meaningful against the background of what does not occur. And by limiting ourselves specifically to stylistic alternatives, we can pinpoint the inferences from the text which are the basis of literary appreciation. Naturally, when we think of unwritten possibilities, we mean those realisations which 'could have been' purely in terms of the language: we do not presume to delve into the psychology of the author, or to tamper with the text itself.

A second, perhaps more plaintive, voice says: 'Is this not too much of a laboratory experiment? What hope is there of saying anything about a whole work, if each small sentence deserves to be scrutinised in this way?' The rejoinder must be: although we may generally have neither the time nor the inclination to look at literary language under the microscope in this way, the fact that it can be done is important, and the doing of it cannot fail to sharpen observation, by making us aware of how larger effects are built up from smaller ones. In Chapter 3 we looked at the general interrelation of stylistic effects over a passage of some extent; in Chapter 2 we considered the 'macro-effects' of style as manifested in whole texts; and now, in this chapter, we have examined the 'micro-effects' which are ultimately presupposed by these more extended approaches to style.

If a reader feels that such minutiae are unimportant, writers, at least, do not. One way in which we can look over a writer's shoulder, and observe the process of composition, is by examining alterations made both in manuscript, and in revised editions of a work. A study of these emendations reveals countless examples of the replacement of one stylistic variant by another. Passages [17] and [18] are respectively the unemended and emended versions of a short extract from Chapter 17 of Samuel Butler's *The Way of All Flesh* (changes of wording have been italicised).[8] The extract concerns the birth of the book's hero, to the younger son of George Pontifex:

[17] *Now, therefore, that the good news* [*viz* of the birth of Theobald Pontifex's son] *came it* was doubly welcome and caused as much delight at Elmhurst as *in Woburn Square* [*it caused dismay*], where the John Pontifexes were *now* living.

Here, indeed, this freak of fortune was felt to be all the more cruel on account of the impossibility of resenting it openly; but *this was nothing to* the delighted grandfather. He had wanted a *male grandchild* and he had got a *male grandchild; that* should be enough for everybody . . .

[18] *The good news therefore* was doubly welcome and caused as much de-light at Elmhurst *as dismay in Woburn Square,* where the John Pontifexes were *then* living.

Here, indeed, this freak of fortune was felt to be all the more cruel on account of the impossibility of resenting it openly; but the delighted grandfather *cared nothing for what the John Pontifexes might feel or might not feel*; he had wanted a *grandson* and he had got a *grandson; this* should be enough for everybody . . .

Butler's changes tend towards economy and tightness of expression; even the replacement of *male grandchild* by *grandson* is a slight gain in concise-ness. But in one instance, he makes the text longer: this is where he replaces 'this was nothing to the delighted grandfather' by 'the delighted grand-father cared nothing for what the John Pontifexes might feel or might not feel'. The revised clause is not exactly a paraphrase of the original one, since it implies something more: the old man was not just insensitive to his elder son's feelings, but was so insensitive as to be possibly unaware of them. The egotism of the patriarch in search of an heir is intensified; and the repetitive, parallelistic form of the new clause ('. . . might feel or might not feel . . .') matches the parallelism in the following clause ('he had wanted a grandson and he had got a grandson') in suggesting the grandfather's own emphatic and headstrong style of speech. On another occasion, too, the emendation strengthens the force of parallelism: 'as much *delight at Elmhurst* as *dismay in Woburn Square'.* Here, reinforced by the phonological similarity of *delight* and *dismay,* is the full ironic flavour of family greed and discord between father and son: a burden which Ernest, the innocent cause of this disharmony, will carry in his future life.

Some of the revisions are relatively trivial, but collectively, they show that the principle of stylistic variation – that there can be alternative ways of saying 'the same thing' – can explain much that goes into the process of literary composition, as well as much that is involved in the reader's interpretation of the text.

4.5 Levels and functions

We have travelled a long way from the traditional 'dualist' and 'monist' views of style outlined in Chapter 1. The model of style proposed here is 'pluralist' in that it allows for three distinct levels (semantic, syntactic, graphological) at which stylistic choices can be made. This simply follows an orthodox linguist's view of language: style, like language itself, is multilevelled.

There is, however, another sense in which style is complex: not just in the levels of choice, but in the values or significances which are associated with choice. It will be remembered that when the pluralist view of style was first introduced in section 1.5, it was associated with a plurality of language functions, as in the three-fold functional scheme of Halliday, who distinguishes between ideational, interpersonal and textual functions. That is, we have two rather different kinds of plurality to deal with:

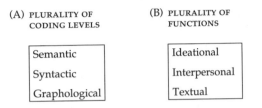

(A) PLURALITY OF CODING LEVELS	(B) PLURALITY OF FUNCTIONS
Semantic	Ideational
Syntactic	Interpersonal
Graphological	Textual

Figure 4.4

Now, there is no one-to-one correspondence between levels and functions (although we shall find, in Chapters 6 and 7, some strong associations between them). The two things are really quite separate. The levels belong to language as a cognitive coding system. The functions are concerned with how this system is *used* for communicative ends. The term 'function', as applied to language, relates the system to the ends which the system serves, or (to put it less teleologically) to the way it is adaptable to the needs of its users. This distinction between the system and its use, between *langue* and *parole*, is what is reflected in the separate triads (A) and (B) in Figure 4.4.

We shall accept Halliday's three functions, although not his precise interpretation of them. The way we shall understand them is this. In ordinary language use, the three functions represent three coexisting ways in which language has to be adapted to its users' communicative needs. First, it has an ideational function: it has to convey a message (in the sense of section 4.2) about 'reality', about the world of experience, from the speaker to the hearer. (Not only propositional language has a message: for example, questions and commands, as well as statements, invoke some extralinguistic reality.) Second, it has an interpersonal function: it must fit appropriately into a speech situation, fulfilling the particular social designs that the speaker has upon the hearer. Third, it has a textual function: it must be well constructed as an utterance or text, so as to serve the decoding needs of the hearer.

We shall have more to say about these functions in later chapters, but will meanwhile point out that these functions and the needs they serve are interrelated: success in interpersonal communication depends in part on success in transmitting a message, which in turn depends in part on success in terms of text production. There is a strong connection between the concept of 'function' and the concept of 'meaning': when we talk of meaning in the broad sense of 'overall significance', we include the implications which an utterance has regarding the intention of the speaker and the effect on the hearer. Thus when we refer to stylistic variation, we are concerned with the three coding levels, and when we refer to stylistic value, we are concerned with the three functions.

'Functional significance' and 'stylistic significance' are equivalent concepts, except that the former tends to be associated with non-literary, and the latter with literary, language. If we speak of the stylistic values of a non-literary text, we are interested in the way in which linguistic choices are adapted to communicative function – to such functions as newspaper reporting, advertising or scientific exposition. The chief difference between this and literature is that the stylistic values of literature cannot be adequately explained in terms of a need-oriented view of language. The function of literature being primarily aesthetic, we must search for explanations of stylistic value – of why this linguistic choice is made rather than that – in terms of considerations internal to the work itself. But the same three macro-functions are the governing principles of stylistic choice in both literary and non-literary language. And hence, to understand stylistic values in literature, we have to pay attention to the functional principles that apply to ordinary language.

4.6 Style and qualitative foregrounding

Our aim so far has been to show that the 'stylistic variant' view of style, which supports the dualist's conviction that style can be distinguished from message, can lead to a more precise understanding of what it means for a writer to choose *this* rather than *that* way of putting things. If we define style in terms of stylistic variants, we assume that language specifies a repertoire or code or possibilities, and that a writer's style consists of preferences exercised within the limits of that code. But we have noted (section 4.1) that creative users of language often overstep these limits to produce original meanings and effects; and that the limits of the code are uncertain, even in grammar, where we might expect to find them determined by clear-cut rules. Does Dickens, for example, overstep the limits of grammar in beginning *Bleak House* with a series of sentences without main verbs?

London. Michaelmas Term lately over, and the Lord Chancellor sitting in Lincoln's Inn Hall. Implacable November weather.

If this telegraphic style goes beyond our standard expectations, it is certainly not such a radical deviation as the opening 'sentence' of Joyce's *Finnegans Wake*, which is the completion of its last:

> riverrun, past Eve and Adam's, from swerve of shore to bend of bay, brings us by a commodius vicus of recirculation back to Howth Castle and Environs.

So deviation is a matter of degree, and at some indefinite point it becomes significant not that a writer has chosen x rather than y or z, but that he has chosen x at all. To put it another way, the quantitative foregrounding (section 2.3) of a prominent pattern of choices within the code shades into the qualitative foregrounding (section 3.1c) which changes the code itself.

It is therefore necessary to bring in another model of style, that of foregrounding, to supplement that of stylistic variants. Our discussion of opacity in section 1.4 has already made this clear. The two views of style are mutually supporting, the one applying to the level of *parole*, and the other to the level of *langue* (section 1.1). Whereas the 'stylistic variants' model locates stylistic effect against a background of other equivalent variants, the foregrounding model locates stylistic effect against a background of more normal or expected expressions which could have occurred. Each model, in its own way, provides a standard for comparing choices, so that the *differentness* of a writer's style can be registered.

To balance section 4.3, therefore, we shall give an illustrative analysis of a passage which is markedly foregrounded. Having quoted the opening of *Gormenghast* in section 1.4 as an example of an opaque style, we shall now return to another passage which occurs shortly after it in the same novel. In the foregrounding model, stylistic value has a slightly different meaning from that which it has in the 'stylistic variants' model: it refers to the special act of interpretation which we make in order to make sense of what would otherwise appear strange and unmotivated. Each qualitative foregrounding implicitly begs a question: what should have led the author to express himself in this exceptional way? For this purpose, the exceptional includes not only the sense deviations we earlier called tropes (section 3.1c), but also the patterns or exceptional regularities of structure that we earlier called schemes. Like stylistic variants, foregounded features can be observed on different levels of the code: tropes, such as metaphor, being chiefly associated with category violations (on the levels of syntax and semantics), and schemes being chiefly associated with structural patterns (on the levels of syntax and phonology). Tropes are therefore matters of content, and schemes matters of expression.

Our passage continues a description of Titus Groan's childhood as heir to the phantasmagorical mansion of Gormenghast:

[19] Who are the characters? (1) And what has he [Titus] learned of them and of his home since that far day when he was born to the Countess of Groan in a room alive with birds? (2).

He has learned an alphabet of arch and aisle: the language of dim stairs and moth-hung rafters (3). Great halls are his dim playgrounds: his fields are quadrangles: his trees are pillars (4).

And he has learned that there are always eyes (5). Eyes that watch (6). Feet that follow, and hands to hold him when he struggles, to lift him when he falls (7). Upon his feet again he stares unsmiling (8). Tall figures elbow (9). Some in jewellery; some in rags (10).

The characters (11).

The quick and the dead (12). The shapes, the voices that throng his mind, for there are days when the living have no substance and the dead are active (13).

[Mervyn Peake, *Gormenghast*, Chapter 1]

Peake, like Mansfield, presents to his readers a 'mock reality'. But his fictional world defies common sense, and frustrates any attempt to separate linguistic means from fictional ends. A difficulty of paraphrase arises even in the first sentence 'Who are the characters?' *Characters* can mean either 'letters, ciphers', or 'people in the fiction', and in spite of the *Who?* which begins the passage, it is not clear which sense is intended here. The second paragraph, with its mention of *alphabet*, answers the question in the former sense, whereas the fifth paragraph, with its liturgical reference to 'the quick and the dead', answers it in the latter. In this way, the two meanings which are logical alternatives are illogically combined.

What is the point of this play on meaning? A pun can act in a similar way to metaphor, pointing to a coalescence of concepts normally distinct. The people who inhabit Gormenghast, ambivalently described as 'figures' and 'shapes', are poised between the two meanings. They are as mysteriously alien to the child as the 'alphabet of arch and aisle', a literal nonsense which he has, nevertheless, learned to make sense of. Disconcertingly, the human world appears to have less reality for him, if anything, than the world of buildings and objects.

Already this illogicality has led us to focus not on a 'mock-reality' but on a mode of experience. It is not how things are that matters, but how they seem. The effect is very different, however, from the beginning of Joyce's *Portrait* (see p. 23), which also presents a child's version of reality, but in the artless style of the child itself. Peake's style is highly *artificial* in a sense that applies to the style of Lyly's *Euphues* (section 1.3.1). It is full of syntactic parallelisms and other kinds of schematic patterning, as the display in Figure 4.5 shows:

He has learned | an | *alphabet* | of | ⌈ *arch* | and
  | | | | | *aisle* |
  | the | *language* | of | ⌈ *dim* | | *stairs* | and
  | | | | *moth-hung* | *rafters.* | (3)

⌈ *Great halls* | | are | his | *dim playgrounds:*
  | | | **X**
his | *fields* | are | *quadrangles:* |
his | *trees* | are | *pillars.* (4) | And

he has learned | that there are always eyes. (5)

⌈ | *Eyes* | that | *watch.* (6) |
  | *Feet* | that | *follow,* | and
  | *hands* | | ⌈ to | *hold* | him | when | | *struggles,* |
  | | | to | *lift* | him | when | he | *falls.* (7)
  | | | Upon his feet again he stares unsmiling. (8)
Tall | *figures* | | *elbow.* (9) | ⌈ Some | in | *jewellery;* |
  | | | | some | in | *rags.* (10)

⌈ The | *characters.* (11)
The | *quick* | | and
the | *dead.* (12)
The | *shapes,*
the | *voices* that throng his mind, for there are days then

⌈ the | *living* | have no substance | and
the | *dead* | are active. | (13)

Figure 4.5
[*Note*: The large 'X' in sentence (4) indicates a chiasmus, or pattern in which the order of elements is reversed; the letters in bold type are used to draw attention to patterns of alliteration and assonance.]

The parallelisms are identified as structural repetitions in which variable elements occur. The simplest examples in the passages are the pattern in (11)–(13) which consists of *the* + N$_1$, *the* + N$_2$, *the* + N$_3$, *the* + N$_4$, *the* + N$_5$, and the pattern in (10) consisting of *some in* + N$_1$, *some in* + N$_2$; in both of these the noun (N) is the only variable element. More complex is the pattern in (1), where the sequence Determiner + N (singular) + *of* + Noun Phrase + *and* + Noun Phrase is repeated. But whatever form a parallelism takes, its effect is to foreground the relation between parallel words and phrases which fill the variable positions. These expressions have been italicised in Figure 4.5.

The relations of meaning foregrounded in this way are in general relationships of similarity or of contrast; they are reinforced, here and there, by alliteration and assonance. We notice that the words tend to fall into natural sets:

113

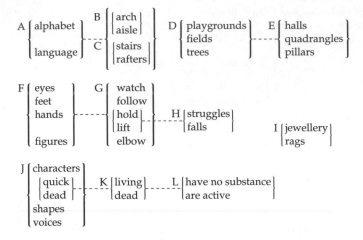

Figure 4.6

It is we, however, who have to work out the connections of similarity and contrast between the expressions in the groups A to L, which thereby become representative of something more general, which could not be expressed by simply adding together the literal senses of the words. Paraphrases can only capture part of what these significances represent: A – represents something like 'things which children have to learn in order to communicate'; B – 'features of buildings (grand and ecclesiastical)'; C – 'features of buildings (plain and domestic)'; D – 'outdoor terrain for boys' amusements'; E – 'grand architectural features', and so on. Within the groups we also find oppositions, for example between *living* and *dead*, and (more subtly) between hostile actions (*elbow*) and protective actions (*lift*), with *watch*, *hold* and *follow* keeping the balance between them. The relationships are not always clear, and we must feel the puzzlement of the young child's attempt to find his bearings in a world of hidden meanings.

More interesting than the vertical connections are the horizontal connections (indicated by dotted lines). These are collocational ties which in many cases defy literal interpretation, and have to be understood metaphorically. For example, the equation through the verb *to be* of groups D and E associates the animate with the inaminate, the natural with the manmade. This direct juxtaposition of incompatibles suggests that in Titus's world such basic categories of experience are not distinct.

The dissolution of common-sense bonds of meaning is taken further when, in (13), we learn that 'there are days when the living have no substance and the dead are active'. This is paradox, rather than metaphor: two directly opposed concepts, life and death, change places with each other. We conclude that, for Titus, not only place but also time fails to recognise the customary separation of the living from the lifeless.

We turn now to foregroundings which are less easy to recognise, because they are less absolute, and do not fit into the traditional rhetorical categories. That 'the living have no substance' has already been implied in the third paragraph, where the nouns *eye, feet, hands* and *figures* are introduced as subjects of verbs which would more appropriately have human subjects such as *men, servants*, etc. The lack of a determiner before these nouns makes them generic, and so makes us feel that the human forces that impinge on Titus's life are vague and insubstantial. They appear to be no different from the 'shapes, the voices that throng the mind'. Further, the transitive verbs *watch, follow* and (more particularly) *elbow* are used intransitively, so that these rather threatening actions not only have a disembodied source, but can be interpreted as having either Titus or his whole surroundings as their target. It is as if Titus lacks the sense of his own identity, as well as that of those around him; and so another conceptual boundary is blurred – that between self and others.

There is also something grammatically unusual (comparable to the opening of *Bleak House*) in the occurrence of a series of parallel graphological sentences which are 'defective' in that they consist of noun phrases alone: these are (10), (11) and (12), and the same construction is continued in (13). The absence of grammatical articulation contributes a further unclarity: it is not clear, for example, how the sentences 'The characters' (11) and 'The quick and the dead' (12) connect both with each other and what has gone before. The links are not logical, but associative, and the clue to them lies in the already noted ambivalence of the word *character*. There is an implied progression from the inanimate world of 'alphabet' and 'language' in (3) to the ambivalently human 'figures' in (9), and thence to the 'quick and the dead' (12) who are clearly human, but poised on the uncertain ground between reality and unreality. The polysemous 'characters' in (11) provides a link in the chain. But it is the gradualness of the progression which requires comment: here is another instance of the author's refusal to acknowledge familiar distinctions taken for granted in the literal use of language.

We hope to have shown, without further analysis, how the burden of interpretation in this passage falls principally on the reader's response to foregrounding. The significance we attach to schemes and tropes is part of an integral process of imaginatively making sense of a strange linguistic experience. Cumulatively, the features we have examined represent the world of a child surrounded and overawed by dimly grasped presences, a world in which the meanings which shape our own response to life are dissolved and reconstituted. We shall return to the way in which linguistic choice determines the nature of mental experience in Chapter 6. At present, however, it is worth observing that the degree of foregrounding in this passage, and the interpretative process it elicits, are of a kind more readily associated with poetry than with prose.

To emphasise the 'poetic' style of the passage, let us also observe that the schematic patterning is extensive on the phonological as well as on the syntactic level, for example in the alliterations and assonances of 'feet . . . follow', 'hands . . . hold', 'alphabet . . . arch . . . aisle', 'lift . . . fall'. More to the point, the passage has a rhythmic regularity which enables it to be written out and scanned as poetry in a quasi-blank-verse metre:

> He has learned an alphabet of arch and aisle:
> The language of dim stairs and moth-hung rafters.
> Great halls are his dim playgrounds: his fields
> Are quadrangles: his trees are pillars.
> And he has learned that there are always eyes.
> Eyes that watch. Feet that follow,
> And hands to hold him when he struggles,
> To lift him when he falls.
> Upon his feet again he stares unsmiling.
> Tall figures elbow. Some in jewellery; some in rags.
> The characters. The quick and the dead. The shapes,
> The voices that throng his mind, for there are days
> When the living have no substance and the dead
> Are active.

This regularity is obviously not fortuitous. But what stylistic value shall we attach to the metricality of prose? Metre raises prose to the level of a musical experience, and it also adds an element of ritual inevitability to the formal patterning of words and structure we have already noted. 'Things are so because they are so', it seems to say. Unlike the infant Stephen in Joyce's *Portrait*, Titus does not appear to us through his own childish language, but through a 'web of ritual' (a phrase which occurs in the paragraph preceding our extract). The formalistic nature of the language helps to express the mystery of unexplained tradition that governs the boy's upbringing.

4.7 The remainder of this book

The *Gormenghast* passage [19] represents a fairly extreme position on the scale of opacity, and when we turn, in the following chapters, to a more detailed study of stylistic values, we shall have little occasion to insist on the distinction we have made between the study of style in terms of foregrounding, and that in terms of stylistic variants. In practice, both models enter into a comprehensive explanation of style and its effects.

In Part Two, we shall aim to give an account of the relation between stylistic choice and significance within a functional framework. For this purpose, it will be useful to divide our attention between three different aspects of a literary work of fiction, corresponding to the three functions:

Chapter 6: Work as MESSAGE   (ideational function)
Chapter 7: Work as TEXT   (textual function)
Chapter 8: Work as DISCOURSE   (interpersonal function)

These three chapters form the nucleus of our investigation of aspects of style. But when we come to the interpersonal function, we not only have to account for the literary work itself as a discourse between author and reader, but we have to reckon with the phenomenon of 'embedded discourse': the occurrence of discourse within discourse, as when the author reports dialogue between fictional characters. In this light, a novel is not a single discourse, but a complex of many discourses. To deal with this extra dimension, we add Chapter 9 on conversation, and Chapter 10 on speech and thought presentation.

Apart from the additional Chapters 11 and 12 (explained in the Preface, pp. xi–xii), the only other chapter to be explained is Chapter 5, 'Language and the fictional world'. This serves as an introduction to Part II, and more particularly as a prelude to Chapter 6, because it deals with the subject of fiction itself: something which is strictly not a matter of style, but which is presupposed by the study of style in fiction writing.

Notes

1. A clear expression of this view is given in w. CHAFE (1970), Chapter 2. Linguists have differed considerably about the precise relation between the various components of the meaning–sound relationship, especially about the relation between semantics and syntax. For a comparison of such views, see J. LYONS (1977), Chapter 10.
2. See H.H. CLARK and E.V. CLARK (1977), Chapters 1–7, especially pp. 85 and 292.
3. This does not mean, however, that accounts of the process of literary composition are irrelevant to stylistics. Many insights into style are provided by writers' own introspective reports on their work: see B. GHISELIN (1952). On the processes of artistic creation in general, see A. KOESTLER (1964).
4. The classical statement of the view that languages determine the way in which their speakers interpret and categorise experience is that of B.L. WHORF (1956). Recent thinking has suggested that there is a great deal more in common between languages in this respect than Whorf acknowledges; but whatever stand one takes on the issue, the fact remains that we conceptualise in terms of the categories our language provides for us. See LEECH (1981), Chapter 12, and CLARK and CLARK (1977), Chapter 14.
5. There is a problem of how to represent in writing the codings at different levels of abstraction. In Figure 4.2 we adopt these conventions: a word in quotation marks is a semantic abstraction (a sense); a word in italics is a syntactic abstraction

(a word form); and a word without either of these markings is a graphological entity (an orthographic word).

6. The semantic difference between *shut* and *close* is shown in such examples as 'I banged the door *shut*' and 'I slowly *closed* the door'. These sentences would sound rather incongruous if the two verbs were exchanged. The difference can be observed more subtly in Keats's line from *The Eve of St Agnes* 'As though a rose should *shut* and be a bud again'. *Shut* here replaces *close* in an earlier draft of the poem.

7. Further illustrations are given in R. QUIRK (1974), Chapter 1.

8. This example comes from W. HILDICK (1965), 102. The square-bracketed words '[it caused dismay]' are not found in the manuscript, but appear to be required as a completion of a clause which Butler deleted before it was finished.

PART TWO

Aspects of Style

CHAPTER 5

Language and the fictional world

5.1 Language, reality and realism

In our study of aspects of style in the following chapters, we continue to follow the principle that the language of literature cannot be understood without a proper appreciation of how ordinary language works. Everyday language is therefore our starting point, in this chapter, for the consideration of the way language is used to convey the 'mock reality' of fiction. And yet, at first glance, nowhere does the distinction between ordinary language and literary language seem so absolute as in the contrast between fact and fiction.

We should be careful, of course, to keep separate in our minds the two notions of 'fiction' and 'literature', although they come together in the scope of this book. Most people would consider Bacon's *Essays* to be literature, but not *The Wombles*, and yet the latter is fictional, and the former is not. Nevertheless, there is a more general sense in which the sanctioning of untruth is the hallmark of literature. John Crowe Ransom argues that 'over every poem which looks like a poem there is a sign which reads: "This road does not lead through to action; fictitious".'[1] Perhaps this could be more carefully and generally expressed as follows: 'Over every work that we approach *as* literature, we erect a sign which reads: "Do not look for the value of this in its correspondence to literal truthfulness".' This applies to literature and to 'sub-literary' activities such as joke-telling and thriller-writing. And it applies *a fortiori* to the narrative genres of literature, where we *expect* that writers will freely use their imagination to conjure up potentialities, rather than actualities, of existence.

So the fictional nature of fiction-writing is important; yet we cannot understand its nature without seeing it as a special case of the ordinary referential, truth-reporting function of language. This can be a way of avoiding the confusion which has bedevilled the discussion of 'realism' in literature. Part of the difficulty has been that to call a novel 'realistic' has seemed to imply a value judgment: that in fiction, realism is a necessity of good literature, or that on the contrary, 'mere realism' is bad: in Oscar Wilde's words, 'The man who calls a spade a spade should be compelled to use one. It is all he is fit for.'[2] We shall avoid such evaluative interpretations of the term 'realistic' in what follows, and will argue that, in any case, there are a number of different concepts of realism to be considered. The main problem, however, is that talk of realism has always seemed to involve measuring a work against some absolute standard of reality – something 'out there' of which a writer could, if need be, give an exact xerographic copy. Harry Levin[3] is closer to the truth when he compares the myth of absolute realism with the myth of absolute liberty: there is no such thing as a 'completely realistic' piece of fiction.

Any description of a state of affairs must use language, and language by its very nature is a vehicle for abstraction and differentiation. To use a noun like *man* or a verb like *run* is to sum up in one term an indefinite multitude of biological or psychological or social facts; and to apply the term *man* to two multitudinous bundles of facts is to lump them together as two instances of the same phenomenon, whatever their many differences. So whenever a writer uses language, he seizes on some features of 'reality' which are crucial for his purpose and disregards others. He cannot give an exact physical portrait of a person: he is bound to ignore this or that wart, mole, pore or whisker. Nor could he take refuge, even if he felt inclined, in scientific explanation, as the ultimate yardstick of reality. Huxley attains a 'scientific realism' of a certain kind when he provides the following description of an event which another writer might have described in the single use of the verb *hear*:

'Bach?' said Lord Edward in a whisper.
Pongileoni's blowing and the scraping of the anonymous fiddlers had shaken the air in the great hall, had set the glass of the windows looking on to it vibrating; and this in turn had shaken the air in Lord Edward's apartment on the further side. The shaking air rattled Lord Edward's *membrana tympani*, the interlocked *malleus*, *incus* and stirrup bones were in motion so as to agitate the membrane of the oval window and raise an infinitesimal storm in the fluid of the labyrinth. The hairy endings of the auditory nerve shuddered like weeds in a rough sea; a vast number of obscure miracles were performed in the brain, and Lord Edward ecstatically whispered 'Bach!' He smiled with pleasure, his eyes lit up.[4]
[Aldous Huxley, *Point Counter Point*, Chapter 3]

But no one could claim that Huxley has here provided a representation of a rock-bottom reality of which the non-scientific word *hear* is an abbreviation.

In the first place, scientific language itself is a kind of language – and a kind which illustrates the inevitable linguistic processes of generalisation and differentiation in one of their most highly developed forms. Second, Huxley is clearly not aiming at a scientific description, but rather a *mock* scientific one, which is both livelier and more comic than a textbook physiological description of the process of audition could have been. It is stylistic joke at the expense of Lord Edward who, a dedicated scientist, is hiding up in his laboratory conducting experiments while his wife entertains her guests with music downstairs. But the eccentric effect of this description brings home very clearly the point that realism is a relative concept; relative, that is, to the purpose of the writer and the effect on the reader. The only thing which matters in fiction is the *illusion* of real experience, and a scientific description, if anything, distances us from that illusion.

The myth of absolute realism arises from a mistaken attempt to compare two incomparable things: language and extralinguistic realities. A more productive line of inquiry is to compare like with like: one linguistic description with another. Hence to elucidate the concept of 'realism' we can fittingly begin by comparing fictional language with language avowedly concerned with the reporting of real events.

5.2 Reality and mock reality

How, in the world of history and public events, does language serve to build up or extend our 'model of reality'? A good starting point is the language of newspaper headlines. One reads a headline 'ANOTHER CONSTABLE HAS TO CHANGE FIRST NAMES', and without reading further, one adds something to one's store of knowledge and understanding. But this piece of learning, although activated by the meanings of the words on the page, can only be explained in terms of our existing model of reality, as an increment to what we already know. The process can best be understood if we imagine the bafflement of a reader who spoke English, but had spent all his life in an alien environment in another galaxy. What Constable? A person named 'Constable' or an officer of the law? (The capitals are of no help.) Why is a change of first names necessary? And which other Constable is in question? If our galactic stranger could get access to the *Encyclopaedia Britannica*, he would discover John Constable, nineteenth-century artist, was more likely to be newsworthy than other people of that name. But only if he could refer to relatively recent newspapers and news bulletins could he discover that some of John Constable's putative works have recently been reattributed to one or other of his sons, and only then could the message of the headline communicate itself to him. Newspaper headlines are an extreme case of the influence of background knowledge on interpretation; think, for example, of the reasons which steer us towards one rather than the other interpretation of the ambiguous headline from the *Guardian*, 'MAN HELPING MURDER POLICE'. But they are a special instance of a quite general phenomenon, that communication on a referential plane relies on a commonality of shared knowledge, whether knowledge of a fairly recent item of news (as in the Constable case), or knowledge which is the common property of mankind, such as that after rain the ground is wet, or that jumping from a high building is a good way of getting hurt.

The following newspaper report, in its narrative function, comes a step closer to fictional discourse; for example, one could imagine it being the basis for a short story:

[1] TOURIST KILLED
   A French Foreign Legion deserter in Northern Corsica shot dead a West German tourist and critically injured his wife. He then kidnapped their daughter and another girl, but freed them unharmed, and killed himself when surrounded by police – Reuter.

   [*The Guardian*, 31 August 1978, p. 4]

What we add to our 'model of reality' on reading this is not just a set of facts in a vacuum, but a structure of fact, explanation and supposition, which draws on our already existing knowledge: for example, what we know of Corsica, or the Foreign Legion. Another thing which influences our ability to make sense of this report is its plausibility. The story will fit our store of knowledge more readily to the extent that it is possible to make plausible connections between one fact and another: for example, Corsica is administratively part of France, and the Foreign Legion is (by romantic notoriety) the sort of organisation from which desertions may be expected. We can imagine the severity of the penalty for desertion, and therefore the desperation of a deserter threatened with capture. We can also read into the story probabilities which make it more explicable: even in this summary piece of reportage, we may guess with some likelihood that the legionnaire's motive, although not stated, was to evade capture, and perhaps to extort money to improve his chances of survival. If we knew more of the story, we could make further inferences, or make inferences with greater confidence. To read and *understand* such a report is to draw conclusions, using our existing knowledge and understanding of the world.

A writer who creates a fiction has to make decisions on such matters as how much information to give, what kind of information to give, and in what order to present the information. These are the sorts of decision which also have to be made in non-fiction reporting, and we may therefore draw out the parallels between 'real' and fictional narration, by considering what might be made of the tragic incident above (a) by a short-story writer, and (b) by a detective given the task of investigating and writing up a report on the incident as a real happening.

5.3 Specification of detail: symbolism and realism

In this brief summary of a real-life calamity, all kinds of questions of a factual kind are implied. A detective investigating the incident, for example, would want to know: What was the precise sequence of events? What did the protagonists say to one another? Precisely when, where, and how did the kidnap, the murder, the release, the suicide take place? *Why* did each event take place? 'Why' is clearly a more abstract question, bringing in antecedent events not reported here, as well as the motivation of the deserter. All these questions, if answered, would add substantial detail to the story; and the choices available to the detective are in essence the same as those available to the story-writer: choices regarding the SPECIFICATION OF DETAIL. What kinds of detail, and how much detail, should be added to fill out the 'model of reality'? But in deciding what to include, the author, unlike the detective, would have artistic criteria of relevance. On the one hand he might omit information of the above kind, in order to leave to the reader the task of guessing, inferring or imagining 'what actually took place'; on the other hand, he might include circumstantial information on the natural environment, the behaviour of the onlookers, the dress of the principal characters, etc.: matters that would be of little interest to the detective, but which might be important to bring out thematic contrasts or symbolic relationships, for example.

In very general terms, criteria of artistic relevance are of two apparently opposed kinds, summed up in the Aristotelian notion that it is the function of literature to express the universal through the particular. On the one hand, there is the impulse to specify such details, in the mock reality, as can be interpreted as standing for something beyond themselves, something universally important in the human condition. In this sense, the message itself, in literature, becomes a code,[5] a symbolic structure. Our Corsican incident, taken over for fictional elaboration, might become in this way an exploration of guilt and freedom. The legionnaire, from a background of guilt and oppression, seeks freedom through violence and crime; the West German tourists seek freedom from the guilty prosperity of their disciplined regimen by escaping to the sunny, unprosperous, lawless Mediterranean. In neither case do the seekers find their goal: freedom for the legionnaire brings more violence and guilt; the tourists finally find that escape to loneliness means insecurity and danger. The two quests come into disastrous conflict, and only the German daughter, released after prolonged involvement with the deserter, learns the wisdom of their reconciliation. Thus the incident might become a dramatisation of general human conflict, and an attempt to resolve, within the 'potential reality' of fiction, a universal problem. And in this generic framework, each character, place and incident could be elaborated in such a way as to be representative, to some extent, of a type or category of human experience; the natural environment, for example – the beautiful brigand-haunted mountains of Corsica – might well become symbolic of the equation of freedom with danger and horror. We can see how the artistic impulse to universalise would lead to the elaboration of detail in specific areas far beyond what a factual explanation would require.

We do not have to invent a fiction, of course, to illustrate this point about symbolism. It is present in every work of fiction worthy of serious consideration, and indeed is the thing which makes fictional literature 'serious'. We briefly return to it in section 5.5. But it is necessary now to balance the impulse towards universality against the impulse towards individuality, which is an equally important factor in the artistic choice of detail. It has been argued by Ernst Cassirer that whereas language tends to abstraction, art 'may be described as a continuous process of concretion'.[6] In other words, art seeks the 'thisness' of things, rather than their general and abstract form. The sense of being in the presence of actual individual things, events, people and places, is the common experience we expect to find in literature, and it is this aspect of the illusion of reality that we may call VERISIMILITUDE.

It might appear that symbolism and verisimilitude are opposed to one another, that one can only be achieved at the expense of the other. But this is not true. Given that language itself generalises or abstracts the qualities of things, it is in the unforeseen combination of attributes that literature achieves both generality and uniqueness. And the contribution of a specific detail may be both symbolic and realistic at once. In the passage from *Odour of Chrysanthemums* in Chapter 3, the colour of the 'dishevelled pink chrysanthemums' becomes symbolic of natural life and beauty against the blackened background of the industrial scene; the movement of the woman and the colt, driven back by the clamour of the train, similarly becomes symbolic of the threat machines pose to life and humanity. But these small details of the scene also contribute to its 'solidity of specification' and to the illusion that we are witnessing an actual piece of reality. What often gives symbolic value is a sense of consistency in the fiction; the same message being expressed through varied instances.

However, it has also been urged that circumstantial detail of a kind which is apparently arbitrary and irrelevant to symbolic meaning (the colour of a chair, the time at which a train leaves, the kind of wood a table is made of, the name of a person) is essential to the technique of prose fiction.[7] Although it may be impossible to give any specific justification of the writer's choice of this rather than that colour, time, name, etc., in a general sense such details make up the individuality of an experience, and so contribute to verisimilitude. In other words, the mock reality is 'well furnished' with data: it includes incidental particularities which give us the sense of knowing places, people, times, occasions, etc. as if we were participants or observers ourselves.

Verisimilitude is closely connected with another aspect of realism, which we may call CREDIBILITY. This is the likelihood, and hence believability, of the fiction as a 'potential reality', given that we apply our expectations and inferences about the real world to fictional happenings. A fiction tends to be credible to the extent that it overlaps with, or is a plausible extension of, our 'real' model of reality. Ordinarily, for example, the fictional world obeys the law of gravity, and the law that language is restricted to the human species; but there are occasions (e.g. in *Gulliver's Travels*) where these are violated. It is the privilege of science fiction, by locating its action in the future, to remain relatively credible, in spite of its violation of the natural laws with which we are familiar: a potential reality of the future is less constrained than one in the present or the past. Even here, transgressions of familiar reality tend to be relatively few, and consistently adhered to. It is worth observing here that CONSISTENCY is an important aid to credibility: an unfamiliar reality which obeys its own set of laws is more credible than one which does not.

The combination of verisimilitude and credibility is a stock-in-trade of mainstream 'realistic' fiction-writing; but it is not to be dismissed as having no artistic function. To keep the fiction well furnished in a way which keeps the reader feeling 'this could be real' is to enter into a contract of good faith with the reader, a convention of authenticity, which has often been taken to be the hallmark of the novel. A writer's quest for such authenticity may be taken to scrupulous extremes, as when Joyce, working on *Ulysses*, wrote to his aunt in Dublin:

> Is it possible for an ordinary person to climb over the area railings of no. 7 Eccles St, either from the path or the steps, lower himself down from the lowest part of the railings till his feet are within 2 feet or 3 of the ground and drop unhurt? I saw it done myself but by a man of rather athletic build. I require this information in detail in order to determine the wording of a paragraph.[8]

But there are occasions where verisimilitude and credibility work in opposite directions:

> [2] I left my poor wife big with child, and accepted an advantageous offer made me, to be captain of the *Adventure*, a stout merchantman, of 350 tons. . . . We set sail from Portsmouth upon the 2nd day of August 1710; on the 14th we met with Captain Pocock, of Bristol, at Teneriffe, who was going to the Bay of Campechy, to cut logwood.
> [*Gulliver's Travels*, IV. 1]

We might ask what does it matter that the captain was called Pocock, that he was from Bristol, that he was going to the Bay of Campechy, that his purpose was to cut logwood, especially when we note that shortly after this passage, Captain Pocock founders and disappears from the narrative. But the painstaking factuality of Gulliver's account, set down in the manner of a ship's log, encourages acceptance of the authenticity of a fictional world in which elsewhere our credulity is stretched to the utmost, with tales of six-inch-high men and talking horses. The fabulous takes place against the background of the believable. This is an instance, at the level of the fictional world, of the artistic device of foregrounding through defeated expectancy (see section 1.4). Just as on the plane of language, so on the plane of fiction-building, a deviation from an expected pattern can be the pointer to special significance. In this case, the reader is lured into accepting the authenticity of a fiction which, on another level, must be dismissed as fabulous. Through this coexistence of commonsense verisimilitude and absurdity, the stage is set for the satirical interpretation of the novel, whereby what is common-sense reality for humankind becomes absurd by the standards of the 'counter-reality' of the fiction.

Specification of detail, whatever its artistic function, is clearly a matter of degree, and there is no such thing as the 'whole story', in the sense that the writer has given us all the conceivable facts of the case. By the same token, credibility and verisimilitude, which have to do with the *kinds* of detail specified, are also matters of degree. Such specification is not restricted to material facts: it also applies to such non-material things as feelings, thoughts and motives, which can all be said, in a general sense, to be part of the 'mock reality'. When it is said that an author is 'omniscient' with respect to his fiction, this means merely that there is no detail which he is not at liberty to specify if he so wishes, whether or not it would be available to the mind of a particular participant or onlooker: he can tell us equally well the exact number of freckles on a person's nose, and the exact memory traces of his brain. The fiction is, after all, entirely his creation. This means also that he is free to make the contents of the fictional world as realistic or unrealistic as he wishes. In this respect, he is entirely different from the detective, who must reconstruct a model which is answerable to the real world in every respect. The other side of the coin is that an author is at liberty to withhold what information he wishes: can leave us in doubt, to guess the likelihood of this or that being the case in the fictional world.

5.4 Real speech and fictional speech

Before we explore more deeply the options open to a writer in the specification of detail, it is important to consider a special case which seems favourable to the view that language can copy reality. This is the case of fictional speech: here, the events being described as part of the mock reality are themselves linguistic, and so language is used to simulate, rather than simply to report, what is going on in the fictional world. Of course, in rendering conversation, a fiction writer is in a very different situation from that of the detective or legal reporter giving an actual transcript of words spoken by real people; there is no specific real speech event against which the report may be measured as a more or less accurate record. But fictional speech may aspire to a special kind of realism, a special kind of authenticity, in representing the *kind* of language which a reader can recognise, by observation, as being characteristic of a particular situation.

5.4.1 Realism in conversation

This kind of realism is the standard by which we judge a writer's 'ear for conversation'; that is, his ability to render in writing the characteristics of spoken conversational language. We are going to find, however, that here again, there is no absolute yardstick of what is realistic, and that indeed the 'ear for conversation', if it is well tuned for literary purposes, will tend to distance itself from the raw realities of spoken discourse.

In the present era of sound-recording, it is relatively easy to transcribe and examine unscripted conversation, and it is often noted that such transcriptions are 'messy' and 'formless' in a way that would be found intolerable in written communication. As an illustration, here is part of a conversation between students about their local cadet force:[9]

A: We've got these – exercises and you've got to take the er butt and erm hold point it away up there and of course (laughter) our aim used to shut it up and down it came.
B: Well I er I joined for these – reasons and plus the er driving you get taught you're taught to drive.   5
C: Well erm also my father says I need a bit of discipline you know.
A: Doesn't (matter what you do).
B: (You won't get any) there (honestly it's just terrific).
C: (No that's why I'm joining) to make him think I'm getting discipline. 10
A: Oh it's great fun there isn't it?
B: Oh but wait – have you – been on a erm drilling yet?
C: No.
B: You just wait.   15

This is of course only a partial transcription of the real properties of speech: for a fuller and more accurate transcription, special notations, including phonetic symbols, symbols for stress, intonation, etc. would have to be used. Nevertheless, it shows the verbal content of the conversation, and marks in an *ad hoc* way some special features of delivery: for example, dashes indicate pauses, and brackets indicate material uttered simultaneously.

The features which obviously make this different from most fictional conversation are, in the first place, those which interfere with and interrupt the fluency of speech. They include:

(i) *Hesitation pauses* (either *filled*, e.g. lines 2 and 4, or *unfilled*, e.g. lines 1 and 13). Filled pauses are those which are plugged by stopgap noises such as *er* and *erm*.
(ii) *False starts*. These can take the form either of a needless repetition of a word (e.g. 'I er I' in line 4), or of a reformulation of what has been said (e.g. 'hold point', line 2; 'you get taught you're taught to drive', line 5). The result is an ungrammatical sequence of words.
(iii) *Syntactic anomalies*. Often we fail to keep control of the syntax of what we are saying, and produce anomalous constructions which, if they are not entirely ungrammatical, would nevertheless be regarded as awkward and unacceptable in written composition. An example is the inconsistent sequence of pronouns and the repetition of *got* in *A*'s first speech: 'We've got . . . you've got to take'.

These may be called features of NORMAL NON-FLUENCY: they are non-fluent in the sense that they fall short of an 'ideal' delivery, and yet they are normal in the sense that they occur habitually in speech; it is difficult to say anything at all interesting without such lapses occurring. The absence of them itself is remarkable, as Yeats reveals in his comment on Wilde's conversation:

> My first meeting with Oscar Wilde was an astonishment. I never before heard a man talking with perfect sentences, as if he had written them all overnight with labour and yet all spontaneous.
>
> [W.B. Yeats, *The Trembling of the Veil*]

The reason for non-fluency is simple: in impromptu speech, we have to plan our utterances in advance (we have to choose which words and structures to use, etc.) and yet we are under pressure to maintain continuous delivery, to keep the conversational ball in the air. Features of non-fluency occur whenever our planning falls behind our delivery. The voiced fillers *er* and *erm*, for example, are useful delaying devices, so that we are able to continue holding the floor while we think of what next to say. These features are such an inevitable accompaniment of speech that a hearer will tend not to notice them: unless they are particularly frequent, they will be edited out of the consciousness as irrelevant to the communication.

In lines 8 and 9, the passage illustrates another 'messy' feature of ordinary speech. Speakers interrupt one another in a battle for the floor, so that more than one person is speaking at once. In addition, there may be frequent and haphazard transitions from one topic to another: the conversation often lacks a sense of 'aim'. In line 10, for example, C sticks doggedly to the topic he was discussing in line 6 (the subject of discipline), ignoring what A and B have said in the meantime.

When we consider the actual form and content of impromptu speech, we notice other characteristics which strike us, against the standard of written communication, as redundant or loosely formulated. Tag constructions such as *you know* (lines 6–7) and initiating signals like *Well* (lines 4 and 6) and *Oh* (lines 12 and 13) seem to add little to the message. Such forms do seem to have an important function, however, in that they signal the 'monitoring' role of the speaker in relation to the message, and also to some extent act as pause-fillers. More obviously interpersonal in their function are tag questions such as *isn't it* (line 12) – an invitation to the listeners to confirm the speaker's observation.

On the syntactic level, conversation tends towards coordination rather than subordination of clauses, for coordination simplifies the planning of sentence structure (*cf* section 7.5.1). The first sentence of the extract, for example, contains a sequence of five clauses linked by *and* (*'n*), and in the whole passage there is no instance of a subordinating conjunction. Apart from this, there is a tendency to use cliché expressions which require no linguistic inventiveness: 'it's just terrific', 'it's great fun', 'you just wait', etc.

Altogether, it may be concluded that real conversation is unlikely to be promising material for literary employment, and that it must strike an observer who has an eye on the aesthetic capabilities of language as sloppy, banal and ill-organised. We come, then, once more to our familiar conclusion about realism: the author of a literary fiction does not aim at a completely realistic representation of the features of ordinary conversation. Nevertheless, it will be valuable to examine two short passages of fictional conversation, to see in what directions a writer tends to depart from a realistic representation of speech.

The following passage is from D.H. Lawrence's short story *The Horse-Dealer's Daughter*. Mabel and her brothers must leave their home because of the collapse of the horse-dealing business started by their father:

[3] 'Have you had a letter from Lucy?' Fred Henry asked of his sister. (1)
   'Last week,' came the neutral reply. (2)
   'And what does she say?' (3)
   There was no answer. (4)
   'Does she *ask* you to go and stop there?' persisted Fred Henry. (5)
   'She says I can if I like.' (6)
   'Well, then, you'd better. (7) Tell her you'll come on Monday.' (8)
   This was received in silence. (9)
   'That's what you'll do then, is it?' said Fred Henry, in some exasperation. (10)
   But she made no answer. (11)

There are no examples in this passage of what we have called 'normal non-fluency', and this is the most obvious way in which, like most fictional dialogue, it fails to resemble the transcription. Such features are in general an impediment, rather than a contribution, to communicative discourse; so they are edited out, and the writer gives us, in this respect, an idealised picture of the coherence of conversation. The passage does, however, contain one or two examples of interaction signals, which tell us something of the relation between the participants. Fred Henry's 'Well, then' in (7) indicates that he is spelling out for his sister the obvious conclusion from what she has just said: it registers a certain degree of impatience with her failure to come to the conclusion herself. The tag question 'is it?' in (10), on the other hand, asks her for her confirmation: having told her to do something without eliciting a response, he is forced into the position of having to solicit an answer – hence the 'exasperation'.

The dialogue in other respects is quite credible, given what we know of the participants. The grammar and lexis are of the very simple kind that might be expected in such a situation, and we can say that Lawrence provides the *illusion* of real conversation. The skill of the novelist lies, however, in the ability to make something so realistically banal as this bear a density of significance in building up the fictional world. The significance comes mainly from the inferences we draw from what is said: inference about the characters, their situation, and their attitude to one another. We note that first, the relation is one of assumed dominance of the brother over the sister: he asks the questions, and tells her what to do. But also the sister asserts her own independence by failing to cooperate with him. She not only gives minimal answers to questions, withholding the information she knows her brother needs, but fails entirely to respond to his command, (9), and two of his questions, (4), and (11). We infer, from her responses, that she does not intend to accept her sister's invitation. The undercurrent of this dialogue is a conflict of wills between the man and the girl, and we learn (without being told) something of the rough, overbearing character of the one, and of the proud, determined nature of the other. These are important in making credible the girl's attempted suicide later on. The dialogue also poses a question, presents us with a minor mystery. Why is Mabel determined not to go and live with her sister? At this stage we can only imagine the reason, but it will be made clearer later on. Lawrence has in fact given us a great deal of meaning in a short space, mainly through inference rather than direct statement.

The way in which dialogue generates such implied meanings will be considered at greater length in Chapter 9; for the present we note it as a special case of the inferential process on which so much of our understanding of a fiction depends. We also learn from this example that even though a writer may use realistically banal language in portraying dialogue, this banality can be artistically functional: a dialogue of very ordinary remarks can be so directed that every sentence has some ulterior literary purpose.

Since features of non-fluency are normally overlooked by participants in real-life conversation, they can be omitted from fictional conversation without impairing the realistic effect. But even these 'errors' can be communicative, in the sense that they may indicate something of the speaker's character or state of mind: frequency of hesitations, for instance, may be a sign of nervousness, tentativeness or careful weighing of words. Features of this kind, when they do occur in fiction, tend to have a communicative purpose. In Kingsley Amis's *Lucky Jim*, Welch, the bumbling history professor, muddles his way through his sentences, and frequently fails to finish them. The following extract shows Welch intervening with unusual vigour, in an attempt to defuse an altercation between his objectionable son Bertrand and Jim Dixon (the Lucky Jim of the title); Dixon has committed the *faux pas* of mistaking Bertrand's present girlfriend for his previous one:

[4] 'I'm terribly sorry if I've made a mistake, but I was under the impression that Miss Loosmore here had something to do with . . .'

He turned to Margaret for aid, but before she could speak Welch, of all people, had come in loudly with: 'Poor old Dixon, ma-ha-ha, must have been confusing this . . . this young lady with Sonia Loosmore, a friend of Bertrand's who let us all down rather badly some time ago. I think Bertrand must have thought you were . . . twitting him or something, Dixon; ba-ha-ha.'

'Well, if he'd taken the trouble to be introduced, this wouldn't have happened,' Bertrand said, still flushed. 'Instead of which, he . . .'

'Don't worry about it, Mr Dixon,' the girl cut in. 'It was only a silly little misunderstanding. I can quite see how it happened. My name's Christine Callaghan. Altogether different, you see.'

'Well, I'm . . . thanks very much for taking it like that. I'm very sorry about it, really I am.'

[Kingsley Amis, *Lucky Jim*, Chapter 4]

Without analysing it in detail, one can see that the unusually realistic effect of this dialogue is due to features of non-fluency. The extract contains two hesitations, two interruptions and one false start; but all these are functional, in giving an impression, in various ways, of the characters' reactions to an embarrassing situation. This is also a good occasion for noting the informal or colloquial character of conversational language. Routine features of informality are abbreviated verb forms and negative forms such as *I'm, I've, he'd, wouldn't*. The lexis is also plainly colloquial, in the use of such idiomatic expressions as 'terribly sorry', 'had something to do with', 'let us down', 'rather badly'. In this, as in other respects, this passage convinces us that it could be a piece of authentic dialogue.

Fictional dialogue imitates the very thing it consists of: language. It is therefore possible to make a linguistic judgment about passages such as [3] and [4], and to say, even though we cannot compare them with any specific original, that they are like the real thing. But with the whole range of English literature in mind, this realism must be placed in a deeper perspective. Successful dramatists from Shakespeare to Shaw and Shaffer have not placed too high a value on it, and often a considered judgment on distinguished literary renderings of the spoken word (e.g. in the work of great nineteenth-century novelists) is that they aspire not so much to realism as to a superior expressiveness of the kind which we do not ordinarily achieve in real life. The ideal conversationalist, Oscar Wilde, has many parallels in fiction.

5.4.2 Dialect and idiolect

When we turn to the characteristics which distinguish the speech of one character from that of another, the same considerations apply: 'The principles of selection and concentration are generally at work to give fictional dialogue a quality quite different from that of real speech.'[10]

Linguists have used the term DIALECT for varieties of language which are linguistically marked off from other varieties and which correspond to geographical, class or other divisions of society. A DIALECT is thus the particular set of linguistic features which a defined subset of the speech community shares; IDIOLECT refers, more specifically, to the linguistic 'thumbprint' of a particular person: to the features of speech that mark him off as one individual from another. As other writers have examined the form and function of idiolect and dialect in fiction in some detail[11] we content ourselves here with a few observations and illustrations of the contribution of fictional speech types as a special aspect of the writer's mock reality, and one that commends itself for study by linguistic methods.

Since we are dealing with a linguistic phenomenon we may characterise it by reference to the various linguistic levels: graphological, syntactic (grammatical and lexical) and semantic. Perhaps the most familiar lexical contribution to characterisation (combined with a graphological marker) is Uriah Heep's harping on the adjective *'umble* in *David Copperfield* – a good example of how even a single word may encapsulate idiolectal expression of character. A less obvious device is Jane Austen's repeated use of vocatives (see section 9.5.1) in the speech of Aunt Norris (*Mansfield Park*), who often ingratiatingly addresses her brother-in-law as 'my dear Sir Thomas'. The more Mrs Norris seeks to influence others, the more liberal her use of vocatives. When, for example, in Chapter 3, Lady Bertram talks about the possibility of giving hospitality and protection to Fanny Price, Mrs Norris is anxious to ensure that no such thing takes place. In nine contributions to the conversation, Lady Bertram uses the vocative 'sister' twice, whereas her other seven remarks have no vocative attached to them. But Mrs Norris uses vocatives in six of her own nine contributions, combining the respectful 'Lady Bertram' with the more cajoling address of 'dear sister' and 'dear Lady Bertram'.

Idiolect and dialect are perhaps most noticeable on the graphological level: from Dickens's rich mine of examples, we may take at random Sam Weller's rendering of *w* as *v* in *Pickwick Papers*: ('there's a pair of Vellingtons a good deal vorn'); Mr Sleary's lisp in *Hard Times*, and Mr Chadband's pronunciation of *truth* as the awesome disyllable *Terewth* (capitalised for further emphasis) in *Bleak House*. The graphology is an indication of phonological correlates, but we have earlier made the point (in sections 4.3.3–4.3.4) that English spelling and punctuation being what they are, these are merely *suggestive* of a particular pronunciation.

Once again, there is no question of absolute realism. This point becomes patently clear when we consider the phenomenon of EYE-DIALECT, where the impression of rendering non-standard speech by non-standard spelling is pure illusion. An example is the spelling *wos* in Poor Jo's 'He wos wery good to me, he wos' in *Bleak House*. *Wos* is in fact an 'illiterate' spelling of the standard pronunciation of *was*, but somehow the social implications of the misspelling are mentally transferred to Jo's manner of speech. Similarly in many novels, lower-class characters 'pronounce' *and* as *an'* or *'n*. But this is a reflection of an elision which occurs naturally in English speech, without respect to dialect. Even a BBC announcer will say 'cats 'n dogs'. If we meet such a non-standard spelling in fiction, it is its non-standardness that strikes us, not the supposed phonetic reality behind it.

The graphological rendering of dialect is so much a matter of impressionistic convention that it is scarcely pertinent to criticise an author for lack of realism in this field. A person unfamiliar with West Country and Yorkshire speech would be hard put to it to reconstruct the actual vowels and consonants of those dialects from examples like these:

'And how long hev this news about me been knowed, Pa'son Tringham?'
[Thomas Hardy, *Tess of the D'Urbervilles*, Chapter 1]

'Tak' these in tuh t'maister, lad,' he said, 'un' bide theare; Aw's gang up tuh my awn rahm.'
[Emily Brontë, *Wuthering Heights*, Chapter 32]

And yet both Hardy and Emily Brontë were scrupulous observers of their local dialects. The goal of authenticity is a reasonable one for an author to adopt, in this as in other aspects of the fiction which overlap with the real world (see section 5.2), but it can result in unintelligibility if taken too far. Charlotte Brontë regarded her sister's rendering of North Country dialect in the speech of Joseph (*Wuthering Heights*) as too faithful, and revised the 1850 edition of the novel in order to make his language more accessible to 'southerns'. When we find that Dickens and other writers are inconsistent in their inclusion of dialect markers, it is reasonable to conclude not that they are careless, but that they are more interested in the illusion, the living flavour, of dialect, rather than with its exact reproduction.

These points are illustrated in the following piece of conversation (from *Bleak House*, Chapter 16), where poor Jo, the crossing-sweeper, is being quizzed by a strange woman (whom we later suppose to be Lady Dedlock) about the whereabouts of Nemo's grave:

> 'Is this place of abomination consecrated ground?'
> 'I don't know nothink of consequential ground,' says Jo, still staring . . .
> 'Is it blessed?'
> 'I'm blest if I know,' says Jo, staring more than ever; 'but I shouldn't think it warn't. Blest?' repeats Jo, something troubled in his mind. 'It an't done it much good if it is. Blest? I should think it was t'othered myself. But I don't know nothink!'

First, Jo's speech is marked by non-standard features which represent him as a member of the 'lower orders': there are pronunciations like *warn't* for *wasn't*, *nothink* for *nothing*; double negatives such as 'I don't know nothink'; the malapropism *consequential* for *consecrated*. In fact, such features are more frequent in Jo's speech than in that of any other character in the novel, and symbolise his status at the opposite pole to the Dedlocks, at the very bottom of the social scale, where ignorance combines with misery and destitution. It may be that some of the written versions of Jo's words are closer than the conventional spellings to the relevant dialect, e.g. *nothink*. But other likely candidates (such as *meself* for *myself*) are not employed. The change of spelling from *blessed* to *blest* is particularly interesting. It is only in rather special circumstances, as in the beatitudes ('Blessed be the peacemakers') that this word is pronounced as two syllables, and so we cannot conclude that Jo's pronunciation of it differs in this respect from Lady Dedlock's, particularly as in one instance he is apparently echoing her. But the graphology indicates that they are different, and it is to this that the reader reacts in registering the contrast between the dialects of the two speakers.

The functions of dialect and idiolect are various. Referring back to section 5.3, we may suggest an association between dialect (which concerns the general characteristics of a group of speakers) and symbolism (the tendency to universalise or typify) – likewise between idiolect (the individualising features of language) and verisimilitude (the tendency to evoke reality by particularising). But there is more to it than this. One of the factors to be reckoned with is the distancing and stigmatising effect of using non-standard forms of language, including deviant spellings. The very fact of using such forms implies that the character deviates from the norm of the author's own standard language. Hence non-standard speech is typically associated with objects of comedy and satire; characters whom we see from the outside only. Some of Dickens's inconsistencies in the use of dialect can be attributed to this cause: for example, illiterate Lizzie Hexam, in *Our Mutual Friend*, speaks almost entirely in standard English, in contrast to the non-standard speech of her equally illiterate father. But then Lizzie is destined to be the novel's heroine, and it could scarcely be allowed for a nineteenth-century heroine to speak dialect. Similar cases of 'dialect suppression' are those of George Eliot's Adam Bede and Hardy's Tess. Such inconsistencies can be cynically explained in terms of Victorian delicacy or snobbery; but an equally good reason is the linguistic one, that non-standard language often implies remoteness from the author's own language, and hence from the central standards of judgment in a novel.

5.4.3 Speech and character

Idiolect can also be an expression of character, an aspect of the fictional world which deserves a great deal of attention in itself. Here we are content to point out that the characters which people the mock reality are, like everything else it contains, formed according to the general principles outlined in sections 5.2–5.3, regarding specification of detail. The details of their appearance, behaviour and personal qualities may be specified to a greater or lesser extent; they may be relatively realistic (in the sense of being credible and consistent) or not; they may be relatively universal in their characteristics (representative of character 'types') or may be relatively individuated. We must also recognise the importance of inference in the determination of character: in novels, as in real life, a person's motives and character are inferred from outward behaviour: from actions, from demeanour, and also from speech.

Speech is such a revealing indicator of character that a common resort of novelists is to IMAGINARY SPEECH, as a way of conveying the hidden purport of a person's behaviour. Here is part of Smollett's portrait of Sir Giles Squirrel:

[5] The baronet's disposition seemed to be cast in the true English mould. He was sour, silent and contemptuous; his very looks indicated a consciousness of superior wealth, and he never opened his mouth, except to make some dry, sarcastic, national reflection. . . . In a word, though his tongue was silent on the subject, his whole demeanour was continually saying, 'You are all a pack of poor, lousy rascals, who have a design upon my purse: 'tis true, I could buy your whole generation; but, I won't be bubbled, d'ye see; I am aware of your flattery, and upon my guard against all your knavish pranks; and I come into your company for my own amusement only.'
[Tobias Smollett, *The Adventures of Ferdinand Count Fathom*, Chapter 22]

Such imaginary speech is also a favourite device of Dickens, and illustrates that writer's 'abiding interest . . . in the act of expression, in whatever aspect and of whatever kind'.[12] Dickens's use of utterance as a reflection of character is one notable manifestation of the generic principle in his writing. For him, observable reality is, for all its vivid and multifarious particularity, symbolic of deeper realities of mood and spirit. Thus the description of Josiah Bounderby's appearance is at one with his style of speaking: both are emanations of a character typified as 'a man perfectly devoid of sentiment', 'the Bully of humility':

[6] A man made out of a coarse material, which seemed to have been stretched to make so much of him. A man with a great puffed head and forehead, swelled veins in his temples, and such a strained skin to his face that it seemed to hold his eyes open, and lift his eyebrows up. A man with a pervading appearance on him of being inflated like a balloon, and ready to start. A man who could never sufficiently vaunt himself a self-made man. A man who was always proclaiming, through that brassy speaking-trumpet of a voice of his, his old ignorance and his old poverty.

[Charles Dickens, *Hard Times*, Part 1, Chapter 4]

When the 'brassy speaking-trumpet' speaks, it comes out with:

[7] Tell Josiah Bounderby of Coketown, of your district schools and your model schools, and your training schools, and your whole kettle-of-fish of schools; and Josiah Bounderby of Coketown, tells you plainly, all right, all correct, – he hadn't such advantages . . .

[*Ibid*]

His habit of referring to himself in the third-person as 'Josiah Bounderby of Coketown' is, with his balloon-like aspect, an indicator of his inflated self-esteem; whereas the 'stretching' of 'coarse material' seems an exact metaphor not only for his appearance, but for the huffing-and-puffing manner in which his speech issues in repetitive bursts. The parallelisms in [7] serve only the purpose of blustering grandiloquence:

Tell Josiah Bounderby of Coketown . . .
and Josiah Bounderby tells . . .

your district schools
and your model schools
and your whole kettle-of-fish of schools . . .

all right,
all correct . . .

And as if to insist on the continuity of speech and character, Dickens's description of Bounderby in [6], with its repetition of 'A man' at the beginning of each sentence, shows the same parallelistic emphasis.

5.5 The rendering of the fiction

In section 5.3 we suggested that there is an analogical relation between the plane of language and the plane of the fictional world, and this analogy we now briefly develop, in order to understand a fiction as a particular realisation of more abstract patterns or NARRATIVE STRUCTURES. Just as letters can be symbols for sounds, or words for meanings, so Bounderby's words can be a symbol of his character, and Bounderby's character itself can be a symbol of a type: the hard, self-made capitalist, the villain of the Industrial Revolution. The analogy, though fruitful, has evident limitations. Only in allegory does a fiction have a consistently symbolic character: in a novel, to reduce a piece of mock reality to a symbolic meaning is to winnow part of the corn away with the chaff. Bounderby cannot be explained away as a symbol, for he is, ultimately and irreducibly, Bounderby.[13]

Nevertheless, the mock reality becomes significant in a literary sense by virtue of our recognition that its elements add up to more than an arbitrary slice of 'what might have happened': that they arrange themselves into patterns or structures representative of human experience in an abstract, archetypal way.[14] The analogy between structures of language and structures of narrative has been developed with subtlety by French structuralists such as Barthes, Todorov and Greimas.[15] The 'grammar of narrative' as studied by these and other structuralist writers will not concern us here, but seeing the fictional world as representative, in this way, of abstract schemata, enables us to pursue the analogy between choices of rendering made on the fictional plane, and stylistic choices made on the linguistic plane. The elements of fictional technique we now consider may, in a broad sense, be said to constitute a 'style' of fiction creation: a matter of *how* it is rendered, rather than of *what* it is. Such aspects of fictional technique belong to what Russian critics have called the SJUZHET, the 'story as shaped and edited by the story-teller',[16] as distinguished from the FABULA, the story as a mere chronology of events. Just as we have distinguished three functions of stylistic choice – the interpersonal, textual and ideational (section 4.5) – so we shall distinguish three corresponding functions in the rendering of fictions: point of view, sequencing and descriptive focus.

5.5.1 Fictional point of view

Corresponding to the interpersonal function of style, there is the slanting of the fictional world towards 'reality' as apprehended by a particular participant, or set of participants, in the fiction. We shall call this FICTIONAL POINT OF VIEW, to distinguish it from the discoursal point of view (discussed in section 8.2), and we shall call the person whose point of view is represented a REFLECTOR[17] of the fiction.

Suppose the police officers investigating our Corsican incident [1] could gain access to only one eye-witness: reconstructed truth would then be limited to what this witness happened to have observed or inferred about the incident. A fiction writer, although not compelled to take one person's point of view, can voluntarily limit his 'omniscience' to those things which belong to one person's model of reality. He can also vary the fictional point of view, sometimes claiming authorial omniscience, sometimes giving us one character's version of events, sometimes that of another. He can even take the point of view of an animal, or of a man on the point of death, bypassing the problem of authenticity: how could such an account have been *told* to anybody? In *The Short Happy Life of Francis Macomber*, Hemingway does both these things, for at one point in a lion hunt, he lets us see things through the eyes of the lion; and the events immediately preceding Macomber's death are seen through the mind of Macomber himself.

Fictional point of view, by the standard of authorial omniscience, can be regarded as a selective withholding of information, or relinquishing of omniscience. It is different in principle from what is more commonly understood as point of view in fiction, and what we later discuss as DISCOURSAL POINT OF VIEW (see section 8.2): the telling of the story through the *words* or *thoughts* of a particular person. There is a difference, let us say, between the police officer's report of what happened, derived from the evidence of one witness, and that witness's own account of what happened, as it might be given in a court of law. But there is also a clear connection between these two conceptions of point of view: if events are recorded through the words or thoughts of a character, they are by that fact limited to what that character could reasonably be expected to know or infer. Discoursal point of view, that is, *implies* a parallel restriction of fictional point of view.

The demarcation of fictional point of view is difficult to determine where the narrative refers to psychological events and states: to perceptions, volitions, emotions, thoughts, judgments. Statements such as 'Margaret was angry', 'Ben was listening to the music', 'The attacker threatened John with a knife' can strictly only be verified by someone who has access to a person's mind: even verbs like *threaten* and *listen* involve the unobservable element of intention. But it is natural and almost automatic human activity to infer such mental phenomena from outward behaviour, and so there is no necessary implication of an 'inside view' when such expressions are used. In the following passage from Bennett's *Clayhanger*, we have a clear impression (consistent with the rest of the novel) of seeing things from Edwin's point of view, even though there are a number of references to what is going on in his sisters' minds:

[8] Edwin went to the doorway of the drawing-room and stood there. Clara, in her Sunday bonnet, was seated at the ancient piano; it had always been she who had played the accompaniments. Maggie, nursing one of the babies, sat on another chair, and leaned towards the page in order to make out the words. She had half-forgotten the words, and Clara was no longer at ease in the piano part, and their voices were shaky and unruly, and the piano itself was exceedingly bad. A very indifferent performance of indifferent music! And yet it touched Edwin. He could not deny that by its beauty and by the sentiment of old times it touched him. He moved a little forward in the doorway. Clara glanced at him, and winked. Now he could see his father. Darius was standing at some distance behind his daughters and his grandchild, and staring at them. And the tears rained down from his red eyes, and then his emotion overcame him and he blubbered, just as the duet finished.

[Arnold Bennett, *Clayhanger*, Book iii, Chapter 12, iii]

Strictly, expressions like 'half-forgotten', 'was ... at ease', 'in order to', imply that the narrator can see inside the minds of Maggie and Clara, as well as of Edwin. But on the other hand, an observer such as Edwin would feel entitled to use such expressions, on the evidence of behaviour. So these do not necessarily count against the view that Edwin is the reflector. More positively, what puts us in Edwin's position is, first, the references to Edwin's inner self, and second, the way in which information in the passage is sequenced. The former are of a kind which could *not* be readily judged from external behaviour ('it *touched* Edwin', 'He could not *deny*') and so by default we must assume privileged access to Edwin's consciousness. The sequencing of information is another important cue, because the details of the inside of the room are given at the point in the story where we assume Edwin must have become aware of them. We are told Edwin went to the doorway, and are *then* told about the piano-playing that he could observe; later, we are told 'Now he could see his father', and a description of his father's demeanour follows.

This illustrates one kind of limitation of omniscience, the limitation to the 'inside view'. There is also the opposite phenomenon of fictional point of view, where the author limits his narrative to an external view of a character, achieving an effect of 'estrangement' by denying himself knowledge of what is inside the character's mind.[18]

5.5.2 Fictional sequencing

As the last example shows, there is an intimate relation between fictional point of view and the order in which information is presented. Fictional SEQUENCING is an aspect of a more general topic which, in its stylistic dimension, belongs to the textual function of language as considered in

Chapter 7. At this point, let us simply acknowledge the obvious fact that a fictive world is not something that the writer can convey in one fell swoop to the reader. The narrative therefore has to progress along a one-way track, gradually building up a fuller store of knowledge and understanding of the events, places, characters, etc. of the fiction. So every novel is, in a way, not a single mock reality but a whole cumulative progression of mock realities, each chapter, paragraph and sentence being incremental to what has gone before. One major kind of choice a writer has to make, in rendering the fiction, is therefore that of sequencing. No doubt a dominant consideration, in determining this choice, is plain chronology: A is presented before B, because A happens (in the fiction) before B. This is the order followed in the news report [1], and may be considered the neutral order for the telling of any story. But as we saw in the passage from James's *The Pupil* (see pp. 81–2), other principles, such as psychological immediacy, can take precedence over chronology. And if the story is told from a fictional point of view, the most important sequencing factor is not objective chronology, but PSYCHOLOGICAL SEQUENCING, the order in which a character comes to learn about the components of the fiction. In the more or less standard formula of whodunit fiction, we follow the fictional point of view of the detective throughout, and so the mystery of the identity of the murderer, something which in chronological terms should have been declared at the outset of the novel, is preserved until the end. On a smaller scale, we have already illustrated this 'psychological sequencing' in [8], and the following passage from Joyce's *The Dead* shows its effect more clearly:[19]

[9] Gabriel had not gone to the door with the others. He was in the dark part of the hall gazing up the staircase. A woman was standing near the top of the first flight, in the shadow also. He could not see her face but he could see the terracotta and salmon-pink panels of her skirt which the shadow made appear black and white. It was his wife.

Why does Joyce withhold initially the information that the woman is Gabriel's wife? The obvious answer is that at that stage Gabriel himself does not recognise her. We seem to be with Gabriel, looking up the stairs towards a vague figure in the shadow, face hidden. The sequence of impression is: first, a woman in the shadow; second, the details of the dress; third, the recognition. The effect would have been nullified if Joyce had begun his third sentence: 'His wife was standing . . .' This is a small-scale illustration of the principle that artistic choice on the fictional plane consists not only of judging what details to include and which to withhold, but also of judging at what stages to disclose information.

In addition to the two principles of chronological and psychological sequencing, attention must be given to a third factor of PRESENTATIONAL

SEQUENCING. The author considers: 'What is the appropriate order in which the reader should learn the elements of the fiction?' On the whole, this will tend to coincide with chronological or psychological sequencing, but in principle it is independent. We can think of a fiction from the reader's point of view as a very complicated model kit, in which the pieces of the model can be glued together in many different orders, but where some orders are more 'logical' or 'natural' than others. For example, if the model were of a sailing ship, one would not normally assemble the rigging until one had assembled the masts and yards to which the rigging is attached. In a similar way, some parts of the fiction are naturally dependent on others. A later event will not be intelligible unless an earlier event is known; an effect will not be intelligible without its cause; a person's behaviour may not be intelligible unless we know that person's character and motives. The best order of presentation, if one wants to facilitate the reader's processing of information, both in fiction writing and in general expository writing, is to go from elements which presuppose the least prior knowledge to those which presuppose the most.[20] When this order is abandoned, we can be sure the author has some good reason for doing so.

In the model kit analogy, the author is the person who writes the detailed linear instructions for assembling the model. But he is at liberty to play tricks with the model-builder, holding back information which is necessary for understanding an earlier piece of the narrative until later. This heightens the element of mystery or suspense which is an important ingredient in all story-telling. At any point in the narrative, the reader will be in the position of being certain of some things, and of being uncertain of others, and it is through this interplay of things known and things guessed, anticipated, or inferred, that the story progresses and holds its interest for the reader. A point of particular concentration is the beginning of the fiction, which, according to the principle above, ought to be the point of least presupposition. This is indeed the principle followed in the time-honoured formula of the fairytale:

[10] Once upon a time there was a miller who had a very beautiful daughter.

This sentence, which begins the story of *Rumpelstiltskin*, contains in the linguistic sense no presuppositions: a signal of this is the three-fold occurrence of the indefinite article, which begs no questions of prior knowledge. But it is more characteristic of modern fiction (as we saw in the Lawrence and James passages in sections 3.4 and 3.5) to introduce the fiction *in medias res*, at a point where certain things are already taken for granted, although the reader can only work them out for himself by reading on.

Hemingway's narration of *The Short Happy Life of Francis Macomber* begins half way through the story, where the Macombers and Wilson have returned to camp after the debacle of the lion-hunt, thrusting us straight into a situation of disequilibrium and dramatic tension. Even the opening sentence is full of dramatic portent:

[11] It was now lunchtime and they were all sitting under the double green fly of the dining tent pretending that nothing had happened.

In contrast to [10], this sentence contains four definite expressions: *the* (twice), *now*, *they*. Since definite expressions are only used on the assumption of shared knowledge about the identity of the referent, these expressions in effect say to the reader: 'You already know when "now" is, who "they" are, where "the dining tent" is; in fact you are already a party to the situation.' Moreover, the verb *pretend* carries the presupposition that 'something has happened', although we do not yet know what it is. By this device, the author sets up a complex mock reality, with its implications of past, present and future, right from the start. Sinclair, in quoting [11], comments: 'The reader is a long way behind, and has to construct a provisional universe.'[21] In a sense, all the way through a story, the reader has to continue constructing his provisional universe or mock reality. In presentational sequencing, as well as in the other aspects of sequencing, the author's artistic sense often shows in the way information is withheld, rather than in the way it is revealed.

The end of the novel, again according to the 'natural' principle of information presentation, should be the point at which the fiction reaches completion, in the sense that nothing (nothing of importance, that is) remains provisional: all questions are answered, all presuppositions are satisfied, all mysteries are solved. In this the fiction achieves coherence. But here again the concept of foregrounding may be applied to the fictional plane: the writer may frustrate conventional expectations both by taking things for granted at the beginning of the story and by leaving things unresolved at the conclusion.

5.5.3 Descriptive focus

We come finally to an area of fictional technique where the mock reality interacts with the ideational choices of meaning through which it is portrayed. Two particular contrasts will be considered: that between physical and abstract description, and that between subjective and objective description. What we call an 'event' in real life is often a composite of these factors; and therefore a description of it can concentrate on one aspect, and ignore another. This is what is meant by DESCRIPTIVE FOCUS.

'Physical' and 'abstract' are terms which can be used without much thought, and so it is as well to be aware of what we mean by them. A physical description concentrates on things which have space/time extension, and have physical properties such as size, shape, colour, movement, speed, etc. which can in principle be registered by the senses. An abstract description (although the term 'abstract' has other uses than this) concentrates on mental and social properties, states, and events. For example, 'perceive', 'forgive', 'possess', 'be married to', 'government', 'threat' and 'teacher' are all (at least primarily) abstract concepts: although they have physical concomitants, they cannot be defined in purely concrete terms (we could not, for example, define marriage in terms of cohabitation). In some areas, the physical and the abstract are virtually inextricable: a verb of speaking such as *ask* involves both a mental event and the physical act of utterance; a kinship term such as *father* has both a biological meaning ('progenitor') and a social meaning, defining the rights and obligations of fatherhood. So the difference between the physical and the abstract in practice is not an absolute distinction, but a matter of degree and emphasis. Sentences [12] and [13] below could be descriptions of the same event, although one is almost entirely physical and the other almost entirely abstract:

[12] A man in a gilded headdress walked forward, smiling, and raised his hand to them.
[13] They were greeted by the chief of the tribe.

But perhaps the most neutral kind of description in fiction is one that combines both physical and abstract elements of an event:

[14] The chief walked forward and raised his hand in greeting.

Once again, the role of inference must be stressed: we cannot help interpreting physical facts in terms of their abstract significance – a raised hand as a sign of greeting, a smile as a sign of friendship. Nor can we avoid imagining the physical accompaniments of mental and social phenomena – the phrase 'chief of the tribe' will evoke a picture of a man in grand costume.

There is also a common ground between subjective and objective description. Adjectives such as *hard, smooth, dark, light, large, small, loud, soft* refer to objective physical attributes, and yet they are also subjective in the sense that they may be subjectively perceived by the senses: an object *feels* hard, *looks* dark, *sounds* loud. But clearly the subjective and objective do not necessarily match; a large object may appear small from a distance; a light object may appear dark in the shadow; and, for that matter, we may subjectively be aware of things which have no objective existence at all. Thus a writer may concentrate on describing the sensory or imaginative aspects of things, leaving us to work out what they are really like 'out there'.

Descriptive focus can have varying effects in literature. As [12] shows, the effect of concentrating on physical description in human matters and refraining from 'ordinary world' inferences can be one of estrangement, as if we are observers from an alien culture, uninitiated into the human significance of events. This effect takes a particularly extreme form in Gulliver's description of his first encounter with the Yahoos:

> Their heads and breasts were covered with a thick hair, some frizzled, and others lank; they had beards like goats, and a long ridge of hair down their backs and the fore-parts of their legs and feet; but the rest of their bodies were bare, so that I might see their skins, which were of a brown buff colour. They had no tails, and were accustomed to sit as well as to lie down, and often stood on their hind feet... The females were not so large as the males; they had long lank hair on their heads, but none on their faces, nor anything more than a sort of down on the rest of their bodies. The hair of both sexes was of several colours, brown, red, black, and yellow.
>
> [Jonathan Swift, *Gulliver's Travels*, iv.1]

We recognise the Yahoos as a slightly hairier version of the human species, and yet the physical description is so distasteful, that we must ruefully agree with Gulliver when he goes on to say: 'Upon the whole, I never beheld, in all my travels, so disagreeable an animal, nor one against which I conceived so strong an antipathy'.

On the other hand, physical description can invite an empathic response from the reader. It is part of Hemingway's technique of dispassionate understatement, which is evident in his use, in *The Short Happy Life of Francis Macomber*, of physical signals to indicate Margot's rejection of her husband after the lion-hunt:

> Macomber's wife had not looked at him nor he at her and he had sat by her in the back seat with Wilson sitting in the front seat. Once he had reached over and taken his wife's hand without looking at her and she had removed her hand from his. Looking across the stream to where the gun-bearers were skinning out the lion he could see that she had been able to see the whole thing. While they sat there his wife had reached forward and put her hand on Wilson's shoulder. He turned and she had leaned forward over the low seat and kissed him on the mouth.

The gesture of removing her hand from Macomber's and kissing Wilson speak for themselves. The concentration of physical details has a more intense and poignant effect in the earlier description of the wounded lion:

> Thirty-five yards into the grass the big lion lay flattened out along the ground. His ears were back and his only movement was a slight

twitching up and down of his long, black-tufted tail. He had turned at bay as soon as he had reached this cover and he was sick with the wound through his full belly, and weakening with the wound through his lungs that brought a thin foamy red to his mouth each time he breathed. His flanks were wet and hot and flies were on the little openings the solid bullets had made in his tawny hide, and his big yellow eyes, narrowed with hate, looked straight ahead, only blinking when the pain came as he breathed, and his claws dug in the soft baked earth.

In the main, this passage gives an objective record, the adjectives in particular adding specificity: *big, long, black-tufted, thin, foamy, wet, hot, solid, tawny, big, yellow, soft, baked.* Hemingway does not tell us what to feel, but our imaginations work on these details to evoke on the one hand a pitying sense of the animal's suffering, and on the other hand, a realisation of the menace that the lion holds for the hunters who now have to track him down. The emotion generated by this apparently flat description is quite complex and ambivalent. This is in keeping with Hemingway's theory of omission, whereby the significance of the text comes through what is unstated, but implied, as much as through the meanings of the words on the page: 'the omitted part would strengthen the story and make people feel something more than they understand'.

When we move from objective physical description to subjective sensory description, the impact is more direct. 'He walloped Stephen's hand with a pandy-bat' is a physical description; but the impression is quite different when Joyce describes that event in *A Portrait of the Artist as a Young Man* (Chapter 1):

A hot burning stinging tingling blow like the loud crack of a broken stick made his trembling hand crumple together like a leaf in the fire: and at the sound and the pain scalding tears were driven into his eyes His whole body was shaking with fright, his arm was shaking and his crumpled burning livid hand shook like a loose leaf in the air. A cry sprang to his lips, a prayer to be let off. But though the tears scalded his eyes and his limbs quivered with pain and fright he held back the hot tears and the cry that scalded his throat.

In contrast to the Hemingway, this strikes one as the opposite of understatement: a striving to do justice in words to the full intensity of an experience. Experiences are unique, whereas word-meanings are general. So to record the imprint of living experience, Joyce resorts to the interassociative meanings of simile and metaphor, mingling tactile vocabulary (*stinging, tingling, scalding, burning,* etc.), auditory vocabulary (*loud, crack, sound, cry*), and kinesthetic vocabulary (*trembling, shaking, quivered, crumpled*). One area of sensation is translated into and invigorated by another, the whole effect being supercharged by grammatical and lexical repetition. And as if to represent how the enveloping pain excludes all else from consciousness, even the giver and recipient of the blow, the description makes no reference at all to Stephen's assailant, and Stephen himself only appears in the passage through references to his body, fragmented, like his shattered spirit, into parts: 'his . . . hand', 'his arm', 'his limbs', 'his lips', 'his throat'.

The gap between sensory and physical description can be marked, as these passages illustrate. To give us the illusion of direct experience, a writer often turns, as Joyce does, to affective language, and the analogical language of simile and metaphor. If the kind of realism aimed at in the Hemingway passage might be described as OBJECTIVITY, the term which applies most readily to the subjective realism of the Joyce passage is VIVIDNESS. Clearly both of these are important elements in fiction writing, and once again it is appreciated that there is no one absolute standard of what it means to be 'realistic'. A writer may give prominence to physical or abstract, subjective or objective phenomena, according to his fictional ontology, but these emphases are simply preferences to specify details of one kind, and not of another. The insistence, for example, that the ultimate reality is that of sensation would put a low value on the works of such writers as Jane Austen, George Eliot and Henry James, for whom the most important realities are on the abstract planes of social, moral and psychological existence.

5.6 Conclusion

In considering the fiction as mock reality we have, in this chapter, distinguished five notions of realism which may, in their own way, contribute to the realistic illusion: credibility (section 5.3), verisimilitude (section 5.3), authenticity (sections 5.3–5.4), objectivity (section 5.5.3) and vividness (section 5.5.3). Realism is therefore a many-sided phenomenon, and its place in fiction must also be balanced against the functions of fiction as 'second-order symbolisation', as discussed in sections 5.3 and 5.5.

The authorial choices we have discussed in sections 5.5.1–5.5.3 belong to fictional technique, rather than stylistic technique: degree of specification, fictional point of view and fictional sequencing can be found in film and, to some extent, in the non-linguistic elements of the dramatic arts, as well as in prose fiction. Descriptive focus, on the other hand, is limited to literature, since other media of artistic expression are sensory; only literature, through its medium of language, can range over the whole data of human experience. Descriptive focus, in this respect, acts as a transition between this chapter and the next, in which we return to strictly stylistic concerns, and investigate the way in which language, through choices of meaning, represents a particular view of the fictional world.

Notes

1. J.C. RANSOM (1938a), 131.
2. O. WILDE, *The Picture of Dorian Gray*, Chapter 17.
3. 'Absolute liberty is as meaningless as realism in a vacuum. Both are relative terms.' H. LEVIN (1966), 66.
4. This passage is discussed from a different point of view by E.L. EPSTEIN (1978), 2–3.
5. The idea of the message as a 'second-order symbolisation' (e.g. a reference to a flower symbolising beauty, transitoriness, friendship, etc.) is implicit in most discussions of symbolism in literature. It has been expounded in both theory and practice by R. BARTHES (1957) and elsewhere. See an introductory discussion in T. HAWKES (1977), 130–134, and BARTHES (1971).
6. E. CASSIRER (1944), 144.
7. For example, F.W. BATESON and B. SHAKEVITCH (1962). For a different point of view, see the discussion of this issue of realistic particularity in D. LODGE (1966), 43–46.
8. Quoted in LODGE (1966), 41. Joyce remarked that if Dublin were destroyed by some massive disaster, its plan could be reconstructed from his novel.
9. From a conversation recorded for research purposes by John Sinclair in Edinburgh, and quoted with his permission.
10. N. PAGE (1973), 16.
11. See PAGE (1973), Chapters 3–4, and more specialised studies such as G.L. BROOK (1970), Chapters 2–5.
12. R. QUIRK (1959), 7.
13. In this respect we differ even from the view interestingly discussed by R. FOWLER (1977), 30–38, that characters can be defined in terms of their semantic make-up in terms of roles and 'semes' (or semantic components), rather as an identikit face is assembled from a large number of stereotype features. The 'illusion of reality' is, we would argue, all-important for character, as well as for other aspects of the fictional world. This means that we do not rely merely on stereotypes in interpreting character, but use inference (especially inference from the character's speech) to derive a sense of individual personality.
14. The term 'archetypal' is applied to recurrent, quasi-mythical themes in literature. See N. FRYE (1957), 131–239, and A. KOESTLER (1964), 353–354.
15. Helpful introductions to structuralism and its relation to stylistics are given in FOWLER (1977), HAWKES (1977) and CULLER (1975). All three books have useful reading lists on the subject.
16. See FOWLER (1978), 78.
17. Instead of the term 'reflector', 'focaliser' is often used.
18. On estrangement, see *ibid*, 90–92.
19. For a discussion of this passage in relation to point of view, see W. BOOTH (1961), 153.
20. See B.J.F. MEYER (1975).
21. J. MCH. SINCLAIR (1975), 87.

CHAPTER 6

Mind style

The difference between the subject of the last chapter and the subject of this can be summarised as follows: the fictional world is *what* is apprehended, whereas our present concern is with *how* that world is apprehended, or conceptualised. The two things are, in fact, opposite sides of the same coin. Any conceptualisation of a world presupposes both a world to refer to, and a mind through which that world is reflected. In practice, the two things may be difficult to separate. But we can recognise a clear difference in these two examples:

[1] It was a bright cold day in April, and the clocks were striking 13.

[George Orwell, *1984*]

[2] Bob Cowley's outstretched talons gripped the black deep-sounding chords.

[James Joyce, *Ulysses*, Penguin edn, p. 282]

Both these sentences are odd, but for different reasons. Sentence [1], which opens Orwell's *1984*, is linguistically transparent, and the only strange thing about it is the fictional world it postulates: a world in which clocks behave differently from the clocks we know. Sentence [2] is a description, from Joyce's *Ulysses*, of someone playing the piano. Here it is not the fictional world that causes surprise: the sentence describes a familiar activity. The strangeness is in the way Joyce causes the action to be perceived. The pianist's hand poised above the keys becomes the talon of a bird of prey, and it grips not the keys (even this would be an odd description) but the chords, which are thereby turned into physical objects. Another synaesthesia arises through the attribution of colour, blackness, to the chords. The sentence thus produces a merger, in one impression, of three senses: touch, vision and sound.

Sentence [2] is a particularly striking case of the phenomenon sometimes called 'world-view', but for which we will prefer Fowler's term MIND STYLE (see section 1.5):

> Cumulatively, consistent structural options, agreeing in cutting the presented world to one pattern or another, give rise to an impression of a world-view, what I shall call a 'mind style'.[1]

It is commonplace that a writer's style reveals that particular writer's habitual way of experiencing and interpreting things: we might say, for example, that the passages analysed in sections 3.3–3.5 exemplify respectively something of the world-views of Conrad, Lawrence and James. But the term 'mind style' can also be applied to more restricted domains of style: for example, the Lok-language of Golding's *The Inheritors* (see p. 26) belongs not to its author's work as a whole, but to one novel, and in fact to one character within the novel. So mind style, in this context, is a realisation of a narrative point of view. More narrowly still, mind style can be associated with quite local stylistic effects, for example in the description of a character or a landscape. Although here we are mainly concerned with cumulative tendencies of stylistic choice, even a single sentence, such as [2], might be said to encapsulate a mind style.

The need to separate fictional world from mind style becomes more obvious to the extent that a writer's way of representing the world deviates from a common-sense version of reality. Joyce's sentence [2] is linguistically foregrounded: the collocations 'Cowley's . . . talon', 'gripped the . . . chords' and 'black . . . chords' violate the selection restrictions requiring that *talon* does not go with a human possessor, that *grip* does not have an abstract object, and that *black* does not accompany an abstract noun. Joyce causes a reader to rearrange standard linguistic categories through metaphorical interpretation. But even in apparently normal pieces of writing, the writer slants us towards a particular 'mental set': there is no kind of writing that can be regarded as perfectly neutral and objective. We therefore progress, in this chapter, from mind styles which can easily strike a reader as natural and uncontrived (section 6.2), to those which clearly impose an unorthodox conception of the fictional world (section 6.3).

Before examining some examples, we must note that although mind style is essentially a question of semantics, it can only be observed through formal construction of language in terms of grammar and lexis. This is also true, of course, of features of the fictional world. Superficially, there is no difference between [1] and [2] in this respect: just as the oddity of Joyce's sentence is apparent in such deviant collocations as '*gripped* the . . . *chords*', so that of Orwell's is apparent in the deviant collocation of the verb *strike* with the numeral *13*. The important thing is to explain the interpretation of this oddity, and this means considering what other choices of language might have been relevantly made.

It is therefore appropriate to begin the examination of mind style with the question of semantic choice and for this purpose we select, as a case study, choice in the area of participant relations.

6.1 How linguistic choices affect mind style

One important aspect of mind style is that of participant relations in the clause.[2] It is at this level that semantic matters like agency and responsibility are indicated. To examine the effect of changes in participant relations more closely, let us look at the middle clause of the following sentence:

[3] The reflexes are taking over; *the left foot comes down with firm even pressure on the clutch pedal* while the right feeds in gas.

[Christopher Isherwood, *A Single Man*, Chapter 1]

In writing this clause Isherwood has chosen from a myriad of stylistic possibilities. Examples [4–8], below, however, are some of the possible alternatives in terms of participant relations:

[4] he comes down with his left foot with firm even pressure . . .
[5] he presses his left foot down with firm even pressure . . .
[6] he presses down with firm even pressure . . .
[7] the left foot presses itself down with firm even pressure . . .
[8] the left foot presses down with firm even pressure . . .

In the formulation Isherwood actually chose, the character's (George's) foot appears to do something automatically and of its own accord. Alternatives [4–8] depict a range of possibilities where the action can appear to be performed by George or his foot, automatically or non-automatically, and with or without some form of conscious effort. The various possibilities and their interrelations are seen in Figure 6.1 below:

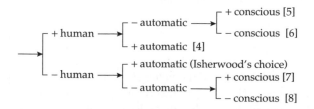

Figure 6.1

In these examples variation occurs within the overall structure of a transitive clause (i.e. a clause with a transitive verb and direct object (e.g. 'John loves Mary') as opposed to an intransitive (e.g. 'John runs well') or a linking clause (e.g. 'John is happy')). In [4–6] there is a human actor, whereas in the original and [7] and [8], it is the foot itself which produces the action; [7] and [8], are both distinguished from Isherwood's clause by the use of an intentional or non-automatic verb (*presses*) as opposed to Isherwood's choice of an automatic verb (*comes down*); [7] and [8], like [5] and [6], are distinguishable from one another by virtue of whether the action is conscious or not. This differentiation is possible because of the option of coding the initiatior of the action and the actor as if they were identical ([6] and [8]), or as if they were separate ([5] and [7]).

Isherwood's use of a bodily part instead of a person as an actor in a clause is a fairly common device for suggesting that the part of the body involved acts of its own accord. This changes the way in which we ascribe motivation for acts, and in situations where the action described is morally reprehensible this device can be used to play down the blame attributed to a character for his actions. Consider the following sentence from John Steinbeck's *Of Mice and Men* [Chapter 5]:

> She screamed then, and Lennie's other hand closed over her mouth and nose.

We know that Lennie is beginning to smother Curley's wife, but Steinbeck's way of putting it seems to relieve Lennie of much of the blame for his action. This is partly because Lennie's hand is the actor in the second clause, and partly because the coordination and sequencing leads us to infer that the woman's screaming somehow causes the action (see section 7.7.1). Since Lennie is represented as a simpleton, it is appropriate in the story that his responsibility should be diminished in this way.

So far we have examined how differing choices at the level of participant relations in *one clause* can indicate varying conceptualisations of the same event. But as the rest of this chapter will make clear, conceptual variation can be controlled by other syntactic and semantic means; moreover, the choices do not have to be restricted to one particular clause. The term 'mind style' is particularly appropriate where the choices made are consistent through a text or part of a text. Such a consistent choice of a particular stylistic variable might be on the part of a novelist, a narrator, or a character. Michael Halliday and Roger Fowler have examined the mind styles of particular characters.[3] In the rest of this chapter we will compare a number of authorial mind styles, and close with an extended analysis of a particular narrator's mind style.

6.2 A comparison of three normal mind styles

There are many ways in which a writer can indicate his view of the mock reality that he is describing besides his manipulation of participant relations within the clause. The best way of examining such control would be to compare descriptions by different writers of the same scene or set of events. However, as it is more or less impossible to find such examples we propose instead to compare three descriptions of characters from near the beginnings of novels or stories. First of all, let us look at Steinbeck's description of Tom Joad from *The Grapes of Wrath* (Chapter 2):

> His eyes were very dark brown and there was a hint of brown pigment in his eyeballs. His cheek-bones were high and wide, and strong deep lines cut down his cheeks, in curves beside his mouth. His lower lip was long, and since his teeth protruded, the lips stretched to cover them, for this man kept his lips closed. His hands were hard, with broad fingers and nails as thick and ridged as little clam shells. The space between thumb and forefinger and the hams of his hands were shiny with callus.

This description shows a preference for simple lexical and syntactic structure. The sentences are short and exhibit a repeated use of the linking x *be* y structure where x is a short noun phrase with a concrete head noun referring to a bodily part, and where y is an adjective phrase having a headword which indicates a simple perceptual quality perceived directly by the senses of sight or touch (*high, long, hard* etc.). There is a marked absence of morphologically complex and abstract nouns and adjectives, and there are no verbs of perception. These positive and negative aspects all contribute to the feeling that we are being given a simple, objective, external and factual description. The reality which Steinbeck sees is, we feel, being *transcribed* so that we can perceive it directly. Note the difference obtained if non-factive, psychological[4] verbs are introduced either directly into the clause or into another clause dominating it:

[9] His hands looked hard, with broad fingers and nails which seemed as thick as . . .

Immediately the description becomes much less 'objective'; it appears that we are getting a more personal and therefore incomplete and possibly inaccurate description: whereas Steinbeck's original appears to us as obvious unmitigated fact. The preference for state verbs (six out of the ten verbs are instances of *be*) gives the impression that what is being described is immobile, rather like a photograph. However, although this appears to be a fairly neutral style of description, it represents only one of many possible mind styles. Compare it with James Joyce's description of Lenehan at the beginning of *Two Gallants*:

> The other, who walked on the verge of the path and was at times obliged to step on to the road, owing to his companion's rudeness, wore an amused, listening face. He was squat and ruddy. A yachting cap was shoved far back from his forehead, and the narrative to which he listened made constant waves of expression break forth over his face from the corners of his nose and eyes and mouth. Little jets of wheezing laughter followed one another out of his convulsed body. His eyes, twinkling with cunning enjoyment, glanced at every moment towards his companion's face.

Lenehan's outward appearance is described much less statically than Tom Joad's. Only one of the eleven main verbs is the copula *be*. Instead we find a preference for verbs of movement – *break forth, followed, glanced*. There are simple physical and perceptual terms, as in 'he was squat and ruddy' but the non-stative *wore* is used instead of *had* in 'he wore an amused, listening face'. Nouns referring to bodily parts are modified by adjectives expressing attitudes and states of mind, e.g. 'amused listening face'. We are also told that Lenehan's eyes twinkled *with cunning enjoyment*, instead of, say, *at the story*. Both the noun and the adjective by which Joyce chooses to modify it are abstract and refer to emotional states and feelings rather than things. As a result of such choices his description, in contrast with that of Steinbeck, appears more full of active feelings and attitudes and less full of palpable objects.

Joyce's description is not only more active than Steinbeck's but is active in a very particular way. A comparison of this passage with the Isherwood clause [3] on p. 152 reveals some similarities. A number of the clauses here have a part of the character or some abstract feeling as actor:

listening *face*[5]
waves of expression break forth over his face
little jets of wheezing *laughter* followed
his eyes laughed
(*his eyes*) twinkling

Most of these expressions are individually unremarkable. Ordinary people quite often talk of people having laughing or twinkling eyes. But it is significant that Joyce chooses the same type of structure over and over again to impart a particular flavour to the description. Lenehan appears not to be a 'doer' in his own right. Instead, the role of actor is assumed by his emotions and the parts of his face. But Lenehan is also unlike Isherwood's George in that the actions he, or parts of him, produce seem always to be initiated by some outside force. This is particularly obvious in two structures:

> The other . . . was at times *obliged* to step on to the road, owing to his companion's rudeness
> the narrative to which he listened *made* constant waves of expression break forth

In both of these constructions the clause which contains the movement produced by Lenehan occurs as object of the main clause where someone or something else is the actor. From this we understand that Lenehan's actions are merely *re*actions to outside events. Once this is realised other, less obvious, examples can be seen to fit the same pattern. For instance the jets of wheezing laughter and the twinkling of Lenehan's eyes are also reactions to the story his friend is relating. The picture of Lenehan as someone who is prompted into action by others rather than on his own initiative is in marked contrast to that of the other of the two gallants, Corley. A typical sentence from his description immediately shows a man in control of his actions:

> He walked with his hands by his sides, holding himself erect and swaying his head from side to side.

This contrast is very important for Joyce's strategy in the story. Corley is the conscious man of action, whereas Lenehan is always on the sidelines. Lenehan is also depicted as a *voyeur* figure, and this can be seen from the large number of sentences in which he appears as subject to verbs of perception and cognition rather than action in the story. This contrast is integral to the ironic effect at the end of the narrative. Corley demonstrates to Lenehan how it is possible to gain money by seducing a woman, and the tale ends with Corley showing his 'disciple' a gold sovereign he has just obtained in this way. But the reader infers that Lenehan will not be able to follow his friend's precept not just because of what he says and does but also because of the manner in which he has been consistently portrayed throughout the story.[6]

One of the reasons that Joyce's description appears less 'objective' than Steinbeck's is its relative lack of directness. Not only is the vocabulary more abstract, but the syntax is also more complex. For example, the noun phrases in Lenehan's description characteristically contain more modification of the head noun, especially by relative clauses. But even Joyce's style seems simplicity itself when compared with that of Henry James in *The Birthplace*:

> Their friend, Mr Grant-Jackson, a highly preponderant pushing person, great in discussion and arrangement, abrupt in overture, unexpected, if

not perverse in attitude, and almost equally acclaimed and objected to in the wide midland region to which he had taught, as the phrase was, the size of his foot – their friend had launched his bolt quite out of the blue and had thereby so shaken them as to make them fear almost more than hope.

The average sentence lengths of the previous two passages were twenty-three and twenty-five words respectively. Here the one sentence in front of us is seventy-six words long. In terms of clause structure it is fairly simple, its complexity arising from the huge noun phrase in apposition to *their friend*: It consists of a proper name, Mr Grant-Jackson, postmodified by a string of relative clauses with their subject pronouns and *be* verbs deleted. Thus what could have been a string of *x be y* main clauses, rather like the Steinbeck description (e.g. 'Their friend was Mr Grant-Jackson. He was a highly preponderant, pushing person . . .'), becomes a complex structure holding up the onset of the verb *had launched* for some considerable time. Lexically the sentence is characterised by highly abstract nouns and adjectives. We learn nothing of Mr Grant-Jackson's physical appearance (except perhaps by suggestion from the term *preponderant* (see pp. 158–9) but a great deal about his character, attitude and standing in the world. Moreover, those abstract terms are selected to be as formal as possible. *Person* is chosen instead of *man*, *discussion* instead of *talk*, *acclaimed and objected to* instead of *liked* and *disliked*.

Henry James's world here, like that of the passage discussed in section 3.5, is one which depends on the exact discrimination of attitudes and social relations. He adds precision by converting what would normally be non-gradable adjectives and adverbs into gradable ones by the use of adverbs of degree ('*highly* preponderant', '*almost* equally', 'fear *almost* more than hope'). The fineness of the description also appears in the use of alternative ascriptions (e.g. 'unexpected, if not perverse in attitude') as if there is no one English word which is exact enough for his need. Indeed, when the description becomes rather less fine and the terminology less rarified, as in 'to which he had taught, as the phrase was, the size of his foot' he makes a point of interpolating a phrase to indicate that the choice of words is not really his.

By moving from Steinbeck through Joyce to James, we have moved from a view of the world where perceptual physical detail is uppermost and has its own reified existence to one where such detail is related in a complex way to emotion and attitude, and finally to a view of the world where physical description is virtually superseded by attention to the exactness of social relations and qualities of character. If the choices which build up this view of things are repeatedly used by a writer in a number of works then they become part of what critics regard as his typical 'style'. In other words, it is not just his preference for certain kinds of linguistic expression which is typical, but also the mind style which this represents. For example, abstractness and complexity of syntactic embedding are well-known characteristics of the *style* of Henry James (see section 3.5),[7] and it is also these characteristics that give rise to the complex social vision which James creates.

6.3 Some more unusual mind styles

All three styles examined in section 6.2 are relatively normal, in the sense that they require a reader to adopt a view of things which is not noticeably at variance with the view we take of the real world. Of the three, Steinbeck's description seems to be the most neutral, the most objective of all, as if he were simply providing a passive record, like a photograph, of a man's appearance. But just as there is no absolute realism, so there is no absolute photographic objectivity in the conceptualisation of a fictional world. In fact, Steinbeck's portrayal of Tom Joad is not itself completely external or photographic. 'His hands were hard' gives us tactile, not visual, information, and 'this man kept his lips closed' depicts a quality of the man which is surely a matter of habit, not recoverable from a click of the camera shutter. We are also told that Joad's teeth protruded, something which would not be visually evident, if he 'kept his lips closed'! So there is more in Steinbeck's description, literally speaking, than meets the eye.

There are, however, more marked kinds of mind style which clearly take liberties with the semantic categories which we use for interpreting the world. We see some signs of this tendency in James's description of Mr Grant-Jackson, where the adjectives seem to be applied to social behaviour, and yet also have physical implications: 'a highly *preponderant, pushing* person, *great* in discussion and arrangement, *abrupt* in overture'. Like most adjectives denoting abstract qualities, these involve metaphorical extensions of concrete meanings: for example, the meaning of *pushing* is transferred from the notion of exerting physical force on others, to that of exerting psychological force; *preponderant* ('exerting superior weight or influence') similarly derives its abstract meaning from the idea of physical weight; *great* is an even more obvious example of metaphorical abstraction. James uses these adjectives in a rather ambivalent way: in that they all modify the noun *person*, they can theoretically be given either a concrete or an abstract interpretation; but an abstract interpretation is imposed by conventional meaning and by various clues of context, notably the attachment of the abstract prepositional phrases 'in discussion and arrangement', and the completion of the list of qualities by the wholly abstract phrase 'unexpected, if not perverse in attitude'. We may therefore feel justified in calling these adjectives of abstract reference, yet the power of the accompanying physical connotations is such that James has also suggested something of the physical appearance and behaviour of the man. There are grounds for saying that he has brought about a degree of fusion between the normally separate concepts of 'concrete' and 'abstract'.

We now examine three examples where there is a more obvious and definitive rearrangement of semantic categories. The first case we shall consider, although an evident deviation from a common-sense view of things, is such a strong current in literary expression (and particularly in the literature of the Romantic movement) that it has been given a name: 'the pathetic fallacy'. This is the attribution of human characteristics to inanimate nature, a kind of metaphor which is routinely found in expressions such as 'the cruel sea', but which occurs more pervasively in descriptions such as that which Hardy gives of Egdon Heath at the beginning of *The Return of the Native*. Here is a short extract from it:

The spot was, indeed, *a near relation of night*, and when *night showed itself* an apparent tendency to *gravitate together* could be perceived in its shades and the scene. The sombre stretch of rounds and hollows seemed to *rise* and *meet the evening gloom* in pure *sympathy, the heath exhaling darkness* as rapidly as the heavens *precipitated* it. And so the obscurity in the air and the obscurity in the land *closed together* in a *black fraternisation* towards which *each advanced* half-way.

The place became full of *watchful intentness* now; for when other things *sank brooding to sleep* the heath appeared slowly *to awake* and *listen*. Every night its *Titanic* form seemed *to await something*; but *it had waited* thus, *unmoved*, during so many centuries, through the crises of so many things, that it could only be imagined *to await* one last crisis – the final overthrow.
[Book 1, Chapter 1]

Each of the italicised expressions (there are twenty in all) suggests in some measure the animation or the personhood of natural phenomena. In its weakest and least specific form, the pathetic fallacy is manifested in the use of inanimate nouns as actors, for example as implied subjects of verbs of motion: 'The sombre stretch of rounds and hollows seemed *to rise* and *meet* the evening gloom'. More specific are expressions which attribute motive and feeling to inanimate nature: 'in pure sympathy', 'full of watchful intentness'. In the first paragraph, there is a whole cluster of metaphors (seven in all) attributing some reciprocal bond between the heath and the darkness of night; in the second paragraph, there is a further cluster of eight metaphors ascribing a quasi-humanity to the heath. The verbs are the chief carriers of metaphor; in fact, the only verbs which do not have this function (apart from one instance of *become*) are those which imply a human observer and interpreter: *seemed, appeared, could be imagined, could be perceived*. The use of the passive with deleted agent in these last two examples shows how thoroughly humanity has been effaced from the scene. The extract gives an entirely consistent picture of nature animated by movement, motive, awareness, while man becomes merely a potential onlooker.

The personifying metaphor is so consistently employed that 'metaphor' almost ceases to be the appropriate term: it is as if our literal sense of the division between animate man and inanimate nature has been eliminated. This partly accounts for the power of this description and its Hardyesque quality as a setting for a rural tragedy. On the one hand, the treatment of nature as humanlike suggests the oneness of humanity and its environment; on the other, the only affinity overtly *expressed* in the passage is such that humanity can have no share in it – the 'black fraternisation' between the heath and the night. Hence the personification of nature produces a tension between reassurance and alienation.

In one respect this is an overstatement. Hardy keeps one foot in the literal world by mixing metaphor with quasisimile (see section 3.3): the words *seemed, appeared, apparent, imagined* indicate that the anthropomorphism may be only a 'manner of speaking'. Yet notice how easily the transition between quasisimile and metaphor is made:

> Every night its Titanic form *seemed to await* something; but it *had waited* thus, unmoved, during so many centuries . . .

The first clause makes the waiting a matter of 'seeming', while the second makes it a matter of fact. In this way, Hardy induces a kind of half-belief in the brooding presence of the heath; it is like a village superstition which a rational mind might dismiss, but which might revenge itself on an unbeliever.

Our second example, from William Faulkner's short story *The Bear*, also involves a realignment of a major conceptual boundary:

> There was a man and a dog too this time. Two beasts, counting Old Ben, the bear, and two men, counting Boon Hogganbeck, in whom some of the same blood ran which ran in Sam Fathers, even though Boon's was a plebeian strain of it and only Sam and Old Ben and the mongrel Lion were taintless and incorruptible.

At the beginning of this story the beings in it are classified into men and beasts. But *beasts* is modified by *counting Old Ben, the bear*, and *men* by *counting Boon Hogganbeck*. These two clauses are parallel to each other and contain the same kinds of assumption. There appears to be some doubt whether Boon Hogganbeck should be counted as a man rather than an animal in spite of his having a name, and equally some doubt whether the bear should be counted as an animal rather than a man: indeed he, like Boon, is given a name, and is thus at least partly anthropomorphised. In other words Faulkner seems to assume that beings cannot be neatly divided into beasts and humans. On the contrary, there appear to be some beings who could belong to either set. This conflation of categories is also brought out at the end of the second sentence in the coordination in 'only Sam and Old Ben and the mongrel Lion were taintless and incorruptible'. Here Faulkner makes a point of not reducing the first conjunction (as in 'Sam, Old Ben, and the mongrel Lion') in order to give equal weight to all three of the beings referred to, and introduces the name *Lion* for the dog in order to increase the parallel further. Hence the class of beings who were taintless and incorruptible (one of whom is described as *mongrel!*) includes a man, a beast and an in-between, to all of which Faulkner gives proper names, and refers pronominally throughout the story by means of *he* and *him*. In Faulkner's world animals and men are thus portrayed not as being distinct, but as being class-related. This way of dividing up the cosmos is at odds with the stereotyped categories of our language, but it can hardly be called less objective or true than those of Steinbeck or Joyce. Indeed, when we read Faulkner casually we may not even notice the way in which he has rearranged our view of the world for us.

A more extreme example is John Cowper Powys's *A Glastonbury Romance*:

At the striking of noon on a certain fifth of March, there occurred within a causal radius of Brandon railway station and yet beyond the deepest pools of emptiness between the uttermost stellar systems one of those infinitesimal ripples in the creative silence of the First Cause which always occur when an exceptional stir of heightened consciousness agitates any living organism in this astronomical universe. Something passed at that moment, a wave, a motion, a vibration too tenuous to be called magnetic, too subliminal to be called spiritual, between the soul of a particular human being who was emerging from a third-class carriage of the twelve-nineteen train from London and the divine-diabolic soul of the First Cause of all life.

[Chapter 1]

Powys describes a world in which humans and divine beings appear to exist on the same plane. This can be seen in terms of participant relations, where the mind of the Creator can act directly upon an individual, and where His soul and that of a human being are integrally related:

. . . an exceptional stir of heightened consciousness agitates any living organism . . .
Something passed . . . between the soul of a particular human being . . . and the divine-diabolic soul of the First Cause of all life.

This improbable juxtaposition is also apparent in Powys's depiction of place relations. In 'within a causal radius of Brandon railway station', an apparently precise and tangible geographical location is made obscure by the odd use of 'causal', and is in turn coordinated with 'beyond the deepest pools of emptiness between the uttermost stellar systems', a phrase which is lexically abstract and indeterminate in spite of a syntactic structure which would seem to indicate spatial precision. This *apparent* precision is a characteristic of the passage. Powys refers to the character we later know as John Crow as 'a particular human being who was emerging from a third-class carriage of the twelve-nineteen train from London', where the *being* is not named, although he is delimited very precisely in terms of place and time by the defining relative clause. With 'the divine-diabolic soul of the First Cause of all life' on the other hand, we are given a name for an immaterial being who exists outside place and time, if he exists at all. *Something* is elaborated into 'a wave, a motion, a vibration, too tenuous to be called magnetic, too subliminal to be called spiritual', where each abstract noun is defined in terms of another abstract noun referring to a type of slight movement. The oddity is that this movement is apparently suspended somewhere between physical ('magnetic') and metaphysical ('spiritual') existence. The reader is left with the feeling that 'something' has been very precisely defined, but without knowing exactly what it is.

6.4 A very unusual mind style

The way in which Powys depicts his world is to say the least, eccentric. But even so, it is doubtful whether the casual reader takes the trouble to examine it, such is the power of the general assumption that the author is our guide, not only to what the fiction contains, but also to how it is to be interpreted. For a novelist's mind style to be perceived by the reader as deviant it must presumably be very deviant indeed. Character mind styles are more readily discernible as odd; we accept quite easily that a character might have a faulty or limited view of things, and of course we often have the mind styles of other characters as a comparative yardstick. The way in which Lok views the world in Golding's *The Inheritors* (see section 1.5) is an obvious case where we are prompted to compare his view of the world with a more 'normal' account seen through the eyes of the tribe which overthrows Lok and his companions.

Novels which have a narrator or reflector who is differentiated from the author (see section 8.1.2) also allow the possibility of a more positive invitation to perceive a particular mind style as deviant. We will close this chapter with an interesting example of just such an invitation. Faulkner's *The Sound and the Fury* has four different narrators, one of whom, Benjy, is mentally subnormal. Because we compare his mind style with that of the other narrators and because Benjy uses language in an extremely deviant way, we are forced to 'reinterpret' his descriptions in order to understand them. In fact, the reader may have to reread this passage from the beginning of the novel a number of times before he realises that Benjy is describing a game of golf:

Through the fence, between the curling flower spaces, I could see them hitting (1). They were coming toward where the flag was and I went along the fence (2). Luster was hunting in the grass by the flower tree (3). They took the flag out, and they were hitting (4). Then they put the flag back and they went to the table, and he hit and the other hit (5). Then they went on, and I went along the fence (6). Luster came away from the flower tree and we went along the fence and they stopped and we stopped and I looked through the fence while Luster was hunting in the grass (7).

'Here, caddie' (8). He hit (9). They went away across the pasture (10). I held to the fence and watched them going away (11).

'Listen at you, now,' Luster said (12). 'Ain't you something, thirty-three years old, going on that way (13). After I done went all the way to town to buy you that cake (14). Hush up that moaning (15). Ain't you going to help me find that quarter so I can go to the show tonight?' (16).

They were hitting little, across the pasture (17). I went back along the fence to where the flag was (18). It flapped on the bright grass and the trees (19).

'Come on,' Luster said (20). 'We done looked there (21). They ain't no more coming right now (22). Let's go down to the branch and find that quarter before them niggers finds it' (23).

It was red, flapping on the pasture (24). Then there was a bird slanting and tilting on it (25). Luster threw (26). The flag flapped on the bright grass and the trees (27). I held to the fence (28).

[William Faulkner, *The Sound and the Fury*, 7 April 1928]

6.4.1 General structure

The first thing to notice about this passage is that it is easily divided into two types of 'text', namely Benjy's narrative and the direct speech of the other characters. This division is reinforced by the paragraph structure. Paragraphs three and five are composed of Luster's speech with minimal reporting clauses. Paragraphs one, four and six are entirely made up of narrative. The only 'mixed' paragraph is two, where the first sentence is the direct speech of one of the participants in the game. This sentence provides an important clue for the reader because it contains the only instance, *caddie*, of a technical term associated with golf. As we are examining Benjy's mind style we will restrict ourselves to the narrative sentences (1–7), (9–11), (17–18) and (24–28).

6.4.2 Lexis

Benjy does not use a single golfing term to describe the game he is watching (he haunts the golf course in order to hear the word *caddie* because the sister he loves is called *Caddy*) and hence has to substitute 'common core' terms for technical ones (e.g. *table* for *tee*). This is one sign of the limited world which he inhabits. Another general way in which this is indicated is by the extreme simplicity of his language. In Benjy's 186 words there are no instances at all of words of more than two syllables; 80.5 per cent of the words are monosyllabic, the remaining 19.5 per cent being disyllabic. Simplicity can also be seen in the choice of types of words. All thirty-four nouns that Benjy uses are concrete, with the possible exception of *spaces* which, however, refers to physical location. There are only four adjectives, *curling*, *little*, *bright* and *red*, all of which are primarily visual. Hence Benjy's world appears to be a simple concrete one, dominated by the sense of sight.

It is also an extremely restricted world, as can be seen by the frequency of lexical repetition. Ten words account for the thirty-four noun occurrences in the text: *fence* (eight), *flag* (five), *grass* (four), *Luster* (four), *tree* (four), *flower* (three), *pasture* (three), *bird* (one), *space* (one), *table* (one). Only three nouns are not repeated. The seven which are repeated all occur three times or more, *fence* occurring on average once every twenty-three words. If the pronouns were taken into account the passage would appear even more repetitious. For example, all three of the instances of *it* refer to *flag*. As there are only four adjectives (but one of these occurs twice) we can glean relatively little evidence of repetition there. But examination of the verbs is more profitable. *Hit* occurs five times in various forms, *go* eight times, *flapping* three times, and *hunting* and *held* twice each. In fact the extent of the repetition is even wider than such figures would suggest because whole clauses and phrases are also repeated:

I went along the fence (three times)   I held to the fence (twice)
Luster was hunting in the grass (twice)   the flower tree (twice)
where the flag was (twice)   the bright grass (twice)

Hence an examination of the lexis indicates a simple and extremely restricted mind style, with little ability to use abstract terms or terms related to the thing described.

6.4.3 Syntax

The simplicity observed in the lexis is reinforced by a degree of naive simplicity in syntax. The average sentence is only ten words long (whereas the simplest of the three passages discussed in Chapter 3, the Lawrence passage, had an average of twenty words per sentence), and of the eighteen sentences which Benjy uses ten are simple, seven are compound and only two are complex. *Where the flag was* does occur twice as a prepositional complement but even so the overall simplicity is very apparent. Moreover, the childlike Benjy shows a tendency common in the writing of young children to string sequences of paratactic and coordinated main clauses together instead of resorting to subordination or sentence division. This can be seen in sentences (5) and (7) particularly, but (6) will serve as a convenient example. Faulkner could have used the subordinating conjunction *as* instead of the coordinator *and*, for example, 'Then, as they went on, I went along the fence'. The subordinated version makes the logical connections between the clauses more explicit and also makes the relative communicative weight of the clauses clear. Benjy's version is much more undifferentiated (see sections 7.5 and 7.5.1).

Benjy's syntax also shows positive deviance from the sentence patterning of English. Like Lok in Halliday's analysis (see section 1.5), Benjy appears to have an imperfect understanding of cause and effect. But, unlike Lok, he does not avoid the use of transitive verbs. Rather, he uses them freely as if they were intransitives, as in 'he hit and the other hit'. We know from our general knowledge of golf that it is a ball which is being struck. But because of the way in which Benjy uses transitive verbs without objects he appears to perceive no purpose in the golfers' actions. Each of the five instances of *hit* occurs without an object. Another centrally transitive verb, *threw*, is similarly treated, and *hunting* is also used intransitively.

The way in which Benjy treats transitive verbs is not the only syntactic oddity in the text. He uses the adjective *little* as if it were an adverb, 'they were hitting little, across the pasture' (17), and we are twice told that the flag flapped 'on the bright grass and the trees' (19, 27). The most predictable kind of prepositional phrase to complete 'the flag flapped . . .' would be one beginning with *in* as in 'the flag flapped in the breeze', where three-dimensionality is assumed. Benjy's usage makes it appear that the flag is actually on both the grass (horizontal plane) and the trees (vertical plane). Hence he appears to have a two-dimensional view of what we think of as a three-dimensional universe. A similar oddity occurs in the very first sentence, where he sees the golfers apparently between the spaces separating the flowers rather than between the flowers themselves. In his world, primacy seems to be given to the visual field in which objects reside rather than the objects themselves. So the golfers come not towards the flag, but towards 'where the flag was'.

6.4.4 Textual relations

The evidence from the vocabulary and syntactic patterns in Benjy's language gives us a picture of someone who is simple and childlike, and who views the world in a very different way from us. A quick examination of the textual relations in the passage (anticipating our next chapter) confirms the childlike nature of the narrator by showing his inability to synthesise information reasonably for his reader's benefit. The golfers, for example, are always referred to pronominally, with no reference forwards or back to a lexically full phrase like *the golfers* in order to specify the reference of the pronouns. The tendency noted earlier towards coordination and away from subordination means that the clauses within sentences are not arranged to distinguish major from minor information. The avoidance of the normal rules for the deletion of identical items and the substitution in coordinated structures of proforms also suggests an immature grasp of the conventions for distinguishing old and new information. This can be seen in the choice of 'he hit and the other hit' instead of 'he hit and so did the other'. This inability of Benjy's to produce reasonable text partly accounts for the apparent absence of a narrator–reader relationship in the passage: the illusion is thus created that we are 'overhearing' Benjy's fairly rudimentary ordering of his direct sensory impressions.

Benjy's language, like Lok's language (section 1.5), exhibits a 'primitive' mind style, lacking many of the categories we make use of in interpreting our universe. In addition to the restrictions we have noted, there are, for example, no indefinite determiners or pronouns in the passage; there are few verb forms apart from the simple past tense; there are practically no adverbials apart from those of place. Such limitations mean that we cannot make sense of the fictional world, including some fictional world inferences (e.g. the significance of the word *caddie*), until we have read further. This extract illustrates particularly clearly the distinction between mind style – the 'view of the world' a text postulates – and the fictional world itself. But while stressing the negative aspects of Benjy's style, we should also mention that its deviant features express some more positive, poetic qualities. The poetry is particularly noticeable in phrases like 'between the curling flower spaces' and 'a bird slanting and tilting'. With its childlike vision, such language borders on poetry in recapturing a pristine awareness of things.

Notes

1. R. FOWLER (1977), 76.
2. The terminology which we adopt for participant roles follows M.A.K. HALLIDAY (1967). Halliday notes that in 'he marched the prisoners' the prisoners are actors, but *he* is the initiator of the action. In 'the prisoners marched', however, the participant roles of initiator and actor are combined.
3. See section 1.5 and R. FOWLER (1977), 103–113.
4. On psychological verbs, see Note c, p. 89. The term 'non-factive' and related terms are explained in section 3.2, note (iv). See also G. LEECH (1981) pp. 301–318.

5. A transformational analysis of this phrase would show that its underlying structure is that of a clause with *face* as subject and *listen* as the verb: '(his) face was listening . . .'.
6. For an extended analysis of this story see C. KENNEDY (1976).
7. See, for example, I. WATT (1969) and S. CHATMAN (1972).

CHAPTER 7

The rhetoric of text

It is now time to extend our view of language to include what Halliday calls the interpersonal and textual functions of language. But we conceive of them rather differently from Halliday, as matters of pragmatics and rhetoric,[1] that is, as ways in which users implement the cognitive or ideational code of language for communicative ends.

7.1 The rhetoric of text and discourse

A distinction may be drawn between communication as DISCOURSE and as TEXT.[2] Discourse is linguistic communication seen as a transaction between speaker and hearer, as an interpersonal activity whose form is determined by its social purpose. Text is linguistic communication (either spoken or written) seen simply as a message coded in its auditory or visual medium. Thus in speech, a 'text' or utterance is a linear pattern of sound waves; in writing, a text is a linear sequence of visible marks on paper; when read out it becomes a linear pattern of sound waves. But it is of course not a random sequence of noises or marks, being coded in *a certain language*. Therefore there is nothing odd in talking about the linguistic properties of texts (as linguists frequently do, and as we did in Chapter 2). Although a written text consists physically only of marks on paper, it has implicit linguistic properties such as graphological and syntactic form, by virtue of which it can be decoded. Building on Figures 4.1 and 4.2, we may represent our view of language as follows:

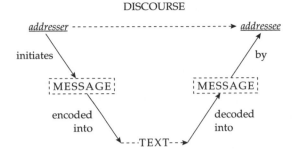

Figure 7.1

If the communication is successful on an ideational plane, then the message on the right of the figure (as stored in the addressee's model of reality) is more or less identical to that which appears on the left. However, there are additional standards of success which apply to the planes of discourse and text. It is the set of principles for achieving communicative ends at these levels that we refer to as the RHETORIC of text and discourse. 'Rhetoric' is used here in the traditional sense of the 'art or skill of effective communication'.

7.2 The linearity of text

We find once again that the best way to understand the principles of literary communication is to see them as deriving in all essentials from principles applied in everyday language. Rhetoric in ordinary language use can be seen as a set of principles or guidelines for getting things done by means of language. These are not rules of the kind which define the grammar of a language; rather, they are normative rules, or rules of good or effective performance, and like all such rules, they can be broken – indeed, other considerations may make it advisable to break them. This is natural and unavoidable, since, as we shall see, such rules frequently make conflicting claims on the language user. They may also be observed with a greater or lesser degree of success. For these reasons, it will avoid confusion if we call them not rules, but PRINCIPLES.[3]

In this chapter we are concerned with the rhetoric of text, which means that in practice we are dealing with the superficial expressive form of language, as it is determined by syntax, phonology and graphology. This places us in the province of syntactic and phonological/graphological style as discussed in sections 4.3.2 and 4.3.3. To understand more clearly the scope of this chapter, let us imagine that a writer has already decided the sense of what he wants to say. Then our present task is to answer the following question: what considerations will induce him to say it in one way rather than another? For this purpose our interpretation of style is close to that of dualists such as Ohmann (section 1.3.2): we are interested in choice between paraphrases.

Texts are communications seen as physical transactions between address-ers and addressees. By 'physical' we mean occurring in an auditory (speech) or visual (writing) medium. The overriding property of texts is linearity: speech occurs linearly in time, and writing, imitating speech, occurs linearly in space. The 'tyranny of succession' is most dominant in the ephemeral medium of speech, since a sound, a word, a sentence which has once been uttered cannot be erased or recalled: the speaker is bound to encode, and the hearer to decode, in ongoing time. In writing, the permanence of the text allows re-editing by the writer and rereading by the reader; but a reader, like a hearer, must decode in a fixed order – the text, for both, is not a static object, but a dynamic phenomenon, something which is EXPERIENCED IN TIME.[4] In this respect, as in others (see section 4.3.4) we shall find that the dynamics of speech are a necessary background to the study of written texts.

Linearity is such an obvious characteristic of texts that it is easy to over-look its important implications for language and for style. Since speech is acoustically 'ongoing', it is necessary for the hearer, in decoding the stream of sound, to segment it into units. A message has to be broken down into 'parcels of information', and the key unit for this purpose in speech is the TONE UNIT, or unit of intonation. Tone units are subdivided into smaller units (rhythm units, syllables, phonemes), and form part of larger, less clearly defined, units which we may think of as the speech equivalent of paragraphs. So linearity entails segmentation, and segmentation involves a hierarchy of units. Hierarchisation in turn means that certain parts of the text are perceived as more salient, or highlighted, than others. From the point of view of phonology, therefore, three important factors in the dynamics of text are sequence, segmentation and salience.

We shall find that these three factors are also basic to the form of written texts. For example, although writing has no units corresponding precisely to tone units, an analogous segmenting function is performed in written texts by punctuation. The pieces of text which are separated by punctua-tion (e.g. the pieces of language occurring between commas) may be called GRAPHIC UNITS.

7.3 The principle of end-focus

In the tone unit, there is a general tendency for GIVEN information to precede NEW information: that is, for the speaker to proceed from a start-ing point of information which is assumed to be shared by the hearer, to information which is assumed to be 'news' to the hearer, and there-fore communicatively more salient. The part where new information is introduced is marked by NUCLEAR STRESS, which is the focal point of the tone unit. The principle that 'last is most important' means that the nuclear tone's neutral position is at the end of the tone unit, specifically, on the last lexical item, or 'content word':

[1a] She completely DENÌED it.   [2a] He's gradually IMPRÒVING.
[1b] She denied it COMPLÈTELY.   [2b] He's improving GRÀDUALLY.

These pairs of sentences show that the normal effect of putting an adverb at the end is to make it bear the nuclear stress (the grave accent symbolises a falling tone on the nucleus), and to make it the main focus of attention in the sentence. The difference this makes is brought out if we imagine [1a] and [1b] as answers to the following questions:

[3a] Did Joan admit the offence?   No, . . .
[3b] Did Joan deny the offence?   Yes, . . .

Plainly [1a] is the appropriate answer for [3a], and [1b] for [3b], because in [3a] the 'denial' is new information, whereas in [3b] it is already assumed in the question, and is therefore given.

The principle that new information is reserved to the end of the tone unit will be called the principle of END-FOCUS.[5] It is a rhetorical principle in the sense that it presumably facilitates the decoding of the message;[6] but a speaker is under no necessity to place the nucleus at the end: another possible variant of [1a] would be: 'She COMPLÈTELY denied it'. But this would be a less obviously interpretable sentence, and would imply a very special kind of context. The point is that the principle of end-focus (like all rhetorical principles) is observed in neutral circumstances; that is, under the condition of 'all other things being equal'.

Although end-focus belongs to phonology, it clearly has important implications in syntax, where the ordering of the elements of the message is largely determined. It can, for example, influence the choice between active and passive sentences:

[4a] John wrote the whole BÒOK.
[4b] The whole book was written by JÒHN.

With end-focus, these two sentences will presuppose different contexts; for example, [4a] would answer the question 'What did John write?', while [4b] would answer the question 'Who wrote the book?'

Similarly, end-focus, although realised by intonation, has implications for written language. In writing, the kind of emphasis indicated by the nucleus is sometimes signalled by italics: 'We *shall* succeed.' But this is never used for regular end-focus: it is a very special device used expressively (for example in fictional dialogue) to give the flavour of spoken emphasis; in general, the nucleus has no counterpart in graphology. It seems strange, therefore, to claim that end-focus has much to do with written texts. But it can be argued that it is if anything more important in writing than in speech, because in the absence of intonation signals, the only thing we can rely upon as a signal of information focus is syntactic order. In other words, the reader naturally looks for new information at the end of the graphic unit, and writing is less successful (all other things being equal) to the extent that it frustrates this expectation. This conclusion can be tried out on the following:

[5a] Instead of morphine, the patient was given opium.
[5b] Instead of morphine, opium was given to the patient.

The principle of end-focus predicts that the reader will find [5a] a 'happier' sentence than [5b]: one will expect the focus to occur at the end, and whereas this is appropriate for [5a] ('... was given ÒPIUM'), it would result in a nonsensical reading of [5b] ('was given to the PÀTIENT'). End-focus, therefore, is one of the principles which guides the sequencing of elements in a written text: we can accept this without assuming that it is always obeyed, and without assuming that intonation plays a direct role in our processing of written language.

7.4 Segmentation

A tone unit constitutes, in speech, a single 'chunk' of information; and, to a considerable extent, the speaker is free to segment his utterance into such 'chunks' as he likes. But the choices he makes will also make a difference to the decoding of the message. Consider, for example, what happens when the following sentence is split respectively into two and three tone units (the acute accent indicates a rising tone):

[6a] Next WÉEK I'm starting a job in LÒNDON.
[6b] Next WÉEK I'm starting a JÒB in LÒNDON.

[6a] presents two pieces of information: (i) 'Something is happening next week', and (ii) 'What is happening next week is that I am starting a job in London'; [6b], on the other hand, presents three: (i) 'Something is happening next week', (ii) 'What is happening next week is that I am starting a job', and (iii) 'The place where I am starting a job is London'. Sentence [6b] would only be uttered by someone for whom getting a job was a piece of news in itself: for example, by someone who had been out of work. But the choices available in one case may not be available in another:

[7a] Next MÓNDAY   I'm spending the day in LÒNDON.
[7b] Next MÒNDAY   I'm spending the DÀY   in LÒNDON.

The stress [7b] is textually absurd, because 'spending the day' cannot have any news value in itself. The sentence would not sound meaningful if pronounced as in [7b].

The organisation of written language into graphic units is rather similar. The contrast between [6a] and [6b] can be captured in writing by the use of an extra punctuation mark:

[8a] Next week, I'm starting a job in London.
[8b] Next week, I'm starting a job – in London.

But because graphic units tend to be longer than tone units, [8b] seems unusually emphatic, and perhaps the normal written rendering would have no internal punctuation at all:

[8c] Next week I'm starting a job in London.

However, the same general principles of segmentation apply to both speech and writing. Note, in this connection, that the absurdity of [7b] is matched by an oddity in the written form of [9]:

[9]   Next Monday, I'm spending the day – in London.

7.4.1 The 'rhythm of prose'

In keeping with earlier remarks on phonology (section 4.1), we may assume that written prose has an implicit, 'unspoken' intonation, of which punctuation marks are written indicators.[7] This certainly seems to be what many writers on prose style have in mind when they discuss the 'rhythm of prose'. When the length of graphic units follows a regular pattern, the text seems to progress with a measured dynamic movement. In the passage on the death of Paul Dombey quoted earlier (pp. 47–8), this may be part of the reason for the air of peaceful solemnity that Dickens manages to convey:

[10] His fancy had a strange tendency to wander to the river,
      which he knew was flowing through the great city;
      and now he thought how black it was,
      and how deep it would look,
      reflecting the host of stars –
      and more than all –
      how steadily it rolled away to meet the sea.

When the graphic units are set out like this, in the manner of poetry, we notice that they follow a pattern of decreasing length, bringing the effect of an increase of tempo towards a climax, until the last unit, being longer, relaxes the tension towards a 'dying fall'. ('Rhythm' is more strictly applied, however, to the pattern formed by the sequence of stressed and unstressed syllables. Notice that rhythm in this metrical sense contributes to the effect of the sentence: the last two graphic units can be read as a rhyming couplet, 'And more than all – how steadily/It rolled away to meet the sea'.)

A very different rhythmic effect is that of the following passage from D.H. Lawrence's *Studies in Classic American Literature*. Richard Ohmann calls Lawrence's style here 'brusque and emphatic',[8] and no doubt much of this impression comes from the author's tendency to use very short graphic units, with heavy punctuation:

[11] The renegade hates life itself. He wants the death of life. So these many 'reformers' and 'idealists' who glorify the savages in America. They are death-birds, life-haters. Renegades.
    We can't go back. And Melville couldn't. Much as he hated the civilized humanity he knew. He couldn't go back to the savages. He wanted to. He tried to. And he couldn't.
    Because, in the first place, it made him sick.

[New York edn, 1955, p. 149]

Lawrence's style of punctuation is here abnormally emphatic: he disjoins by full-stops constructions which syntactically form part of the same sentence. The punctuation itself has an important stylistic role, as may be seen by a comparison of the last part of [11] rewritten with more orthodox punctuation:

[12] He wanted to, he tried to, and he couldn't – because in the first place, it made him sick.

The comparison shows that graphological style is not just a question of where the punctuation occurs, but how heavy it is. Example [12] differs from its original in terms not of the graphic units themselves, but of the weight of punctuation. The full stop, the 'heaviest' punctuation mark, has the greatest separative force; hence the effect of using full stops in [11] is to emphasise the autonomy of each piece of information, which is thereby asserted with the maximum force. If Lawrence had written 'They are death-birds, life-haters, renegades', he would have weakened the savage emphasis on *renegades* which he achieves by making it stand as a separate graphological sentence. Here segmentation interacts with salience. Both

174

density and weight of punctuation are signals suggesting the rhythm and intonation one would use in reading the text aloud.

7.4.2 Segmentation and syntax

Example [11] reminds us that the three main factors of textual organisation – segmentation, sequence and salience – exist on the level of syntax, as well as on the levels of phonology and graphology. We will find that in respect of these factors, there is a partial, but not a complete, match between the levels. For example, segmentation on both the syntactic and graphological levels involves a major unit we call a SENTENCE. On the syntactic level, a sentence (ignoring some areas of indeterminacy) may be defined as an independent syntactic unit, either simple (consisting of one clause) or complex (consisting of more than one); in a complex sentence, the clauses are related to one another either by subordination or by coordination. On the graphological level, a sentence is simply a unit beginning with a capital letter and ending with a full stop. In the popular conception of what a sentence is, it is assumed that these two definitions are the same: that syntactic sentences and graphological sentences are (or at least ought to be) co-extensive. But the Lawrence example shows that this need not be the case; the last two lines of [11] contain four graphological sentences, but only one syntactic sentence. As the more orthodox punctuation of [12] suggests, the two notions of sentencehood usually match, but in principle they are matters of independent choice.

With this in mind, we now consider segmentation on the level of syntax. If a text is broken down into a series of minimal sentences, the result is that each clause stands on its own feet, and is accorded equal importance with the others:

[13a] Jim threw the ball. The ball broke a window. The noise attracted the owner's attention. The owner scolded Jim.

By various devices of coordination, subordination, pronoun substitution, etc. these ideas can be combined into a smaller number of sentences, or into a single sentence:

[13b] Throwing the ball, Jim broke a window. The noise attracted the attention of the owner, who scolded him.

[13c] When Jim threw the ball and broke the window, he was scolded by the owner, whose attention had been attracted by the noise.

These paraphrases do not merely differ in terms of segmentation; they also differ in the use of subordination, coordination, and in the ordering of clauses. The difference can be represented as shown in Figure 7.2.

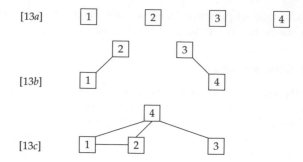

Figure 7.2
[Oblique lines represent subordination, and horizontal linking lines coordination.]

Obviously there exist many other possibilities of syntactic paraphrase, even with this simple example. But the point is sufficiently illustrated in [13*b*] and [13*c*] that the question of segmentation leads on to questions of salience and sequence: in forming complex sentences, we face decisions as to whether to promote one clause above another in the syntactic hierarchy (a matter of salience), and whether to place one clause before or after another (a matter of sequence). Let us consider what stylistic values are associated with these decisions.

7.5 Simple and complex sentences

Should a writer use simple, one-clause sentences, as in [13*a*], or should he build his separate units into more complex sentence structures, as in [13*c*]? There is no general answer to this question, since different considerations will apply in different circumstances. But we can make the general point that complex sentences are to be preferred if the aim of the writer is to present us with a complex structure of ideas, a complex reading experience. 'The complex form gives and withholds information, subordinates some ideas to others more important, coordinates those of equal weight, and ties into a neat package as many suggestions, modifiers, and asides as the mind can attend to in one stretch.'[9] A succession of simple sentences, on the other hand, leaves only one of our three variables to play with: that of sequence. Thus [13*a*] represents a naive narrative style in which there is no indication of the relationship between events, or of their relative importance.

There are occasions, however, where simple sentences are just what is needed:

[14] She saw there an object. That object was the gallows. She was afraid of the gallows.

[Joseph Conrad, *The Secret Agent*, Chapter 12]

These three sentences occur at the climactic point in the novel where Mrs Verloc realises the full consequence of her actions in murdering her husband. They record with brutal simplicity and clarity the three separate impressions (perception of object → identification of object → fear of object) which pass through Mrs Verloc's mind in logical progression, dramatising the mounting horror of her discovery. The dramatic force of this step-by-step revelation would be dissipated in a complex sentence such as 'She saw there an object she was afraid of – the gallows' or 'The object she saw there – the gallows – frightened her'.

Contrast the very different effect of:

[15] The tireless resilient voice that had just lobbed this singular remark over the Bella Vista bar window-sill into the square was, though its owner remained unseen, unmistakable and achingly familiar as the spacious flower-boxed balconied hotel itself, and as unreal, Yvonne thought.

[Malcolm Lowry, *Under the Volcano*, Chapter 2]

Lowry's sentence presents us with a more difficult and adventurous reading experience than the three simple sentences of [14]. Here too we have a sequence of impressions, but they are integrated in a single complex awareness of a number of things which must be going on in the mind of Yvonne, beginning with the voice (the immediate object of perception), moving on to the attendant circumstances of that perception (expressed in subordinate clauses), then to the impression the voice made ('unmistakable . . . familiar . . . unreal'), and finally to the perceiver herself, Yvonne. The two passages contrast in ordering: [14] working from the person ('She') to the percept ('the gallows'), and [15] working from percept ('the . . . voice') to person ('Yvonne'). But this is incidental to the contrast between simplicity and complexity: the difference between experiencing events one by one, and experiencing them as an articulate and complex whole.

7.5.1 Coordination and subordination

The major devices for linking ideas together into a complex sentence are coordination and subordination. Coordination gives clauses (and other units) equal syntactic status, whereas subordination places one clause in a dependent status, as part of the main clause. Subordination is thus, syntactically, the opposite of salience, since the effect of making a clause subordinate is to background it: to demote the phenomenon it describes into a 'subservient circumstance' which cannot be understood except in terms of its part in the main clause. Often a subordinate clause is less salient in the sense of expressing information which is at least partially known or presupposed in advance. In [13c], for instance, the effect of placing two events in a subordinate clause ('When Jim threw the ball and broke the window') is to imply that the hearer already knows something about them. A similar effect would be created by the relative clause 'The ball *which Jim threw*'. We thus may enunciate a general principle of subordination (which is not without its exceptions):

If A is subordinate to B, then A is the circumstantial background against which B is highlighted.

It is one of the more routine virtues of prose-writing that a writer brings about, by coordination and subordination, an appropriate salience and backgrounding of parts of the sentence. But as with other rhetorical principles, this principle of subordination may be violated:

Curley's fist was swinging when Lennie reached for it.
[John Steinbeck, *Of Mice and Men*, Chapter 3]

The second clause of this sentence described the turning point in the fight between Lennie and Curley, and yet Lennie's action is backgrounded by its subordinate status. On the face of it, Steinbeck would have done better to write something like: 'As Curley's fist was swinging, Lennie reached for it.' But what he did write fits in very well with his overall strategy in the novel, that of absolving Lennie of responsibility for his actions. By downgrading Lennie's part in the fight, he makes it seem an inadvertent and blameless reaction to Curley's onslaught. A more complex example of a similar kind is this:

[16] The system worked just fine for everybody, especially for Doc Daneeka, who found himself with all the time he needed to watch old Major — — de Coverley pitching horseshoes in his private horseshoe-pitching pit, still wearing the transparent eye patch Doc Daneeka had fashioned for him from the strip of celluloid stolen from Major Major's orderly room window months before when Major —— de Coverley had returned from Rome with an injured cornea after renting two apartments there for the officers and enlisted men to use on their rest leaves.
[Joseph Heller, *Catch 22*, Chapter 4]

This sentence is representative of a syntactic technique which is used again and again in *Catch 22*. There seems to be something rather perverse about its structure: the elements which we feel deserve to be in the foreground are subordinated, and therefore backgrounded. The sentence begins with the subject, verb and complement of the main clause, and then nose-dives into a chain-like structure of subordinate clauses (especially non-finite clauses), each dependent on its predecessor. The syntactic chaining expresses a chain of bizarre relationships between one character and another, in keeping with the eccentric design of this novel, in which characters and events are linked through apparently irrational peculiarities of behaviour. As the fiction is elaborated, we find that each character is animated by a crazy, paradoxical logic of his own, in terms of which his idiosyncracies are explicable. To put all these idiosyncratic details in subordinate clauses is to treat them as presupposed, predictable, part of the normal scene. So Heller's sentence structure fits into the topsy-turvy vision of the novel: it says, in effect, 'In terms of the prevailing logic of *Catch 22*, craziness is run-of-the-mill and taken for granted.'

7.5.2 The principle of climax: 'last is most important'

We have now encountered two principles of saliency, the principle of end-focus, which is phonological, and the principle of subordination, which is syntactic. They operate on different levels, and are independent of one another. However, they are linked by a further phonological principle, which has important repercussions in syntax, and which we call the PRINCIPLE OF CLIMAX:

In a sequence of interrelated tone units, the final position tends to be the major focus of information.

This principle can be seen as an extension of the end-focus principle, for it says for a sequence of tone-units what the end-focus principle says for individual tone-units, that 'last is most important'.

Each tone unit, as we have said, represents a unit of information; but such units are of varying autonomy, and usually it is the falling tone (`), with its implications of finality, which carries the most weight of information:[10]

[17] After the gale died DÓWN   we were picked up by a CÒASTER.

The most natural reading of [17] places a rising tone (or a fall-rise tone) at the end of the subordinate clause, and a falling tone at the end of the main clause.

In this case, the highlighting of intonation merely duplicates the highlighting of syntactic structure. The independent effect of the climax principle can be illustrated, however, with coordinate clauses, which are syntactically of equal status:

[18] The gale died DÓWN   and we were picked up by a CÒASTER.

Here the opposite placing (... DÒWN ... CÓASTER) would be practically impossible: there is clearly a natural progression from the incomplete information point signalled by the rise, to the complete information point

179

signalled by the fall. The same principle would apply if there were more than two coordinate constructions:

[19] The gale died DÓWN   the daylight CÁME   and we were picked up by a CÒASTER.

But there is also a further possibility, that each clause has a falling tone:

[20] The gale died DÒWN   and we were picked up by a CÒASTER.

The contrast between [18] and [20] shows the inconclusive effect of the rising tone. In [18] something must be added to 'The gale died down' to complete it; but in [20] this clause sounds complete in itself: the second clause is phonologically a fresh departure. Thus the two clauses have equal informational weight.

Punctuation also provides a means for distinguishing finality from non-finality. The contrast between [18] and [20] could, for example, be made by using a comma in [18] and a full stop or (more likely) a semi-colon in [20]. Returning to [11], it is probable that the assertive finality of the falling tone accounts for much of the brusque assertiveness of Lawrence's 'tone of voice'. Given the correlation between falling tone and the full stop, the following is a likely reading for the passage:

[21] We CÀN'T go back   And MÈLVILLE couldn't   Much as he hated the civilized humanity he KNÈW   He CÒULDN'T go back to the savages He WÀNTED to   He TRÌED to   And he CÒULDN'T.

We will have something to say later (in section 7.6) about the position of the nuclei here: there are violations of the end-focus principle which give the impression of a spoken text (the speaking voice of Lawrence) rather than of a written one. But more immediately, it is relevant to compare this passage with one which is more traditionally typical of well-written prose: a sentence which is 'well constructed' because it observes both the principles of end-focus and climax:

[22] Eleven hundred and sixty-three years after the foundation of RÓME, the imperial CÍTY, which had subdued and civilized so considerable a part of MANKÍND, was delivered to the licentious fury of the tribes of Germany and SCÝTHIA.

[Edward Gibbon, *Decline and Fall*, Chapter 31]

We have indicated in this sentence not only the punctuation, but also the nuclear tones which would precede each punctuation mark in a neutral reading.[11] The sentence is thus divided into four graphic units, leading up to the climactic unit, or point of finality, at the end. In a classically well-behaved sentence, we expect the parts of the sentence to be presented in the general order of increasing semantic weight, in obedience to the principle of climax. And Gibbon, practitioner of the classical prose virtues, does not disappoint us. The first graphic unit, a factual reference to the foundation of Rome, is scarcely newsworthy in the context of the book: it is a familiar territory which provides the sentence with its point of departure. The second unit, a piece of elegant variation, adds no new piece of information, but adds weight by invoking the later, more glorious image of Rome as centre of an empire. The import of this honorific title 'imperial city' is developed more grandly in the relative clause which constitutes the third unit. But the fourth, the predicate of the main clause, is the true climax, not confirming the glory of Rome, but rather, by a dramatic reversal or peripeteia, destroying it. In terms of the expectations set up by the rest of the sentence, it is informationally highly 'newsworthy'.

Gibbon in this sentence gives an insight into how literary rhetoric grows out of the rhetoric of everyday communication. From the purely functional principle that 'last means most important' it is only one step further to the literary principle that the message be presented in a way which achieves dramatic effect; and this is what Gibbon manages here, by recapitulating in one brief sentence the tragic path of Rome's rise and fall.

7.5.3 Periodic sentence structure

Gibbon's sentence [22] is also climactic in another sense: it saves the main part of the main clause to the end, and thus reinforces the highlighting of final position with the highlighting of syntactic form. This is the kind of sentence structure which is traditionally called PERIODIC. A periodic sentence in a strict sense is one which saves its main clause to the end. But as it is unusual for sentences of any complexity to have this form in English, we use the term 'periodic' more loosely, and say that any sentence has a periodic structure if anticipatory constituents play a major part in it.

By ANTICIPATORY CONSTITUENT we mean any subordinate or dependent constituent which is non-final.[12] Consider the following pairs:

[23] The truth is [that they have suffered through negligence].
[24] [That they have suffered through negligence] is the truth.
[25] Sophia sailed into the room [with her eyes ablaze].
[26] [With her eyes ablaze], Sophia sailed into the room.

Both [24] and [26] contain a major anticipatory constituent: in [24], a subordinate clause has initial position as subject of the main clause; in [26] the adverbial has initial position in the clause it modifies. The corresponding dependent constituents in [23] and [25] are in the final position in the clause, and may therefore be called TRAILING constituents. Parenthetical dependent constituents (those occurring in a medial position) belong to the anticipatory category:

[27] Sophia, [with her eyes ablaze], sailed into the room.

This sentence, with its parenthetical adverbial, is to be classed with [26] rather than with [25].

Anticipatory constituents bring an element of suspense into syntax. A dependent constituent is one which cannot stand on its own, and hence cannot be interpreted in isolation. An anticipatory constituent must therefore be held in the memory until the major constituent of which it is a part has been interpreted. Trailing constituents, on the other hand, do not involve such suspense: we can interpret them as we go along.

The element of suspense clearly depends on the size of the anticipatory constituent: the longer the constituent is, the greater the burden upon the memory, and the greater the tension. On the whole, short anticipatory constituents such as adjectives preceding a noun are not significant; it is the major constituents – clauses and phrases – which contribute to the periodic structure of sentences.

Since anticipatory constituents place a burden on the reader's memory in decoding the sentence, we might wonder why periodic structure has been an influential model in the history of prose writing. One reason is that periodic sentences (as we saw with the Gibbon example) have a dramatic quality: they combine the principle of climax with the principle of subordination, and so progress from a build-up of tension to a final climactic point of resolution. We can see something of this build-up effect in the *Euphues* example (section 1.3.1), and in the Lowry example [15] in this chapter. A more remarkable dramatic effect is that created by this periodic sentence, in which Dickens describes the fomenting of the 1780 Gordon riots:

[28] But when vague rumours got abroad, that in this Protestant association a secret power was mustering against the government for undefined and mighty purposes; when the air was filled with whispers of a confederacy among the Popish powers to degrade and enslave England, establish an Inquisition in London, and turn the pens of Smithfield Market into stakes and cauldrons; when terrors and alarms which no man understood were perpetually broached, both in and out of Parliament, by one enthusiast who did not understand himself, and bygone bugbears which had lain quietly in their graves for centuries, were raised again to haunt the ignorant and credulous; when all this was done, as it were, in the dark, and secret invitations to join the Great Protestant Association in defence of religion, life, and liberty, were dropped in the public ways, thrust under the house-doors, tossed in at

windows, and pressed into the hands of those who trod the streets by
night; when they glared from every wall, and shone on every post and
pillar, so that stocks and stones appeared infected with the common
fear, urging all men to join together blindfold in resistance of they
knew not what, they knew not why; – then the mania spread indeed,
and the body, still increasing every day, grew forty thousand strong.

[Charles Dickens, *Barnaby Rudge*, Chapter 7]

The sentence is essentially an elaboration of the anticipatory pattern 'When
x, then *y*'. But the 'When *x*' part of the pattern is so extended through
parallel coordination and subordination that it contains over twenty clauses.
Thus the syntactic suspense grows and grows, dramatising the rising tide
of fear which will culminate in public violence. But this also shows that
periodic structuring can backfire on the author: such a tremendous climax
is expected, that when the 'then *y*' part of the pattern arrives, we may well
feel that it does not fulfil its promise. At least to a modern reader, hardened
by bulletins of rioting millions, the final clause 'and the body . . . grew forty
thousand strong' falls rather flat.

Apart from its dramatic quality, the periodic sentence has the related
virtue of concentrating significance at one point in the sentence. Since the
interpretation of anticipatory constituents is delayed, in an ideal periodic
sentence enlightenment comes, retrospectively, at the end, where all the
elements of meaning fit synoptically into a whole. A periodic sentence
offers, in this sense, a way of escaping from the 'tyranny of succession', for
although meanings are necessarily presented sequentially, periodic structure requires us to hold them all in the mind simultaneously. Thus an
apparently needless complication of style, such as James's predilection for
parenthetical constructions, may find its justification in the impression it
gives of complex wholeness:

[29] At the end of the ten minutes he was to spend with her his impression
– with all it had thrown off and all it had taken in – was complete.

[Henry James, *The Ambassadors*, Chapter 14]

The final word *complete* here takes under its umbrella the meaning of the
whole sentence. The dependence of interpretation is mutual: the rest of
the sentence cannot be interpreted until we reach *complete*, and we cannot
understand the full implications of *complete* until we have understood the
rest of the sentence. Hence the full realisation of what the sentence means
comes at the end with momentary entirety.

7.5.4 Loose sentence structure

A periodic sentence may therefore be artfully constructed for its integral
effect on the reader. But artfulness is close to artifice, and we now have to

acknowledge that periodic structure achieves its effects at great cost, in that it contravenes a presumed principle of sentence construction. We may call this principle the MEMORY PRINCIPLE, and express it in the imperative mood as follows:

> Reduce the burden on the reader's immediate syntactic memory by avoiding major anticipatory constituents.[13]

In keeping with this principle, the most common type of complex sentence has what has been traditionally called a LOOSE structure: that is, a structure in which trailing constituents predominate over anticipatory constituents. Loose structure is 'natural' in that it makes things easy for the addressee, and incidentally for the addresser, by reducing the amount of syntactic information that has to be stored in decoding. We can decode the syntax as we go, holding in the memory only the immediately preceding grammatical context:

[30] He stood in the doorway´ with the taste of alcohol on his tongue´ watching a thin girl´ in a red rubber cap´ giggle under the floodlighting´.

[Graham Greene, *Brighton Rock*, Part 5, Chapter 1]

All the major constituents in this sentence occurring between points marked ´ are trailing constituents, and we see this in the fact that ´ in each case marks a point of potential completion, a point at which the whole of what precedes can be interpreted as a sentence. This is a good example, then, of a loose sentence.

To the category of trailing constituents may be added the non-initial constituents of a coordinate structure: here again (as we saw with example [20]) it is possible to interpret one coordinated constituent without the next:

[31] He seized the doctor's hand´ and shook it warmly.

In summary, then, anticipatory and trailing constituents can be identified as follows:

A ANTICIPATORY	B TRAILING
1 initial dependent constituents	1 final dependent constituents
2 parenthetical constituents	2 non-initial coordinate constituents

A loose sentence, in which constituents of type B predominate, lacks the anticipatory tension of the periodic sentence. The qualities associated with loose structure are, not surprisingly, easiness, relaxation, informality: the qualities one expects, in fact, in a fairly unconsidered use of language:

[32] This morning I was troubled with my Lord Hinchingbroke's sending to borrow £200 of me; *but* I did answer that I had none, *nor* could borrow any; *for* I am resolved I will not be undone for any body, *though* I would do much for my Lord Sandwich, *for* it is to answer a bill of exchange of his; *and* I perceive he hath made use of all other means in the world to do it, *but* I am resolved to serve him, *but* not ruin myself.
[Samuel Pepys, *Diary*, 9 Dec. 1667]

A loose sentence, like this one, can be very complex (in terms of number of words, number of clauses, etc.) without causing difficulties of comprehension. The linear chain of ideas follows the linear progress of the text, like a train with its linked wagons moving along a railway track. The links are the conjunctions, which are marked in italics in the above example.

Not surprisingly, loose structure is characteristic of a literary style which aims at natural simplicity and directness, rather than rhetorical effect. A representative example is the opening paragraph of D.H. Lawrence's *Women in Love*:

[33] Ursula and Gudrun Brangwen sat one morning in the window-bay of their father's house´ in Beldover´, working and talking´. Ursula was stitching a piece of brightly-coloured embroidery´, and Gudrun was drawing´ upon a board´ which she held on her knee´. They were mostly silent´, talking´ as their thoughts strayed through their minds´.

Once again, the symbol ´ is used to mark the boundaries of major trailing constituents. As the relation between successive sentences involves no anticipatory structure, it is quite appropriate to extend the concept of loose structure from individual sentences to a whole sequence of sentences, such as [33].

Periodic and loose structure are two poles between which styles of sentence structure can vary. Looking back over the history of English prose, we can perhaps say that the most neutral style of writing is one that combines both anticipatory and trailing elements, and thus achieves a balance between 'art' and 'nature'.

7.6 Addresser-based rhetoric: writing imitating speech

The rhetoric of text, as we have considered it, is addressee-based: this means that the principles of good textual behaviour (although they may make conflicting claims on the writer) have functions which can be explained in terms of the reader's needs and responses. However, literary writing also makes use of an addresser-based rhetoric, which reflects the exigencies of encoding.

In ordinary speech, the speaker is in the position of having to 'think on his feet', of having to encode the message under pressure of time. This means that he does not necessarily have time to obey the rhetorical principles we have discussed. In some respects, what is easy from the decoding point of view is also easy from the encoding point of view: the 'principle of memory', for example, reflects a constraint which applies to speaker as much as to hearer (see section 5.4.1), and this explains why impromptu spoken language tends to be extremely 'loose' in its structure. In other cases, the pressures of the encoding process in speech can override the principles of addressee-based rhetoric: in particular, the 'last is most important' principle clashes with a tendency for the speaker to mention what is most important first. As speakers, we are rarely able to plan the whole of our utterance in advance, so we tend to begin with the thing which is uppermost in our mind, the thing which, from our point of view, is the focal nub of the message. This 'first is most important' principle accounts for some syntactic inversions and dislocations characteristic of ordinary speech: 'That dinner you cooked last night – I really enjoyed it'; 'Got a cold have you?'; 'Relaxation you call it!' The same factor accounts for frequent disregard in spoken English of the end-focus principle: for example, the last sentence quoted would be pronounced with the nucleus in non-final position:

[34] RELAXÀTION you call it.

Although a prose writer is not in the position of having to 'think on his feet' in this way, he may wish to cultivate the impression of spontaneity and vigour which is associated with impromptu speech. This is to be expected, for instance, in fictional dialogue and in stream-of-consciousness narrative. But it may also be an ingredient of the authorial 'tone of voice'. We noticed in [21] that Lawrence's style implied the violation of end-focus in such sentences as:

[35] We CÀN'T go back.
[36] He CÒULDN'T go back to the savages.

where the final part of each clause ('go back', 'go back to the savages') is given or implied by the preceding context, and therefore cannot be treated as the focus of information. The early placing of the nucleus adds to the forceful, declamatory effect of the passage, and confirms the feeling that Lawrence is adapting written language to produce the expressive qualities of speech.

Another case of addresser-based rhetoric is the use of parentheses, especially parenthetical constructions which are syntactically dislocated from their context. A parenthetical constituent, as we have said, runs counter to the memory principle: the addressee has to keep in store the rest of the sentence while the parenthesis is being elaborated. But from a speaker's point of view, a parenthesis is in part a recuperatory mechanism, a way of digressing from the main structure of the sentence in order to include something which, with more forethought, could have been integrated into the syntax of the sentence. The following passage from Norman Mailer's documentary novel *The Armies of the Night* includes parentheses and other features of syntax (such as parataxis and verbless sentences) which suggest the improvisatory flow of speech. The occasion he describes is the march on the Pentagon in protest against the Vietnamese war; here he refers to himself in the third person, and evokes his own feelings as a participant in the march:

[37] They were prancing past this hill, they were streaming to battle (1). Going to battle! (2) He realized that he had not taken in precisely this thin high sensuous breath of pleasure in close to twenty-four years, not since the first time he had gone into combat, and found to his surprise that the walk towards the fire fight was one of the more agreeable – if stricken – moments of his life (3). Later, in the skirmish itself it was less agreeable – he had perspired so profusely he had hardly been able to see through his sweat – much later, months later, combat was disagreeable; it managed to consist of large doses of fatigue, the intestinal agitations of the tropics, endless promenades through mud, and general apathy towards whether one lived or not (4). But the first breath had left a feather on his memory; it was in the wind now; he realized that an odd, yes a *zany* part of him had been expecting quietly and confidently for years, that before he was done, he would lead an army (5). The lives of Leon Trotsky and Ernest Hemingway had done nothing to dispel this expectation (6).

[Norman Mailer, *The Armies of the Night*, Book 1, Part III, Chapter 2]

We notice here, as in the Lawrence passage, that reading aloud would entail some rather unusual placings of the nucleus. In sentence (4), *agreeable* occurs three times at the end of a graphic unit, and so a shift from end-focus can scarcely be avoided: 'more AGRÉEABLE . . . DÌsagreeable . . . LÈss agreeable.' The exhilaration of the experience is appropriately conveyed through a jaunty freshness of style, as if the impressions are tumbling out as fast as the writer can get them on paper.

7.7 Iconicity: the imitation principle

This brings us to a more general consideration of the imitative aspect of literary texts. Up to now we have been dealing with aspects of textual rhetoric which apply both to non-literary and literary writing. But if there is one quality which particularly characterises the rhetoric of text in literature, it is that literature follows the 'principle of imitation': in other words, literary expression tends to have not only a PRESENTATIONAL function (directed towards the reader's role as decoder) but a REPRESENTATIONAL function (miming the meaning that it expresses).

Here we must touch on the iconic element of language in general. A code is iconic to the extent that it imitates, in its signals or textual forms, the meanings that they represent. The code of traffic signs is largely iconic: a crossroads is signalled by a cross, a narrowing road by converging lines, etc. The maritime flag code, on the other hand, is non-iconic: there is no connection between the colour and design of a flag and the meaning (such as 'I am altering course to port') which it is used to signify. One of the tenets of modern linguistics is that language is essentially non-iconic, that the form–meaning relationship is arbitrary. It has of course been acknowledged that language contains certain iconic elements: well-known examples are onomatopoeic words such as *cuckoo, whisper, bang*; and phonaesthetic series such as *clutch, cling, clamp, clog, clinch; gleam, glimmer, glitter, glare, glow, gloaming*. But iconicity of this kind has been dismissed as marginal if not trivial in relation to the arbitrariness of language as a whole. Moreover, it is by no means free from arbitrariness in itself, since the iconic values of sounds are not wholly imitative, being constrained by the limits of the code itself. Thus they are only suggestive of meaning in the presence of a suitable semantic stimulus: the sound evokes, rather than directly represents, its meaning.

Against this orthodox view it can be urged that iconicity is inherent in language in a way that the mention of odd words like *miaow* and *thunder* does not begin to show. The phonetic shape of words is in fact one of the less promising areas in which to explore the phenomenon of language imitating nature. Words are conventional and stereotyped units; but beneath the level of words, poets have always known how to exploit the symbolic and evocative value of sounds; and it has been suggested by Bolinger[14] that above the word, iconicity takes a 'quantum leap', the syntactic relations between words characteristically imitating relations between the objects and events which those words signify. We shall give two important instances of this syntactic iconicity: chronological sequencing, and juxtaposition.

Here again, then, the communicative values of literature can be seen as a special exploitation of values which are inherent in the language of everyday use. Let us consider the sequencing of elements in a text. One factor which influences ordering is the principle of chronological sequencing which says that textual time imitates real time: that if A comes before B in the model of reality, then A comes before B in the text. This is a particularly convincing case of syntactic iconicity, because if A and B refer to events, the sequence 'A and B' is sufficient to enforce the interpretation that the former event precedes the latter. This is why [38] is nonsensical in contrast to [39]:

[38] The lone ranger rode off into the sunset, mounted, and saddled his horse.

[39] The lone ranger saddled his horse, mounted, and rode off into the sunset.

Other iconic principles of ordering are derivable from this one. It is natural, for example, for cause to precede effect in a text, because this is indeed the way things happen in real time:

[40] Tom ran out of money, and had to find another job.

The reversal of this sentence ('Tom had to find another job, and ran out of money') means something quite different, if it means anything at all. Iconicity is a principle, not a rule, because we can always find exceptions to its operation. In fact the conjunction *because* enables the cause–effect relation to be reversed: it is in the absence of such overt signals that the iconic principle takes over.

A further step leads to the claim that it is 'natural' for the subject of a verb to precede its object.[15] In a sentence which contains an object, the subject typically refers to the agent, or causer, of the event, and the object to the person or thing which suffers the consequences of the event. Hence in a clause like 'God made heaven and earth', or 'The dog ate the bone', initial position is given to the initiator, whose action or inherent force brings the event to pass.

These preferences are to some extent built into language, for example the placing of the subject before the object is built into the dominant S–V–O order of English clauses. (Other languages have V–S–O or S–O–V, but languages with O–S orderings are very rare.) Presumably, then, we are conditioned to expect that language, for all its arbitrariness, is in various ways an iconic mirror of reality. It is in the nature of literature to exploit these iconic possibilities: to bring out associations between form and meaning which are ordinarily dormant. Pope declares that 'The sound must seem an echo to the sense', but iconicity penetrates more deeply than this aphorism suggests. It embraces not only onomatopoeia and sound symbolism, but the miming or enactment of meaning through patterns of rhythm and syntax.[16]

Chapter 5 talked of the 'illusion of reality', and it can now be seen how textual rhetoric contributes to this. The iconic force in language produces an ENACTMENT of the fictional reality through the form of the text. This brings realistic illusion to life in a new dimension: as readers we do not merely receive a report of the fictional world; we enter into it iconically, as

189

a dramatic performance, through the experience of reading. It has been emphasised that reading is an experience that happens in time; and so, before considering other iconic elements in prose style, it will be fitting to give attention to the mimetic force of sequencing.

7.7.1 Three principles of sequencing

We now consider the interrelation between three principles of sequencing which have been touched on in this chapter, and which correspond to the three kinds of fictional sequencing discussed in section 5.5.2: PRESENTATIONAL, CHRONOLOGICAL and PSYCHOLOGICAL sequencing. The first of these is non-iconic, unless we interpret iconicity liberally to apply to imitation of the reader's thought processes: it is determination of sequence by addressee-based considerations, as exemplified by the principle of climax. The second, as we have seen, is iconic in the sense that it imitates the purported sequence of events in the fictional world. The third is also iconic, and has been exemplified in the principle 'first is most important' mentioned in section 7.6: this is where the syntactic order appears to represent the order in which things spontaneously arise in the consciousness of the author. But from this, the principle of psychological sequencing may be generalised to all cases where textual order reflects the order in which impressions occur in the mind. It thus covers the imitation of a fictional narrator's or reflector's thought processes, as found pre-eminently in 'stream of consciousness' prose. Example [14] from Conrad's *The Secret Agent* has already provided an instance of it:

[14] She saw there an object. That object was the gallows. She was afraid of the gallows.

In an earlier passage from the same novel, as Anne Cluysenaar has shown in some detail,[17] the handling of psychological time is more subtle, involving effects which anticipate the slow-motion and still techniques of the cinema:

[41] He saw partly on the ceiling and partly on the wall the moving shadow of an arm with a clenched hand holding a carving knife (1). It flickered up and down (2). Its movements were leisurely (3). They were leisurely enough for Mr Verloc to recognize the limb and the weapon (4).

They were leisurely enough for him to take in the full meaning of the portent, and to taste the flavour of death rising in his gorge (5). His wife had gone raving mad – murdering mad (6). They were leisurely enough for the first paralysing effect of this discovery to pass away before a resolute determination to come out victorious from the ghastly struggle with that armed lunatic (7). They were leisurely enough for Mr Verloc to elaborate a plan of defence, involving a dash behind the table, and the felling of the woman to the ground with a heavy wooden chair (8). But they were not leisurely enough to allow Mr Verloc the time to move either hand or foot (9). The knife was already planted in his breast (10).

[Joseph Conrad, *The Secret Agent*, Chapter 14]

Here, in the description of Mrs Verloc's murder of her husband, we see things through the mind of the victim: an unexpected entry into the mind of Mr Verloc in an episode which is told predominantly from his wife's point of view. The first sentence gives, as if in slow motion, the perceptual record of Mr Verloc's eye as it progressively makes sense of what it sees, beginning with the location ('partly on the ceiling and partly on the wall'), moving to the vague apprehension of the shadow, then, growing more specific, to the arm, the hand, and the carving knife. The sentence gradually funnels down to a point. In sentence (2), the murder is committed almost casually, in five words: 'It flickered up and down'; the verb *flicker*, signifying a brief movement of light and shadow, indicates the speed, but scarcely the violence of the act. But in the next series of sentences, (3–9), the reel, as it were, is wound back: we experience again, as if in a temporal vacuum, the last moments of Mr Verloc's living consciousness, elaborated through the repeated word *leisurely* and the parallel sentences opening: 'They were leisurely enough . . .' The word *leisurely* in itself is apparently out of place: how can a 'flicker' be leisurely, and how can a death blow be described with an adverb suggesting the absence of energy, tension and purpose? But in this lies the point of the description: Mrs Verloc has performed the act as if in a dream, as if impelled by an external force, and her unsuspecting husband apprehends it in the same spirit. In the mind of a man about to leave the temporal world, time pauses on the brink of the precipice. This imaginative experience could not be a part of the reader's response without the postulate that text time imitates psychological time.

The stylistic implications of sequence are most apparent when, as in [41], our expectations about time are frustrated. On the basis of chronological sequencing, the following sentence makes a rather incongruous impression:

[42] Upon which he [the footman] clapt the door in my face, telling me, I must learn better manners before I could have access to his master.

[Tobias Smollett, *Roderick Random*, Chapter 14]

If we assume that the main clause enacts its meaning before the participial clause does so, we get the (presumably unintended) picture of the footman addressing Random through the shut door. A more interesting case, one of abnormal psychological sequencing, is the following:

[43] Through an open window a streak of ruddy sunlight caresses the rump of a naked lady who reclines calm as a hardboiled egg on a bed of spinach in a giltframed picture behind the bar.

[John Dos Passos, *Manhattan Transfer*, First section, 2]

This is a striking sentence in a number of ways, demonstrating a linguistic technique which has something in common with expressionism in art and imagism in poetry: it projects a subjective sensory reality through the distortion of the linguistic medium. One of the 'distorting' effects comes from the ordering of impressions, which seems to follow the eye of an observer obliquely downwards from the window, via the picture, to the bar. The trailing syntax, here, also seems iconic, progressively deepening the embedding of one structure inside another to suggest the downward trail of visual connections:

```
the rump
    (of a naked lady
        (who reclines calm
            (as a hardboiled egg
                (on a bed
                    (of spinach
                        (in a giltframed picture
                            (behind the bar)))))))
```

What is odd about the ordering is that it reverses the normal way of perceiving – and describing – the contents of a room. Most rooms have a natural centre of focus, connected with their function, and this is what our eyes locate first. In a bar room, the centre of focus is naturally enough the bar, and other objects tend to take their orientation from it, ordering themselves from focal point to the periphery. Dos Passos's view of the room is a disorientating one, which gives pure perception priority over function. The eye seizes first on a perceptual high point: the open window, with its shaft of light; and from this, it follows a track which ultimately leads to the thing we ought to have noticed first – the bar. It is part of the disorientation that what is new and unpresupposed ('*an* open window . . . *a* streak . . . *a* naked lady . . .') precedes what is taken for granted ('*the* bar'): definite and indefinite articles reverse their expected roles. It is also part of the disorientation that parts are initially perceived in isolation from the wholes to which they belong: the illuminated rump strikes the eye before the lady it belongs to.

7.7.2 Juxtaposition

Not all that is strange about [43] can be attributed to sequencing. Another, related, aspect of iconicity – juxtaposition – comes into play. Juxtaposition can be iconic in the sense that words which are close in the text may evoke an impression of closeness or connectedness in the fiction – not only closeness of time, but psychological or locative relatedness. The hierarchical structuring of syntax frequently ensures that this iconic principle is upheld: for instance, in

[44] [A schooner manned by forty men] sailed into [Portsmouth harbour].

the two noun phrases (delimited by square brackets) keep related things together in the sentence: the men belong spatially with the schooner, and the harbour with Portsmouth. In [44a], on the other hand, the subject noun phrase is divided into two discontinuous parts:

[44a] A schooner sailed into Portsmouth harbour *manned by forty men*.

Such discontinuous constructions violate the juxtaposition principle: they upset the natural semantic connections between things. We tolerate them in ordinary language where they serve some other purpose, e.g., the principle of end-focus or climax:

[45] The time came for everyone to LÈAVE.

But in the following examples (also from *Manhattan Transfer*) the motivation comes rather from a more subtle form of iconicity:

[46] There were six men at the table in the lunch room eating fast *with their hats on the backs of their heads*.

[First section, 2]

[47] He seized the nurse's hand and shook *it showing all his uneven yellow teeth in a smile*.

[First section, 1]

In [46], the men are separated from their hats by the action of eating at the table. A reader who makes sense of this in terms of the principle of juxtaposition will treat as a constituent the sequence 'eating fast with their hats . . . heads', and so will build a connection between the two parts of this expression. The obvious connection is haste: the men are in such a hurry to eat their dinner that they cannot spare the time to take their hats off.

In [47], the connection between the hand-shaking and the jagged smile is forced by juxtaposition and reinforced by alliteration: 'shook . . . showing'. But the sentence somehow turns two cordial gestures into uncouth, hostile ones, and this is partly achieved by the delay of the smile to the end. Up to the last word, the sentence reads threateningly:

[47*a*] He seized the nurse's hand and shook it showing all his uneven teeth
in a . . .

We would almost expect a *snarl* rather than a *smile* as an appropriate
conclusion. The aggressive connotations of *seize, shook* and *uneven teeth*
interanimate one another, so that by postponing the key word *smile*, Dos
Passos seems to trick the reader into a wholly negative response.

Returning to [43], we can now see how there, too, the combined effects of
juxtaposition and sequencing are to lead the reader into making associative, chiefly sensory, connections which short-circuit the logic of syntax.
In this, Dos Passos capitalises on the multiple ambiguity of structure
which allows each of the following prepositional phrases to act either as a
postmodifier or as an adverbial:

on a bed of spinach . . .
in a giltframed picture . . .
behind the bar.

Since each of these phrases has two syntactic functions, the sentence can in
fact be parsed in six different ways! But we will be content to illustrate two
interpretations, one in which all the prepositional phrases are adverbials,
and one in which they are all postmodifiers (bracketing shows the relevant
constituent structure):

[43*a*] . . . a naked lady who reclines (calm as a hardboiled egg) (on a bed of
spinach) (in a giltframed picture) (behind the bar).
[43*b*] . . . a naked lady who reclines (calm as (a hardboiled egg (on a bed of
spinach (in a giltframed picture (behind the bar)))))

In [43*a*], the lady reclines on a bed of spinach, the lady reclines in a
giltframed picture, and the lady reclines behind the bar. In [43*b*], the
hardboiled egg is on a bed of spinach, and the bed of spinach is in a
giltframed picture, and the giltframed picture is behind the bar. Perhaps
the most intelligible interpretation is a compromise between these two:
one in which the hardboiled egg is on a bed of spinach, the lady reclines
in a giltframed picture, and the giltframed picture is behind the bar. But
the ambiguities are fruitful, creating a verbal *trompe l'oeil* in which there
is interplay between the perceptual movements of the eye and the
metaphorical connections of the imagination. Is there a hardboiled egg
in the giltframed picture? And is there a real naked lady reclining on a
real bed of spinach behind the bar? Probably not, but the gaudy sensory
world of Manhattan, spectacular without meaning, allows for such obscene
marvels.

7.7.3 Other forms of iconicity

The possibilities of 'form enacting meaning' are virtually unlimited – as unlimited, let us say, as the author's imaginative power over the expressiveness of language, and as the reader's capacity to see connections. In this respect, iconicity has a power like that of metaphor: it rests on the intuitive recognition of similarities between one field of reference (the form of language) and another. But this very open-endedness is a danger. It is all too easy – as is well known in the case of onomatopoeia – to use the undoubted iconic suggestibility of language as a *carte blanche* for justifying private and whimsical responses.

While we must be on our guard against this tendency, we must also recognise that the more powerful forms of iconicity often take the form of a highly specific, if not idiosyncratic, adaptation of linguistic expression to literary function. To illustrate this, we take one final example of the iconic rule of syntax:

> For in this long digression which I was accidentally led into, as in all my digressions (one only excepted) there is a masterstroke of digressive skill, the merit of which has all along, I fear, been overlooked by my reader, – not for want of penetration in him, – but because 'tis an excellence seldom looked for, or expected indeed, in a digression; – and it is this: That though my digressions are all fair, as you observe, – and that I fly off from what I am about, as far and as often too as any writer in Great Britain; Yet I constantly take care to order affairs so that my main business does not stand still in my absence.
>
> [Lawrence Sterne, *Tristram Shandy*, Vol. 1, Chapter 22]

Sterne almost provides here an apology for his *Tristram Shandy*, which is not so much a novel as a celebration of accident and irrelevance. The narrator purports to be telling his own history, but manages instead to produce a discourse in which digressions triumph over the main narrative. The discourse becomes self-reflexive, for its supposed author becomes entrammeled in the need to expound the nature of his own role and his view of story-writing. In this sense, too, the above extract is homological: it expatiates on the digressiveness of which it is itself an instance. But more to the point, the syntax of the sentence enacts on a small scale the digressiveness which it at once praises, and exemplifies in the main context of the narrative. The syntactic icon of digression is a parenthetical constituent; and in the following layout (parenthetical constituents being placed in square brackets), we see them taking over the main structure of the sentence:

> ... in this long digression, [which I was ... led into as in all my digressions [one only excepted]] there is a masterstroke ... [I fear] ... [or expected indeed] ... that [though my digressions are all fair [as you observe] and

that I fly off from what I am about, as far [and as often too] as any writer in Great Britain]; yet I . . .

But from *Yet* . . . onwards, the narrator emerges from his quagmire of parentheses within parentheses, and makes triumphantly for dry land. What threatened to be incoherent turns out, in the end, to have a goal. This is iconic on two levels: in the narrow scope of the sentence, the syntax dramatises its own meaning, which is that digression is both, perversely, an end in itself, and also a means to the end of advancing the fiction; and on a large scale, the syntax is an icon of the author's *modus operandi* in the whole work.

7.8 Cohesion

The rhetoric of text controls, as we saw in section 7.4, the way in which the message is segmented into units. Segmentation, however, implies its opposite – COHESION. The units must be implicitly or explicitly bound together; they must not be just a random collection of sentences. The connectivity of the elements of a text is essentially a matter of meaning and reference; but we are interested, here, in the formal means by which these connections are signalled. One kind of cohesion is syntactic inclusion: two noun phrases 'the princess' and 'the hunter' may be related by being part of the same clause: 'The princess loved the hunter'; but our concern now is with the linear connectivity which takes place between sentences, as well as within them: 'The princess loved the hunter. *But she* could not marry *him*.' The second sentence illustrates the two major kinds of linear cohesion: the pronouns *she* and *him* are examples of CROSS-REFERENCE, and the conjunction *but* is an example of LINKAGE. By cross-reference we understand the various means which language uses to indicate that 'the same thing' is being referred to or mentioned in different parts of the text. Linkage, on the other hand, is the use of overt connectors: coordinating conjunctions, subordinating conjunctions, and linking adverbials.

The following is a list of the most important cohesive devices in English:[18]

A: Cross-reference
1 *Definite reference*
   (a) personal pronouns: *he, she, it, they,* etc.
   (b) the definite article *the*
   (c) deictics: *this, that, these, those,* etc.
   (d) implied: *same, different, other, else, such,* etc.
2 *Substitution*: pro-forms such as *one, ones, do* and *so* which substitute for other linguistic expressions.
3 *Ellipsis*: omission or deletion of elements whose meaning is 'understood' because it is recoverable from the context.

4 *Formal repetition*: repeated use of an expression (morpheme, lexical item, proper name, phrase, etc.) which has already occurred in the context.
5 *Elegant variation*: use of an alternative expression (not a pronoun or a substitute) as a replacement for an expression in the context.

[*Note*: By CONTEXT we mean the relevant preceding (or sometimes following) part of the text.]

B: Linkage
6 *Coordinating conjunctions*: *and, or, but, both . . . and, neither . . . nor*, etc.
7 *Linking adverbials*: *for, so, yet, however, therefore, meanwhile, for example*, etc.

The list is incomplete, but will, we hope, be useful for reference. Notice that the items listed under A1 (definite reference) are not necessarily cohesive: these items refer to things which are in some sense contextually 'given', but the givenness can be supplied by extralinguistic, as well as linguistic context. When they are cohesive, such items may be said to CO-REFER to some other expression in the text.

Cohesion is an important part of what makes a text, both in literary and non-literary writing, but it is not always an important aspect of literary style. In literary fiction it can most often be seen as a background to more significant style markers, just as the framework which makes a building hang together is rarely the most interesting part of its architecture. To illustrate this *obbligato* working of cohesion, we choose part of the description of the Marabar Caves in E.M. Forster's *A Passage to India* (Chapter 12):

[48] Only *the wall* of *the* circular *chamber* has been polished *thus* (1). The *sides* of the tunnel are left rough, *they* impinge as an afterthought upon *the* internal perfection (2). An entrance was necessary, *so* mankind made *one* (3). *But elsewhere, deeper* in *the* granite, *are* there certain *chambers* that have no entrances (4)? *Chambers* never unsealed since the arrival of the gods (5). Local report declares that *these exceed* in number *those* that can be visited, as the dead *exceed* the living – four hundred of *them, four thousand* or *million* (6). *Nothing* is inside *them, they* were sealed up before the creation of pestilence or treasure; if mankind grew curious and excavated, *nothing, nothing* would be added to the sum of good or evil (7). One of *them* is rumoured within the boulder that *swings* on the summit of *the highest of the hills*; a bubble-shaped cave that has *neither* ceiling *nor* floor, and mirrors *its* own darkness in every direction infinitely (8). If *the* boulder falls and *smashes, the cave* will *smash too – empty* as an Easter egg (9). *The* boulder because of its *hollowness sways* in the wind, *and* even moves when a crow perches upon *it*: *hence* its name *and* the *name* of *its stupendous pedestal*: the Kawa Dol (10).[19]

The passage provides examples of the kinds of cohesion we have listed.

A: Cross-reference

1 *Definite reference*
   (a) *personal pronouns*: (2) *they* (co-referring to 'the sides'); (6) *them* (co-referring to 'chambers'); (10) *it* (co-referring to 'the boulder') etc.
   (b) *the definite article*: (9) *'the* boulder' (co-referring to 'the boulder that swings on the highest of the hills'); *'the* cave' (co-referring to 'a bubble-shaped cave') etc.
   (c) *deictics*: (1) *thus*; (6) *these*; *those*.
   (d) *implied*: (4) *elsewhere* (i.e. in a different place from that already mentioned); *deeper* (i.e. deeper than this).
2 *Substitution*: (3) *one* (= 'an entrance').
3 *Ellipsis*: (6) *four thousand* (= four thousand of them); *or million* (= four million of them); etc.
4 *Formal repetition*: (1) *chamber*, (4) *chambers*; (7) *nothing, nothing, nothing*; (6) *exceed, exceed*; (9) *smash, smash*, etc.
5 *'Elegant' variation*: (1) *the wall* – (2) *the sides*; (9) *empty* – (10) *hollowness*; (8) *swings* – (10) *sways*; (8) *the highest of the hills* – (10) *its stupendous pedestal*.

B: Linkage

6 *Coordinating conjunctions*: (4) *but*; (8) *neither . . . nor*; etc.
7 *Linking adverbials*: (3) *so*; (9) *too*; (10) *hence*.

7.8.1 Cross-reference

Cross-reference may be a device either for a repetition of meaning or for a repetition of reference. The most explicit kind of repetition, in each case, is what we have called 'formal repetition', the simple repetition of words or phrases. But cohesion frequently involves the principle of REDUCTION, whereby language allows us to condense our messages, avoiding the repeated expression of repeated ideas. The most common form of reduction is by means of third-person pronouns, of which there are nine examples in [48] above: for example, *it* in (10) repeats the reference to 'the boulder' in the same sentence. Semantic repetition can, similarly, be reduced by substitution or ellipsis; thus Forster's repetition of the verb *exceed* in (6) could have been avoided in two ways:

[49] Local report declares that these *exceed* in number those that can be visited

198

Where choice of reduction exists, we are generally guided, at a practical level, by two principles which may be phrased as follows:

'Do not reduce where reduction leads to unclarity.'
'Otherwise, reduce as much as possible.'

In other words, it is a good thing, on the whole, to make your message concise, so long as this can be done without loss of clarity.[20] But even in workaday prose, there are two other principles of a more aesthetic kind which interfere with this maxim. In the first place, there is a principle of variety: too much repetition, either of lexical items or of reduced forms, can be tedious, and hence ELEGANT VARIATION becomes an allowable, and indeed welcome, device of cross-reference. We have already seen in the discussion of Henry James (section 3.5) that this can become a powerful thematic device in literature. It can take the form either of a repetition of meaning (by the use of a synonymous or almost synonymous expression) or of a repetition of reference. In [48], the former is illustrated by the verbs *swing* and *sway*, which are virtual synonyms in the context. The latter is illustrated by the use of the phrase 'its stupendous pedestal' (10), referring back to 'the highest of the hills'.

A second principle favours the use of formal repetition even where the alternative of reduction would be possible and acceptable. We might name this the principle of EXPRESSIVE REPETITION, seeing it as a kind of aesthetic counterbalance to that of elegant variation. Repetition is expressive in that it gives emphasis or emotive heightening to the repeated meaning.[21]

Perhaps Forster was instinctively following this principle when he chose the first of three alternatives in [49]. Here, as is often the case, formal repetition is a means of strengthening a syntactic parallelism: 'A *exceeds* B, as C *exceeds* D'. The parallelism is potent because it compares the undiscovered caves to the unseen dead: a cosmic image which adds to the portrayal of the Caves as a place where everything is reduced to a mystic infinity of nothingness. Appropriately, the word *nothing* itself is repeated three times in (7), one of these repetitions being an 'asyntactic' repetition ('*Nothing, nothing* would be added . . .) which has a purely rhetorical value.

For a more complex example of expressively redundant repetition, we may look back to our earlier Conrad example:

[14] She saw there an object. That object was *the gallows*. She was afraid of *the gallows*.

The repetition of *the gallows* here is all the more striking because it appears dysfunctional in two ways: it resists both the principle of reduction and the principle of end-focus. According to the normal convention, the second occurrence of 'the gallows' cannot bear nuclear stress because it is old information, and so the pronunciation would have to be: 'She was AFRÀID of the gallows'. But by these apparent violations of textual principles, the repetition becomes doubly expressive of the horror with which Mrs Verloc regards the image that her mind has conjured up.

Returning to Forster, we note that the last two paragraphs of *A Passage to India* provide another impressive example of repetition (this time combined with pronominal reduction):

[50] 'Why can't we be friends now?' said the other, holding him affection-
ately. 'It's *what I want*. It's *what you want*.'

But the horses *didn't want it* – they swerved apart; the earth *didn't want it*, sending up rocks through which riders must pass single file; the temples, the tank, the jail, the palace, the birds, the carrion, the Guest House, that came into view as they issued from the gap and saw Mau beneath: they *didn't want it*, they said in their hundred voices, '*No, not yet*,' and the sky said '*No, not there*.'

The effect of this ending can only be fully explained by reference to cohesion. The last paragraph is built chiefly on a series of parallelistic statements: 'A didn't want it; B didn't want it; C didn't want it . . .' The repeated words 'want it' refer back to the balanced sentences in the former paragraph: '*It*'s what I *want*. *It*'s what you *want*.' And *it* here in turn refers back to 'Why can't we be friends?' said by the Englishman Fielding to the Indian Aziz. So the whole paragraph looks back to this farewell conversation between friends resigning themselves to the irreconcilability of East and West. In this way, Forster leads us away from a specific human encounter, by stages, to a conclusion which relates it to the intangibilities of society, culture, environment which prevent the reconciliation. The parallelism begins with the two men, then moves progressively to their horses, to the earth on which they tread, to the immediate setting of an Indian town, and ultimately to the overarching sky. The personification which runs through this receding parallelism is more than a vain figure of speech; it summons up the many episodes in the book (notably that of the Marabar Caves) in which inscrutable nature, the very land and sky of India, blends with Indian civilisation to enforce its influence on man's motives and actions. Reduction also plays a part in this effect: the piling up of noun phrases ('the temples, the tank, the jail . . .), each with its predicate 'didn't want it' deleted, makes the forces against reconciliation seem overwhelming. A last and telling example of ellipsis comes in the final utterances 'No, not yet,' and 'No, not there'. The implied omission 'you can . . . be friends' links them directly, as answers, to Fielding's humanly unanswered question with which the passage begins. This connection brings together the human and the symbolic dimensions of the novel in a final statement of its theme.

7.8.2 Linkage

It will be noted that [48] contains few examples of linkage and, of these, only one (*but*) is a link between graphological sentences. We suggest that in the history of fiction writing, there has been a progressive tendency, over the past three hundred years, to dispense with such logical connections between sentences, and to rely instead upon INFERRED connections.

Something of this may be seen by comparing almost any modern novel with the following passage from *The Pilgrim's Progress*, in which Mercy rejects the courtship of Mr Brisk:

> Mercy *then* revealed the business to the maidens that were of the house, *and* inquired of them concerning him, *for* they did know him better than she. *So* they told her, that he was a very busy young man, *and* one that pretended to religion; *but* was, as they feared, a stranger to the power of that which was good.
>
> Nay *then*, said Mercy, I will look no more on him; *for* I purpose never to have a clog to my soul.
>
> Prudence *then* replied that there needed no great matter of discouragement to be given to him, her continuing *so* as she had begun to do *for* the poor would quickly cool his courage.
>
> [John Bunyan, *The Pilgrim's Progress*, Dent 1943; p. 243]

Part of the archaic flavour of this passage, for a modern reader, comes from the abundance of linking words (italicised). We should not ignore purely historical explanations for this (the influence of the Bible on Bunyan's style is one factor), but at the same time we should observe the stylistic value of linkage, which is to make the text into a *logically articulated* discourse; little is left to the reader's imagination. Bunyan's fiction, as an allegory, is answerable less to any principle of realistic illusion than to the transcendent principle of Christian doctrine; in this sense, Mercy's coyness towards Mr Brisk is inexorable. The connectives, too, give the style an inexorable quality: they steer the reader along a well-signposted road.

In contrast, the most conspicuous feature of linkage in modern fiction is its absence: or, speaking less paradoxically, we may observe that the modern novelist tends to rely on INFERRED LINKAGE, or simple juxtaposition, rather than on overt signals. Semantically, linkage may be placed on a scale of cohesiveness: the most cohesive signals are connectives like *therefore*, which makes a fairly explicit relation between two clauses: that of reason. *And*, on the other hand, is the vaguest of connectives – it might be called a 'general purpose link', in that it merely says that two ideas have a positive connection, and leaves the reader to work out what it is. But the end-point of the scale is inferred linkage, and its importance in fiction is a reflection of the general reliance on inference in the interpretation of fictional texts (see sections 4.2 and 5.2).

To illustrate, let us take two examples of inferred linkage from [48]:

The sides of the tunnel are left rough, they impinge as an afterthought
upon the internal perfection. (2)
Nothing is inside them, they were sealed up before the creation of pestilence or treasure . . . (7)

The implied connection between the clauses could be made explicit in the
first case by *so*, and in the second case by *because*. But these connectives
would overdetermine the relation between the two ideas, which is happily
left vague, so that the connection between them is imaginatively registered,
like an electric spark jumping a gap.

For a more extreme manifestation of this tendency, it is natural to turn to
the stream-of-consciousness prose of James Joyce. This passage of interior
monologue is from the Hades episode of *Ulysses*:

[51] Whores in Turkish graveyards. Learn anything if taken young. You
might pick up a young widow here. Men like that. Love among the
tombstones. Romeo. Spice of pleasure. In the midst of death we are in
life. Both ends meet. Tantalizing for the poor dead. Smell of frilled
beefsteaks to the starving gnawing their vitals. Desire to grig people.
Molly wanted to do it at the window. Eight children he has anyway.
[Penguin, 1978, p. 110]

The connections in this case cannot be made by a simple conjunction or
adverb such as *so* or *because*. The width of the associative gap between
sentences is increased by the fact that the sentences themselves are often
syntactically and cohesively incomplete: noun phrases lack verbs, verbs
lack subjects, etc.; also personal pronouns (such as *he* in the last sentence)
have no co-referent. Joyce captures the working of the consciousness at a
level below that of complete verbalisation, and just as the impulses of the
mind lack logical articulation, so also does Joyce's prose. For example, the
one word *Romeo* signifies little in itself; it can only be linked to the rest of
the text by associative recall of the scene in Shakespeare's play in which
Romeo embraces Juliet in the tomb.

While the Joyce passage illustrates the extreme of inexplicitness, we finally
turn to a style which, in modern fiction-writing, is exceptional in the opposite direction. The following passage from Samuel Beckett's *Watt* (from the
beginning of Part II) seems to contain too many connections:

[52] Mr Knott never *left the grounds*, as far as Watt could judge (1). *Watt*
thought it unlikely that *Mr Knott* could *leave the grounds*, without
its coming to his notice (2). *But he* did not reject the possibility of
Mr Knott's leaving the grounds, without *his being any the wiser* (3). *But*
the *unlikelihood, on the one hand* of *Mr Knott's leaving the grounds*, and *on*

the other of *his doing so without* exciting the general comment, seemed very great, to *Watt* (4).

Mr Knott is the mysterious God figure for whom Watt works and whom he never gets to know, although they share the same premises. This paragraph is typical of a book in which the occurrence or non-occurrence of events, however trivial, becomes the basis for a philosophical, almost theological, superstructure of argument and self-questioning in the mind of Watt. This strange orientation of the fiction is reflected in the frequency of cohesive devices, both of cross-reference and of linkage.

The abundance of cross-reference means that the style is immensely repetitive. Formal repetition of morphemes, words and phrases is the most obvious sign of this: 'left the grounds . . . leave the grounds . . . leaving the grounds'; but other devices also contribute. The idea of 'leaving the grounds' is further repeated in the *its* of (2), and in the substitution of 'doing so' in (4):

. . . without *its* (= Mr Knott's leaving the grounds) coming to his notice . . .
. . . and on the other of *his doing so* (= Mr Knott's leaving the grounds) . . .

Elegant variation also plays a part: 'without his being any the wiser' in (3) clearly means more or less the same as 'without its coming to his notice' in (2). On the other hand, 'without exciting the general comment' in (4) is not quite synonymous, since it implies some public notice being given to Mr Knott's comings and goings. The oddity of this is that in Watt's solipsistic world there ought to be no room for such public observations. But in spite of the disconcerting effect of such mental twists, the paragraph essentially runs over the same subject matter in several slightly different ways: it is a logical dance which always seems to come back to the same starting-point.

Part of this dance is executed through linkage: the *but* which begins (3) is countermanded by the *but* which begins (4). 'On the one hand' and 'on the other hand' in (4) balance one improbability against another. It is also notable that each sentence contains a carefully weighed element of uncertainty: 'as far as Watt could judge', 'did not reject the possibility', 'thought it unlikely', 'the likelihood . . . seemed very great'. The passage comes close to being a parody of philosophical analysis. The unusual prominence of cohesion is a sign that this text is concerned not with building up the realistic illusion of a mock reality, but rather with the very processes of truth-seeking and inference which (as we saw in sections 4.2, 4.3.1 and 5.2) underlie the realistic illusion. In this respect, it resembles a philosophical text more than a narrative one.

Another intriguing feature of cohesion in the style of *Watt* is absence of variation in referring to characters: Watt is always named as *Watt* and Mr Knott as *Mr Knott*. (Compare the opposite tendency in the style of

Henry James; see p. 85.) Apart from bringing out the punning and rhyming character of the names (*Watt* = *what*; *Knott* = *not*), this abstemiousness seems to make Watt and Knott into 'primitive terms' of the argument: where most things are uncertain, the existence of Watt and Knott seems to be unquestioned, and in no need of amplification. A similar tendency can be seen in the word-for-word repetition of 'leave the grounds': this rather strange locution appears to have the status of an *a priori* concept in Watt's thinking. Here again there is an element of parody, for ordinary common-sense logic proceeds on just such a basis of unexamined concepts. The peculiarity of Watt's vision of life is that he is inclined to take for granted what others would challenge, and to challenge what others would take for granted.

7.9 Conclusion

We have examined in this chapter the principles which govern a writer's production of a linear and coherent text. This examination has concentrated on five general factors: segmentation, salience, sequence, iconicity and cohesion. Our aim has been to show how even the most mundane features of textual form can be exploited for heightened expression in literature. Perhaps two aspects of this exploitation may be singled out in conclusion. First, there is in literature an exceptional development of the iconic, imitative resources of language; and second, as we have seen in the last example from *Watt*, a literary text may bring new significance by foregrounding, by the violation of textual expectations.

In the next chapter our concept of rhetoric is broadened to take in the principles which govern the use of language as interpersonal discourse.

Notes

1. The term 'pragmatics', originating in philosophy (see LYONS, 1977) is now generally applied to the study of the relation between language and its users (speakers and hearers), or more specifically, to the contextual conditions governing the speaker's choice of an utterance, and the hearer's interpretation of it. In linking this to rhetoric, we take the view that such conditions can, in large measure, be expressed in terms of principles or maxims of linguistic behaviour: that is, they can be formulated in terms of goals of successful or effective communication by means of language. The best known of such principles is the Cooperative Principle of Grice (see section 9.1.2). This conception of rhetoric proposes a natural continuity between 'rhetoric' in its ordinary language sense, and as applied to literature. It is developed further in G. LEECH, (1980), 9–29.
2. On the distinction between literature as 'text' and as 'discourse', see H.G. WIDDOWSON (1975), p. 6 and Chapters 2–4; also R. FOWLER (1977), 45–47. Widdowson's and Fowler's understandings of these terms differ in detail from our own, but, like ours, correlate roughly with Halliday's concepts of the textual and interpersonal functions of language.

3. See note 1 above.
4. An approach to literary criticism which stresses this experience of a text as happening in time is that of S.E. FISH (1970). Fish illustrates the importance of analysing 'the developing responses of the words as they succeed one another on the page' (p. 143), going so far as to claim that 'the experience of an utterance . . . *is* its meaning' (p. 131).
5. Our account of end-focus and of given/new information is much simplified; see further S. GREENBAUM and R. QUIRK (1990), Chapter 18. These concepts are derived primarily from the work of M.A.K. HALLIDAY, e.g. (1968).
6. The psycholinguistic basis for this is unclear; see, however, A. CUTLER (1976) and A.H. WOLD (1978), esp Chapter 9.
7. This assumes an active view of the decoding process, of 'analysis by synthesis', which is confirmed by psycholinguisitic research. See H.H. CLARK and E.V. CLARK (1977), Chapter 5, esp. 214; also D. DEW and P. JENSEN (1977), Chapter 10.
8. This passage is discussed by R. OHMANN (1964), 275, and by FOWLER, *op. cit.*, 61–65.
9. J. BARZUN (1975), 156.
10. The preference for placing a falling tone in final position does not show in speech as clearly as the 'principle of climax' might suggest. This is possibly because of the 'addresser-based' factor discussed in section 7.6 below. See, however, the positive evidence of R. QUIRK (1968), esp. 135.
11. There might well be other nuclear tones than those marked in [22]. Another point to bear in mind is that 'new' information, although signalled by the nucleus, may have a wider scope than the nucleus-bearing word alone, and may in some cases extend over the whole information unit.
12. Here again, in the treatment of anticipatory constituents, we have simplified considerably. There are two related issues: the position of obligatory constituents, and the position of optional constituents. The former issue is related to Yngve's 'depth hypothesis' (see note 13); the latter is discussed by J. MCH. SINCLAIR (1972) under the headings of *arrest* and *extension*.
13. *Cf* V. YNGVE (1961).
14. D. BOLINGER (1980), Chapter 3.
15. J.H. GREENBERG's (1963b) study of universals of syntactic order reports that subject precedes object in 98 per cent of the languages examined. The passive construction, of course, enables us to reverse the normal order of 'doer' and 'done-to'.
16. Syntactic iconicity or mimesis in literary style has been interestingly investigated by E.L. EPSTEIN (1975). On phonetic mimesis, see EPSTEIN (1978), 25–37.
17. See A. CLUYSENAAR (1976), 77, 79–80.
18. The most detailed treatment of cohesion is that of M.A.K. HALLIDAY and R. HASAN (1976). See also S. GREENBAUM and R. QUIRK (1990), Chapter 19, and with special reference to literature, W. GUTWINSKI (1976).
19. In [48], we have marked as cohesive only those cases of coordination which link main clauses or sentences. For coordination, and for some other categories, it is difficult to draw a line between what we have called 'linear cohesion', and cohesion defined by syntactic constituency. HALLIDAY and HASAN (1976) limit their study of cohesion to relations between sentences, but this seems rather restrictive for purposes of literary analysis.
20. This can be related to Grice's maxims of 'Manner' and 'Quantity'; see section 9.1.2.
21. On the stylistic function of repetition, see G. LEECH (1969), Chapter 5.

CHAPTER 8

Discourse and the discourse situation

8.1 The discourse situation of literature

L anguage is a vehicle of communication whereby one person conveys messages to another for a range of different purposes, e.g., informing, ordering, persuading, reassuring. The way the message is used to achieve such ends may, in ordinary speech situations, be called 'the rhetoric of discourse'. But in a novel or short story, the rhetoric of discourse has a rather different implication. Here the writer has the goal of 'informing' the reader about a particular fictional world; but also he needs to achieve a rapport with his readers, an identity of viewpoint whereby the contents of the fiction will be interpreted and evaluated in an appropriate way. Some of the problems of achieving the latter aim arise from the fact that a novel or short story is in the written medium.

Typically, a spoken utterance takes place in a discourse situation containing the following factors:

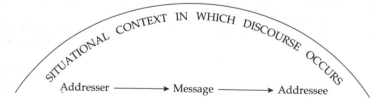

Figure 8.1

As Figure 8.1 implies, the production and reception of a spoken message normally take place within a single context of time and space. But clearly this is not true of a written discourse such as a letter. Further, the addresser and addressee in a discourse situation are normally distinct; but they need not be. If you write a shopping list to remind yourself what to buy, the addresser and addressee are the same. For all published texts, on the other hand, there is usually one addresser but a large number of addressees, the vast majority of whom the writer has never met. Literature is thus a kind of discourse where the writer can assume relatively little about the receiver of his message or the context in which it will be received.

One result of the relative uncertainty of the situational context of the literary message is its degree of redundancy. In order to make sure that the point is put across, the novelist tends to say the same thing in a number of different ways, and at different levels of structure. Conrad's *Nostromo*, for example, is a novel where 'material interest' is portrayed as an influence which isolates people from each other. The silver mine, owned by the Englishman, Charles Gould, helps to subvert his marriage, and corrupts Nostromo, the hero of the story, thus destroying his position as symbol of the aspirations of his people. Most of the characters in the novel are isolated from one another. Martin Decoud is ironically made editor of the newspaper (an organ of communication) while he keeps secret his plans to leave Costaguana. Nostromo, the 'man of the people', is isolated both spiritually and physically from them by his lone quest to rescue the silver from the mine. Indeed, everyone thinks that he has drowned in the attempt. The many instantiations of isolation at the level of plot are reinforced by the way in which events are described, for example when Decoud and Nostromo find Señor Hirsch in the lighter, pretending to be dead:

Decoud, to his immense astonishment, recognized Señor Hirsch, the hide merchant from Esmeralda. Nostromo, too, had recognized him. And they gazed at each other across the body, lying with its naked feet higher than its head, in an absurd pretence of sleep, faintness or death.

[Part 2, Chapter 7]

Instead of choosing to represent Decoud's and Nostromo's perceptions together by saying 'they recognized . . .', Conrad states their realisations separately. Then, instead of looking at Hirsch, the two men gaze at each other with the body keeping them symbolically apart. Both incident and mode of description combine to embody one of the major themes of the novel.

8.1.1 Implied author and implied reader

Although the author of a novel is in the dark about his readers from many points of view, he can of course assume that he shares with his readers a common fund of knowledge and experience. We have already shown (in section 4.3.1) that quite a lot of general background knowledge of the world about us is needed to interpret even the simplest of sentences in a novel. This background knowledge can include not just common inferences, like the fact that when people stop breathing they die, but also knowledge of certain well-known historical events and literary works, and even quotations from the latter. Hence Powys can reasonably hope that when William Zoyland tells Tom Barter in *A Glastonbury Romance* that 'you look to me as if you know a hawk from a hernshaw' his reader will pick up the line from *Hamlet* which is misquoted and spot an irony. A writer will also allude to things which it is reasonable to expect the educated readers of his day to know, but which a later reader (e.g., a twentieth-century reader of an eighteenth-century novel) will have to make himself positively aware of. When Fielding wrote *Shamela* he could assume that his readers would be well acquainted with Richardson's *Pamela*. If the modern reader has not read *Pamela* he will have to read it in order to put himself in the position of Fielding's assumed reader and to be able to appreciate the satire.

Because the author can assume knowledge which any particular reader might not necessarily have, we have to conclude that the addressee in literary communication is not the reader, but what Wayne Booth has called the 'mock reader', or what can be more conveniently termed the IMPLIED READER;[1] a hypothetical personage who shares with the author not just background knowledge but also a set of presuppositions, sympathies and standards of what is pleasant and unpleasant, good and bad, right and wrong. For a reader to 'suspend his disbelief' and become the appropriate reader he has not just to make himself aware of certain *facts*, but also to make all kinds of allowances – linguistic, social, moral – for the reader whom the author is addressing. An obvious *linguistic* 'allowance' is the way in which we deal with obsolete or obsolescent usage. Old-fashioned undergarments are invariably funny: the term *drawers*, when applied to articles of ladies' clothing, can hardly be used today without eliciting a grin. But the word apparently had no such comic association for James Joyce:

> Her long slender bare legs were delicate as a crane's and pure save where an emerald trail of seaweed had fashioned itself as a sign upon her flesh. Her thighs, fuller and soft-hued as ivory, were bared almost to the hips, where the white fringes of her drawers were like feathering of soft white down.
>
> [*A Portrait of the Artist as a Young Man*, Chapter 4]

In order to be able to respond sensitively to the poetic description of the girl that Stephen sees on the seashore, the modern reader must take account of changes in meaning between Joyce's usage and his own. Similarly, he will have to allow for social changes from one era to another. When Jane Austen wrote *Mansfield Park* she could assume that her readers had a view of society where the male was dominant, and where women never pushed themselves forward. Accordingly, Fanny Price never tells Edmund of her love for him, but waits passively and fearfully for him to declare that he loves her. Many readers object to Fanny's attitude, saying that she is too much of a doormat to be credible. But arguably this is to import inappropriately modern views of society into the reception of a nineteenth-century novel.

Booth has also noticed that just as there is an implied reader between the reader and the work, so there is what he has called an IMPLIED AUTHOR between the author and the text. Otherwise we would have to ascribe automatically the views expressed through a work to the author himself. But the fact that the seducer, Humbert Humbert, is given sympathetic treatment in *Lolita* does not allow us to infer that the writer, Nabokov, approves of men who take advantage of young girls. Authors may very often believe the views which they are putting forward, but there is no necessary reason why they should, and in the normal situation, where we do not know the author's views from some external source, it is not reasonable to make the transference from the work to the person who wrote it. It is this fallacy which tempted critics earlier in the twentieth century to accuse some writers of insincerity.

Just as there is a 'sincerity gap' in the production of the literary message, so there is in its reception. When Sterne in *Tristram Shandy* addresses his reader thus:

> Now in order to clear up the mist which hangs upon these three pages, I must endeavour to be as clear as possible myself.
> Rub your hands thrice across your foreheads – blow your noses – cleanse your emunctories – sneeze, my good people! – God bless you –
> Now give me all the help you can.
>
> [Vol. 9, Chapter 20]

not even the most willing of his readers is likely to carry out the instructions he is given. And it would be naive to assume that Sterne believed his readers would take him at his word and do his bidding. Literary communication does not 'take effect' in the way that non-literary messages do. As Henry Widdowson puts it:

> . . . a piece of literary discourse is in suspense from the usual process of social interaction whereby senders address messages directly to receivers. The literary message does not arise in the normal course of social activity as do other messages, it arises from no previous situation and requires no response, it does not serve as a link between people or as a means of furthering the business of ordinary social life.[2]

The discourse situation with which we are concerned is thus a rather odd, embedded one, where an *implied author* communicates a message disengaged from an immediate situational context to an addressee (*implied reader*) who cannot talk back.

We usually do not know the opinion of the real author except by inference from what he writes; and there will often be no practical need for us
to distinguish between the reader and the implied reader because we, as
readers, happen to have the requisite knowledge, beliefs and preconcep-
tions. Because of this, and for terminological ease, we refer normally to
author and *reader*. But it should always be borne in mind that *author* means
implied author and *reader* means *implied reader*:

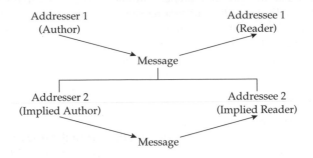

Figure 8.2

The potential conflation of these two levels of discourse is an instance of a
general principle which we elaborate below. Literary discourse can function
simultaneously on many levels, but unless there are signals to the contrary,
the reader will assume a merger of the different levels 'by default'. That is,
our interpretation of the discourse situation is as simple as is compatible
with the evidence.

8.1.2 Authors and narrators

(a) I-narrators
Authors and readers are not the only figures involved in the discourse
situation of the novel. Critics have for a long time distinguished between
the author and the narrator, and the narrator may well be talking to someone distinct from the reader. This is very clear in an I-narration novel such
as Emily Brontë's *Wuthering Heights*, which apparently takes the form of a
diary which Mr Lockwood writes to himself:

> 1801 – I have just returned from a visit to my landlord – the solitary
> neighbour that I shall be troubled with. This is certainly a beautiful
> country!
>
> [Chapter 1]

This narration itself contains long passages reporting Nellie Dean's narration of the events of the story to Mr Lockwood:

About twelve o'clock, that night, was born the Catherine you saw at Wuthering Heights: a puny, seven months' child; and two hours after the mother died, having never recovered sufficient consciousness to miss Heathcliff, or know Edgar.

[Chapter 16]

Hence the discourse structure of Nellie Dean's narration is:

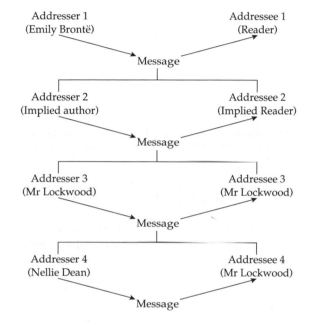

Figure 8.3

It will be noted that Mr Lockwood appears as an addressee at both level 3 and level 4 in the diagram. He is addressed by Mrs Dean at the most embedded level of discourse, and in turn addresses himself when he reports the conversation in his diary. This collapsing of levels, resulting in this case in an asymmetrical structure, is very common in novel-writing. Any one novel does not necessarily make use of all the theoretical distinctions available to it in terms of its discourse structure. For example, *David Copperfield* is narrated by an I-narrator, David, apparently to an interlocutor; but because there is no direct evidence of someone listening to David, we tend to assume that he is talking directly to us. As there is also no obvious reason to distinguish between author and implied author, and reader and implied reader in this novel, its resulting perceived discourse structure is:

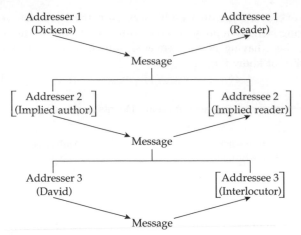

Figure 8.4
Note: Square brackets around a discourse participant indicate that that category is collapsed into the equivalent participant in the immediately superordinate level of discourse structure.

In *David Copperfield*, the collapsing on the 'addressee' side of the diagram takes place more or less by default. But sometimes we can see direct evidence of that reduction, as in 'Reader, I married him' (*Jane Eyre*, Chapter 38). Some novels make full use of the distinction between the author level and the narrator level. In Richardson's *Clarissa*, for example, there are a number of I-narrators and confidants, none of whom can be assumed to be the author or the reader.

Once it is noticed that there can be a series of narrators, each possibly associated with a different discourse structure in terms of the amount of collapsing allowed, it can be seen that novels, as discourses, can have highly individual architectures. This is especially so when we realise that a particular narrator can address different interlocutors at different points in his story, this address sometimes allowing collapsing and sometimes not. In Nabokov's *Lolita*, Humbert Humbert's addressee can be the reader, the jury at his trial, or even Lolita herself:

> Ladies and gentlemen of the jury, exhibit number one is what the seraphs, the misinformed, simple, noble-winged seraphs envied. Look at this tangle of thorns. [Part 1, Chapter 1]

> Reader! what I heard was but the melody of children at play . . .
> [Part 2, Chapter 36]

> Be true to your Dick. Do not let other fellows touch you. Do not talk to strangers. I hope that you will love your baby. I hope that it will be a boy.
> [Part 2, Chapter 36]

The choice of a first-person narrator where the 'I' is also a primary character in the story produces a personal relationship with the reader which inevitably tends to bias the reader in favour of the narrator/character. This can be seen very easily in novels like *Jane Eyre*. It is even possible by the use of this device to convert the reader to views he would not normally hold for the duration of the story (hence the need to postulate an implied reader). In *Lolita* our sympathy for Humbert Humbert can be so great that we manage to accept the murder he commits and his seduction of a minor. It is not however the case that we have total sympathy with the I-narrator whatever the deed. To see this we have only to consider Anthony Burgess's *A Clockwork Orange*:

> He was sort of flattened to the wall and his platties were a disgrace, all creased and untidy and covered in cal and mud and filth and stuff. So we got hold of him with a few good horrorshow tolchocks . . .
>
> [Part 1, Chapter 2]

Much of the fascination which this story holds comes from the clash between the sympathy determined by the first-person narration and the manner in which the actions of Alex and his friends are portrayed. It is not just the actions but also the way in which they are depicted that is important; otherwise we would not be able to condone murder in *Lolita*. Even so, it is difficult for us to accept that a tramp's untidiness is a reasonable cause to beat him up. Interestingly enough, the 'hero' of *A Clockwork Orange* is partly alienated from us by virtue of the fact that he speaks a variety of English full of very un-English looking words (*cf* section 5.4.2).

(b) Third-person narration

So far, in this section we have concentrated on novels with first-person narrators. But it is more usual for a novelist to employ an 'impersonal' style of narration, which is in the third person, i.e., where reference by the narrator to himself is avoided. This passage from George Eliot's *Middlemarch* is an example:

> Miss Brooke had that kind of beauty which seems to be thrown into relief by poor dress. Her hand and wrist were so finely formed that she could wear sleeves not less bare of style than those in which the Blessed Virgin appeared to Italian painters. [Chapter 1]

The first advantage of this third person form is that the absence of an 'I' invites the reader to assume that there is no explicit 'you'. The narration is therefore presented to the reader directly, without an intermediary. The lack of an 'I' also invites the reader to collapse the addresser side of the novel's discourse structure, so that implied author and narrator become merged. It is for this reason that most third-person narrators are, for the purposes of the fiction, omniscient: because they stand in the place of the implied author they take on his absolute knowledge. This can be seen most clearly by comparing the first- and third-person narrations in novels like *The Sound and the Fury* and *Bleak House*, which have both types within a single work. Indeed, when the third-person narrator forsakes his omniscience for some reason or other, the result is very marked. In *Bleak House*, when he is recounting the death of Mr Tulkinghorn, Dickens pretends that he does not know that the event has occurred, putting himself in the position of passer-by who realises step by step what has happened: 'What's that? Who fired a gun or pistol? Where was it?' The typical declarative structure of the narrative sentence is replaced by a series of questions in which the focus of interrogation gradually becomes more clear. The second sentence actually contains two places where information is apparently lacking, the *wh*-word, as in the other sentences, and the *or*-coordination of *gun or pistol*. Dickens seems to be unaware not only of who fired the shot, but also what kind of weapon the shot came from. He keeps up this conceit for some time, wondering what might account for the disturbance:

> Has Mr Tulkinghorn been disturbed? His windows are dark and quiet, and his door is shut. It must be something unusual indeed to bring him out of his shell. Nothing is heard of him, nothing is seen of him. What power of cannon might it take to shake that rusty old man out of his immovable composure?   [Chapter 48]

Here the question form is supplemented by the occurrence of the modal verbs *must* and *might*, expressing opinions on the possible state of affairs, and the demonstrative pronoun *that* indicating immediacy of context, as if Dickens is sharing with his reader the role of mystified onlooker.

The main feature which marks the unusual stance of the narrator in the above passage is the use of questions. We normally expect third-person narrators to relate events and descriptions by the use of statements. Questions imply both an asker and an addressee who, theoretically at least, has the power to react and reply. It is this fact which allows the question to be used by novelists to make direct addresses to the reader, inviting judgments on the events they relate and the characters they describe, or giving us opinions on the world in general:

[1] Instead of wondering at this result of misery in Mr Casaubon, I think it quite ordinary. Will not a tiny speck very close to our vision blot out the glory of the world, and leave only a margin by which we see the blot? I know no speck so troublesome as self.

[George Eliot, *Middlemarch*, Chapter 42]

George Eliot's style of narration favours the rhetorical question, which implies its own answer: 'Will not . . . ?' above implies 'Yes, it will'. Thus she appeals to the reader's own experience, inviting us to share her insight. A different kind of rhetorical question is illustrated in a later chapter of *Middlemarch*:

> The bias of human nature to be slow in correspondence triumphs even over the present quickening in the general pace of things: what wonder then that in 1832 old Sir Godwin Lydgate was slow to write a letter which was of consequence to others rather than to himself?
>
> [Chapter 65]

This style of direct address to the reader is marked off formally from the rest of the text not just by the use of rhetorical questions, but also by the change of tense from past (the norm for the relation of stories in novels) to the generic, 'timeless' present and possibly, as in the first extract, by the change from third to first person. George Eliot thus makes her presence tangibly felt, ostensibly guiding the reader towards particular judgments on characters and events. We are made aware of the fact that she is an addresser giving a message to us as addressees.

On the other hand, the author might choose not to make such intrusions, and by the consistent use of a third-person narrator 'appear to disappear'. He cannot disappear altogether, of course, because the presence of a message inevitably implies an addresser who has produced it. And it is to that addresser that we must attribute the choice of what actions are performed, what the characters say, and so on. For this reason it is misleading to argue, as Ford Maddox Ford did, that 'the novelist must not, by taking sides, exhibit his preferences. . . . He has . . . to render and not to tell.'[3] Because messages are, by their very nature, communicated by an addresser, the novelist can never really let the novel tell itself. But he can make it appear to do so, by the selection of the linguistic features that go with one mode of address rather than another.

8.1.3 Narrators and characters

In section 8.1.2 (*a*) we noted that novels can contain at least three levels of discourse embedded one inside another, operating at the levels of author and reader, implied author and implied reader, and narrator and interlocutor. But there is yet another general level of discourse in the novel which we have not yet examined, for embedded within the talk between the narrator and his interlocutor are the conversations which the characters have with one another and which that narrator reports. Hence Figure 8.5, showing the final discourse relations involved in the novel, looks like this:

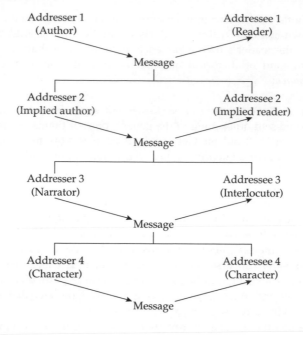

Addresser 1
(Author)

Addressee 1
(Reader)

Message

Addresser 2
(Implied author)

Addressee 2
(Implied reader)

Message

Addresser 3
(Narrator)

Addressee 3
(Interlocutor)

Message

Addresser 4
(Character)

Addressee 4
(Character)

Message

Figure 8.5

In *Nostromo*, which has a third-person omniscient narrator, the conversations between the characters are ultimately a part of the message from author to reader. Hence the following fragment of a conversation between Nostromo and his friends can be seen as yet another instantiation of his isolation (through misunderstanding) from them:

'You have done your best to kill me with fear,' cried Signora Teresa. She wanted to say something more, but her voice failed her. Linda raised her eyes to her face for a moment, but old Giorgio shouted apologetically: 'She is a little upset.'
Outside Nostromo shouted back with another laugh:
'She cannot upset me.'

[Part 1, Chapter 4]

Signora Teresa indicates her chagrin to Nostromo and he apparently misinterprets this as an attempt to throw him off balance. This is obvious in a change in the use of *upset*: Giorgio uses it as an adjective, attributing that quality to his wife, but Nostromo uses it as a verb, as if he is the affected and Signora Teresa the affecting participant.

The use of third-person narration generally separates the level of character discourse from that of narrator discourse. But the choice of a first-person narration allows a further kind of merger of roles. In *Bleak House*, the Esther Summerson narration is told through the eyes of someone who is also a character in the story. In Faulkner's *As I lay Dying* there is a whole series of I-narrations by narrator characters. A traditionally favoured device which allows a series of I-narrations from different characters is the epistolary novel, in which the fictional world is presented to the reader by a series of letters from one character to another. In all these cases, as in most I-narration novels, there is a merger of the character's and narrator's levels of discourse. This kind of conflation is very marked in the following extract from a letter by Anna Howe to Clarissa Harlowe in Richardson's *Clarissa*. Anna has locked herself in her room to write to Clarissa about Lovelace. But she is interrupted by her mother:

If this ever-active, ever-mischievous monkey of a man, this Lovelace, contrived as you suspect – But here comes my mother again (1). – Ay, stay a little longer, my mamma, if you please (2). I can but be suspected! (3). I can but be chidden for making you wait (4); and chidden I am sure to be, whether I do or not, in the way you, my good mamma, are Antony'd into (5).

Bless me! – how impatient she is! – how she thunders at the door! (6). This moment, madam (7). How came I to double-lock myself in! What have I done with the key? (8). Deuce take the key! (9). Dear Madam! You flutter one so! (10)

[Vol. 2, Letter 1]

(The numbers in parentheses refer to separate utterances made to different addressees.)

This text consists of an interlacing of remarks made directly to Clarissa about the situation, reports of what Anna says to her mother and thoughts that she addresses to herself, all (because of the pervasive use of the present tense) apparently reported at the moment they are uttered:

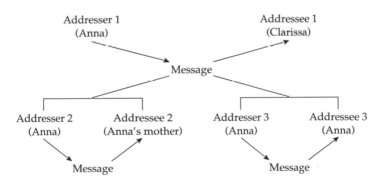

Figure 8.6

Utterances (1) and (6) are made by Anna to Clarissa. They are marked off by third-person reference to her mother (*she*, *my mother*). Utterances (2), (4), (7) and (10) are directed purportedly at her mother. They share the present tense with (1) and (6), but are characterised by the use of the second-person pronoun *you* and vocatives like *my mamma* and *madam*. (5) and (9) exhibit the formal characteristics of utterances directed by Anna to her mother, but the tone of the remarks is obviously inappropriate, and so we interpret them as remarks (i.e., thoughts) made by Anna to herself *as if* they were said to her mother. It is through utterances such as these that her antagonistic attitude towards her mother is made most explicit. Once (5) and (9) are seen to be a representation of Anna's thoughts, (2), (4), (7) and (10) can also have this interpretation of *sotto voce* apostrophe. Utterances (3) and (8) do not contain either second- or third-person reference and so are ambiguous in another respect: (3) 'I can but be suspected' could be a remark about the immediate situation made directly to Clarissa or one made to herself and reported to Clarissa by its being written down; (8) 'How came I to double-lock myself in! What have I done with the key!' is appropriate structurally either to Anna's self-directed thoughts or talk to her mother. As we assume that she locked herself in on purpose we are almost certain to rule out the former interpretation. But the formal merger of the types of 'talk' helps to suggest a conflation of the levels of discourse, which in turn is instrumental in conveying the confusion and immediacy of the situation. Indeed, even utterances which are formally ascribable to one mode become potentially double-edged. Hence (6), 'Bless me! – how impatient she is! – how she thunders at the door', which we have argued is formally marked as an address to Clarissa can at the same time be seen as an evocation of Anna's thoughts in reaction to her mother's knocking. It is clear that levels of discourse, particularly where the author withholds the signals of transition from one level to another, can be a rich source of ambiguity and complexity of interpretation.

8.2 Point of view and value language

The term 'point of view' has often been used in novel criticism to refer to the various factors of discourse situation already discussed. We can define DISCOURSAL POINT OF VIEW as the relationship, expressed through discourse structure, between the implied author or some other addresser, and the fiction. This leads on naturally to consideration of other critical terms such as *irony* (section 8.4), *tone* (section 8.5) and *distance* (section 8.5) which imply attitude and judgment. We have already seen how an author can make his attitude towards character and action clear by direct address; but the author's point of view can also be given 'bias' within the narration itself by the use of language which, either in its sense or its connotations, expresses some element of value. In this description of Mr and Mrs John Dashwood from Chapter 1 of Jane Austen's *Sense and Sensibility*, a large proportion of the nouns and adjectives (those italicised) have 'good' or 'bad' meanings:

[2] He was not an *ill-disposed* young man, unless to be rather *cold hearted*, and rather *selfish*, is to be *ill-disposed*: but he was, in general, well *respected*; he conducted himself with *propriety* in the discharge of his ordinary *duties*. Had he married a more *amiable* woman, he might have been made still more *respectable* than he was: – he might even have been made *amiable* himself; for he was very young when he married, and very *fond* of his wife. But Mrs John Dashwood was a strong *caricature* of himself; – more *narrow-minded* and *selfish*.

The author leaves us in no doubt as to her view of these two characters; and on the assumption that the author is not only omniscient on matters of 'fact', but all-seeing in matters of judgment, we are inclined to accept her word for it, and to expect her estimation to be fulfilled in later events in the novel. We learn from this paragraph that Mr Dashwood is not an admirable character, and that his wife is even less so. But looking more carefully, we can distinguish different scales or spheres of value: there is a sphere of moral disposition (*ill-disposed, cold hearted, selfish, amiable, narrow-minded*); there is also a purely social scale of accepted behaviour, of standing in the community (*respected, propriety, duties, respectable*). The only 'good' word on the moral scale is *amiable*, and since this occurs in counterfactual contexts ('Had he married . . .', 'he might have been . . .'), we conclude that amiability is *not* one of Mr Dashwood's qualities. A third evaluative sphere makes a brief appearance with the word *fond*, which is expressive of a positive emotive attitude: when we learn that John Dashwood was 'fond of his wife', this, like his respectability, acts in mitigation of his moral failings. The author's judgment of the two characters is so clearly stated that it might be diagrammed. Figure 8.7 is a simple (and much simplified) example of how an author can direct a reader's value responses to the characters and events in a novel. Simple as it is, it shows elements of complexity which will be present in a novel which claims any degree of realistic insight into character. It shows how our 'value picture' of a character, or for that matter of a whole fiction, can be built up into a composition of associated and contrasted kinds of value judgments.

A rather more complex characterisation is afforded by the beginning of Jane Austen's *Emma*. We see the events of the novel through Emma, and therefore tend to sympathise with her; but from the very first clause of the

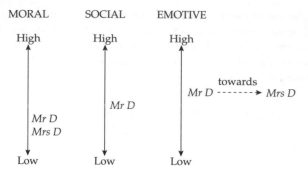

Figure 8.7

novel Jane Austen is careful to undercut an apparently glowing description of her so that we see her as attractive but by no means perfect:

[3] Emma Woodhouse, handsome, clever, and rich, with a comfortable home and happy disposition, seemed to unite some of the best blessings of existence . . .

[Chapter 1]

The three parallel adjectives which describe Emma are not all of the same type. 'Handsome' and 'clever' are merit terms and also real attributes of her. Wealth, on the other hand, is something conferred upon her by the accident of her birth. Similarly, by coordinating the parallel phrases 'comfortable home' and 'happy disposition' Jane Austen invites us to contemplate the relationship between the two states and suggests that Emma's happy disposition is at least partly a result of her comfortable home. This might also lead us to examine the possible causal relation between handsomeness, cleverness and wealth. The uneasiness that the alert reader is likely to feel after reading the subject noun phrase is underlined in the rest of the clause. The overt merit quality of 'best blessings of existence' is undermined by the rhetorical flavouring imparted to the phrase by the alliterative and assonantal patterns it exhibits. Moreover, the determiner shows that we are only dealing with 'some' of those blessings (perhaps only those conferred by the accident of birth?). In the verb phrase the factive verb *unite* is dominated by the non-factive *seem*, suggesting that all is not necessarily as it appears on the surface. Wealth, comfort, etc. do not guarantee happiness, after all, and the result is a complex, double-edged value picture of Emma.

What we have just been referring to as the VALUE PICTURE of a novel is the evaluative counterpart of the mock-reality which it conveys. As the *Emma* example shows, it is derived, like the fiction itself, not only from direct statement and attribution but from other clues. Of paramount importance in this picture are the inferences which we draw from characters' words and behaviour. If we are told, for instance, that a husband gets drunk every night and beats his wife, we cannot help disapproving of him. When Mr and Mrs Dashwood after their introduction in [2] go on to deprive Mr Dashwood's mother of her intended share of her husband's inheritance, our poor opinion of them is confirmed. If we call these 'value inferences', it seems a reasonable extension of the term 'inference' as applied to the mock-reality (section 5.2). But the area of uncertainty is greater: authors cannot rely on shared standards of judgment in quite the same way as they can rely on shared factual knowledge. Just as Jane Austen would find it difficult to come to terms with the sexual morality of *Lolita*, so modern readers may be reluctant to accept the apparent implications of the term 'respectable' for Jane Austen. Hence our value picture of a fiction depends considerably on the light in which characters and events are presented to us. The very exposure (as in *Lolita*) to a character's point of view – his thoughts, emotions, experience – tends to establish an identification with that character, and an alignment with his value picture. There appears to be an inevitable association between shared experience, understanding, sympathy and shared values: *tout comprendre, c'est tout pardonner*. But this is only one aspect of a writer's control over a reader's attitudes to the elements of the narrative: we shall examine others.

8.3 Multiplicity of values

The multifaceted nature of our value picture is a matter not only of coexisting spheres of value, but of coexisting levels of discourse. We have seen in Figure 8.5 that a novel can contain an embedded hierarchy of discourses, and that there is a potential (but not necessary) distinction between character, narrator, implied author and real author. We have also noted that unless there are clues to the contrary, these levels of discourse are conflated. The same can be said about the value pictures associated with these levels. In some novels with a first person hero, such as *David Copperfield*, there is little need to distinguish the values of the first-person character (David as child and young man), the narrator (David as adult), the implied author ('Dickens') and the real author (Dickens): they all take the same attitude, for example, in liking Peggotty and disliking Mr Murdstone.

We do not, of course, necessarily *know* what the *real* Dickens felt about his characters. But leaving aside biographical evidence of his attitudes, we must acknowledge that in spite of differences in the standards of different ages, groups and individuals, there are SHARED VALUES to which writers can appeal.

As fellow human-beings, Charles Dickens and his readers will tend to have a prejudice (to put it no higher than that) in favour of people who are kind to children, and against people who are cruel to them. Unless the real author and reader shared such prejudices, there would be no way into the value picture of the implied author, and of the novel itself.

There are, however, cases where the standards of judgment on one level contrast with those on another level. One case is that which Booth[4] calls the 'unreliable narrator', citing the example of the Jason section of Faulkner's *The Sound and the Fury*:

> 'I aint gwine let him [beat you],' Dilsey says, 'Don't you worry, honey.' She held to my arm. Then the belt came out and I jerked loose and flung her away. She stumbled into the table. She was so old she couldn't do any more than move hardly. But that's all right: we need somebody in the kitchen to eat up the grub the young ones can't tote off. She came hobbling between us, trying to hold me again. 'Hit me, den,' she says, 'ef nothin else but hitting somebody wont do you. Hit me,' she says. 'You think I won't?' I says . . .   [April Sixth, 1928]

As Jason, trying to beat his niece, is hindered by the aged servant Dilsey, neither the actions he attributes to himself nor the sentiments he expresses can be reconciled with our shared values. It is as certain that Jason is morally flawed as that Benjy in the same novel (section 6.4) is cognitively flawed. In both cases the reader's response is on two levels: we respond as interlocutors to Jason's self-incriminating monologue, and also as implied readers participating in the implied author's judgment on it. Another kind of value contrast Booth illustrates from *Emma*,[5] where the corrective to the heroine's point of view is provided in part by another character, that of the 'reliable' character Mr Knightley.

In such cases of value contrast there is what Booth calls a 'secret communion' between (implied) author and (implied) reader. This conspiracy is founded on shared standards of evaluation, and on the manner in which these are controlled and developed through the novel. It may be that the assumption of agreement between addresser and addressee is one of the features that distinguish fictional discourse from other kinds of discourse (e.g. conversation, political propaganda). It is not that we as readers cannot disagree with the values portrayed by the author, but that if we are made conscious of disagreement, this is a sign of the author's failure to carry us with him: like suspension of disbelief, suspension of dissent seems to be a sacrifice which readers are ready to accept in embarking on the adventure of reading a novel.

8.4 Irony

This 'secret communion' between author and reader is the basis of IRONY, and in fact we have no hesitation in describing as 'ironic', despite their evident differences, the effects of point of view we have identified in *The Sound and the Fury* and *Emma*. For fictional purposes irony can be defined as a double significance which arises from the contrast in values associated with two different points of view. So defined, irony is a wide-ranging phenomenon which can be manifested in a single sentence, or can extend over a whole novel. The most usual kind is that which involves a contrast between a point of view stated or implied in some part of the fiction, and the assumed point of view of the author, and hence of the reader.

On a small scale, such irony may be located in details of lexis and syntax. We have already noted this in the opening sentence of *Emma* [3], and will illustrate it further with a classically clear-cut example:

[4] Heark ye, Clinker, you are a most notorious offender – You stand *convicted of sickness, hunger, wretchedness, and want.*

[Tobias Smollett, *Humphry Clinker*, Penguin p. 113]

Here, as is often the case, irony shows itself in a 'collocative clash', that is, a combination of words which conflicts with our expectations. After 'You stand convicted of . . .', the only nouns normally allowable are names of crimes, such as *larceny, bigamy, burglary*, etc. Instead, Smollett uses words from another value set: words referring to misfortunes. So the value picture this sentence seems to present is one in which misfortune is equated with crime. This is the overt and patently unacceptable meaning; the covert meaning is the one which author and reader share by virtue of their 'secret communion': a satirical sense of the opposition between their own norms and the perverted norm to which the speaker pays lip-service. Collocative clash is also a clue to irony in:

[5] He had a good healthy sense of *meum*, and as little of *tuum* as he could help.

|Samuel Butler, *The Way of All Flesh*, Chapter 2]

'A *good healthy* sense of . . .' contains two value terms which are incompatible with the implication of selfishness in *meum*. The irony is further underlined by the antithesis of *meum* and *tuum*, and the more subtle innuendo of 'as little . . . as he could help': normally the things which we 'can't help' are unpleasant, but in this case the character restrains himself from the desirable emotion of generosity. It is worth noting here that irony derives much of its force from conventions of politeness and euphemism: the stiletto in a jewelled case is a more discreetly effective weapon than the bludgeon. In the same way, Butler's criticism gains a veneer of scholarly delicacy from the Latin words *meum* ('mine') and *tuum* ('yours').

The sequencing of impressions is also important to irony. If we run [4] or [5] in slow motion, the irony hits us as a sudden reversal of expectation, after the words 'You stand convicted of' and 'a good healthy sense of' respectively. On a slightly larger scale, this sense of 'being led up the garden path' is present in the following passage:

[6] Smith said that Roy was a time server (1). He said he was a snob (2). He said he was a humbug (3).

Smith was wrong here (4). The most shining characteristic of Alroy Kear was his sincerity (5). No one can be a humbug for five-and-twenty years (6). Hypocrisy is the most difficult and nerve-racking vice that any man can pursue; it needs an unceasing vigilance and a rare detachment of spirit (7). It cannot, like adultery or gluttony, be practised at spare moments; it is a whole-time job (8).

[Somerset Maugham, *Cakes and Ale*, Chapter 1]

The repeated parallelism 'X said that Y was a Z' in (1)–(3) is the first clue that Maugham is aiming for a rhetorical build-up. The irony would be much weaker if such patterning were eliminated, for example by the following paraphrase:

[6a] Smith was mistaken in saying that Roy was a time-server, a snob, and a humbug, for sincerity was Alroy's most shining characteristic . . .

But [6a], by its reordering, also loses the dramatic effect of gradually enticing the reader towards a sudden reversal of judgment. The way Maugham leads one by the nose in sentences (3)–(6) can be represented by the putative reactions of a naive reader:

(3) Aha! This merely confirms my impression that Roy is an absolute cad.
(4) Really? Then Roy is not so bad after all?
(5) Sincere? Surely not? You can't mean he was as exemplary as that?
(6) (sudden reversal) Ah-oh! So after all, he is a worse cad than I thought in the first place. The only reason he is sincere is that he's too *lazy* to be a hypocrite.

Moving on to sentences (7) and (8), it is once more by collocative collision that we get the full flavour of the narrator's sardonic, man-of-the-world wit. In normal usage, one 'pursues' occupations and hobbies, but hardly 'vices'; one 'practises' such things as philanthropy and self-denial, but not 'adultery' and 'gluttony'. And when we read that hypocrisy is a 'difficult and nerve-racking vice', it is as if the commission of the seven deadly sins is regarded as a duty not to be shunned. By these unorthodox juxtapositions, Maugham proposes a distortion of accepted values: VICE = VIRTUE.

In these examples, there is a clear division between what *we* think, and what the language says. But irony is too broad a term of literary appreciation to be accommodated in the formula of a satirical reversal of values. In what follows, we place irony within the more general context of TONE. Both are widely used critical terms which can benefit from definition in terms of the rhetoric of discourse.

8.5 Authorial tone

In a broad sense, AUTHORIAL TONE means 'the stance or attitude taken by an (implied) author towards his readers, and towards (parts of) his message'. If we add to this the postulate of 'secret communion', of the equivalence of authors' and readers' points of view, the essence of tone can be captured in Figure 8.8.

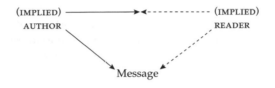

Figure 8.8

We assume here a symmetry between the attitudes the author expresses, and the attitudes elicited from the reader, as if the reader's situation is a mirror-image of the author's. It is by virtue of this symmetry that critics can reasonably talk about 'the tone of a novel' or 'the tone of a passage', thereby merging the theoretically distinct attitudes of author and reader. The symmetry is in fact not complete, but it is a useful starting point. How do we justify it?

The notion of DISTANCE is the key to this symmetry of tone. On the one hand, the authorial address to the reader may be relatively distant, formal, public, or else relatively intimate, colloquial, private. One can contrast, for instance, the authorial manner of Fielding in *Tom Jones* with that of Sterne's eponymous narrator in *Tristram Shandy*. Fielding maintains the polite distance of an eighteenth-century gentleman discoursing at ease with his public: his utmost familiarity is 'Examine your heart, my good reader...' [Book 5, Chapter 1]. But Sterne can button-hole, joke with, and cajole the reader as one would address an intimate: '...don't fly off, ... and as we jog on, either laugh with me, or at me, or in short, do anything, – only keep your temper' [Book 1, Chapter 6]. This kind of familiarity and distance is, of course, mutual: to the extent that the author is distanced from the reader, the reader is distanced from the author.

On the other hand, the relation between author and subject matter is also one of variable distance, which, as already suggested, is a function of the difference between the knowledge, sympathy and values of the implied author, and those of the characters and society which he portrays. The reader, in sharing a 'secret communion' with the author, is also assumed to share these differences. So in this respect too the two sides of Figure 8.8 balance one another.

But now let us take account of respects in which the author–reader relation is not symmetrical. As unfolder of the fiction (see section 5.5.2) the author may grant and withhold information; as ironist, he may, like Jane Austen (see p. 220) and Somerset Maugham (see p. 224), artfully delay and disguise the judgment of character. In these and other respects, the author takes the role of a guide, a mentor, or a stage-manager, controlling the reader's response. Our passages from *Dombey and Son* (section 2.7) showed how Dickens, the great stage-manager–novelist, changes his style, and thereby his tone, and so regulates the reader's sympathy and distance from one part of the novel to another. This control is most evident when the author directly addresses the reader about the contents of the fiction, as George Eliot does in Middlemarch (see p. 214). As if to forestall a response of wonderment in the reader, she rejects this response and replaces it by her own:

> Instead of wondering at this result of misery in Mr Casaubon, I think it quite ordinary.

She then resorts to one of her favourite devices of reader-control, the rhetorical question:

> Will not a tiny speck very close to our vision blot out the glory of the world, and leave only a margin by which we see the blot?

The question is a direct appeal to the reader: she invites us to agree with a general observation about human psychology, made more persuasive by its metaphorical form. If we accept the wisdom of her insight, we will also admit that Mr Casaubon's reaction to events is plausible, and so continue to accept George Eliot's guiding assessment of his character. The appeal to shared knowledge and wisdom can also be made by more unobtrusive means:

[7] Grandcourt's speeches this morning were, as usual, all of *that brief sort which never fails to make a conversational figure when the speaker is held important in his circle*. Stopping so soon, they gave signs of a suppressed and formidable ability to say more, and have also the *meritorious quality of allowing lengthiness to others*.

[George Eliot, *Daniel Deronda*, Chapter 13]

In this passage concerning the wealthy Grandcourt's courtship of Gwendolen, there are two generic propositions which invite the reader's ironic assent. Both are concealed in noun phrases. The first proposition is 'there is a brief sort of speech which never fails to make a conversational figure when the speaker is held important in his circle'; the second is: 'the quality of allowing lengthiness to others is meritorious'. By warning us that she is less impressed than Grandcourt's interlocutors by his taciturnity, George Eliot adjusts our response to what is to come. We are given a presentiment of the brutish disposition to which Gwendolen, soon to embark on a disastrous marriage, is blind.

To illustrate the subtlety of flexibility and authorial tone, we can do no better than to draw further exemplification from George Eliot's technique in this same novel. The stylistic ingredients of this technique include those already noticed: evaluative terms and evaluative inferences; ironic contrast and reversal; direct appeal to the reader through rhetorical questions and the like; indirect appeal to the reader through generic statements and other references to a commonality of experience and judgment. All these lead to a complex weighing up of one attitude against another, especially of sympathetic identification against ironic distance. The authorial tone is subtle, complex and variable in a way which gives solidity to the presence of the implied author, George Eliot *qua* novelist, whose involvement with the fiction seems to strive for a resolution of the competing claims of charity, truth and justice to all.

Authorial tone, like authorial point of view, therefore takes on a multiplicity of values. The irony of [7] is only one point in a spectrum of tone, which can extend in theory from pure compassion to pure denunciation, but in practice contains some measure, however slight, of both. Similarly, irony is not all of one piece, but can register varying degrees of distance or severity, ranging from a satirical bitterness to a benevolent awareness of the contradictory impulses which can undermine good intentions in even the best-motivated of characters. Somewhere between these two poles we would place the following passage, in which Eliot describes Gwendolen's uncle Mr Gascoigne:

[8] He had some agreeable virtues, some striking advantages, and the failings that were imputed to him all leaned toward the side of success (1).
    One of his advantages was a fine person, which perhaps was even more impressive at fifty-seven than it had been earlier in life (2). There were no distinctively clerical lines in the face, no official reserve or ostentatious benignity of expression, no tricks of starchiness or of affected ease: in his Inverness cape he could not have been identified except as a gentleman with handsome dark features, a nose which began with an intention to be aquiline but suddenly became straight, and iron-grey hair (3). Perhaps he owed this freedom from the sort of professional

make-up which penetrates skin tones and gestures and defies all drapery, to the fact that he had once been Captain Gaskin, having taken orders and a diphthong but shortly before his engagement to Miss Armyn (4). If anyone objected that his preparation for the clerical function was inadequate, his friends might have asked who made a better figure in it, who preached better or had more authority in his parish? (5). He had a native gift for administration, being tolerant both of opinions and conduct, because he felt himself able to overrule them, and was free from the irritations of conscious feebleness (6). . . . Indeed, the worst imputation thrown out against him was worldliness: it could not be proved that he forsook the less fortunate, but it was not denied that the friendships he cultivated were of a kind likely to be useful to the father of six sons and two daughters; and bitter observers – for in Wessex, say ten years ago, there were persons whose bitterness may now seem incredible – remarked that the colour of his opinions had changed in consistency with this principle of action (7). But cheerful, successful worldliness has a false air of being more selfish than the acrid unsuccessful kind, whose secret history is summed up in the terrible words, 'Sold, but not paid for' (8).

[*Daniel Deronda*, Chapter 3]

If we call this a three-dimensional description of character, the geometric metaphor is not ill-founded, since the impression of seeing Mr Gascoigne 'in the round' comes from the convergence of different points of view on a single object. There are three points of view: first, the overtly sympathetic stance of the author, who is determined to see Mr Gascoigne in the best light that is compatible with the evidence; second, the negative attitude imputed to 'bitter observers'; and, third, the implied author's point of view which emerges from the balancing of these sympathetic and unsympathetic assessments: this is the point of view we arrive at in appreciating that George Eliot is being simultaneously sympathetic and ironic.

The first sentence gives this three-fold impression in a nutshell. It coordinates two terms for good qualities (*virtues, advantages*) with one for bad qualities (*failings*); but the *failings* are only *imputed*, and are mitigated by their association with another positive value term: *success*. On the surface, therefore, the author acknowledges only what is good in Mr Gascoigne, while also acknowledging that others might think differently. Less prominent, however, are the clues of irony. A man of God is naturally to be evaluated in terms of *virtues* rather than *advantages*, and yet the adjective which modifies the former, *agreeable*, is one of social rather than moral commendation; while *striking*, which modifies *advantages*, is the more forceful adjective. Already there is a suspicion that worldly values are more appropriate than other-worldly values to a favourable estimate of the rector. But more damning than this is the term *success*, which is purely worldly, and might be judged, from a strict Christian standpoint, to detract from, rather than enhance, Mr Gascoigne's qualities as a clergyman. Yet by linking this to the other qualities by *and*, George Eliot appears to add it to the positive side of the balance sheet. It is at this point that the approbatory portrait begins to be significantly tarnished, and this process continues into the next paragraph, where we discover that the 'advantages' worthy of first mention are matters of outward appearance and demeanour, in which Mr Gascoigne's unrectorly qualities are singled out for commendation. We find that the author, to praise this cleric, has had to adopt a somewhat anti-clerical attitude.

We shall not pursue this analysis further, but will merely note that the undercurrent of irony persists through the passage, and can be traced in the small details of language; most bluntly, perhaps, in the ill-assorted, sylleptic coordination of 'had taken *orders* and a *diphthong*' in (4). But the charitable portrait of Mr Gascoigne is not altogether effaced, and we are free to discount, if we wish, the 'incredible bitterness' of those who would calumniate him. The ultimate effect is one of an equitable balance of attitudes.

8.6 Conclusion

In examining fiction-writing as discourse between author and reader, we have reached the outer limit of the study of style. All other levels of stylistic choice presuppose the choices which the author makes regarding discourse; that is, regarding his involvement with the reader in the fiction. The stylistic values we have directly considered in this connection are those of point of view, distance and tone. These concern the question: What does the (implied) author mean by (i.e., mean us to understand by) the fiction? And because of the assumed 'communion' between author and reader, this question becomes indistinguishable in practice from that of 'What does the reader understand the author to mean by it?' But since the significance of the literary artefact as a whole is interpreted in discourse terms, stylistic values at all levels become, in the final analysis, contributions to the way a literary work is interpreted as a transaction between author and reader.

This viewpoint is readily appreciated in the case of 'intrusive authors' such as George Eliot, who explicitly take on the role of guide, presenter and interpreter. What is less obvious is that even in novels where the author forgoes the right to direct our response in this way, the implications of authorial presence – of point of view, distance, tone – are still in play. We are justified, for example, in saying that Joyce's technique is ironic when he treats the sordidly mundane affairs of Gerty MacDowell in a style which is a pastiche of pulp romantic fiction:

Style in Fiction

The summer evening had begun to fold the world in its mysterious embrace . . .
His eyes misty with unshed tears Master Tommy came to her call for their big sister's word was law with the twins . . .
Cissy's quick motherwit guessed what was amiss and she whispered to Edy Boardman to take him there behind the pushcar where the gentlemen couldn't see and to mind he didn't wet his new tan shoes.

[James Joyce, *Ulysses*, Penguin, pp. 344–346]

The difference between the 'interfering' author and the 'disappearing' one is not that the one exists in the novel while the other does not, but rather that the one declares his presence directly, while the other does so only through the inferences we inevitably draw from the way the fiction is presented. It is simply a question of different styles of discourse.

Our study of style would end here if it were not the case that discourse has its own hierarchical complexity, as shown in Figure 8.5. We turn, in the next two chapters, to the way the 'subdiscourses' of monologue and conversation are interpreted as parts of the overarching discourse which is the novel itself.

Notes

1. W.C. BOOTH (1961), 138–9. See also W. ISER (1974) and (1978), 27–38.
2. H. G. WIDDOWSON (1975), 51.
3. FORD MADDOX FORD, *The English Novel: from the earliest days to the death of Joseph Conrad* (1930), 121, quoted in BOOTH (1961), 25.
4. See BOOTH (1961), 306–8.
5. BOOTH (1961), Chapter 9.

Conversation in the novel

In the last chapter we noted that the novel consists of a series of discourse situations, one embedded inside another, where addressers produce messages for addressees. The most deeply embedded of these levels, where character talks to character, is unlike the others in that the messages can be passed in either direction. Interchange at this level is also an important feature to consider if only because large portions of almost any novel consist of talk between characters. But as we shall see in section 9.3, an analysis of how characters communicate with one another can also contribute to our understanding of the higher-level, one-sided 'conversation' between author and reader.

What follows is an interpretation, for stylistic purposes, of some recent work by linguists, philosophers and others, on the subject of conversation.

9.1 Pragmatics and the interpretation of conversation

Some parts of conversations are pretty unremarkable, and can be understood almost entirely from our knowledge of syntax and lexis. The following fragment, for example, comes from E.M. Forster's short story *The Celestial Omnibus*:

'About when do you start?' He tried to sound nonchalant.
'At sunrise.'
'How far do you go?'
'The whole way.'
'And can I have a return ticket which will bring me all the way back?'
'You can.'

The boy in the story asks perfectly straightforward questions of the driver of the celestial omnibus, and receives tailor-made answers. The situation itself is odd, because the bus is bound for heaven, but the question and answer sequence is ordinary enough. So, in its way, is the following conversation between Nicholas Urfe and Mr Conchis from *The Magus* by John Fowles:

> 'I shall see you next spring then?'
> 'Perhaps.'
> 'I have a two-year contract at the school.'
> 'Ah.' ...
> ... 'Will she be here next year?'
> 'You will not see her.'
> 'But will she be here?'

> [first edn, Chapter 55]

Nicholas asks questions, and the mysterious Mr Conchis provides the answers. But this time there is an obvious undercurrent to the conversation, perceived by both reader and characters. Mr Conchis never gives a straight answer. The declarative form of Nicholas's first query expects confirmation, but Conchis's reply is totally neutral. When Nicholas supports his first remark with evidence that he will still be on the island, thus indicating that it is likely that they will meet again if Conchis intends to return, Conchis does not reply at all, but merely shows that he has understood what has been said. Later on, when Nicholas asks whether the girl he has known as Julie will be there the following year, Conchis is also evasive. If she will not be there it follows naturally that Nicholas will not see her. But the fact that Nicholas will not see her does not, of course, imply that she will not be there. Conchis has again given nothing away, and Nicholas obviously realises this when he repeats his question 'But will she be here?' The repeated pattern allows the reader, like Nicholas, to *deduce* that Conchis is being evasive and that Nicholas cannot be sure that he will meet either Conchis or Julie again. The conversation thus instantiates one of *The Magus*'s major thematic preoccupations. Throughout the novel Nicholas repeatedly attempts and fails to follow the two mystery characters and solve the riddle of their identity and role.

The conversation between the two characters in *The Magus* is ordinary enough. It could easily occur in real life. But notice that the value we have stated for Conchis's remarks cannot be arrived at merely through an understanding of the syntactic and lexical structure of the exchange. We also have to use PRAGMATIC interpretative strategies. Indeed, even the Forster example may no longer seem as simple as at first sight. The reply 'the whole way' is only a precise enough answer to the question 'How far do you go?' if it can be assumed that both participants know the destination of the bus, an assumption which is somewhat open to doubt in the story. In order to understand the interaction of character and character in dialogue, then, it will be useful to see how we can profitably apply the work of those who have developed the pragmatic analysis of ordinary conversation.

9.1.1 Speech acts

The pragmatic analysis of language can be broadly understood to be the investigation into that aspect of meaning which is derived not from the formal properties of words and constructions, but from the way in which utterances are used and how they relate to the context in which they are uttered. One important concept which relates utterance meaning to context is that of the SPEECH ACT, as developed by J.L. Austin and J.R. Searle.[1] Since Searle's work is the more recent, we will confine our attention to his kind of analysis. Searle's starting point is the observation that when people utter sentences they also perform *acts* of various kinds, such as declaring, asking, requesting, commanding, promising and so on. Sometimes the kind of act performed is made obvious by the presence of a *performative* verb as in the request 'I *beg* you to come here'. However, this is not usually the case: 'Please come here' is as much a request as 'I ask you to come here', and is more likely to occur in actual conversation. Speech acts, as this example already shows, are in principle independent of syntactic and semantic categories; for example, to make a request, we may use many different syntactic forms, which overtly, in their semantic content, mean different things:

[1] Please come here   (imperative)
[2] Could you come here   (interrogative)
[3] I'd like you to come here   (declarative)

In most contexts sentences [1]–[3] would have approximately the same force as speech acts, although they have different syntactic forms, and differ in sense and tone. We must therefore keep separate the pragmatic force of an utterance and its semantic sense. While semantics is concerned with the representation through the language system of referential 'reality' (see sections 5.1–5.3), pragmatics is concerned with the enactment, through language, of 'situational reality'. The two 'realities' are not totally distinct, of course, and in fact it is the function of an important class of elements called DEICTICS (*this, that, here, there, now, then, I, you*, present and past tenses, etc.) to refer directly or indirectly to elements of the situation.

To see the relevance of speech act analysis to our understanding of conversation in the novel we will examine a passage from Jane Austen's *Pride and Prejudice*. Mrs Bennet, whose zeal for matchmaking has been frustrated by her daughter's rebuff of Mr Collins, addresses her unsympathetic husband:

[4] 'O Mr Bennet, you are wanted immediately; we are all in an uproar. You must come and make Lizzy marry Mr Collins, for she vows she will not have him, and if you do not make haste he will change his mind and not have *her* . . . (1)

'I have not the pleasure of understanding you,' said he, when she had finished her speech. 'Of what are you talking?' (2)

'Of Mr Collins and Lizzy. Lizzy declares she will not have Mr Collins, and Mr Collins begins to say that he will not have Lizzy.' (3)

'And what am I to do on the occasion? . . . It seems a hopeless business.' (4)

'Speak to Lizzy about it yourself. Tell her that you insist upon her marrying him.' (5)

Mr Bennet rang the bell, and Miss Elizabeth was summoned to the library.

'Come here, child,' cried her father as she appeared. 'I have sent for you on an affair of importance. I understand that Mr Collins has made you an offer of marriage. Is it true?' (6)

Elizabeth replied that it was (7). 'Very well – and this offer of marriage you have refused?' (8)

'I have, sir.' (9)

'Very well. We come to the point. Your mother insists upon your accepting it. (10) Is it not so, Mrs Bennet?' (11)

'Yes, or I will never see her again.' (12)

'An unhappy alternative is before you, Elizabeth. From this day you must be a stranger to one of your parents. Your mother will never see you again if you do *not* marry Mr Collins, and I will never see you again if you *do*. (13)

[Chapter 20]

(Our numbers here indicate not sentences, but conversational 'turns' delimited by a change of speaker or addressee.)

Suppose we were asked to report this dialogue to another person, without directly quoting each speech. We could do so by turning it into a stylised indirect speech (see section 10.1.1), using speech act verbs to convey roughly the interpersonal force of what is said:

Mrs Bennet TOLD Mr Bennet that he was wanted . . . ;
she then EXHORTED him to make Lizzy marry . . . ;
and she EXPLAINED to him that Lizzy vowed she would not have Mr Collins . . . ;
She WARNED him that if he did not make haste . . . (1);
Mr Bennet CLAIMED that he did not understand . . . ;
He ASKED her what she was talking about . . . (2);
Mrs Bennet REPEATED that . . . (3)

Such a rendering gives some idea of the ongoing nature of the linguistic transactions between Mr and Mrs Bennet, and indeed it appears that we as readers must perform an analysis of this kind in order to understand what is going on in the passage; but as it stands it does not take us very far. One problem is that the labels attached to the speech acts are to some extent arbitrary – there is, as we shall see, no one-to-one correspondence between speech act verbs and the pragmatic force of speech acts. Another drawback is that much of the significance of what is said lies in overtones which are too subtle to be captured by this type of paraphrase.

What the analysis does show is that a speech act is not necessarily embodied in a sentence or in a speech by a single character: speech acts, as units on the pragmatic level of analysis, do not have to correspond to easily recognisable units of syntactic or textual analysis. Moreover, the concept of the speech act becomes more useful when we consider that every speech act has conditions of appropriateness (or FELICITY CONDITIONS). For example, there is something inappropriate and slightly absurd (even to Jane Austen and her contemporaries) about Mrs Bennet's bidding her husband to order Elizabeth to marry. One cannot reasonably order someone to do something unless one is in a position to do so (a private cannot order a general) and unless what is demanded is feasible (you cannot order someone to leap over a house). In this case it is not at all obvious that a wife can normally order her husband, nor that a father can force a daughter to marry against her will. However, the felicity conditions for speech acts may change from one society or time to another: a hundred years ago it would have been unreasonable to order someone to fly to Paris. In contrast there have, at least until recently, been societies or parts of societies where it was thought reasonable for fathers to order their daughters to marry. To appreciate the force of Mr and Mrs Bennet's remarks, we have to adjust to the norms of their age and culture.

Speech acts also have conditions of success; a command or a question is successful if it elicits an appropriate response. Thus the first part of Mrs Bennet's demand 'speak to Lizzie . . . yourself' (5) is acceded to, but the second part 'Tell her that you insist . . .' is not. Instead, Mr Bennet merely asks his wife to confirm, in Elizabeth's presence, that *she* insists on the marriage. This she does, reinforcing her earlier remark with a threat: 'Yes, or I will never see her again' (12). The threat is capped by Mr Bennet at the end of the passage, when with mischievous humour, he imposes a counterthreat on his daughter, thus placing Elizabeth in a comic dilemma, and foiling his wife's demand.

The ironic turn of this last sentence is the stronger because up to that time Mr Bennet has given no hint that he will not take his wife's part. He has already, however, implied a disbelief of his wife's earlier explanation, by cross-examining his daughter on the information his wife has already given him. Thus, throughout the passage, the conditions of success for

Mrs Bennet's speech acts are unfulfilled: her demand is ignored, her assertions are (by implication) doubted, and her threat is finally thwarted.

9.1.2 Conversational implicature

Just as in semantics, so in pragmatics, much of what we learn comes from inferences from the language, rather than from what is openly said. When Mr Bennet says 'Of what are you talking?' (2) we can conclude either that he has not heard or understood what his wife has said (something which would follow directly from the appropriateness conditions of questions), or we can conclude that he is pretending not to understand (either as an ironic reflection on his wife's incoherence, or because the news is so surprising). A similar ambivalence attaches to his next question 'And what am I to do on the occasion?' (4) which might be a genuine request for advice or, more likely, a rhetorical question with the implied force 'There is nothing I *can* do'. In either case, he brings into doubt the assumptions which underlie Mrs Bennet's quasi-imperative, 'You must come and make Lizzy marry Mr Collins' (2). Mr Bennet's subsequent questions ('Is it true?' (6), 'Very well – and this offer of marriage you have refused?' (8). 'Is it not so, Mrs Bennet?' (11)) are also somewhat out of the ordinary, since they require confirmation of facts of which he has already been apprised. From what we have learned, both here and elsewhere, of Mr Bennet's character and his relations with his wife, it is more likely that we will read into these questions more than they appear to mean: they are not mere innocent requests for information. In such cases, the 'extra meanings' that we infer, and which account for the gap between overt sense and pragmatic force, may be called IMPLICATURES.

The term 'implicature' was proposed by the philosopher H.P. Grice. He suggested that when people converse with one another they acknowledge a kind of tacit agreement to cooperate conversationally towards mutual ends. This agreement he calls the COOPERATIVE PRINCIPLE. When one abides by the cooperative principle one conforms to various rules, or MAXIMS, as Grice calls them. One must tell the truth, and make remarks which are relevant to the conversation, for example. Grice suggested four conversational maxims:

(i) *The maxim of quantity*
   Give the required amount of information – not too much or too little.
(ii) *The maxim of quality*
   Do not say that for which you lack evidence or which you believe to be false.
(iii) *The maxim of relation*
   Make your contributions relevant to the purpose in hand.
(iv) *The maxim of manner*
   Avoid obscurity, ambiguity and unnecessary prolixity, and be orderly.[2]

The important point about these conversational maxims is that unlike *rules* (e.g., grammatical rules) they are often violated. In this sense they are *rhetorical principles* (*cf* our remarks in section 7.1). Sometimes the violations may be clandestine, as when someone tells a lie and is not found out by the hearer; but, more important, the maxims are also broken ostentatiously, so that it is obvious to all of the participants in the conversation. When this happens the listener perceives the difference between what the speaker says and what he means by what he says, the particular meaning deduced for the latter being the implicature. Let us examine a simple example from Agatha Christie's *Destination Unknown* [Chapter 1]:

'What about the wife – you've tried her?'
'Several times.'
'Can't she help?'
The other shrugged his shoulders.
'She hasn't so far.'
'You think she knows something?'

Jessop's answer to Wharton's first question is perfectly straightforward. However, his response to the second breaks the maxims of quantity and manner (it is quite common for a contribution to a conversation to break more than one maxim at a time). It breaks the maxim of manner because if he had the information asked for, *yes* or *no* would have been the shortest and most uncomplicated reply. The maxim of quantity is broken because Jessop does not give as informative an answer as he might. 'She can't help' would have entailed the actual reply, but 'She hasn't helped' does not entail 'She can't help'. One good reason for breaking one of the maxims is to avoid violating one of the others. In this case Wharton notices that Jessop is apparently breaking the cooperative principle and interprets this violation as being necessitated by his not breaking the maxim of quality. Jessop is not sure of the answer and therefore cannot truly reply *yes* or *no*. Wharton reasonably concludes from his colleague's reply not only that the woman has not helped so far but also that she might be of some use in the future. In real life the deduction of implicatures is often aided by the use of kinesic signals – e.g., gestures like eyebrow-raising or head movement. If someone says 'John is being very helpful today' and raises his eyebrows at the same time, he can suggest that John has an ulterior motive for his action. In this case Agatha Christie gives us the kinesic information ('shrugged his shoulders') in her narrative description, thus helping us to understand Jessop's implicature. The two characters are obeying the cooperative principle even though maxims are being violated.

Another example which appears to break both the maxims of manner and quantity comes later in *Destination Unknown*:

'He's supposed to be a cousin by marriage of Tom Betterton.'
'Supposed?'
'Let us say, more correctly, that if he is who he says he is, he is a cousin of the late Mrs Betterton.'   [Chapter 4]

Again, in order to avoid breaking the maxim of quality by saying 'he is a cousin by marriage of Tom Betterton', which he suspects is false, Jessop uses a more complex and less definite locution. Hilary Craven echoes the added part of the sentence in order to indicate that she has understood the implicature, and to ask for further clarification. Although this particular strategy is not really covered by Grice's maxims, it can be treated in an analogous fashion. Typically people employ echo questions to indicate that they are not sure whether they have heard or understood the relevant part of the previous remark properly. There is no obvious reason to suppose that Hilary has not heard the sentence correctly, or that it is difficult for her to understand. Hence we, like Jessop, treat the echo as a request for more explicit information.[3]

The breaking of the maxims of quantity and quality can be seen in the following extract from *Wuthering Heights* where Nelly Dean and Isabella are talking about Heathcliff:

'Hush, hush! He's a human being,' I said. 'Be more charitable; there are worse men than he is yet!'
'He's not a human being,' she retorted, 'and he has no claim on my charity. I gave him my heart, and he took and pinched it to death, and flung it back to me.'   [Chapter 17]

When Nelly Dean calls Heathcliff a 'human being' she breaks the maxim of quantity by stating what is self-evidently true and therefore redundant. The implicature, made apparent by what follows, is that he deserves to be treated with the sympathy and consideration that human beings usually afford to each other. Isabella breaks the maxim of quality a number of times by uttering what is literally untrue, namely that Heathcliff is not a human being, and that he has torn out her heart and killed it. It is through the implicative force of metaphor and hyperbole that she indicates the extent of her ill-treatment by her husband and the depth of her resentment towards him.

A further example of a statement which is self-evidently untrue is Leamas's reply to Liz in John Le Carré's *The Spy Who Came in From the Cold*, when she asks him if he has any feelings for the innocent East German to whose death he has contributed:

'But what about Fiedler – don't you feel anything for him?'
'This is a war,' Leamas replied.   [Chapter 25]

Here Leamas breaks not only the maxim of quality, but also the maxim of relation, by not answering the question. But on a deeper level, via the maxims of relation and quality, we see that he does answer it: by saying that there is a war when there is not, and also when it is not relevant he implicates that having feelings for victims in espionage is, as in war, inappropriate, and that he must not allow himself to have them. It is apparent that Liz understands this when she comments 'You don't want to. You're trying to persuade yourself.'

The interpretation of implicatures assumes that the cooperative principle is only superficially violated: at a deeper level it is being obeyed. But it is open to the participants to violate the principle more fundamentally; to decide not to cooperate. One example of this is Mabel's refusal to reply to her brother in *The Horse Dealer's Daughter*, quoted in Chapter 5 (see p. 131). Another is the conversation from *The Magus*, in this chapter (see p. 232): there Conchis was clearly not giving as much information as Nicholas felt he could, and it was this fact that allowed him (and the reader) to deduce that Conchis was being evasive. This refusal to play the cooperative game can also be seen in Alan Sillitoe's *The Loneliness of the Long Distance Runner*, when the detective quizzes Smith on the break-in that has just taken place in Papplewick Street. Both participants know that Smith is responsible, and also that the policeman cannot prove it:

> 'Well, you know where Papplewick Street is, don't you?' the copper asked me taking no notice of mam.
> 'Ain't it off Alfreton Road?' I asked him back, helpful and bright.
> 'You know there's a baker's half-way down on the left-hand side, don't you?'
> 'Ain't it next door to a pub, then?' I wanted to know. He answered me sharp: 'No, it bloody well ain't ' Coppers always lose their tempers as quick as this . . .
>
> [W.H. Allen, 1975, p. 31]

Each time the policeman invites Smith to give him information which they both know he has at his disposal, Smith avoids giving him the answer by pretending to make guesses which they both know are incorrect. The overtones of this extract can only be accounted for by combining Grice's analysis with Searle's conception of speech acts. The policeman makes queries using negative tag questions ('. . . don't you . . . don't you . . .'). This is a kind of speech act which combines assertion and interrogation: the policeman states what he believes to be true, and invites Smith to confirm it. A felicity condition of such a speech act is that the speaker believes that both he and the hearer know the answer to the question. But instead of confirming as required, Smith replies in his turn by asking questions – thus denying the premise of shared knowledge on which the policeman's interrogation is based. The detective's loss of temper is easily understood when we realise that Smith has turned the tables on him, posing questions where, in his role of suspect, he should be giving answers.

Two important points have been illustrated in these passages of dialogue. One is that Gricean implicature can be seen as the basis, in ordinary conversation, of traditional rhetorical figures such as metaphor, hyperbole and irony. Such figures are, negatively speaking, ways of 'failing to say what one means', and the motivation for such obliquity lies in interpersonal factors which are at odds with the principle of cooperation: factors of attitude, tension and conflict. A second point is that pragmatic force is not so much a function of the situation itself objectively considered, as of the way participants construe the situation. Besides a 'model of reality', participants in a discourse also construct a 'model of context' which includes their conceptions of relations with the interlocutor. Implicatures are contributions which are made to this 'model' as conversation proceeds. When characters are at cross-purposes (as in the Sillitoe passage), their models are at variance. Such variance is the basis of the dramatic interest in conversational dialogue.

9.2 Pragmatics and thought

Because thoughts are addressed to oneself or to the void it might seem, at first sight, that pragmatic analysis would not be able to aid significantly our understanding of the flow of character thought. But although there can be, by definition, no interlocutor when minds are depicted, writers often represent them as if there were. In this way thought becomes a form of suspended action; or even a form of suspended *interaction* between characters:

> That girl, thought Mrs Dempster (who saved crusts for the squirrels and often ate her lunch in Regent's Park), don't know a thing yet (1). . . . She had had a hard time of it, and couldn't help smiling at a girl like that (2). You'll get married, for you're pretty enough, thought Mrs Dempster (3). Get married, she thought, and then you'll know (4). . . . For really, what with eating, drinking, and mating, the bad days and good, life had been no mere matter of roses (5). . . . But, she implored, pity. Pity, for the loss of roses. Pity she asked of Maisie Johnson, standing by the hyacinth beds (6).
>
> [Virginia Woolf, *Mrs Dalloway*, Hogarth Press, 1976 edn, p. 31]

Mrs Dempster is pondering the figure of Maisie Johnson, whom she can see across the park. At a number of points that reflection takes the form of self-address. In (1), for example, Mrs Dempster appears to be giving herself information. In conversation, a speaker (A) will only give his interlocutor

(B) information, if he believes that B does not already have it, and needs to know it. In this case, Mrs Dempster must already have the information in order to convey it to herself, and because of this we conclude that Virginia Woolf is trying to depict not just a character 'talking' to herself, but also a series of realisations, which as they surface, appear to the thinker to be particularly significant. At other places Mrs Dempster thinks in a form which makes her appear to address Maisie. She apparently *advises* Maisie that she will get married (3), and *warns* her that it is not a good idea (4). Making the thought process conversational in this way makes it seem conscious and palpable, and as the speech acts which occur here are of the kind which are used normally to effect action by another person or to arouse a response in others (i.e., to change the world, however slightly), Mrs Dempster's mind seems peculiarly active. In Virginia Woolf's novels this often results in a stark contrast between inner and outer reality. It does so when at the end of this passage Mrs Dempster apparently *pleads* with Maisie. This strong emotional activity (heightened by other features, such as lexical repetition) is juxtaposed with information about the physical world ('standing by the hyacinth beds' (6)) depicted in obviously static terms.

Even when there is no apparent addressee for a character's thoughts, pragmatic analysis can still be a useful tool of interpretation. The maxim of relation is particularly pertinent in describing the sequencing of apparently unrelated pieces of information in Joyce's 'stream of consciousness' writing:

[5] A kidney oozed bloodgouts on the willowpatterned dish: the last (1). He stood by the nextdoor girl at the counter (2). Would she buy it too, calling the items from a slip in her hand (3). Chapped: washing soda (4). And a pound and a half of Denny's sausages (5). His eyes rested on her vigorous hips (6). Woods his name is (7). Wonder what he does (8). Wife is oldish (9). New blood (10). No followers allowed (11).

[*Ulysses*, Penguin edn, p. 61]

After two sentences of narrative – except perhaps for 'the last' in (1) – this passage slips into an internal representation of Leopold Bloom's thoughts. Sentence (4) is extremely truncated, consisting merely of a participial adjective and a noun phrase. This discourse is not really structured for a listener, breaking the maxims of quantity and manner; and it is via the maxim of relation that we formulate the hypothesis that Bloom is observing that it is the girl's hands that are chapped, and that this was caused by washing soda. Sentence (5), 'And a pound and a half of Denny's sausages' clearly breaks the maxim of relation in spite of its apparently cohesive initial *and*. We can no longer relate this sentence to the immediately previous one, but must assume that Joyce is obeying the cooperative principle even if Bloom is not. The coordinator helps us to interpret the sentence as an item from the girl's shopping list, which happens to be overheard by Bloom at this point and therefore impinges on his consciousness. Bloom's visual perception of the girl's hips in (6) is followed by a remark totally unrelated to any of the previous sentences; but the maxim of relation demands that it be made relevant. This requirement can be met by our assuming that Bloom's focus of attention has now moved from the kitchen girl to her employer.

Another major jump in topic occurs between sentences (9) and (10), 'Wife is oldish. New blood.' This example deserves special attention because there are two possible ways of making it cohere with the surrounding text. We could interpret (10), via lexical repetition, as another perception of the kidneys referred to in (1). Alternatively, Bloom may be thinking that as Woods's wife is 'oldish', he may be having sexual relations with his servant. This hypothesis is strengthened by 'No followers allowed' (11), a common phrase of Joyce's time to indicate that female servants were not allowed men friends. Even so, the associative connection with the meat in the butcher's shop is not totally removed, and we may even surmise that the phrase comes into Bloom's mind partly because of his being in the butcher's shop. This ambiguity with its richness of suggestion makes one wonder if Grice's inclusion of the injunction 'avoid ambiguity' in the maxim of manner is adequately formulated to cope with literary prose. But it is apparent that the maxim of relation is essential to our understanding as sensitive readers. On the surface this passage could hardly be called a coherent 'text'. But if we assume (as a cooperative reader must) that Joyce is obeying the cooperative principle, we construe the apparently unrelated observations in a manner which does allow a uniform interpretation. It is by trading on the maxim of relation that Joyce is able to depict the stream of a character's mind, skipping associatively from one perception or thought to the next.

9.3 'Conversation' between authors and readers

It will be clear from our discussion of the *Ulysses* passage [5] in particular, that the pragmatic model of understanding can apply not only to character–character discourse, but also to the way in which authors convey messages to their readers. Indeed, because the novel is a written form, it is arguable that adherence to the cooperative principle must be assumed even more strongly than for everyday talk exchanges: because the writer has plenty of time to choose exactly what to say, there should be no glaring errors, and criticism assumes as a starting point that everything in the novel 'counts'. Sometimes an author conveys what he wants to say directly, and sometimes via interchange between characters. In both kinds of case we can expect conversational implicatures and other inferential strategies to be used.

The employment of sentences in the generic present (see section 8.5) is a clear example of author–reader implicature. When the author breaks away from the narrative past, and adopts the aphoristic present tense, we must assume some relevance to the narrative: e.g., that the narrative illustrates the general truth in question. It is with such a sentence that Jane Austen begins *Pride and Prejudice*:

> It is a truth universally acknowledged that a single man in possession of a good fortune must be in want of a wife.

But here the implicatures are less direct. Surely no one can accept such a 'truth' as 'universally acknowledged'. In other words, Jane Austen breaks the maxim of quality. So how do we make sense of what she says? We assume that the author is speaking ironically, and understand her roughly as follows: 'Although this is not a universal truth, the social conventions of money and marriage are such that a lot of people go about behaving as if it were true.' This sets the tone for the rest of the novel, so that when we see Mrs Bennet trying to marry off her daughters to any moneyed man within sight, we recognise the norm of behaviour that is being satirised.

The reader is thus invited, in a novel, to draw implicatures both from character speech and authorial commentary. But this two-level response also leads to a third kind of implicature; one that is derived by the reader from character speech, very often in circumstances where the characters themselves may be assumed not to be 'in the know'. This is the novelistic equivalent of what on the stage is often referred to as 'dramatic irony'. One example occurs at the beginning of Dorothy Parker's story *Here We Are*:[4]

> 'Well!' the young man said.
> 'Well!' she said.
> 'Well, here we are,' he said.
> 'Here we are,' she said. 'Aren't we?'
> 'I should say we were,' he said. 'Eeyop. Here we are.'
> 'Well!' she said.
> 'Well!' he said. 'Well. How does it feel to be an old married lady?'

Here the two newlyweds are so embarrassed by their situation that they can produce nothing but informationless sentences: phatic communion. It is not, however, obvious that either of them is aware of the other's hesitancy; they are *expressing*, rather than *implicating*, embarrassment. In ordinary conversation, then, phatic communion would seem to be a counter-example to Grice's theory; the maxim of quantity is broken in such talk not to convey implicatures; rather, phatic communion is a way of expressing social cohesion, starting off conversations, and the like. But at the level of the interchange between author and reader an implicature does pass. It is the reader who notes the breach of the quantity maxim and interprets this as embarrassment.

If philosophers such as Grice and Searle have contributed new dimensions to the understanding of human behaviour in conversation, further illumination has been provided by work in sociology and sociolinguistics: for example, in the dynamics of turn-taking in conversation.[5] It is this aspect of conversational behaviour that helps to elucidate the following exchange from Ken Kesey's *One Flew Over the Cuckoo's Nest* (Part 1):

> 'Am I to take it that there's not a man among you that has committed some act that he has never admitted?' She reached in the basket for the log book. 'Must we go over past history?'
>
> That triggered something, some acoustic device in the walls, rigged to turn on at just the sound of those words coming from her mouth. The Acutes stiffened. Their mouths opened in unison. Her sweeping eyes stopped on the first man along the wall.
>
> His mouth worked. 'I robbed a cash register in a service station.'
>
> She moved to the next man.
>
> 'I tried to take my little sister to bed.'
>
> Her eyes clicked to the next man; each one jumped like a shooting-gallery target.
>
> 'I – one time – wanted to take my brother to bed.'

The reader is obviously intended to perceive the rigid control that Nurse Duckett exercises over her patients in the mental hospital, and to disapprove of the authoritarian world which she has created. Why is this so? In everyday conversations like the one we examined in section 5.4.1, the participants are on roughly equal terms when negotiating whose turn it is to speak next. But in other, more controlled situations, the turn-taking is more carefully regulated. In a doctor's surgery, for example, the doctor speaks first, asking questions, and the patient takes up the secondary, answering role. In this kind of situation there are only two participants, but the same principle of control can apply to larger groups. Sinclair and Coulthard have noted that in school classrooms, where there is a large number of participants, the teacher controls the right to talk by asking questions to which he or she already knows the answers, and by nominating which child is to reply either verbally or by kinesic signals like pointing or nodding.[6] This closely resembles the kind of situation that Kesey depicts above, except that this 'school' has the remorseless regimen of a modern Dotheboys Hall. The nurse nominates who is to speak, and has also determined the general nature of the responses. The patients must announce some past act of which they are ashamed. She is thus completely in control, treating a group of fully grown men as if they were guilty children, and hence demeaning them both by what she forces them to say and by how she does it.

We also note the extreme asymmetry of the situation through peculiarities of speech act behaviour. Nurse Duckett's two utterances are questions, but clearly they are 'loaded' questions which require no answer, and really function as threats. In contrast, the Acutes make statements which appear to be replies to an unasked question. The normal rules of cooperative interchange are abandoned, and through this Kesey implicates to the reader, more powerfully than he could communicate by direct statement, that Nurse Duckett is a tyrant, and that the Acutes are in her power.

9.4 An extended pragmatic analysis

The kinds of analysis which we have been outlining in this chapter so far, like other kinds of analysis shown in this book, enable us to explain and justify the intuitive reactions of a reader to fictional dialogue. To see how these methods apply to a more extended analysis, we turn to another passage from *One Flew Over The Cuckoo's Nest*:

[6] The guys file by and get a capsule in a paper cup – throw it to the back of the throat and get the cup filled with water by the little nurse and wash the capsule down (1). On rare occasions some fool might ask what he's being required to swallow (2).

'Wait just a shake, honey; what are these two little red capsules in here with my vitamin?' (3)

I know him (4). He's a big, griping Acute, already getting the reputation of being a troublemaker (5).

'It's just medication, Mr Taber, good for you (6). Down it goes, now.' (7)

'But I mean what *kind* of medication (8). Christ, I can see that they're pills —' (9)

'Just swallow it all, shall we, Mr Taber – just for me?' (10) She takes a quick look at the Big Nurse to see how the little flirting technique she is using is accepted, then looks back at the Acute (11). He still isn't ready to swallow something he don't know what is, not even just for her (12).

'Miss, I don't like to create trouble (13). But I don't like to swallow something without knowing what it is, neither (14). How do I know this isn't one of those funny pills that makes me something I'm not?' (15)

'Don't get upset, Mr Taber —' (16)

'Upset?' (17) All I want to *know*, for the lova Jesus —' (18).

But the Big Nurse has come up quietly, locked her hand on his arm, paralyses him all the way to the shoulder (19). 'That's all right, Miss Flinn,' she says (20). 'If Mr Taber chooses to act like a child, he may have to be treated as such (21). We've tried to be kind and considerate with him (22). Obviously, that's not the answer (23). Hostility, hostility, that's the thanks we get (24). You can go, Mr Taber, if you don't wish to take your medication orally (25).

'All I wanted to *know*, for the —' (26)

'You can go.' (27)

He goes off, grumbling, when she frees his arm, and spends the morning moping around the latrine, wondering about those capsules (28).

[Part 1]

This passage, like the previous one, demonstrates the authoritarian nature of the mental hospital. What starts as a reasonable request for information ends in the total subjugation of Mr Taber by the Big Nurse.

When Taber asks his first question (3), he suggests by the use of the imperative, its colloquial lexis and the informal vocative *honey* that he is on familiar and roughly equal terms with the nurse. Her reply (6), on the other hand, is politely distanced by the choice of form of address: *Mr Taber*. Moreover, her 'answer' to his question, because it is an attempt to reassure without answering the question, breaks the maxim of quantity – it does not tell Mr Taber anything he does not already know – and possibly the maxim of manner – it is very vague. The implicature for the reader is that the nurse is avoiding telling him what he wants to know, probably because the pill's purpose would not be acceptable to its taker, and is also putting him in his place. She then tries to persuade him to swallow the pill by saying 'Down it goes, now' (7). The speech act status of this sentence is that of a command in spite of its declarative structure. It is as if what she wants to happen has already taken place. It is typical of the coaxing language adults use in controlling children, often used in situations where ultimately the child has no choice.

Having failed to get his question answered, Taber asks it again. His refusal to accept the response he has received can be seen in his use of the antithetical coordinator *but*, and the swear word used in sentence (9), where he states that he already knows what she had told him in (6), and therefore challenges the reasonableness of her reply. The nurse reacts to this challenge by interrupting her patient (note the use of the dash) and by ordering him to swallow the pill. She has refused to answer his question in any way. The tone of her order is still rather like that of a parent to a child, as can be seen in the 'illicit' use of *we*: an imperative is tagged as a cooperative enterprise. But Taber still does not submit to her authority and states more politely (note the change of vocative to *Miss* and his statement that he does not want to cause any trouble) the *reasons* for his questions. He then asks about the possible effect of his pills in (15). The nurse again refuses to answer his question, by telling him not to get upset. Hence, each time Taber asks a question the nurse responds to it by giving him an unconnected command, and so attempts to re-establish her control. But the nurse's speech act is not successful either: Taber does not produce the required response. When she tells him not to get upset he challenges the imperative by echoing the word *upset* and then makes another attempt to deny her control, this time by using the stronger declarative form, bolstered by an oath, which states the motivation for his question (17).

So far, then, the conversation has taken the form of a struggle for control, where neither participant has finally won, and where the opposing speech acts of questioning and commanding are never successful. Now, however, Nurse Duckett interrupts Taber, takes the floor, and ruthlessly exercises her dominance both physically and verbally. In (20–24) she threatens him indirectly by talking to Miss Flinn in his hearing and yet as if he were not present. Her refusal at this point to talk directly to her patient is extremely impolite. The implied suggestion is that she does not consider Mr Taber capable of understanding and acting reasonably.[7]

The Big Nurse (the narrator's way of referring to her makes her into a nameless, totalitarian figure, like Big Brother) shifts the ground from under Taber's feet. No longer is he being ordered about, he is being denounced. A denunciation leaves the 'denouncee' with no part to play. Imperatives have been replaced by statements, including a statement which carries the force of a sarcastic order, 'you can go'. The sting in the tail comes with the last word of sentence (25), *orally*, which breaks the maxim of quantity and also gets considerable effect from its final position, thereby carrying nuclear stress and constituting new information (see section 7.3). The sinister implication is, of course, that Mr Taber does not have the choice of whether to take his medicine or not – merely of whether to take it orally. Nurse Duckett's diatribe leaves Taber without a foothold in the conversation, and at the final mock imperative 'you can go' (27), he deserts the field, vanquished. However, he has to wait until she lets him before he can obey. This is seen by the presence of the clause 'when she frees his arm' after the order. (The chronological sequencing principle (section 7.7.1) indicates that she must have let go of his arm *after* she has told him that he can go.) This brutal put-down, allied to the assumption that Taber's enquiry was a perfectly reasonable one, is part of Kesey's strategy of alienating the reader from the nursing staff of the mental home, and from the Big Nurse in particular.

9.5 Conversational tone

The subject of authorial tone was discussed in section 8.5, and to match it, we shall give some account here of tone in the speech of characters, particularly in its role of indicating the social stance of speaker to hearer. Its importance in dramatising personal relationships has already been seen in [6], where the dynamics of conversation are reflected variously in

Style in Fiction

the politeness, familiarity or rudeness of tone adopted by one character towards another.

In real conversation, tone can be so important as to overrule the actual sense of what is said: 'It wasn't so much what she said, as her tone of voice that I objected to.' The phrase 'tone of voice' here brings out the significance of phonetic factors such as intonation and voice quality; but even if these are unavailable (as they are in written dialogue) tone can be indicated by varied and subtle use of grammatical, lexical and graphological markers, as well as by authorial descriptions of a character's manner of speech.

Stylistic values of tone are essentially scalar: there are scales of politeness, of formality, of emotive key, etc., and these have their positive and negative poles; for example, *politeness* implies its antonym of *familiarity*; *formality* implies its antonym of *informality* or colloquialism. The term *impoliteness* should perhaps be considered not so much the opposite of *politeness*, as a reference to an inappropriate position on the scale: we can be impolite both by being too polite and by being too familiar for the occasion. This leads to an important observation about conversational tone in literature: we judge a character's tone by relating it to some contextual norm of appropriateness (for example, the cheery greeting 'Hi!' may be appropriate when one student addresses another, but not when a student addresses an archbishop) and the interest of tone often lies in the way a character's verbal behaviour deviates from some such norm implicit in the fiction or in the author's presentation of it. This means that we have to be sensitive to norms of tone in reading a novel, and must also be aware of the way in which such norms change from one age to another, and from one situation to another.

9.5.1 An example: references to people

The way in which one character addresses or designates another is a revealing indicator of tone, particularly in novels of the nineteenth century, when distinctions of social status were more explicitly graded in speech than they are today. There is a scale of politeness running roughly from titles of respect (*My lord*, *madam*) to titular prefixes (*Mr*, *Miss*) to surnames (*Smith*, *Brown*) to first names (*Cecilia*, *Thomas*) and to pet names and endearments (*Cissy*, *Tom*, *my dear*); but a wide range of combinations including these and other possibilities can be selected to signal various degrees and kinds of social distance.[8]

Mrs Elton in *Emma* shows her lack of social discrimination in cosily designating her husband 'Mr E.' and above all by the ill-judged familiarity of referring to Mr Knightley without title; social sins which earn the outraged censure of Emma [Chapter 32]:

'Knightley! – I could not have believed it, Knightley! – never seen him in her life before, and call him Knightley!'[9]

This shows a consciousness of the social implications of address which is also reflected in *Dombey and Son* when Dickens's heroine Florence corrects her maid Susan Nipper for an irreverent reference to the aristocratic Skettles family:

'Better late than never, dear Miss Floy,' said Susan, 'and I do say, that even a visit from *them old Skettleses* will be a Godsend.' 'It is very good of *Sir Barnet and Lady Skettles*, Susan,' returned Florence, with a mild correction of that young lady's familiar mention of the family in question, 'to repeat their invitation so kindly.'

[Chapter 23]

But in contrast to that of Mrs Elton, Susan's social transgression is easily pardoned: she asserts a refreshing honesty of feeling in the mercantile world of Mr Dombey, with its loveless preoccupation with status and social distance. Against that background, too, Susan's addressing her beloved mistress as 'dear Miss Floy' (an interesting combination of endearment, title and pet name) stands out as a welcome sign of human affection breaching the barriers of social inequality. There is no doubt that Mr Dombey would disapprove of such intimacy with the 'lower orders'. Condemned to isolation by his unbending sense of dignity and family pride, he can scarcely bring himself to utter an endearment to his wife, even when on the childbed which is also her deathbed, she crowns his ambitions by producing a son [Chapter 1]:

The words ['Dom–bey and Son'] had such a softening influence, that he appended a term of endearment to Mrs Dombey's name (though not without some hesitation, as being a man but little used to that form of address): and said 'Mrs Dombey, my – my dear.'

Major Bagstock, a parasite on Dombey's wealth and influence, interlards his speech with 'Mr Dombey', 'Dombey' and 'Sir', as if the glow of Mr Dombey's *amour propre* requires continual stoking with vocatives:

'Mr Dombey, Sir,' said Major Bagstock, 'Joey B. is not in general a man of sentiment, for Joseph is tough. But Joe has his feelings, Sir, and when they *are* awakened – Damme, Mr Dombey,' cried the Major with sudden ferocity, 'this is weakness, and I won't submit to it!'

[Chapter 20]

At the same time, the Major's flattery takes the disguise of soldierly bluffness, and to dramatise his own role as Dombey's confidant, he punctuates his speech with a range of familiar self-references, from 'Joseph Bagstock' and 'Joey B.' to plain 'Josh' and 'Joe'. His speech to his servant, on the other hand, is wantonly abusive:

> 'Where is my scoundrel?' said the Major, looking wrathfully round the room.
> The Native, who had no particular name, but answered to any vituperative epithet, presented himself instantly at the door and ventured to come no nearer.
> 'You villain!' said the choleric Major, 'where's the breakfast?'
>
> [*ibid*]

At the bottom end of the scale, as this example shows, a person who is sufficiently menial cannot be expected to have a name at all: to claim such a right to individuality would be presumption. This indeed seems to be the attitude of Florence's nurse, whose name, characteristically, Mr Dombey cannot remember when he summons her to take care of the infant Paul:

> '. . . I needn't tell you . . . to take particular care of this young gentleman, Mrs –'
> 'Blockitt, Sir?' suggested the nurse, a simpering piece of faded gentility, who did not presume to state her name as a fact, but merely offered it as a mild suggestion.
>
> [Chapter 1]

And when Paul requires a wet-nurse, Polly Toodle, in order to be accepted in that embarrassingly intimate capacity in the august house of Dombey, is required to leave not only her family, but also her name, behind, and to adopt the colourless pseudonym of *Richards*. This use of surname alone, in addressing a woman, is a particular stigma (even today, we talk of 'Dickens', but usually not of 'Austen' or 'Brontë'). There is the parallel case of young Cissy Jupe, in *Hard Times*, who, like Polly, has to give up her family in order to join the ranks of the socially respectable: in the Gradgrind household she becomes *Jupe*, and at school suffers the ultimate debasement of becoming a mere number: 'girl number twenty'. In all these and many other ways, modes of address in *Dombey and Son* and in Victorian novels generally express the manifold gradience of superiority and inferiority, of intimacy and distance.

9.5.2 Other indicators of politeness

It is generally true that to be polite, one has to be prolix and indirect:[10] the propitiation of the hearer requires the ceremonies of respectful address, apology, circumlocution, hyperbole. Mr Carker, Mr Dombey's sinister manager, betrays his insincerity and hypocritical intentions by an extreme of politeness which borders on servility. Here he is addressing Florence:

> *'I beg pardon'*, said Mr Carker, *'a thousand times*! But I am going down to-morrow morning to Mr Dombey, at Leamington, and if *Miss Dombey* can entrust me with any commission, *need I say how* **very** *happy I shall be?'*
>
> [Chapter 24]

Perhaps his most striking mark of deference is the replacement of *you* by the indirect third-person address of 'Miss Dombey'. The other italicised portions of this speech are redundant from a strictly informational point of view: for example, it is only unctuous politeness which requires Carker to apologise 'a thousand times' for the audacity of opening a conversation with his boss's daughter. His prolixity reaches even greater extremes when he begins to insinuate himself into delicate matters such as Mr Dombey's estrangement from his second wife. The following speech to Mr Dombey could all be reduced in plain language to the brief remark 'So you want me to humble her pride, do you?' – all the rest is obsequious padding:

> 'And – pardon me – do I misconceive you,' said Carker, 'when I think you descry in this, a likely means of humbling Mrs Dombey's pride – I use the word as expressive of a quality which, kept within due bounds, adorns and graces a lady so distinguished for her beauty and accomplishments – and, not to say of punishing her, but of reducing her to the submission you so naturally and justly require?'
>
> [Chapter 42]

Apart from the routine apology 'pardon me', the chief markers of politeness here are parenthetical constructions, euphemisms and hedges (i.e., constructions which in some degree modify and tone down the force of an utterance). The whole of the sentence from 'I use the word . . .' is in fact an elaborate parenthetical disclaimer, containing further parentheses, whereby Carker on the one hand excuses his implied disrespect to Mr Dombey in applying the term *pride* to his wife, and on the other hand turns the nasty suggestion of punishment into a tribute to Mr Dombey's rights as husband. The hedging non-factive verbal constructions 'do I misconceive you', 'I think', and 'you descry', as well as the adjective *likely*, all help to remove the dangerous implications of Mr Carker's remarks from the realm of reality, so that they appear to be mere speculations about what Mr Dombey may have in mind. However, although this overdone ceremoniousness may betray Mr Carker's falseness to us as readers, it is important in the novel's development that Mr Dombey, insulated from genuine human contact by his egotism, takes it simply as fitting homage to his self-esteem, and so fails to detect the villainy beneath the fawning manner.

9.5.3 Politeness and formality

It is not unexpected that Mr Carker's politeness goes with formal rather than colloquial vocabulary (*misconceive, expressive of a quality, distinguished, submission*), and also with syntax which tends towards rhetorical formalism: notice the balancing pairs of 'adorns and graces', 'beauty and accomplishments', 'naturally and justly'. Because these are signs of studied linguistic choice they suggest a lack of spontaneity, and hence, by extension, carry a suspicion of insincerity.

The scale of FORMALITY[11] often correlates, as here, with that of politeness, but the two are in principle distinct. Both convey a sense of distance, but a formal style is associated with the distance of serious public communication (particularly written communication), of language 'on its best behaviour'. Nevertheless, we see in Mr Dombey's speech at Paul's christening how a formality that is inappropriate to situation can produce an effect very similar to that of overpoliteness:

> 'Well, sir,' said Mr Chick, making a desperate plunge, after a long silence, and filling a glass of sherry; 'I shall drink this, if you'll allow me, Sir, to little Paul.'
>
> 'Bless him!' murmured Miss Tox, taking a sip of wine.
>
> 'Dear little Dombey!' murmured Mrs Chick.
>
> 'Mr John,' said Mr Dombey, with severe gravity, 'my son would feel and express himself obliged to you, I have no doubt, if he could appreciate the favour you have done him. He will prove, in time to come, I trust, equal to any responsibility that the obliging disposition of his relations and friends, in private, or the onerous nature of our position, in public, may impose upon him.'
>
> The tone in which this was said admitting of nothing more, Mr Chick relapsed into low spirits and silence.
>
> [Chapter 5]

The unaffected good wishes of his guests elicit from Mr Dombey a heavy-handed speech which is more appropriate in its manner to the boardroom than to a family gathering. His pomposity shows in the Latinate diction, particularly of abstract nouns (*obliging disposition, onerous nature, responsibility, impose, position* – all sounding the note of duty rather than of rejoicing); also in the elaborate parallelism of his second sentence:

the obliging disposition of his relations and friends in private
the onerous nature   of our position   in public

This ironically underlines a dichotomy which Mr Dombey's own life lamentably fails to recognise: the distinction between one's public and private self. He has turned the christening into a public meeting.

Formality does not always have such negative associations. Jane Austen's novels bear the influence of the eighteenth-century view of Dr Johnson that the best conversation was that which most approximated to the written language. There is no implication of pomposity, therefore, in the rather formal style that she assigns to such morally weighty characters as Sir Thomas Bertram in *Mansfield Park*. Rather, such a style is consonant with their dignity and moral seriousness. Some sign of this is seen in the contrast between the speech of Mrs Bennet and that of her husband in our earlier quotation [5] from *Pride and Prejudice*. When Mr Bennet replies to his wife, 'I have not the pleasure of understanding you . . . Of what are you talking?' he used the more formal construction of the question with initial preposition (instead of 'What are you talking of?'); similarly, when he later refers to the subject of Elizabeth's marriage: 'I understand that Mr Collins has made you an offer of marriage', the dignity of his utterance contrasts with his wife's colloquial treatment of the same subject: 'she vows she will not have him'. We notice the same kind of contrast in politeness. Whereas Mrs Bennet importunes her husband unceremoniously with 'You must come and make Lizzy marry Mr Collins', he replies with the somewhat over-emphasised politeness of 'I have not the pleasure of understanding you'. Again, in mode of address, Mrs Bennet uses the familiar *Lizzy*, while Mr Bennet prefers the fuller form *Elizabeth* (which is also, significantly, the form occurring in the authorial narrative). The context encourages us to read into these small signals an implied reproof by Mr Bennet of his wife for light-headed treatment of the grave matter of his daughter's future. Here formality reinforces a norm, rather than reacts against it.

9.6 Conclusion

We have concentrated in this chapter on discourse in terms of the two-way interaction of conversation, whereas in the last chapter we concentrated on the one-way discourse between author and reader. These two levels of discourse, we can now see, are closely interconnected: (a) because the discoursal point of view of the author must be interpreted in the light of the embedded discourses of conversation; and (b) because the strategies of communication (e.g., through implicature) employed in two-way conversation are also used by the author in his 'conversation' with the reader. To a large extent, it is only the greater complexity, multiplicity and subtlety of the novel as discourse which separates it from the most common-place conversational transactions. A further factor in this relation between the two levels of discourse is explored in the next chapter: the *manner*

Style in Fiction

in which conversation and monologue are incorporated into the authorial narrative.

Notes

1. J.L. AUSTIN (1962) and J.R. SEARLE (1969). A convenient summary of Searle's work can be found in SEARLE (1975a).
2. This account of conversational implicature is much simplified. For a fuller statement of Grice's views see H.P. GRICE (1975). An attempt to apply his work to literary texts can be found in M.L. PRATT (1977), especially Chapters 5 and 6.
3. M. COULTHARD (1977), 170–81 shows how Iago uses the echo question in a similar way to help engineer Othello's jealousy of Desdemona in Act III, scene iii of *Othello*.
4. Part of this passage is quoted as the supreme example of the phatic function of language (see section 1.5) by R. JAKOBSON (1961).
5. The most well-known analysts in this field are H. SACKS and E.A. SCHEGLOFF, but their work is spread through a number of articles in various academic journals. For a more accessible account, see COULTHARD (1977), Chapter 4.
6. See J. MCH. SINCLAIR and R.M. COULTHARD (1975), and Chapter 5 COULTHARD, *op cit*. For control mechanisms in interviews, see R. FOWLER *et al.* (1979), Chapter 4.
7. People often address questions which they could reasonably ask of children to their parents instead, and to the friends or parents of disabled people who are quite capable of replying for themselves. The annoyance which this causes was reflected in the ironic title of a series of BBC radio programmes for the blind, *Does He Take Sugar?*
8. For a systematic account of the social implications of modes of address in modern English, see S.M. ERVIN-TRIPP (1969).
9. For further discussion of Jane Austen's use of forms of personal address and reference, see N. PAGE (1972), 52.
10. The fact that politeness interacts with language features related to Grice's cooperative principle is, perhaps, not surprising. Grice himself, *op cit*, has suggested that politeness may be another conversational maxim, and the notion of a politeness principle, complementary to the cooperative principle, has been advanced in by G. LEECH (1983), Chapters 5 and 6. A more detailed and influential account of politeness is that of P. BROWN and S. LEVINSON (1987).
11. A simple account of the relation between formality and other scales is given in G. LEECH and J. SVARTVIK (2002), 30–36.

CHAPTER 10

Speech and thought presentation

In Chapters 5 and 9 we examined character talk in the novel in order to see how it compares with everyday conversation and how contributions to speech exchanges are interpreted by the reader. In effect, this meant that we restricted ourselves to discussion of DIRECT SPEECH. But an author has other modes of presentation of character talk at his disposal; INDIRECT SPEECH, for example. It is to the choice of modes of speech presentation, an area which has received sustained investigation from stylisticians of the novel,[1] that we now turn. As most of the features involved in differentiating modes of character speech are paralleled by similar modes of character THOUGHT, we also include a discussion of this important area. However, although the formal differentia of speech and thought modes are the same, some of their effects are not, and so for the sake of clarity we will discuss them separately.

10.1 The presentation of speech

10.1.1 Direct and indirect speech (DS and IS)

The essential semantic difference between direct and indirect speech is that when one uses direct speech to report what someone has said one quotes the words used verbatim, whereas in indirect report one expresses what was said in one's own words. The formal relationships between these modes of report are most easily shown by seeing how it is possible to convert one into the other. If we take the following example of DIRECT SPEECH (DS):

[1] He said, 'I'll come back here to see you again tomorrow.'

we can easily convert it into INDIRECT SPEECH (IS) as follows:

[2] He said that he would return there to see her the following day.

In the conversion the following changes have taken place:

(i) The inverted commas around the reported speech, which indicate that quotation is occurring, and which mark that quotation off as being syntactically independent of the reporting verb *said* are removed, thus making the reported speech dependent on the reporting verb.
(ii) That dependence is marked explicitly by the introduction of the sub-ordinating conjunction *that*.
(iii) The first- and second-person pronouns change to third-person.
(iv) The tense of the verb undergoes 'backshift', as does the time adverb, *tomorrow*, which becomes *the following day*.
(v) The 'close' deictic adverb *here* changes to the more remote *there*.
(vi) The verb of movement changes from 'towards' to 'away from' (note that it would also have been possible to convert *come* in [1] to *go* in [2], where *go* is neutral, and therefore not marked as 'towards').

The effect of these changes is to remove all those features which are directly related to the embedded speech situation only and to subordinate the reported speech to the verb of saying in the primary speech situation.

In this example the time and place in which the reported and reporting speech events occur are totally distinct. But there will be occasions in conversations (though these are relatively rare in the novel) where some of the extralinguistic referents will be the same for both the primary and the secondary speech situations. The relevant deictics can then remain unchanged. For example, if 'I'll come back here to see you again tomorrow' has been uttered in a hospital and the person who is reporting that utterance to someone else is doing so on the same day and in the same building, his utterance of 'He said that he would come back here to see her again tomorrow' would correctly report that utterance in indirect speech because the 'nearness' indicators (*here*, *tomorrow*) would be relevant to the primary speech situation. (Similarly, *you* would replace *her* in IS if the addressee was identical in the two speech situations.) It follows from this that the mode of speech presentation is determined not by the presence of formal linguistic features alone, but also by our knowledge of extra-linguistic contextual factors.

The effect that is produced when IS is used to report speech is one whereby the person who is reporting the conversation intervenes as an interpreter between the person he is talking to and the words of the person he is reporting, instead of merely quoting verbatim the speech that occurred. What is reported can thus become fully integrated into the narrative. This difference can best be seen in terms of what the reporter commits himself to. If he reports in direct speech he is claiming to report faithfully (*a*) what was stated and (*b*) the exact form of words which were used to utter that statement. If he uses indirect speech he only commits himself to (*a*). A consequence of this difference is that some of the words of the indirect form can be altered without altering its truth claim at all, for instance the motion verb and the place adverbial:

[3] He said that he would *return to the hospital* to see her the following day.

There is thus more than one possible indirect version of a direct string. Moreover, a reader faced with an indirect string cannot automatically retrieve the original direct speech: [3] above could be an indirect version of [1] or any of the following:

[4] 'I will return to the hospital to see you tomorrow.'
[5] 'I'll come back here and see you again tomorrow.'
[6] 'I'll be back again to see you tomorrow, duck.'

This lack of fit between direct and indirect speech means that it is not possible for us to regard variants of speech presentation types as being merely syntactic variants of the same proposition. The 'equivalence' relation which holds between them is of a rather looser kind.[2] Nevertheless, within our broad conception of stylistic variation (see sections 1.6 and 4.2–4.4), these, and other modes of speech presentation, may still be regarded as stylistic variants.

The examples we have discussed so far involve only syntactic and lexical changes; hence in the direct version the reporter claims to be faithfully producing the original speaker's syntactic and lexical structure. An even more faithful reproduction could be made by representing as closely as possible the pronunciation of the original sentence as well. In real speech, voice quality and intonation might be mimicked in order to show speaker attitude, for example the haughtiness with which a particular remark was made, or to indicate a sentence's communicative value where it is not otherwise clear. Thus 'He said, "George, the window is open"' can be said in two different ways, one so that it is merely a remark, and the other where it is a command to close the window. Alternatively, a class or regional accent might be imitated. The English writing system is notoriously bad at representing pronunciation, but novelists do make use of conventional orthographic representations to suggest pronunciations (see section 5.4.1). If the original statement in [1] was uttered by a Cockney an even more faithful representation of it might therefore be:

[7] He said, 'I'll come back 'ere to see yer again tomorrer.'

Similarly, although the majority of prosodic features can only be captured in writing by the insertion of information into the narrative description (e.g., by the use of adverbs as in 'he said *sternly*'), some can be indicated by orthographic convention in the speech itself, as in:

[8] He said, 'I'll come back *here* to see you again tomorrow.'

where an indication of the placement of nuclear stress is made.

So far we have only talked about direct and indirect speech, but novelists do not just have two forms of speech presentation at their disposal. There are at least three other immediate possibilities: a more direct form than DS, a more indirect form than IS, and a mixed form somewhere between the two. And indeed all these forms occur in fiction. They are, respectively, FREE DIRECT SPEECH (FDS), the NARRATIVE REPORT OF SPEECH ACTS (NRSA) and FREE INDIRECT SPEECH (FIS).

10.1.2 Free direct speech (FDS)

Direct speech has two features which show evidence of the narrator's presence, namely the quotation marks and the introductory reporting clause. Accordingly, it is possible to remove either or both of these features, and produce a freer form,[3] which has been called FREE DIRECT SPEECH: one where the characters apparently speak to us more immediately without the narrator as an intermediary:

[9] He said I'll come back here to see you again tomorrow.
[10] 'I'll come back here to see you again tomorrow.'
[11] I'll come back here to see you again tomorrow.

Hemingway is fond of omitting the reporting clause. In *A Clean, Well-Lighted Place* he uses this choice to portray the quick to-and-fro of the conversation between the two waiters:

'He's drunk now,' he said.
'He's drunk every night.'
'What did he want to kill himself for?'
'How should I know.'
'How did he do it?'
'He hung himself with a rope.'
'Who cut him down?'

In fact this is only a portion of some twenty-eight lines of FDS between the initial direct speech and the next narrative sentence. Without the introductory clauses specifying which waiter says what, it becomes difficult to remember which waiter is which, so that confusion is gradually produced in the reader's mind. Indeed, one critic, David Lodge, has argued that this is precisely the point of Hemingway's story:

> Hemingway deliberately encourages the reader to make an initially incorrect discrimination between the two waiters, which, when discovered and corrected, amounts to a kind of peripeteia. Hemingway, in short, is making things deliberately difficult for his readers in this story.[4]

James Joyce, on the other hand, is fond of running speech and narrative together by omitting the inverted commas:

> – And Xenophon looked upon Marathon, Mr Dedalus said, looking again on the fireplace and to the window, and Marathon looked on the sea.
>
> [*Ulysses*, Penguin edn, p. 125]

By continually removing the distinction between speech and narrative report, Joyce creates the impression that they are inseparable and relatively indistinguishable aspects of one state. Dickens uses the most free form of all in *Bleak House* to portray the verdict of accidental death which is brought in at the inquest on Nemo:

> Now. Is there any other witness? No other witness.
>
> Very well, gentlemen! Here's a man unknown, proved to be in the habit of taking opium in large quantities. . . . If you think it is a case of accidental death, you will find a verdict accordingly.
>
> Verdict accordingly. Accidental death. No doubt. Gentlemen, you are discharged. Good afternoon.
>
> [Chapter 11]

Dickens truncates many of the sentences to speed up the effect, as if coroner and jury are gabbling their way heedlessly through a well-worn ritual. The lack of quotation marks and locutionary clauses also produces a kind of ambiguity. We are either given the coroner's words without any of the intervening responses from the jury, or, alternatively, we can read the extract so that sentences like 'No other witness' are attributed to other speakers. In either case, the verdict is arrived at with unseemly haste.

10.1.3 The narrative report of speech acts (NRSA)

The possibility of a form which is more indirect than indirect speech is realised in sentences that merely report that a speech act (or number of speech acts) has occurred, but where the narrator does not have to commit himself entirely to giving the sense of what was said, let alone the form of words in which they were uttered. Hence [1] could have been reported by either of the following:

[12] He promised his return.
[13] He committed himself to another meeting.

where only a minimal account of the statement is given. We call this form the NARRATIVE REPORT OF SPEECH ACTS (NRSA). It is useful for summarising relatively unimportant stretches of conversation, as can be seen from Joyce's *The Dead*:

> Mr D'Arcy came from the pantry, fully swathed and buttoned, and in a repentant tone told them the history of his cold. Everyone gave him advice . . .

The conjoining of 'Mr D'Arcy came . . .' with 'told them the history . . .' helps us to see the exact status of speech act reporting. The speech act is reported in a way that puts it on a par with other kinds of action. When a novelist reports the occurrence of some act or speech act we are apparently seeing the event entirely from his perspective. But as we move along the cline of speech presentation from the more bound to the more free end, his interference seems to become less and less noticeable until, in the most extreme version of FDS, he apparently leaves the characters to talk entirely on their own:

Cline of 'interference' in report

(NRA = Narrative report of action, FIS = Free indirect speech (see below))

Figure 10.1

10.1.4 Free indirect speech (FIS)

As can be seen from Figure 10.1, the form in between DS and IS is called FREE INDIRECT SPEECH (FIS). As its name implies, FIS is normally thought of as a freer version of an ostensibly indirect form. Its most typical manifestation is one where, unlike IS, the reporting clause is omitted, but where the tense and pronoun selection are those associated with IS. Hence, the following are all free indirect versions of [1].

[14] He would return there to see her again the following day.
[15] He would return there to see her again tomorrow.
[16] He would come back there to see her again tomorrow.

Sentence [14] is an example of FIS because of the omission of the reporting clause. That omission allows the reported clause, which is always subordinate in indirect versions, to take on some of the syntactic possibilities of the main clause, and in this respect share some of the features typically associated with DS. This can be seen in [15] and [16], which are successively freer versions of [14] because of the introduction of the 'near' deictics *tomorrow* in [15] and *tomorrow* and *come back* in [16]. As Figure 10.1 implies, FIS has a rather odd status in terms of truth claims and faithfulness. It is in a sort of halfway house position, not claiming to be a reproduction of the original speech, but at the same time being more than a mere indirect rendering of that original. The syntactic features which we have discussed so far are a means of rendering the semantic status of the particular report clear. It is this semantic status which we regard as primary, and which is unclear in the case of FIS. We will return to it later in this section (pp. 265–6) when we discuss the use of lexis and graphology in the aspect of speech presentation type.

FIS usually occurs in the context of sentences of narrative report, and, given the preponderance of the third-person narrator telling his tale in the past tense, its characteristic features in the novel are almost always the presence of third-person pronouns and past tense, which correspond with the form of narrative report and indicate indirectness, along with a number of features, both positive and negative, indicating freeness. Thus it is, as it were, a free form 'purporting' to be IS. A good example is the portrayal of the lawyer Mr Shepherd's speech in *Persuasion*:

'Then I take it for granted,' observed Sir Walter, 'that his face is about as orange as the cuffs and capes of my livery.'
Mr Shepherd hastened to assure him, that Admiral Croft was a very hale, hearty, well-looking man, a little weather-beaten, to be sure, but not much; and quite the gentleman in all his notions and behaviour; – not likely to make the smallest difficulty about terms; – only wanted a comfortable home, and to get into it as soon as possible; – knew he must pay for his convenience; – knew what rent a ready-furnished house of that consequence might fetch; – should not have been surprised if Sir Walter had asked more; – had inquired about the manor; – would be glad of the deputation, certainly, but made no great point of it; – said he sometimes took out a gun, but never killed; – quite the gentleman.

[Chapter 3]

261

Sir Walter's speech is in the direct form, appropriate for the speech of a man totally sure of himself. Mr Shepherd's role, however, is that of the deferential functionary, and so Jane Austen uses the more self-effacing indirect form for him. He begins in IS which then blends into FIS mainly by virtue of the fact that the subordinating conjunction *that* and the subject are not repeated. These negative syntactic indications are reinforced by colloquial lexical forms, especially the fussy lawyer's reiteration of the re-assuring phrase 'quite the gentleman', and the dashes, which indicate that we are only getting snatches of the conversation. Thus we are presented with a form which has indications of an intervening narrator but also some flavour of the original speech. The chopping of the speech brings out the parallels in the form of the statements about the admiral, as if to underline the inexhaustibility of the lawyer's store of eager reassurances. All these factors help to put an ironic distance between the reader and Mr Shepherd, allowing room for us to feel that his persuasiveness is for his own benefit rather than Sir Walter's. This ability to give the flavour of the character's words but also to keep the narrator in an intervening position between character and reader makes FIS an extremely useful vehicle for casting an ironic light on what the character says.

The example we have just examined 'purported' to be IS but developed into FIS. This is the most normal kind of context for FIS. But it is also possible to find more indirect forms masquerading as DS:

> Quit Kellynch Hall. The hint was immediately taken up by Mr Shepherd, whose interest was involved in the reality of Sir Walter's retrenching, and who was perfectly persuaded that nothing would be done without a change of abode. – 'Since the idea had been started in the very quarter which ought to dictate, he had no scruple,' he said, 'in confessing his judgement to be entirely on that side . . .'
>
> [Chapter 2]

This quotation occurs before the previous one in the novel. If anything, the ironic distance between Mr Shepherd and us is even greater here. This is partly because it is easier to notice the formal deviance in this case as the tense and pronoun selection are consistently inappropriate for DS. But the speech also occurs immediately after an authorial statement making Mr Shepherd's role in the proceedings very apparent. This is an important point to notice. The use of FIS does not automatically produce irony; but in the context of Jane Austen's previous statement about Mr Shepherd's interests, the use of a form which creates distance between us and the character's words can only be interpreted as placing them in an ironic light.

From what we have noticed so far, it would seem that FIS always uses past tense and third-person pronouns. But it would be more accurate to say that the pronoun and tense selection has to be *appropriate* to the form of narration in which the FIS occurs. If we look at novels written in the narrative present we can still find examples of FIS. For a good example we may return to the coroner's scene in *Bleak House*, a scene which occurs in that portion of the novel narrated in the present tense through the eyes of a third-person narrator:

> Name, Jo. Nothing else that he knows on. Don't know that everybody has two names. Never heard of sich a think. Don't know that Jo is short for a longer name. Thinks it long enough for *him*. *He* can't find no fault with it. Spell it? No. *He* can't spell it.
>
> [Chapter 11]

Because the occurrence of the present tense is determined by the overall style of narration, the only thing which tells us that this passage is in FIS and not FDS is the use of third-person pronouns and the appropriate markings on the verbs. There are many features of directness. The passage contains responses to questions, echo questions, idiosyncratic spellings to indicate Jo's 'idiolect', and italicisation to show where contrastive stress occurs. Dickens also indicates the rapidity of the cross-questioning by omitting the questions that the coroner produces, thus presenting one side of a piece of interrogation as if it were a monologue. It is easy for us to infer the questions asked from the replies given. The FIS and the suppression of one side of the interchange has an ironic purpose which is consistent with the scene as a whole. We get a compassionate view of Jo while the court is shown as riding roughshod over human values in general, and those unfortunates who cannot stand up for themselves in particular:

> 'This won't do, gentlemen!' says the coroner with a melancholy shake of the head.
>
> 'Don't you think you can receive his evidence, sir?' asks an attentive juryman.
>
> 'Out of the question,' says the coroner. 'You have heard the boy. "Can't exactly say" won't do, you know. We can't take *that* in a court of justice, gentlemen. It's terrible depravity. Put the boy aside.'
>
> Boy put aside, to the great edification of the audience, especially of Little Swills, the comic vocalist.
>
> Now. Is there any other witness? No other witness.
>
> Very well, gentlemen! Here's a man unknown, proved to have been in the habit of taking opium in large quantities for a year and a half, found dead of too much opium. If you think you have any evidence to lead you to the conclusion that he committed suicide, you will come to that conclusion. If you think it is a case of accidental death, you will find a verdict accordingly.
>
> [*Ibid*]

The coroner's view of justice is one where only the views of some people are to be taken into account. The aim of the proceedings seems to be to get things over as quickly as possible rather than to arrive at the correct conclusion.

We have seen that the presence of the past tense is not criterial for the definition of FIS. Similarly, FIS can be found in the first-person mode:

> Hardly had the Farlows gone than a blue-chinned cleric called – and I tried to make the interview as brief as was consistent with neither hurting his feelings nor arousing his doubts. Yes, I would devote all my life to the child's welfare. Here, incidentally, was a little cross that Charlotte Becker had given me when we were both young. I had a female cousin, a respectable spinster in New York. There we would find a good private school for Dolly. Oh, what a crafty Humbert!
>
> [*Lolita*, Part 1, Chapter 23]

The narrator, Humbert Humbert has, unknown to anyone else, murdered Lolita's mother in order to gain complete control of his step-daughter and further his plan to seduce her. It is quite evident from the context that, 'Yes, I would devote all my life to the child's welfare' must be a free indirect (*cf* the past tense and the response word) version of Humbert Humbert's words to the cleric. The general definitional point is the same as before. The presence of third-person pronouns is not essential for FIS. Rather, the pronoun choice must be consistent with the primary discourse situation. In an I-narrator novel, the pronoun selection for FIS will thus inevitably include the possibility of first person.

Of the three features discussed in section 10.1.4 when we defined sentences [14–16] as FIS, the one remaining is that of the absence of the introductory clause of saying. It might be thought that although the presence of past tense and third-person pronouns is not, the absence of a reporting verb is criterial for the presence of FIS. Indeed, many writers on speech presentation[5] have assumed this to be the case. However, we prefer an account where no one particular feature has to be present for FIS to occur. Our definition, then, is one in terms of 'family resemblance' rather than one dependent upon the presence of a particular defining feature.[6] Our main reason for this approach is the occurrence of sentences which exhibit subordination but which would appear to belong to the semantic halfway house reserved for FIS. Consider the following example from Paul Scott's *Staying On*:

[17] He said he must persuade Billy-Boy to build a pool in the hotel compound one day when old Ma Bhoolaboy was out playing bridge so that when her tonga brought her back at night the whole thing would tip in with a bloody great splash.

[Chapter 11]

Here subordination is present, but the selection of colloquial lexical forms like 'old Ma Bhoolaboy' and 'with a bloody great splash' indicate that in the subordinate clause itself we are getting not just an indirect report of the statement which the retired colonel, Tusker, uttered, but also some indication of the form of words which he used. In other words, the sentence begins in the indirect mode in the main clause and then slips into the free indirect mode. Another good example can be found in Conrad's *The Secret Agent* when Comrade Ossipon leaps from the moving train in order to escape from Mrs Verloc:

> He had leaped out at the very end of the platform; and such was his determination in sticking to his desperate plan that he managed by a sort of miracle, performed almost in the air, to slam to the door of the carriage. Only then did he find himself rolling head over heels like a shot rabbit. He was bruised, shaken, pale as death, and out of breath when he got up. But he was calm, and perfectly able to meet the excited crowd of railwaymen who had gathered round him in a moment. He explained, in gentle and convincing tones, that his wife had started at a moment's notice for Brittany to her dying mother; that, of course, she was greatly upset, and considerably concerned at her state; that he was trying to cheer her up, and had absolutely failed to notice at first that the train was moving out. To the general exclamation 'Why didn't you go on to Southampton, then, sir?' he objected the inexperience of a young sister-in-law left alone in the house with three small children, and her alarm at his absence, the telegraph office being closed. He had acted on impulse. 'But I don't think I'll ever try that again,' he concluded . . .
>
> [Chapter 12]

Again, the sentence beginning with 'He explained . . .' exhibits subordination, but appears to offer the degree of faithfulness to the 'original' found in FIS. In this case it is the use of the repetitive construction and the performative adverb *of course* which give the flavour of the original. Because the main clause is short and comes at the beginning of the sentence, the free indirect style of the sequence of subordinate clauses tends to dominate it. This quotation also includes a sentence, 'He had acted on impulse', which appears formally to be a piece of narrative report, but which by *contextual considerations alone* we interpret as being FIS. It is quite apparent from the preceding narrative account that Ossipon had not acted on impulse at all when jumping from the train, but was following a prearranged plan to effect his escape from Mrs Verloc. Hence this sentence must be a free indirect report of his words to the railwaymen.

Norman Page[7] suggests that examples with subordination but which possess lexical or graphological features associated with the original DS are really IS with 'speech colouring'. In other words, he assumes that syntactic features alone determine the speech presentation category. But this kind of account ignores the fact that the claim to faithfulness in sentences like those we discussed above seems to be the same as that found in more central examples of FIS, i.e., those where the marker of subordination is absent. We prefer to say that features from any of the three major linguistic levels might be instrumental in indicating that a particular sentence is in FIS. Indeed, it is possible to construct examples where the only thing which suggests that an utterance is in FIS is a single lexical or graphological feature:

[18] He said that the bloody train had been late.
[19] He told her to leave him alone!

Here, the only features which show that we are dealing with FIS are the swear word in the first sentence and the exclamation mark in the second. Neither of these forms are normally used by narrators in novels, and so inevitably evoke the character's manner of expression.

It was assumed for some time by writers on FIS that it was a form which did not develop until the nineteenth century. Stephen Ullmann, for example, implies that Jane Austen was the first English novelist to use it consistently.[8] But FIS (largely determined by lexis and graphology) was used fairly extensively by Fielding,[9] and can be found in non-literary texts even earlier. For example it occurs regularly in Harrison's 1612 account of the trial of the Lancaster witches.[10] This is not surprising, as recourse to FIS allows a reporter a sense of immediacy not found in IS and, on purely practical grounds, avoids continual repetition of the reporting clause. An interesting transitional example of FIS in the novel can be found in Swift's *Gulliver's Travels* (published in 1726):

> I made bold to tell her Majesty that I owed no other obligation to my late master, than his not dashing out the brains of a poor harmless creature found by chance in his field. . . . That the life I had since led was laborious enough to kill an animal of ten times my strength. That my health was much impaired by the continual drudgery of entertaining the rabble every hour of the day. . . . But as I was out of all fear of being ill treated under the protection of so great and good an empress, the Ornament of Nature, the Darling of the World, the Delight of her Subjects, the Phoenix of the Creation . . .
>
> [Part II, Chapter 3]

In this extract Swift apparently wants to avoid the repetition of 'I made bold to tell her Majesty' but feels that he must make the subordination to the reporting verb apparent. Hence he begins two sentences with the subordinating conjunction *that*. When he reaches the sentence beginning with 'But as I was out . . .' he leaves out the subordinating conjunction too.

Thus, what starts as a struggle between IS and FIS ends in a victory for FIS. This is apparent not just in the absence of subordination but also in the use of merit adjectives and the string of laudatory appellations ('the Ornament of Nature', etc.). As the overall form of narration is in the first person, this also incidentally illustrates the point that IS and FIS need not be restricted to third-person pronouns.

Before we leave the matter of the definition of FIS we must consider the effect of inversion. If we examine a sentence like 'He said he would return there again to see her the following day' we can be in no doubt that it is an example of IS. It is identical to [1] except for the optional omission of the conjunction *that*. However, the inversion of the reporting and reported clauses as in:

[20] He would return there again to see her the following day, he said.

makes the reported clause look at first sight like a central example of FIS.[11] This impression is of course corrected when one comes to the reporting clause, but the original effect is not entirely subsumed, and so constructions like this take on a Janus-like character somewhere in between IS and FIS. The writing of Virginia Woolf is particularly rich in constructions such as these:

He must be off, he said, getting up . . .
[*Mrs Dalloway*, 1976 edn, p. 132]

The effect in examples like this is not particularly striking because the reported clause contains no positive indications of freeness and because the analogy with DS, where inversion is common, plays down the contrast. But in cases where there are more positive features indicating freeness in the reported clause, the sudden appearance of a reporting clause in a communicatively dynamic position at the end of the sentence, after what the reader has taken in as an obviously central example of FIS, can be quite striking:

What department did she want? Elizabeth interrupted her.
[*Mrs Dalloway*, 1976 edn, p. 143]

Here, the exclamatory and interrogative forms seesaw the reader from a relatively free rendering to an indirect position from which to view what is said. The effect can be even more startling when the reported material is longer than in the cases we have examined here.

Inversion also has a role to play in other speech presentation forms. In DS it is quite normal to put the reported speech before the locutionary clause. But in FDS the placing of speech before a clause of saying appears more free than the reverse order. Compare:

267

No, that is true, said Sally...

[*Mrs Dalloway*, 1976 edn, p. 212]

with its rearranged equivalent:

Sally said, No, that is true...

But although inversion has a role to play in such cases as these, it is clear that the most complex and interesting examples occur in IS and FIS.

10.1.5 The effects and uses of FIS

We have already noted some of the uses of FIS in the passages we have discussed, especially the ironic effect in the passages from *Persuasion* and *Bleak House*. The irony arises because FIS is normally viewed as a form where the authorial voice is interposed between the reader and what the character says, so that the reader is distanced from the character's words. This is explicable if it is assumed that DS is a norm or baseline for the portrayal of speech (see section 10.3).

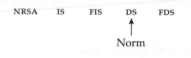

Figure 10.2

As we saw in the Hemingway example [12], any movement to the right of DS on the above scale will produce an effect of freeness, as if the author has vacated the stage and left it to the characters; whereas any movement to the left of the norm will usually be interpreted as a movement away from verbatim report and towards 'interference'. It is this distancing which allows FIS to be used as a vehicle for irony. But that irony does not have to be at the expense of the speaking character. In the coroner's scene in *Bleak House* it is not Jo that we feel at odds with, but his inquisitors. And although FIS is often used for irony it does not have to be, as this extract from Virginia Woolf's *Mrs Dalloway* shows:

'But what are you going to do?' she asked him. Oh, the lawyers and solicitors, Messrs. Hooper and Grateley of Lincoln's Inn, they were going to do it, he said.

[p. 52]

Peter has just told Clarissa that he is in love with a married woman, and that he has come to London to see about the divorce. Clarissa is startled by the information, and she is accorded direct speech. Peter, on the other hand, is very offhand about the matter. His reply is distanced by its presentation in FIS and its unemotive tone is emphasised by the interpolation of the unnecessary information of the name of his solicitors. The effect, however, is not one of irony. Instead, the contrast between the modes of speech presentation puts one, so to speak, in the shadow of the other, and so allows us to infer different characters' attitudes towards the information presented.

This shows how FIS can contrast with other speech modes in the author's control of the 'light and shade' of conversation, the highlighting and backgrounding of speech according to the role and attitude of characters. This variation can also be used for more large-scale strategic purposes; for example, to channel our sympathies towards one character or set of characters and away from another (this is of course implicit in the use of irony). An example of this strategic use is the courtroom scene in *A Tale of Two Cities* where, as Michael Gregory has shown, Dickens uses mainly FIS to portray the speeches of those characters hostile to the central characters of the novel. This choice allows him to cast an ironic light on what they say. When the friendly witnesses take the stand, however, DS is used and, 'they are, as it were, allowed to speak for themselves'.[12] This division of modes of speech presentation thus becomes an important vehicle which Dickens uses to control our sympathies over a relatively sustained period. Charles Jones has also suggested that Conrad uses variation of speech presentation in *The Secret Agent* to help indicate changes in the role of his characters. After her murder of her husband, the proportions of Winnie Verloc's speech change from roughly 50 per cent direct and 50 per cent more indirect forms to a state of affairs where 95 per cent of her words are presented through DS. This display of apparent garrulousness reduces the 'robust anarchist' Ossipon to a state of inward doubt, where the majority of his thoughts are presented through categories towards the indirect end of the scale.[13]

Although the use of FIS normally involves some kind of distancing, there are occasions when it does not. These are usually situations where the preceding context has used even more indirect forms, and where the introduction of FIS is perceived against this localised norm as a movement towards directness. In this example from Fielding's *Tom Jones*, for instance:

> Here, while he was venting his grief in private, he heard a violent uproar below stairs; and soon after a female voice begged him for heaven's sake to come and prevent murder.
>
> [Book XIII, Chapter 5]

Tom's thought and perception are reported in a very indirect form, namely that of the NARRATIVE REPORT OF A THOUGHT ACT (the equivalent for character thought of NRSA; see sections 10.1.3 and 10.2.1). When the words of the female voice appear in FIS, the contrast in form with what has gone before adds to the urgency of the plea.

To sum up, FIS is often used as a vehicle for irony because its occurrence on the indirect side of the DS norm on the speech presentation scale allows for the introduction of two points of view. But this indirectness does not automatically involve irony, and indeed, in the context of a set of more indirect locutions, the effect of FIS may well be one of relative directness. Its uses, therefore, are many and varied, sometimes operating at a relatively minor level in the interpretation of dialogue, sometimes being used for larger-scale tactical effect. These varied effects can be explained naturally if FIS is seen, by virtue of its intermediate position on the scale, as contrasting in different ways with alternative speech modes.

10.2 The presentation of thought

Although we have so far concentrated on the novelist's presentation of speech, it would be fair to say that many leading novelists of the nineteenth and twentieth centuries have been deeply concerned with the portrayal of 'internal speech'. This is because one of the major concerns of the novelist for the last hundred years or more has been how to present vividly the flow of thought through a character's mind. Hence thought presentation has come to be inextricably linked with what is usually known as 'stream of consciousness writing'. The modes of speech and thought presentation are very similar formally, but it should always be remembered that the representation of the thoughts of characters, even in an extremely indirect form (like NARRATIVE REPORT OF THOUGHT ACTS – see section 10.2.1), is ultimately an artifice. We cannot see inside the minds of other people, but if the motivations for the actions and attitudes of characters are to be made clear to the reader, the representation of their thoughts, like the use of soliloquy on stage, is a necessary licence. Once it is accepted that it is reasonable for a novelist to tell us what is in the minds of fictional characters, then it is not surprising that there emerge various experimental techniques like FREE INDIRECT THOUGHT or Joyce's Bloom-language in *Ulysses*. They are attempts not just to report what the character thinks, but also to render the character's immediate experience or consciousness of those thoughts.

10.2.1 The categorisation of thought presentation

The categories available to the writer in presenting the thoughts of his characters are the same as those for the presentation of speech, and are distinguished from one another by similar means. In our abbreviations below we use 'T' for 'thought'.

[21] Does she still love me? (Free Direct Thought: FDT)
[22] He wondered, 'Does she still love me?' (Direct Thought: DT)

[23] Did she still love him? (Free Indirect Thought: FIT)

[24] He wondered if she still loved him. (Indirect Thought: IT)

[25] He wondered about her love for him. (Narrative Report of a Thought Act: NRTA)

In the various possibilities above, the FDT example is like the DT example but with the introductory reporting clause removed. The FIT version differs from that of DT by virtue of the back-shift of the tense and the conversion of the first-person pronoun to the third person (indirect features) and also by the absence of a reporting clause and the retention of the interrogative form and question mark (direct features). The IT version has an introductory reporting clause, explicit subordination, and a declarative form for the reported clause. The NRTA sentence incorporates what minimal report there is within the main clause by nominalising the reported clause. It should be apparent from our examples that the thought presentation modes, like those for speech, can be distinguished by features from any of the three levels of grammar, lexis and graphology.

A writer who decides to let us know the thoughts of a character at all, even by the mere use of thought act reporting, is inviting us to see things from that character's point of view. Moving along the scale towards the 'free' end of the thought presentation continuum, we apparently get the 'verbatim' thoughts of the characters with less and less intervention on the writer's part. As with speech presentation, the crucial factor is the semantic status of the type of thought presentation used, and the categories may be differentiated by one or more of a group of formal features. It is apparent, for example, that in I-narrator novels (where the author makes us view everything from that character's stance) the first-person pronoun can occur in FIT because it is appropriate to both the primary and the reported discourse situation. This can be seen in Dickens's *David Copperfield*:

> Three years. Long in the aggregate, though short as they went by. And home was very dear to me, and Agnes too – but she was not mine – she was never to be mine. She might have been, but that was past!
>
> [Chapter 58]

This passage is also an example of something which we saw earlier with regard to FIS, and which is fairly common in FIT: it is impossible to tell by the use of formal linguistic criteria alone whether one is reading the thoughts of the character or the views of the narrator/author. The tense and pronoun selection are appropriate to either, and as we have an I-narrator, the interpolation, exclamation and truncated sentences could all indicate his emotional involvement. Actually David does marry Agnes in the end, so the only possible interpretation in retrospect is that we are being presented with a vivid characterisation of the younger David's thoughts. The reader

271

might well feel cheated when he finds out that Dickens at last manages to produce the happy ending which he seems to deny here. But this would only be a justifiable complaint if the passage were authorial report: if it is interpreted as FIT, then of course Dickens cannot be held responsible for the truth of the beliefs he attributes to his hero.

Sometimes the lack of formal discriminating features can actually give rise to critical dispute over the status of the sentences in a novel. Mary Lascelles in *Jane Austen and her Art* believed that the following lines from *Persuasion* are either authorial statement or the free indirect presentation of Frederick Wentworth's words in conversation with his sister:

> He had thought her wretchedly altered, and, in the first moment of appeal, had spoken as he felt. He had not forgiven Anne Elliot. She had used him ill; deserted and disappointed him; and worse, she had shewn a feebleness of character in doing so, which his own decided, confident temper could not endure. [Chapter 7]

She claims that Jane Austen's move here is a mistake, 'an oversight',[14] because it illicitly breaks the consistent portrayal of events from Anne's point of view. But Wayne Booth in *The Rhetoric of Fiction* proposes a third possibility, namely that the sentences involved are Wentworth's FIT, and that in this 'momentary inside view' we learn Wentworth's mistaken interpretation of the events of the novel, a mistake which he does not realise until the end of the story. In other words: 'It is deliberate manipulation of inside views in order to destroy our conventional security. We are thus made ready 'to go along with Anne in her long and painful road to the discovery that Frederick loves her after all'.[15]

The sentences involved are thus three-way ambiguous in terms of mode of presentation. Booth's analysis seems preferable, not on any formal grounds, but because his account is the only one which gives a satisfactory motivation for the shift in viewpoint which Mary Lascelles notices.

This negative feature of speech and thought presentation, that it is often difficult to tell which mode is being used, is something that can be positively exploited in the manipulation of point of view. It allows an author to slip from narrative statement to interior portrayal without the reader noticing what has occurred, and as the reader has little choice but to take on trust the views of the narrator, when character and narrator are merged in this way he tends to take over the view of the character too. The unobtrusive change from one mode to another, sometimes called 'slipping', can occur more than once inside one sentence. Indeed Leaska[16] has discovered one example in Virginia Woolf's *To The Lighthouse* where slipping occurs seven times. We were effectively dealing with slipping from IS to FIS when we earlier discussed sentences like the one from Paul Scott's *Staying On* (see [17] in section 10.1.4), which began with a clause of saying and therefore because of the subordination at first sight appeared to be indirect, but which had positive free features in the subordinate clause. The same kind of phenomenon can, of course, be found in thought presentation, and, as in the portrayal of speech, the inversion of the main and subordinate clauses tends to make the change more noticeable. An example is the first sentence of the following quotation from *Mrs Dalloway*:

> And there the motor car stood, with drawn blinds, and upon them a curious pattern like a tree, Septimus thought, and this gradual drawing together of everything to one centre before his eyes, as if some horror had come almost to the surface and was about to burst into flames, terrified him. The world wavered and quivered and threatened to burst into flames. It is I who am blocking the way, he thought.   [p. 18]

Because the reported clause is fairly long, the effect of the reporting clause, when it comes, is quite unexpected. A consequence of this kind of change in thought presentation is that Septimus's thoughts suddenly appear to be much more conscious than we first assumed. After the main clause the sentence slips back into FIS again with the use of the 'near' deictic *this*. This passage also exploits the possibility of inversion in FDT in the last sentence.

10.2.2 The relationship between inner speech and point of view

When an author chooses to represent the thoughts of a character, in whatever form, we are invited to see things from that character's POINT OF VIEW: he becomes the REFLECTOR of the fiction (section 5.5.1). But before we examine the ways in which the portrayal of those thoughts can be presented through categories of thought presentation, it will be worth reiterating a point that we made in Chapter 5, namely that the reverse does not apply: it is possible to view things from a particular character's point of view without representing his thoughts. This could be seen in our discussion of the passage from Arnold Bennett's *Clayhanger* (p. 330), where we noted that Edwin was a reflector even though the presentation of his thoughts was kept to a minimum and though we were given information about the mental events of other characters. Another example is from D.H. Lawrence's short story *You Touched Me*:

> In the morning she could feel the consciousness in his eyes, when she came downstairs. She tried to bear herself as if nothing at all had happened, and she succeeded. She had the calm self-control, self-indifference, of one who has suffered and borne her suffering. She looked at him from her darkish, almost drugged blue eyes, she met the spark of consciousness in his eyes, and quenched it. And with her long, fine hand she put the sugar in her coffee.

In this extract there is continual reference to Matilda's inner self. But it is her state of mind, not the direct experience of her thoughts that is represented. Besides expressions like 'she had the calm self-control', which describes her inner state, Matilda is also continually the subject of intentional verbs like *tried, looked, met*.

A character's point of view can also be represented without the state of his mind being described. Instead, the author portrays scenes and events as they would have looked to the character concerned. In the following extract from *Tess of the D'Urbervilles* we see Tess's departure from the viewpoint of her family:

> They saw her white shape draw near to the spring-cart, on which her box was already placed. But before she had quite reached it another vehicle shot out from a clump of trees on the summit, came round the bend of the road there, passed the luggage-cart, and halted beside Tess, who looked up as if in great surprise.
>
> [Phase the First, Chapter 7]

The most obvious indication that the omniscient narrator is restricting himself to the perception of Tess's family is the fact that the first sentence is dominated by 'they saw'. But in any case, Hardy restricts the perceptions themselves by using linguistic forms which are only appropriate to the characters. Hence, instead of saying 'they saw Tess' we find 'they saw her white shape'. We see what they see with their eyes and no more. Similarly, at the end of the last sentence, Tess looks up 'as if in great surprise'. The omniscient narrator would know whether Tess was surprised or not, and so the *as if* locution would be unnecessary for him. Again, therefore, we must assume that we are being invited to look at the scene before us from the limited point of view of Tess's family.

10.2.3 Uses of the categories of thought presentation

Because any portrayal of character thought must involve the presence of an omniscient narrator, the more direct forms of presentation, DT and FDT, take on a somewhat different value from their speech counterparts. In the presentation of speech, the use of DS or FDS produces the impression that the character is talking in our presence, with less and less authorial intervention. Similarly, in DT and FDT authorial intervention appears minimal; but as the result is effectively a monologue, with the character 'talking' to himself, the thoughts he produces acquire a conscious quality:

> He asked himself what is a woman standing on the stairs in the shadow, listening to distant music, a symbol of.
>
> [*The Dead*]

Here Joyce makes his 'hero' Gabriel *consider*, with apparent verbal articulation, the significance of the scene in front of him. In the following example from *Mrs Dalloway*, FDT and inversion are combined:

> I know all that, Peter thought; I know what I'm up against, he thought, running his finger along the blade of his knife, Clarissa and Dalloway and all the rest of them; but I'll show Clarissa – and then to his utter surprise, suddenly thrown by those uncontrollable forces, thrown through the air, he burst into tears . . . [p. 52]

The conscious qualities of FDT and inversion are used to indicate how in control of his thought Peter is, or rather how in control he thinks he is; for immediately after these deliberations his emotions take him over completely. Even when the discourse involved is relatively incoherent FDT has a conscious feel to it:

> Her ear too is a shell, the peeping lobe there. Been to the seaside. Lovely seaside girls. Skin tanned raw. Should have put on coldcream first make it brown. Buttered toast. O and that lotion mustn't forget.
>
> [*Ulysses*, Penguin edn, p. 280]

This is the most extreme kind of FDT, with no reporting verb or quotation marks. It is the truncated quality of the sentences and the sudden associative changes of topic which give the impression that the thoughts are half-formed and fairly inchoate. But the use of the FDT form makes it seem that Bloom, like us, is watching his thoughts as they go by.

Because FDT is relatively easy to distinguish it can also be used to represent sudden strength of realisation, as in this extract from Lowry's *Under the Volcano*:

> Yet one felt that really they were wrapped in each other's arms by this river at dusk among gold stars. Yvonne, he thought, with sudden tenderness, where are you, my darling? Darling . . . For a moment he had thought her by his side. [Chapter 7]

The switches from FIT to FDT and back again to NRTA are made apparent by the sentence boundaries and the sequence of dots after *darling* as well as by the tense and pronoun changes. The use of FDT, with some of it occurring before the reporting verb, mirrors the abrupt change in emotional key indicated lexically by 'with sudden tenderness'. Like the direct forms, the free indirect form takes on a different value when we turn from the presentation of speech to the presentation of thought. Instead of indicating a move towards the narrator, it signifies a movement towards the exact representation of a character's thought as it occurs:

> He picked up the dagger and drew the beautiful thing lightly through his fingers. It was sharp, polished, dangerous, marvellously integrated and sweetly proportioned.
>
> [Iris Murdoch, *An Unofficial Rose*, Part Two, Chapter 9]

If it were not for the value-laden adjectives and adverbs *beautiful, marvellously* and *sweetly*, this sentence would be straight narrative report. Iris Murdoch could also have chosen to give us Penn's thoughts in a more indirect form in sentences like 'He picked up the dagger and drew it through his fingers. He noticed that it was beautiful . . .' Her choice of FIT, on the other hand, makes us feel that we are getting a more vivid and immediate representation of the character's thoughts as they happen. Hence while FIS distances us somewhat from the characters producing the speech, FIT has the opposite effect, apparently putting us directly inside the character's mind. The reason for this is that the norm or baseline for the presentation of thought is IT, whereas the norm for speech is DS:

Figure 10.3

The fact that IT is the norm for thought presentation requires some explanation, if only because in the twentieth century novel at least, it is arguable that FIT is the more common mode. The reason that the IT mode is viewed as the norm has to do with the semantics of reporting. We noted earlier that DS claims to provide a verbatim report of what was said, but that in IS, on the other hand, the writer gives the *substance* of what someone said without commitment to the words used to express it. DS is possible, and indeed common, because it is the mode that represents speech in the form in which it is directly manifest to a listener (we may note, in this connection, the well-established conventions of DS in dramatic texts, as well as in parliamentary and legal reporting). But other people's thoughts are not accessible to such direct perception, and so a mode which only commits the writer to the content of what was thought is much more acceptable as a norm. Thoughts, in general, are not verbally formulated, and so cannot be reported verbatim. Given that the norms for speech and thought presentation are at different points on the continuum, the different values of FIS and FIT can be naturally explained. FIS is a movement leftwards from the norm

in Figure 10.3 and is therefore interpreted as a movement towards authorial intervention, whereas FIT is seen as a move to the right and hence away
from the author's most directly interpretative control and into the active
mind of the character. Because the direct perception of someone else's
thought is not possible, DT is perceived as more artificial than more indirect
forms. When DT is used, the writer is in effect saying, 'This is what the
character would have said if he had made his thoughts explicit'. It is this
explicitness which gives rise to the conscious qualities of DT and FDT, which
we noted earlier.

In spite of the artificial nature of the use of DT, it has been adopted fairly
widely, particularly in more traditional novels, perhaps through analogy
with the dramatic mode of soliloquy, or in an attempt to make character
thought more actual. From this point of view we can think of FIT historically as a natural development, keeping much of the vividness of DT without the artificiality of the 'speaking to oneself' convention. Since FIT gets
the best of both worlds it is understandable that it has become as common
as it has in the twentieth-century novel.

The concern that nineteenth- and twentieth-century novelists had with
portraying the internal drama of the minds of their characters meant that
some of them moved the narrative focus of their *stories* into those minds.
This is very clear in the work of writers like Henry James, Virginia Woolf
and James Joyce. A clear example of this is Joyce's short story *Eveline*, at the
beginning of which we learn that the title character has consented to run
away from home with her lover, Frank. The rest of the story hinges entirely
on whether or not she will actually carry out that decision:

> She had consented to go away, to leave her home. Was that wise? She
> tried to weigh each side of the question. In her home anyway she had
> shelter and food; she had those whom she had known all her life about
> her. Of course she had to work hard, both in the house and at business.
> What would they say of her in the stores when they found out that she
> had run away with a fellow? Say she was a fool perhaps; and her place
> would be filled up by advertisement.

Apart from the third sentence, which is NRTA, this entire paragraph is in
FIT. The first sentence might possibly be narrative report in spite of the
'spontaneous' effect of the repeated infinitive structure. But the fact that
the following sentence, which is a question, and therefore definitely in FIT,
refers back to the first pronominally suggests that that too must be part of
Eveline's thoughts. Eveline in effect carries on a dialogue with herself,
asking questions and trying to answer them disinterestedly. The fact that
she is questioning her decision at all must make us suspect that she is
going to reverse it, and even here, near the beginning of the story, she
seems to find more reasons for staying than for going.

When we examined the choices of mode of speech presentation we noted that it was possible for a writer to make consistent choices with respect to his characters for general strategic purposes within his work. Novelists can use the presentation of thought in a similar way in order to control our sympathies. In Angus Wilson's short story *Raspberry Jam* the central character, a young boy called Johnny, lives in a world of his own. It is evident that his parents do not understand him at all, and his only sympathetic treatment is by two very eccentric old ladies. Wilson controls our sympathy for Johnny by giving us extensive accounts of his thoughts through FIT. His parents and their friends are distanced from us by virtue of the fact that we are never shown inside their minds. We only learn about them through their conversations and direct narrative statement. The two old ladies, who are in an intermediate position, are accorded some FIT, but not as much as Johnny. Towards the end of the story the two old ladies go on a drinking bout because they think they have been snubbed by the vicar. They have been drinking for two days when they realise Johnny is coming to tea. They rush out to get some raspberries for him, and find a young bullfinch that has been stealing the fruit, stuck in the netting. When Johnny arrives for tea they get him drunk too, and then pull the bird gradually to pieces as a punishment for eating the raspberries. Johnny cannot stand this, snatches the bird from them, stamps on it and runs away. Thus at the end of the story the adults whom Johnny has come to trust shock him violently, causing him to reject them. We feel for Johnny at the end of the story, and this tendency is helped by the fact that from the moment when the ladies begin their drinking spree the privilege of FIT presentation is removed from them. Hence Wilson first enlists our sympathy for them through the use of FIT and then removes it in order to mirror for us Johnny's response to their actions.

Modes of speech and thought can interact in many interesting ways, particularly when speech presentation is used to represent thoughts, producing a kind of soliloquy. In *The Old Man and the Sea*, Hemingway uses the interaction of speech and thought presentation to represent two distinct aspects of the old man's mind:

'I'll kill him though,' he said. 'In all his greatness and his glory.'
Although it is unjust, he thought. But I will show him what a man can do and what a man endures.

[Cape edn, p. 61]

'Don't think, old man,' he said aloud. 'Sail on this course and take it when it comes.'
'But I must think, he thought. Because it is all I have left . . .'

[p. 97]

In these extracts, the old man's immediate reactions to the world around him are portrayed through DS. But FDT is used to show the more reflective side of his nature. It is almost as if the reflective, more philosophical, side of the old man carries on a dialogue with the physical, instinctual half, keeping it in check. In this way Hemingway dramatises the elemental struggle in the old man's nature in this story of privation, courage and endurance.

10.3 Conclusion

In conclusion, we must emphasise the almost boundless versatility of speech and thought presentation as a means of varying point of view, tone and distance.

First, the versatility comes from the theoretically limitless embedding process: this somewhat philosophical point is illustrated with humorous pedantry in the Socratic dialogue in *Ulysses* where Joyce expounds the meeting of Bloom's and Stephen's minds:

What, reduced to their simplest reciprocal form, were Bloom's thoughts about Stephen's thoughts about Bloom and Bloom's thoughts about Stephen's thoughts about Bloom's thoughts about Stephen?

He thought that he thought that he was a jew whereas he knew that he knew that he knew that he was not.

[Penguin edn, p. 602]

Like a hall of mirrors, each mirror capable of replicating the image in another, a discourse can embody narrators within narrations, reflectors within reflections, and so on *ad infinitum*. In practical terms, this means that an author has all the resources needed to call up a multiplicity of viewpoints on the same subject matter.

Second, the versatility of speech and thought presentation arises from fine gradations among the speech mode categories, and between them and the author's narrative report. We have seen this potentiality for overlap not only in the scale of speech and thought modes illustrated in Figure 10.2, but in the neutralisation which can take place between FIT and narrative report; that is, between modes at different levels of discourse structure.

The distinction between the author's voice and a voice which comes from inside the fiction can be signalled by slight variations of style which may or may not be perceived as significant by the reader. Consider the opening paragraph of Lawrence's story *The Horse Dealer's Daughter*:

'Well, Mabel, and what are you going to do with yourself?' asked Joe, with foolish flippancy (1). He felt quite safe himself (2). Without listening for an answer, he turned aside, worked a grain of tobacco to the tip of his tongue, and spat it out (3). He did not care about anything, since he felt safe himself (4).

The simple syntax and lexis of sentences (2) and (4) seem to belong to Joe's idiolect rather than to that of the author, who is capable of describing Joe's manner as one of 'foolish flippancy'. It is this stylistic hint, together with the repetition of 'he felt [quite] safe himself', and the suspicion that only Joe's self-deceiving egotism would describe his situation in that way, that encourages us to read these sentences as FIT.

But the same type of colloquialism, later in the story, requires a different kind of interpretation in 'Joe stood with his knees stuck out, in real horsey fashion'. This equine comparison is in keeping with Joe's trade, but is unlikely to be an expression of his own thoughts; rather, Lawrence seems to be ventriloquising Joe's style of speech in describing him: a trick of style which makes us see this oafish horse dealer in, as it were, his own terms. There is a close resemblance, therefore, between FIT and a related phenomenon, the selective imitation of a style of speech by the author, which we may call SPEECH ALLUSION.

We have observed various forms of speech allusion in previous chapters: for example, in Lawrence's sentence 'The miners were being turned up' (see p. 75), and in Dickens's description of Captain Cuttle in terms of nautical phraseology (see p. 50). In its most attenuated form, it may simply show in a single word or phrase; and it need not be associated with a particular character, but may be the expression of communal point of view. It is characteristic of Conrad's writing, for instance, that the use of a specific phrase, characteristic of some group within the novel, comes to accumulate symbolic force by repetition. In *Nostromo*, the central character is named in various ways: as Nostromo, as Gian' Battista (by his fellow countrymen the Violas), as Capataz de Cargadores ('Master of the Wharves') by the people of the neighbourhood. It is this last resounding title that signifies, both for Nostromo and the populace, his powerful and esteemed position as a 'man of the people'. So when Conrad uses this title in the narrative itself (rather than in the speech of the characters) it becomes invested with these same associations, and accumulates under its wing a host of interrelated qualities – power, popularity, courage, munificence, vanity, etc. – which attach to Nostromo both as a public and as a private individual. When the novel ends with:

> . . . the genius of the magnificent Capataz de Cargadores dominated the dark gulf containing his conquests of treasure and love.
>
> [Part 3, Chapter 13]

it is as if the novelist himself adopts the estimate of Nostromo which has been built up both in Nostromo's own eyes and in the eyes of the people of Sulaco for whom he has become a legendary figure. A point of view that belongs to characters within the novel appears to have been absorbed into the narrative. Speech allusion can be more or less noticeable, and can have varying effects from ironic distance to sympathetic identification. But, at its best, it seems to add an intensity of commitment to the narrative style, by its implication of empathy between the author and the inhabitants of the fiction he creates.

This last illustration shows that it is not easy to pin down and catalogue the many variations of point of view achieved through manipulation of the author's voice in relation to the voices of participants in the fiction. These subtle interactions between speech and thought presentation and point of view have become one of the richest and most open-ended areas of interpretative significance in the novel, and thus constitute an extremely fruitful aspect of the study of style in fiction.

Notes

1. A good survey is B. MCHALE (1978). Other useful references can be found in the notes below.
2. R. OHMANN (1964) assumes that direct and indirect speech are transformationally related in a generative grammar, but A. BANFIELD (1973) has convincing arguments against this view.
3. It seems to have been generally assumed by writers on speech presentation that DS and IS are at the extremes of the speech presentation continuum, with FIS and FDS in the middle. But as FDS possesses no indirect features at all, and merely consists of DS without either the locutionary clause or the speech marks (features which indicate the presence of a narrator) its proper place, as its name suggests, is at the free end of the continuum, beyond DS.
4. D. LODGE (1971).
5. See, for example, N. PAGE (1973), 32–35.
6. Hence the definition is like that of Wittgenstein for games in the *Tractatus*. He argues that there is no one feature that all games share, but that there are features in common between football and chess, chess and bridge, bridge and patience etc. Hence patience and football may possibly share no features with each other but belong to the same 'family'.
7. N. PAGE (1973), 32.
8. S. ULLMANN (1957), 99.
9. See A. MCDOWELL (1973).
10. C. LAWRENCE (1978).
11. It appears that the final or medial positioning of the reporting clause changes its syntactic role from a 'main' to a 'comment' clause (see R. QUIRK *et al.* (1985), 15.53–56). The fact that the interrogative form is much more natural with inversion (compare 'How did he do it she asked' with 'She asked how did he do it' and 'She asked how he did it') is evidence that a syntactic change has taken place. Hence it is reasonable to suggest that inverted forms are not IS but in between IS and FIS on the speech presentation continuum.
12. M. GREGORY (1965).
13. C. JONES (1968).
14. M. LASCELLES (1965), 204.
15. W. BOOTH (1961), 252.
16. M.A. LEASKA (1970).

CHAPTER 11

Stylistics and fiction 25 years on

I n this, the first of the two added chapters for this second edition of *Style in Fiction*, we review the developments which have taken place in the field in the last 25 years and how these developments would have changed the book if we were writing it now. In the new final chapter, we analyse a short story by T.F. Powys in the light of the theoretical developments we describe in this chapter.

In section 11.1 we review the changes which have taken place in stylistics in general over the last 25 years and how stylistics relates to newly-developed neighbouring areas of study. We refer to more book publications than journal articles, as books will be more generally available internationally than journals. In section 11.2 we concentrate more specifically on developments in the analysis of prose fiction since the first publication of *Style in Fiction* and so indicate what we think we would have to *add* if we were writing the book from scratch. In section 11.3 we discuss what aspects of the original we feel we would have to *change* if we were writing the book now.

11.1 The development of stylistics as a sub-discipline

The introduction to *Style in Fiction* positions it as a contribution to what, in 1981, was still called the 'new stylistics' and specifically refers to *A Linguistic Guide to English Poetry* (Leech 1969), the volume which was, in effect, its elder sister in the same series. Although stylistics can be seen as a development from two movements early in the twentieth century, namely Russian formalism (*cf* Bann and Bowlt 1973, Erlich 1969, Garvin 1958 and Matejka and Pomorska 1971) and the practical criticism of I.A. Richards (1929) and William Empson (1953), its approach was still felt to be new.

Until 1981, most stylistic analysis had been carried out on poems, and *Style in Fiction* was one of the first book-length explorations of the stylistic analysis of extracts from prose fiction. Drama was virtually undiscussed, and stylistics still did not have enough extant analyses of literary texts to demonstrate adequately its assumption that 'examining the language of a literary text can be a means to a fuller understanding and appreciation of the writer's artistic achievement' (Leech and Short 1981, p. 1).

Now, at the beginning of the new millennium, the situation is very different. Work on the stylistic analysis of poetry has continued (*cf* Bradford 1993, Cook 1994, Freeman 2005, Hasan 1989, Jeffries 1993, Semino 1997, Tsur 1992, 2003, Verdonk 1993, Widdowson 1995a, York 1986), and the linguistic examination of prose fiction has blossomed (*cf* Emmott 1997, Fludernik 1993, Hardy 2003, Hoover 1999, Hori 2004, Simpson 1993, Stockwell 2000, Toolan 2001 [1988], 1990, Verdonk and Weber 1995). Moreover, the stylistic analysis of drama is now more plentiful (*cf* Burton 1980, Culpeper 2001, Culpeper, Short and Verdonk 1998, Freeman forthcoming, Herman 1995). (To the lists of publications in the preceding sentence, we should add relevant contributions in the collections referred to towards the end of this paragraph.) Douthwaite (2000), which is devoted to foregrounding theory, uses many prose examples and analyses, and Simpson (2003) is an innovative account of satire which draws on stylistics, discourse analysis and pragmatics, and applies them to literary and non-literary texts. A very useful dictionary of stylistics (Wales 2000 [1989]) and a number of collections of stylistics articles (e.g. Bex, Burke and Stockwell 2000, Carter 1982, Carter and Simpson 1989, Freeman 1981, van Peer 1988, Short 1989, Toolan 1992 and Weber 1996) have been published, which give a representative flavour of the range and depth of the field. Finally, among other organisations, there is a flourishing international association, the *Poetics and Linguistics Association* (http://www.pala.ac.uk), which has stylistics at the centre of its interests. Moreover, there are more journals which concentrate on stylistics-related articles, of which *Language and Literature, Style* and the *Journal of Literary Semantics* are probably the most influential. Among journals relating to text and discourse, *Text & Talk* (formerly named *Text*) and *The Journal of Pragmatics* take stylistics articles relevant to their areas of concentration. *Language and Literature* (a key journal for our field) and *The Year's Work in English Studies* carry annual summaries of recent work published in stylistics, and *Style* also presents occasional annotated bibliographies of relevant areas.

There have also been useful advances in neighbouring areas of study which are important to stylistics. Linguistic pragmatics (including politeness analysis and discourse analysis) is much more developed than it was in 1981, leading to more sophisticated stylistic work on fiction and drama in particular. Indeed, the use of pragmatics has become so prevalant in stylistics since the early 1980s that it would be fair to say that stylistics has undergone a 'pragmatic turn', which started around the time we were writing the first edition of *Style in Fiction*. In addition, other sub-disciplines have sprung up which overlap to some degree with the aims of stylistics. The field of narratology (e.g. Bal 1997 [1985], Bonheim 1982, 1990, Chatman 1978, Fludernik 1996, Herman 2002, 2003, Prince 1982, Rimmon-Kenan 2002 [1983], Ronen 1994, Ryan 1991, Stanzel 1984, van Peer and Chatman 2001) is probably the most notable for stylisticians interested in the study of prose fiction, as it has contributed much to the understanding of viewpoint, plot structure and fictional worlds, areas in which stylistics has long had an interest.

Another, more general, area worthy of note is what is usually called 'empirical literary studies'. Of course stylistics itself is empirical, in the sense that it attempts to analyse texts as accurately and objectively as possible, taking into account what we know about textual structure and the nature of language processing. Empirical literary studies, on the other hand, undertake analyses of informant responses of the kind psychologists typically perform. This is done to see what empirical evidence there is to support or disconfirm particular accounts of reader reactions to individual texts, and so to understand more fully the processes by which literary texts are interpreted (*cf* Bortolussi and Dixon 2003, Emmott, Sanford and Morrow 2006, Gerrig 1993, Hakemulder 2000, Zwaan 1993). The aims of empirical literary studies thus also overlap with those of stylistics, and stylistics is in a good position to provide detailed interpretative accounts to be tested out by those involved in empirical literary studies. Indeed, some academics (e.g. van Peer 1986) perform both stylistic analysis and informant work.

Although most stylisticians have focused on the analysis of literary texts, many have also extended their interest to the analysis of non-literary texts too (e.g. Cook 1992, Freeborn 1996). Not surprisingly, then, there has been a general overlap between the work of stylisticians and those interested in language varieties and the study of register. Another related approach is that which now most frequently goes under the title 'critical discourse analysis' (CDA), although the term 'critical linguistics' has also sometimes been used to refer to our own area of study. CDA shares a considerable number of analytical tools with stylistics, though it is more closely associated with the linguistic school of M.A.K. Halliday (*cf*, e.g., Halliday and Matthiessen 2004) than the more eclectic stylistics enterprise with which this book is associated. The defining difference of CDA is that it analyses (usually non-literary) texts in order to expose what the authors usually see as unjustified socio-political assumptions encoded non-obviously in the text concerned (e.g. Fairclough 1989, 1995, 2000, 2003, Fowler 1991, Wodak and Meyer 2001). In this respect it has interesting correlations with the deconstructive and postmodernist styles of analysis practised by some modern literary theorists. CDA approaches to the stylistic analysis of literary texts can be seen in Birch (1989, 1991) and Weber (1992). Although, in principle, CDA could be applied to any text and from any ideological perspective, there is a tendency for it to be practised by those with a left-wing political persuasion, and the stylistician Henry Widdowson has criticised critical discourse analysts for, among other things, effectively knowing what interpretation they are going to 'impose' on a text before they have even read it (see Widdowson 1995b, 1996, 2000 and Fairclough 1996, with whom Widdowson has debated the issue).

A fast-developing area which is having an increasing effect on contemporary stylistics is corpus linguistics (*cf* Biber 1988, Biber, Conrad and Reppen 1998, McEnery and Wilson 1996, Sinclair 2004, Thomas and Short 1996). Although, in its earlier years, corpus linguistics set itself the task of creating large and varied corpora of (extracts from) a wide range of written and spoken texts in order to investigate central aspects of language like lexis and grammar, of late we have seen the growth of corpus applications to literature. Louw (1993, 1997) has used large corpora of English to establish what he calls the typical 'semantic prosody' of particular words, i.e. the typical contexts in which particular words occur, as a way of establishing the generalised associations we have for a word, and whether its semantic prosody in a particular text parallels, or contrasts with, its more typical semantic prosody. This technique is particularly useful in the study of poetry, but can also be used effectively with texts from other literary genres. In the remainder of this paragraph, we mention publications illustrating a wide range of applications of corpus-based techniques to literary style. Hori (2004) examines collocational patterns in the novels of Charles Dickens, Hoover (1999) uses the British National Corpus (BNC) and a specially-constructed corpus of novels to test the claims that Halliday (1971) made about Golding's *The Inheritors* (see pp. 25–6), Hardy (2003) combines a corpus approach with qualitative stylistic analysis to elucidate style and thematic world-view concerns in the fiction of Flannery O'Connor, and Stubbs (2005) discusses the benefits of a corpus-based approach for stylistics, using Conrad's *Heart of Darkness* as an example. Semino and Short (2004) use a manually tagged corpus to develop more accurate and complete models of discourse presentation in literary and non-literary narrative (for further details see section 11.3). Others are developing a corpus-based approach to the study of metaphor (see the 2001 special issue of *Language and Literature* 11, 1) in order to see how exactly linguistic recognition of metaphor in texts can be related to the conceptual constructs of cognitive metaphor theory associated with Lakoff and others (e.g. Lakoff and Johnson 1980, Lakoff and Turner 1989, Turner 1996).

The use of relatively sophisticated computational techniques in corpus linguistics might lead to fears that the computer is 'taking over' the domain of literary language in a way that leaves little scope for individual response and interpretation. This fear would be unfounded, however, as corpus techniques are (at least at present) incapable of simulating the human capacity to understand and interpret. The contributions of corpus linguistics can be put more positively as follows: it allows us to carry out fast, exhaustive and accurate searches of texts, to undertake certain kinds of quantitative processing, including the comparison of different texts in terms of key vocabulary, and so on. The computer remains the servant of the human mind and sensibility. Procedures such as contextual concordance searches and frequency counts can be carried out on easily recognisable features of texts, such as vocabulary items, collocations and simple grammatical categories, but for more abstract levels of analysis (such as that of discourse presentation categories mentioned above), the human analyst has to annotate the text manually. The 'corpus turn' in stylistics, if it can be called such, is partly due to the fact that an enormous range of literary texts in English are now available in electronic form, and basic processing tasks can be carried out with relatively little difficulty on the entire oeuvre of major writers of the past, such as Shakespeare, Austen, James and Dickens.

The 'cognitive turn' within linguistics is, if anything, a more substantial influence, applying to much more than metaphor (see Ungerer and Schmid (forthcoming) for a useful introduction to work in the field). The mental spaces and blending theory of Fauconnier (1985), for example, has been developed so that it applies to literature as well as language more generally, and is becoming more influential in stylistics. As before, we find a wide range of applications to literature of a fast developing research paradigm. Fauconnier and Turner (2002) include chapters giving blending theory accounts of fictional worlds and of character portrayal. Turner (1996) sees the 'literary mind' as central to language, its origins and development. A recent issue of *Language and Literature* ((15), 1, 2006) is devoted to blending theory accounts of literary texts, and its editor has also used the theory to examine travel narratives by Jonathan Raban (Dancygier, 2005). Just as the 'cognitive turn' within linguistics has become more general, so has the 'cognitive turn' within stylistics. Stockwell (2002) provides a useful introductory account, and Semino and Culpeper (2002) and Gavins and Steen (2003) give an indication of the range of work in what is increasingly being known as 'cognitive stylistics'. An area which is clearly relevant to viewpoint analysis is 'deictic shift theory', which tries to explain how readers move perceptually from one deictic centre to another as they read (for example, from their own deictic centre to that of a character in a novel, and from that character's deictic centre to another's, or to the same character's different deictic centre in a 'flashback' within the novel). See papers in Duchan, Bruder and Hewitt (1995) and Stockwell (2002, pp. 46–55).

It is not just that new academic areas within literary studies and linguistics have grown up around stylistics, giving it new things to relate to. To some degree, since 1981, stylistics itself has also changed what it concentrates on, and in ways which have made the name 'stylistics' more difficult to live with. *Style in Fiction* begins with two chapters devoted almost entirely to the elucidation of the notion of 'style'. This was because although the stylistics of poetry was concerned rather more with meaning, the study of prose had been dominated up to 1980 by the issues of (a) how to identify and account for style in general and (b) how to characterise and differentiate the styles of particular authors. But things were already changing in 1981: this can be seen in the way that Chapter 3 of *Style in Fiction* uses linguistic analysis to exemplify not only style, but also meaning and effect, in the three short story openings examined. Since then, the study of authorial style has moved away from the mainstream. (However, the corpus stylistics approach referred to above is currently leading to a revival of interest, while authorship detection studies, using computational methods, have continued throughout our period, as is demonstrated by an examination of back numbers of the *Journal of Literary and Linguistic Computing*.) The mainstream stylisticians have concentrated much more on trying to explain how, when we read, we get from the words on the page to the meanings in our heads and effects in our hearts. The result has been that 'stylistics' no longer transparently describes what most people who call themselves stylisticians do. There have been various attempts to change the name of the enterprise to, for example, 'discourse stylistics', 'critical linguistics', 'literary pragmatics' or 'literary linguistics'. But because stylistics covers such a wide range of analytical activities (including the stylistic analysis of non-literary texts), none of the alternatives seem properly to fit the bill either. So although the term 'stylistics' no longer appears to represent the area of study very accurately, it is still in fairly common use, and we are happy to live with it.

As a sub-discipline, stylistics sits athwart the boundary between linguistic and literary study, and sitting on a fence always has its drawbacks. One obvious such drawback is that those in the middle of the two big fields which the fence connects/divides may not even know you are there. Many mainstream descriptive and theoretical linguists and almost all of the literary critical community are unaware of stylistics or else studiously ignore it, even though it has useful things to say to both groups. Detailed analyses of texts often point up interesting problems for particular descriptive and theoretical accounts of language, and detailed analyses of particular texts have an obvious relevance for literary scholars studying the relevant authors or periods. But the ignorance of neighbouring colleagues may still be preferable to outright hostility, which has also been a mark of the relations between stylistics and the major academic subjects it connects to. The pugnacious 'debate' between Roger Fowler and the literary critic F.W. Bateson (the contributions to which are collected together in Fowler, 1971) formed a backdrop to our original writing of *Style in Fiction*, and Bateson's attack on the stylistics enterprise has since been repeated by a number of others. For contributions to the 'debate' begun by Stanley Fish (1996 [1973]), see Toolan

(1996 [1990]), Hoover (1999, pp. 19–52) and Stubbs (2005). For a similar debate initiated by Mackay (1996), see Short *et al.* (1998), Mackay (1999) and Short and van Peer (1999).

Although these border disputes clear the air from time to time, they never seem to change the minds of those engaged in them. One of us who has been involved in the most recent such debate has found it a rather fruitless experience. There is a tendency for the proponents in such debates to attack straw men, by giving outdated accounts of the other side (for example, the common accusation that modern stylistics is 'formalist' in spite of the fact that it makes considerable use of informal pragmatic inference and makes reference to psychological processing in its accounts). Hence although we have provided references above for those who want to follow up on these debates, we would prefer to get on with what we enjoy and do best; analysing texts and exploring particular descriptive and theoretical issues (of which there are plenty to examine).

The last general area we would like to comment on in this section is that of pedagogy. If stylistics is to be of any practical benefit, it must be because it helps others to understand and appreciate particular texts in detail and to perform their own analyses of other texts. For this reason, the needs of students have never been far from the thoughts of most stylisticians. *Style in Fiction*, with its detailed and exemplificatory textual analyses, was always intended to be a useful book for students as well as a contribution to the academic study of language in literature. This can be seen not only in its analysis of extended pieces of text, but in the provision of passages for further discussion at the end of the book and in the development of a checklist of linguistic and stylistic categories at the end of Chapter 3. This checklist was designed to help students become more systematic and detailed in their own analyses, and it is an approach which has been developed further in Short (1996). Since the publication of *Style in Fiction* we have seen a number of introductory books on stylistics. Bradford (1997), Fowler (1996 [1986]), Short (1996), Simpson (1997) and Toolan (1997) are all textbooks which cover the stylistic analysis of all three literary genres, and Simpson (2004) is a cross-genre, activity-based introduction which also contains readings from works by other stylisticians. A number of scholars have developed stylistics-related pedagogical approaches to the integration of language and literature teaching, both in mother-tongue and second/foreign language learning contexts (e.g. Brumfit and Carter 1986, Carter and McRae 1996, Short 1989 and Widdowson 1995a). This pedagogical focus has also been seen in scholarly journals: *Style* (37, 1, 2003) is devoted to stylistics pedagogy and *Language and Literature* (15, 3, 2006) is a special issue on Short's freely-available web-based introductory stylistics course (http://www.lancs.ac.uk/fass/projects/stylistics/start.htm) together with a series of pedagogical investigations worldwide on student reactions in using it.

11.2 New developments in the stylistic analysis of prose fiction and what, with hindsight, we would add to *Style in Fiction*

Let us assume that the general aim of stylistics is an attempt to explain how readers get from the words of a text to (a) an understanding of it and (b) a felt response to it. We can then see that a large part of what is involved in the enterprise with respect to prose fiction texts is the attempt to connect textual analysis and processes of reader inference to the important general non-linguistic literary critical concepts which, when taken together, comprise the understanding of, and response to, novels and stories. We probably cannot produce an exhaustive list of these non-linguistic critical concepts, but the following would surely have to be included and given a prominent place: (i) style, (ii) point of view, (iii) story/plot, (iv) fictional worlds, (v) character, (vi) theme and (vii) evaluation and appreciation. When *Style in Fiction* was written we concentrated mainly on (i)–(ii). We did not ignore (iii)–(vi), and indeed Chapter 5 was devoted to language in relation to fictional worlds. But 'story', 'plot', 'character' and 'characterisation', 'theme' and 'evaluation' did not get references in the index, let alone chapters or sections devoted to them, even though it could be argued that the analyses of particular passages often elucidated character and theme, and suggested indirectly some of the reasons why the texts concerned should be highly valued. The book was organised around the concept of style, with considerable stretches (including Chapters 6, 8 and 10 and significant parts of Chapters 5 and 9) being devoted to linguistic aspects of viewpoint. This restriction is not surprising, given the state of knowledge at the time the book was written. A little was known about the linguistics of plot and the creation of fictional worlds, but hardly anything was known about how readers construe character when they read, and, even now, relatively little has been written about theme and evaluation in the stylistics tradition (although we note Short and Semino (forthcoming) on evaluation, and Louwerse and van Peer (2002) on theme).

If we were writing *Style in Fiction* now, it is clear from what we have said in section 11.1 that we would need to take deictic shift theory into account when discussing viewpoint, and corpus stylistics when discussing style. In addition, we would add major chapters on story/plot and character/characterisation, elaborate and re-cast the chapter on the fictional world, and also be more explicit about the relationship of our textual analyses to theme and evaluation.

11.2.1 Story/plot

When *Style in Fiction* was first published, Anglo-American literary criticism had tended to ignore story and plot, largely because of an assumption that story and plot, unlike style, were uninteresting to literary scholarship. As E.M. Forster (1974 [1927], pp. 40–41) had influentially put it:

> ... Yes – oh dear yes – the novel tells a story. That is the fundamental aspect without which it could not exist. That is the highest factor common to all novels, and I wish that it was not so, that it could be something different – melody, or perception of the truth, not this low atavistic form.
>
> For the more we look at the story (the story that is a story, mind) the more we disentangle it from the finer growths that it supports, the less shall we find to admire. It runs like a backbone – or may I say a tapeworm, for its beginning and end are arbitrary...

But by the 1960s structuralist and formalist influences from outside the English-speaking world had brought a new interest in story structure. The rise of structuralism in French literary studies was strongly influenced by the work of the anthropologist Lévi-Strauss (e.g. Lévi-Strauss 1963). From Russian formalism came Propp's *Morphology of the Folktale* (published in Russian in 1928, but, until the late 1960s, virtually inaccessible in the West). By the time we wrote *Style in Fiction*, Lévi-Strauss believed that the structure of myths was connected inextricably to their role, as he saw it, of mediating the contradictory assumptions held by particular societies; and he saw these oppositions as being represented in stories by, among other things, oppositions between different kinds of events in the myths. This re-connected story and plot structure with overall textual meaning in an interesting way (see Hendricks (1972) for a stimulating application of this approach to a story by Ambrose Bierce). In a parallel development, Propp had shown that narrative genres (in particular Russian folktales) could be distinguished by a sophisticated analysis of the event-structures of the stories. The structuralist tradition explored, in a number of seminal works, the 'grammar' of stories, using analogies with the structures and derivations of sentences in generative grammar. Indeed, before the publication of *Style in Fiction*, influential works by Prince (1973) and Todorov (1969) had included the word 'grammar' in their titles. Other influences in the structural analysis of story and plot were Barthes (1977 [1966]), Chatman (1969), Brémond (1973) and Labov and Waletsky (1967). Since the early structuralist work a number of influential books devoted to narrative, Bal (1997 [1985]), Chatman (1978), Fludernik (1996), Herman (2002), Prince (1982), Ricoeur (1983), Rimmon-Kenan (2002) and Toolan (2001 [1988]) have all given space to the discussion of story structure, and other works have been specifically devoted to the technical study of plot, e.g. Dry (1981, 1983) and Pavel (1985). But, by and large, in stylistics the interest in such work has waned since, because the 'structuralist' approach was too formalistic or reductive to deliver results sensitive enough to account for readers' perceptions of what was happening in stories in literary texts.

Although interest in the analysis of story and plot has waned in stylistics, it is clearly of great importance for future developments of the field, and this is why we devote some space to it here. The key to success will probably involve an amalgam of (i) structuralist approaches, (ii) more inferential accounts derived from the work done in linguistic pragmatics and cognitive stylistics over the last twenty years, and (iii) foregrounding theory. An influential narratologist, David Herman (2002) has argued persuasively that work on what he calls 'story logic' (which involves character and viewpoint as well as story) needs to be based on inference by readers, which in effect will connect narratology, including structural narratology, to pragmatics and cognitive linguistics.

It would appear that our ability to be able to 'see' story structure 'through' the sentences of a text comes about through a combination of, or interaction between, what the psychologists call 'bottom-up' and 'top-down' processing. Roland Barthes (1977 [1966]) and W.O. Hendricks (1973a) tried to identify which clause-types typically contribute to the onward movement of stories. The action theory associated with Teun van Dijk (see below) is also highly relevant here, as is the work of discourse analysts like Michael Hoey (1983, 1991) working mainly on the structure of non-literary texts. Not surprisingly, there is a tendency for sentences and clauses which have (i) dynamic transitive verbs and (ii) main characters as subject or object to be important in plot development. Indeed, Fowler (1977, pp. 23–25), following Greimas, suggested that the constructional principles of narratives and sentences are the same, just as more recent work in blending theory also tends to assume an analogical 'fit' between basic linguistic structures and a wide range of cognitive phenomena. But it is not that difficult to find (a) examples of such sentences which are *not* important in the development of story in a particular text, and (b) 'descriptive' sentences which *do* turn out to be crucially important. For example, 'John kissed his wife', although it is a transitive structure with human agents, is unlikely to be an important action in driving a story forward precisely because it is a prototypical (and so backgrounded) action for husbands to perform, and so will not carry much 'story weight' unless it is marked within a particular story as being significant in some way. Similarly, although sentences like 'The door was open' and 'The room was full of wonderful things' are stative descriptions of the kind which do not prototypically push a story forward, it is not too difficult to invent a context where they could mark important story transitions. Imagine, for example, that some explorers had been trying, without success, to open a door in an ancient Egyptian tomb. Then, when they arrive the next day, 'The door was open. The room was full of wonderful things.' The first of the two state descriptions indicates a significant change of state in the world of the fiction, and the second state description allows us to infer (a) that the characters have finally managed to enter the room and (b) that what they have found is likely to be significant in plot terms. In this sort of way, structuralist, pragmatic and foregrounding accounts could be interestingly allied in careful textual analysis. A completely adequate account will also need to take into account the effects of schematic assumptions on the interpretation of utterances, and the findings of action theory (van Dijk 1977, pp. 167–188, 1981, pp. 120–145, Kintsch and van Dijk 1983). Van Dijk points out that even apparently simple actions are complex, consisting of '. . . *three phases*: the *mental conditions* (wishes, desires, decisions, purposes, intentions – of which the internal structure is still pretty obscure, and irrelevant for our discussion), the *actual doing*, and the *consequences* of the doing (purposed or not): state, event or process' (1981, p. 120). Pragmatically, it is possible to represent an action by stating the consequence of that action (*cf* the 'door was open' example above) or the prior intention of the relevant actor (*cf* 'He decided to open the door') without describing the action itself. Moreover, simple actions are in turn linked in sequences, and are sub-parts of higher-level compound or complex actions.

For example, when George kills his simpleton friend, Lennie, near the end of Steinbeck's *Of Mice and Men* because he does not want the pursuing lynch mob to get Lennie first (see the discussion of the examples from this novel in sections 6.1 and 7.5.1 for some of the context leading up to the lynch mob's blood lust), the description of the act of shooting Lennie is broken down for dramatic, foregrounded and slow-motion effect into simpler sub-parts, the pointing of the gun at the back of Lennie's head, and so on. And the fact that George raises and lowers the gun more than once helps us to infer the battle inside his mind between (a) his wish/intention to shoot Lennie when he is not looking in order to save him from of dying in terror at the hands of the lynch mob and (b) his wish/obligation not to be the instrument of his friend's death (we will return to textual 'worlds', such as these, in section 11.2.2 below).

The quotations below are extracted from the last three pages of the novel. In the intervening text, the lynch mob is getting closer and closer. To ensure Lennie dies happy, George tells him the details of their shared dream (a dream which he has repeatedly re-told throughout the novel) of having a small farm of their own. Meanwhile, Lennie, sitting in front of him, looks out over the Salinas valley:

> He reached in his side pocket and brought out Carlson's Luger; he snapped off the safety, and the hand and the gun lay on the ground behind Lennie's back. He looked at the back of Lennie's head, at the place where the spine and skull were joined. . . .

> . . . George raised the gun and his hand shook, and he dropped his hand to the ground again. . . .

> . . . George looked down at the gun. . . .

... The voices came close now. George raised the gun and listened to the voices.

Lennie begged, 'Le's do it now. Le's get that place now.'

'Sure, right now. I gotta. We gotta.'

And George raised the gun and steadied it, and he brought the muzzle of it close to the back of Lennie's head. The hand shook violently, but his face set and his hand steadied. He pulled the trigger. The crash of the shot rolled up the hills and rolled down again. Lennie jarred, and then settled slowly forward to the sand, and he lay without quivering.

[John Steinbeck, *Of Mice and Men*, Chapter VI]

The suspense is created here in two ways. First, Steinbeck pulls apart textually (a) the preliminary and intentional phases and (b) the performance phase of the sub-parts of the macro-action. Second, he describes George trying, and failing, to perform the terrible deed. Then, when the lynch mob are almost upon them, George finally manages it. The dramatic irony of the ambiguity of the pronoun 'it' in Lennie's final request and the ellipsis in George's reply ('I gotta. We gotta.') increase the pathos of the scene, and Steinbeck creates more suspense at the very end of the description by telling us of the echoing sound of the gun before he describes the effect of the shot on Lennie himself. Even then, he does not tell us straightforwardly that Lennie is dead, but of course it is inferred. Here we see how foregrounding, action theory, and the inferencing of cognitive theory and pragmatics come together.

So far we have used the terms 'story' and 'plot' more or less interchangeably. This is in spite of the fact that critics usually think of plots as being more interesting critically than stories, and so we should explain our usage. The critical attitude just referred to probably derives from E.M. Forster (1974 [1927]), where he famously suggested that plots, unlike stories, exhibited relations of cause and effect. His examples were:

Story: 'The king died and then the queen died.'
Plot: 'The king died and then the queen died of grief.'

Forster says that the plot example has cause and effect, and this is clearly specified in the adverbial phrase in the second sentence. But the problem with the opposition he proposes, and which has held so much sway in the world of Anglo-American literary criticism, is that, in spite of what Forster says, it is difficult not to construct a cause and effect relation between the two sentences of the 'story' example too. This will be seen more obviously if we change Forster's example slightly to:

'The king died and then the queen cried.'

Although there is no overt connection, readers will infer one, using the pragmatic maxim of relation (Grice 1975) or the principle of relevance (Sperber and Wilson 1986). It is just about possible to imagine that the queen cried for no reason at all, or for some reason not referred to in the text (perhaps she was peeling onions?), but the likeliest inference, given our schematic knowledge about deaths in families, is that she cried because the king died. Some story structures are clearly more basic than others. For example, if we are told at the beginning of a story what is going to happen at, or near, the end, we will relate that re-ordered presentation of the events to the order in which they 'must have occurred' chronologically (the *fabula* in Russian Formalist terms), and perceive the achronological re-ordering (the *sjuzhet* in Russian Formalist terms) as significant in our understanding of the text. For example, *Marabou Stork Nightmares* by Irvine Welsh begins with the first-person narrator in hospital, in a drug-induced coma. Most of the remainder of the novel is his narration of events earlier in his life, which are read as an account of how he ended up in the coma, as well as explaining why, at the end of the novel, he is brutally murdered while still in his coma. As with the sentences 'The door was open. The room was full of wonderful things.' above, the significance of cause-and-effect relations and unusual orderings in the presentation of events seems to need careful pragmatic and foregrounding analysis.

We came very close to adding a chapter on the analysis of story and plot to the first edition of *Style in Fiction*. Indeed, we even performed initial analyses, which we have never published, on 'The Bucket and the Rope' by T.F. Powys (which we now discuss in Chapter 12) and part of 'The Short Happy Life of Francis Macomber' by Ernest Hemingway. But *Style in Fiction* was already considerably longer than we had intended, story analysis did not sit easily with the structure or title of our book, and, in spite of our interest in it, we were not convinced that we had enough analytical tools at our disposal to provide a satisfying account in the kind of detail we had provided elsewhere in the volume. But 25 years on, the possibility of combining structural, pragmatic and foregrounding analysis in the study of stories and story-telling looks like an area ripe for development.

11.2.2 Fictional worlds, text worlds, mental spaces

There have been interesting developments since 1981 in the study of how, when we read fiction, we infer, and operate interpretatively with, the fictional world 'in' or 'behind' the text (see Pavel 1986, for instance). In narratology, there have been advances within what is often called 'possible worlds theory', the study of how the main world of the fiction 'interacts' with other, closely related, 'possible worlds', for example the 'belief worlds' or 'wish worlds' of particular characters. Clashes between the various possible worlds (e.g. the wish of a character to change the status quo) can effectively drive the plot of a story forward and at the same time help us to infer contrasting and/or parallel relations among characters. Interesting exponents of this possible-worlds approach are Eco (1990), Ryan (1991) and Ronen (1994), though this narratological work could be usefully connected more explicitly to the detailed linguistic structure of the texts considered. Semino (1997) concentrates mainly on fictional worlds in poems, but her approach sits much more clearly within the stylistics tradition and could easily be extended to other genres. She interestingly combines, in one approach to the study of fictional worlds, three different kinds of analysis: (a) the narratological possible-worlds approach of Ryan (1991), (b) the psychological approach of schema theory, and (c) the linguistic-stylistic approach, and in particular the study of deixis. It is clear that as stylistics develops it is moving to integrate linguistic, psychological and more literary approaches, and Semino's work is an excellent exemplar of this.

Another influential approach to the study of fictional worlds is that associated with Paul Werth and his followers, and perhaps best seen in Werth (1999). Hidalgo Downing (2000) uses Werth's approach, among others, in a useful study of *Catch 22* by Joseph Heller, and Gavins (2003) uses it to analyse Donald Barthelme's *Snow White*. The term Werth uses is 'text world' rather than 'fictional world', as he is concerned with inference into worlds 'behind' any text, fictional or non-fictional. But a number of his examples are from well-known fictional texts, and his approach to 'text world construction', although it is by no means perfect, and was still under development when he died, is admirable in its focus on charting in considerable detail how readers get from the precise linguistic configuration of a text, via processes of inference, to the world evinced by that text. This line of research looks most promising, and, if we were trying to write a 'perfect and complete' *Style in Fiction* now, we would almost certainly want to add a chapter on the inference of fictional worlds, possible worlds related to the world of the fiction, and consequent meanings and effects, thus building substantially on what we said about fictional worlds in Chapter 5.

One of the difficulties at the present time is that the accounts of story, action theory, possible worlds and text worlds, which have arisen in different areas of study, overlap with one another, and it is not entirely clear how these approaches can be successfully integrated. Moreover, the mental spaces and blending theory referred to in section 11.1 arguably has the potential to subsume all of these approaches (and indeed the theories of character we describe in section 11.2.3, and much more besides) within its scope. All this raises two issues which will need considerable future research to resolve. First, although theories of general applicability are very attractive in principle, their very generality tends to mean that they become less explanatory in a detailed way when applied to the more particular phenomena of individual texts. So it is not clear, for example, how useful it will be to subsume the other action and worlds theories within the more general mental spaces theory. Second, the action theory, fictional worlds and mental spaces accounts are attractive in literary critical terms because they seem to relate directly to critical concerns like story, fictional worlds and character. But they all have to be 'worked out' in detail on a range of texts before we can be sure that the approaches are reliably replicable from analyst to analyst. Even the text worlds approach, which is perhaps the best connected of all to the linguistic details of textual structure, still has a long way to go before it achieves the detailed analytical precision and reliability associated with more traditional forms of stylistic analysis.

11.2.3 Character and characterisation

Although, by and large, character and characterisation are not addressed as a major organisational topic in *Style in Fiction* (but see section 5.4.3, 'Speech and character') the book contains plenty of analyses which could easily be re-cast as discussions of characterisation. For example, the discussion of speech acts in a passage from *Pride and Prejudice* (see pp. 234–6) is framed to elucidate the conversational behaviour of Mr and Mrs Bennet in one particular interaction. But the conversational behaviour of the two characters in the relevant passage is also reflective of their behaviour throughout the novel and so can easily be seen as indicating their individual characterisations and their character-relations. Similarly, Chapter 6 on mind style, as well the various discussions on different aspects of viewpoint, is clearly relevant to the portrayal of character. At the time we wrote the original book, characterisation was not very high on the agenda of prose fiction study in stylistics, or criticism more generally. Perhaps because of the dominance of the critical discussion of viewpoint in prose fiction, the study of characterisation in twentieth-century criticism was, by and large, more evident in the criticism of drama than that of prose fiction, though it was not very plentiful even there.

The history of the study of characterisation in literary studies is somewhat chequered. Until the twentieth century, there was a tendency in drama criticism, seen most famously in Bradley (1904) and still evident in less sophisticated discussions of characters in fiction, to think of characters as if they were real people, with existences both on stage and off stage. This approach was debunked in the seminal essay 'How many children had Lady Macbeth?' by L.C. Knights (1963 [1946]), which helped to move Anglo-American drama criticism away from the study of character towards the study of textual properties. But reactions from one fallacy often go to the extreme of the opposite fallacy – as is seen in Weinsheimer (1979), who viewed the idea that characters were people-like as completely irrelevant to the criticism of fiction: 'Emma Woodhouse is not a woman nor need be described as if it were.' But this kind of extreme statement seems to fly in the face of what we know about the reading process. Just as readers infer a fictional world 'behind' the text when they read, they also furnish that fictional world with characters as well as other objects, and, not surprisingly, they use their knowledge of, and schematic assumptions about, people in the real world when construing characters in novels. Hence the use of the analysis of conversational behaviour as evidence for characterisation, as in the above-mentioned example from *Pride and Prejudice* (and elsewhere in stylistics) seems helpful, as it is not unlike how we construe personality from real-world conversations. As with literary criticism, most of the stylistic work on characterisation so far has been on dramatic texts, but it is not difficult to apply the type of analysis developed for the stylistics of drama to character interaction in prose texts. The essays by Bennison, Culpeper, Herman, Lowe and Toolan in Culpeper, Short and Verdonk (1998) are all directly relevant to characterisation, as is much of Herman (1995) and Chapters 7 and 8 of Short (1996). Chapter 5 of Rimmon-Kenan (2002 [1983]), Chapter 4 of Toolan (2001 [1988]) and Chapter 11 of Toolan (1990) are on character in the novel, and Person (1999), which is devoted to conversation in fiction, is also relevant. Chapter 5 of Herman (2002) is a suggestive update of narratological accounts of character and Chapter 12 of Fauconnier and Turner (2002) gives an outline of a mental spaces approach.

The most highly articulated stylistic account of character in fiction to date is Culpeper (2001). Although it focuses on drama, this is a book which is likely to become highly influential in stylistic discussion of character in the discussion of the novel. Culpeper brings together a 'top-down' approach to character, based mainly on social cognition and attribution theory within psychology, and the more 'bottom-up' approach seen in much stylistic analysis (which concentrates on particular textual detail and how character and characterisation can be inferred from that textual detail). This approach enables Culpeper to chart a theoretical course between the critical extremes of Bradley on the one hand and Weinsheimer on the other, and to connect detailed analysis of conversational behaviour with social constructs via linguistic inference and schematic approaches to character types. Culpeper's work thus effectively enables us to relate the text-analytical work on character interaction already extant in prose stylistics to the principled elucidation of character and characterisation. Besides working directly within the stylistics tradition, Culpeper also connects his work to useful modern critical accounts of characterisation (e.g. Margolin 1989, 1990 and Pfister 1988) and historical linguistic-stylistic work on characterisation in early literature (e.g. Taavitsainen 1999). He takes into account not just the behaviour of particular characters, but also what other characters say about them (which could, in turn, be linked to narrator statements about characters in prose fiction, although different kinds of narrators will produce some complications). He also (a) distinguishes between behavioural factors which can be character-related and those which need to be 'discounted' because they are contextually determined, and (b) shows how Taavitsainen's notion of 'surge features' can be used analytically to account for why particular stretches of character talk and behaviour are especially relevant to perceptions of character. Interestingly, he also points out that in fictions, unlike the real world, once we have read the whole text we have *all* the behaviour available on which to base judgments about character, and so can come to a properly 'rounded' judgment not easily possible in real life. Not surprisingly, if *Style in Fiction* was being written now there would be a substantial discussion of character and characterisation in the novel, building on the recent work of Culpeper and others, including Culpeper (2002), which outlines a possible cognitive stylistic approach to characterisation. We would need to explore not just a Culpeper-style analysis of how characters talk about themselves and others, and exhibit their character through what they say, but also how we can take the statements about characters by different kinds of narrators into account and how viewpoint blending between a narrator and particular characters would affect the perception of character.

11.3 New developments in the stylistics of prose fiction and what, with hindsight, we would change in *Style in Fiction*

We would like to feel that much of what we wrote 25 years ago has stood the test of time. We would want to stand, by and large, by our discussions of particular textual extracts, and where we disagree with our former selves, it would require too much detailed discussion than we have available here to examine what we would want to alter with respect to individual texts, and why. So below we will concentrate on more theoretical aspects of the stylistic description of prose fiction. We would also want to stand, by and large, by our general account of style (with the additional consideration of corpus-based works, as indicated in section 11.2, for example, in determining norms of style), and its exemplification through particular analyses in Chapters 1–4 of the original book.

However, there has been considerable attention to the stylistics of viewpoint in its widest sense, and the findings in this area, as well as developments in our own thinking, would lead us to various rather more substantial changes in the later chapters of the book, in addition to adding the work on deictic shift theory referred to in section 11.2.

11.3.1 Different kinds of viewpoint and different linguistic indicators of viewpoint

Our first edition made a distinction between (i) *fictional* point of view, that is the viewpoint held by one or more characters whose consciousness is represented through the fiction, and (ii) *discoursal* point of view, that is the relationship between the teller (the 'implied author' or narrator and the fiction being represented). This distinction helped us to be clear about whose viewpoint was being represented and how viewpoints were sometimes blended. We also indicated some of the ways in which viewpoint could be indicated linguistically, but we did not provide a very systematic account of the linguistic features typically involved in viewpoint manipulation or of the different aspects of the notion of viewpoint that are involved when a person's point of view is represented. Now we would want to be more discriminating in both these areas. Simpson (1993, Chapter 2), following Uspensky (1973) and Fowler (1996 [1986]), distinguishes the following different kinds of viewpoint: (i) spatial viewpoint (the physical 'angle' of the viewpoint), (ii) temporal viewpoint, the time 'angle' (Chatman 1978 links (i) and (ii) together to form what he calls perceptual point of view), (iii) psychological viewpoint (what Chatman calls conceptual point of view), and (iv) ideological viewpoint (the socio-political slant put on what is described). To this list we would want to add a fifth kind of viewpoint, (v) social viewpoint (which expresses social relationships between the person whose viewpoint is being represented and other characters), and we would want to note that, within the notion of ideological viewpoint, room needs to be made to take account of *personal* attitudinal values (e.g. that a particular character 'is horrible' or 'looks kind'), as well as those associated with social or political groups. This kind of subdivision of the different elements involved in the concept of viewpoint usefully enables more descriptive precision. We would also want to be more precise about the linguistic features which are prototypically used to indicate viewpoint, in the spirit seen in Fowler (1996 [1986], Chapter 9) and Short (1996, Chapter 9), though we would also want to note that sometimes, as Short (1999) shows, viewpoint can be indicated by linguistic factors very different from the 'list of usual suspects'. Nonetheless, checklists of linguistic features prototypically associated with particular phenomena are useful in helping analysts and students to be more systematic (*cf* Short 1996 *passim*).

11.3.2 Narratological aspects of viewpoint

The distinction between discoursal and fictional point of view mentioned above, with its distinction between the point of view of the teller and that of some character being represented in the story told, brings us to a series of issues concerning discoursal viewpoint, which centres on Chapter 8 of *Style in Fiction*, 'Discourse and the discourse situation'.

The reason that twentieth-century criticism of the novel in particular has focused on the study of viewpoint so much is that, compared with prototypical poems and plays, there are more viewpoints to take into account in the discourse structure of the prototypical novel. The use of the level of

narration means that there is at least one more discourse level (with another addresser and addressee to take into account). We also think that our
characterisation of the various ways in which the different discourse levels
can 'collapse' together in particular novels, leading to different 'discourse
architectures', is helpful in characterising discoursal viewpoint, although
we would want to make it clear that 'discourse architectures' in novels are
not necessarily unchanging, like the architecture of buildings. Indeed, in
particular novels the discourse architecture may change quite a lot, and
in either sudden or subtle ways, which, when charted, can lead to insights
about viewpoint manipulation and the nature of the particular novel examined. A good example of this is the 582-word prologue at the beginning of
Jane Gardam's *Bilgewater* (discussed in some detail in Short, Culpeper and
Semino 2000). This prologue begins, for the first 135 words, with a third-
person narration combined with the fictional viewpoint of a prospective
undergraduate being interviewed for a place at a Cambridge college. Then,
in sentence 14, the narration slips into second-person mode, and by sentence 33, 137 words later (which include 63 words of free direct speech and
free direct thought), the narration has moved to the first-person and the
tense of the narration has shifted from the past to the present (thus causing
a possible ambiguity with free direct thought). Hence we begin with an
apparently objective third-person narration, even though the narrator
describes things from the prospective undergraduate's viewpoint, and are
shifted in stages to a much more intimate and potentially limited and flawed
viewpoint, a shift relatable to a tactic which leads to a surprise at the end of
the novel. These shifts in discourse architecture within a relatively short
passage, as Short, Culpeper and Semino (2000) point out, also raise an
interesting theoretical issue about what it means to say that a particular
(section of a) novel is written in a particular narrative form, and how we
make these overall judgments about kinds of narration. For example, is it
reasonable to say, as we have done above, that the prologue of *Bilgewater*
slips into second-person narration for just a few words? And if it is not,
how should we best describe the shift that takes place?

There are some things, however, that we would want to revisit and possibly change. We no longer share the conviction that the 'implied author'–
'implied reader' level is really needed in the discourse structure of the
novel (and indeed Short (1996) does not use it). It seems to have the status
of a useful heuristic which may well not be theoretically necessary, and is
potentially misleading in that, in spite of the term 'implied', it suggests
a 'reified' addresser and addressee at that level, equivalent to an author,
a narrator or a character (*cf* Nünning 1993). Although critics from Booth
(1961) onwards have used the 'implied author/reader' concepts, it is interesting to note that those writing about non-literary writing (e.g. newspapers, letters) do not seem to feel the need for such concepts. Instead, they
rely on the notion that when we communicate with one another we do not

just instantiate our own viewpoints, but at the same time take into account the viewpoint(s) of those we are communicating with. When describing the narratorial aspect of discoursal viewpoint, we made the traditional critical distinction between first-person and third-person narration. In 1981, there were not many cases of second-person narration in novels. But recently the number has increased somewhat, and narratological research on them has become more extensive (see, for example, Fludernik 1996, Chapters 6 and 7). Now we would need to discuss second-person narrations as well. Interestingly, as the pronoun number ordering might lead one to expect, second-person narrations seem, to some degree at least, to occupy a position between first- and third-person narrations. Such narrations often begin with a third-person-like generic 'you' and then shift as the narration develops, into a second-person equivalent of 'I-narration' (as in *Half Asleep in Frog Pyjamas* by Tom Robbins, for example). But the system of effects of particular forms of narration clearly needs to be reviewed, particularly when it is remembered that in addition to second-person narrations it is also now possible to find plural narration forms (involving 'we' or 'they': see Margolin 1996 and Fludernik 1996, pp. 223–249) and what Fludernik (1996, pp. 249–266) calls 'odd' narrative tenses.

In discussing point of view in Chapter 5 we made use of the notion of a 'reflector' for the 'person whose [fictional] point of view is represented' (see Section 5.5.1, p. 139). The term 'focaliser' has since become a much more popular term for this role. But, as indicated in Short (1999), some of us now have some reservations about using these terms. They tend to suggest that just one person's view is represented in a story, and it is true that one person's point of view often predominates in particular stories. But careful examination of viewpoint shifts in short extracts often shows that the reflector/focaliser may change from sentence to sentence or even within sentences. It is important that we do not unwarily allow terms like 'the focaliser' to prevent us from picking up on such changes and variations, and indeed the possibility of variability in viewpoint is of ever-present importance in fictional prose.

Similar remarks can be applied to the concept of mind style, to which we devoted Chapter 6 of our book. It is arguable that the notion of conceptual viewpoint (see section 11.3.1 and Chatman (1978)) effectively includes the notion of mind style, except that the conceptual viewpoint being expressed is abnormal in some way. And the borderline between mind style and ideological viewpoint is sometimes not easy to maintain. Of course, as with discussions of particular 'implied authors' or focalised viewpoints in particular texts, these remarks do not negate the value of particular discussions of mind styles in particular texts (e.g. Bockting 1995, Semino 2002, 2006, Semino and Swindlehurst 1996). The issue is a more theoretical one of asking, Occam-like, how many terms and concepts we need to describe to account for the phenomena we are examining.

11.3.3 Speech, thought and writing presentation

In 1981 Chapter 10 of *Style in Fiction* represented an advance on previous accounts of discourse presentation in the novel in a number of respects. It brought more analytical precision to the study of discourse presentation than before, and has since been used by a number of other analysts (e.g. Roeh and Nir 1990, Simpson 1993, Thompson 1996). It distinguished speech presentation and thought presentation systematically, by allocating them to separate, parallel scales, showed how the presentational scales connected to narration, and argued for a presentational cline along which the various categories, distinguished by a combination of linguistic and contextual means, were associated with varying degrees of faithfulness to an original. It argued for a placing of the free direct category at the extreme of the 'direct' end of the scale (previous accounts, if they made clear the placings of the various categories in relation to one another at all, tended to situate free direct speech in between direct speech and free indirect speech). It also argued for a new presentational category, the narrator's report of a speech act (and its thought presentation equivalent), to account for sentences like 'She demanded an apology for the tone of his request', which indicates the speech act value (and often the topic of the speech act, as here) of the utterance presented, but not its propositional content, as found in indirect speech. Finally, it tried to explain, via reference to different presentational norms, how the same presentational category could have different effects on the speech and thought presentation scales, with the FIS/FIT contrast being the starkest.

Since that time, research in the area of discourse presentation has continued with some vigour (see, for example, Fludernik 1993, a monumental work which exhaustively describes research up to that date and makes a number of influential theoretical claims) and a reincarnation of *Style in Fiction* now would need to take account of the relevant literature and the advances made. We would particularly want to take account of the findings of the Lancaster speech, writing and thought presentation research projects, which have taken the original *Style in Fiction* model and applied it systematically and exhaustively not only to a corpus of written fictional and non-fictional narratives, but to a corpus of spoken English, in order to see how well it stands up to rigorous application to a wide range of data. The work on the written corpus, which has been reported in Semino and Short (2004) and a series of articles by the research team they led, has shown that, by and large, the original *Style in Fiction* model works well when applied to non-fictional narratives as well as to the fictional narratives it was originally developed for. Among other things, the corpus work has enabled useful comparisons between fictional and non-fictional text types (see Short, Semino and Culpeper 1996 and Short, Semino and Wynne 1999). There is no space to go into much detail here, but the Lancaster corpus work has, among other things, established the need for

(i) another scale of presentation, in addition to those of speech and thought: *writing presentation* (which will be of particular relevance for the epistolary novel), and

(ii) another category on the speech presentation scale to account for sentences even more minimal than the narrator's report of a speech act category, as described above: *narrator's representation of voice* (NV).

The introduction of a narrator's representation of voice category, and its equivalents on the thought and writing presentation scales, to account for sentences where utterance is reported even more minimally (e.g. 'They talked quietly to one another'), effectively completes the range of 'faithfulness claims' that can be made when reporting someone else's speech (or writing):

1. Speech occurred.
2. Speech occurred + speech act (and topic) specified.
3. Speech occurred + speech act (and topic) and propositional content specified.
4. Speech occurred + speech act (and topic), propositional content and the words and structures used to utter that propositional content specified.

More detail can be found in Semino, Short and Culpeper (1997), Short, Semino and Wynne (2002) and Short (2003). Semino, Short and Wynne (1999) discuss how discourse presentation theory and the possible-worlds theory described briefly in section 11.2.2 can be interestingly combined to analyse hypothetical discourse (e.g. a character thinking about what he or she *might* say to someone else, but does not).

11.4 Detail and precision, and the way ahead

Much of what we have been describing in section 11.3 above instantiates the need to take into account the work of the last 25 years, which, building on the previous work of others, has helped us to understand better, and in more detail, particular aspects of the stylistic analysis of fictional (and non-fictional) texts. The areas we have picked out for particular comment, although they are major topics in the stylistics of fiction, are by no means the only areas we could have mentioned. For example, our brief encounter with speech act theory in Chapter 9 would now need to be adapted and expanded to take account of more recent work on indirect speech acts, deviant speech acts, speech act ambiguity and the way in which some speech acts take a number of conversational turns to achieve completion. Another area to which there would be much to add is that of 'textual rhetoric', the subject of Chapter 7: here we would need to take account of recent decades of work on the mental processing of texts, leading to a fuller understanding of narrative from the perspective of reading and comprehension (Emmott 1997, Emmott, Sanford and Morrow 2006). There is plenty more to do in areas we already know quite a lot about, and there are bound to be more insights and new methods of analysis for these areas in the future.

And indeed, even if these 'old' areas were now completely understood (which they are clearly not), there are still aspects of stylistic involvement with novels that we have hardly begun to account for as yet. The stylistic explications of theme and evaluation are the most obvious areas awaiting development. And of course novelists keep on writing interesting new novels for us to analyse too. For those who found the first edition of *Style in Fiction* quite a strenuous read, the new version, if written from scratch, could scarcely avoid being much more so. In reflecting on this we bring the present chapter to a timely end.

CHAPTER 12

'The Bucket and the Rope'

This final additional chapter of our second edition has the goal of filling in two significant gaps in our treatment of style and fiction up to this point. First, we need to illustrate more fully, through concrete textual examples, the newer developments in the stylistics of fiction introduced and explained in Chapter 11. Second, we feel it is important to attempt the stylistic analysis of a whole fictional text. It is a besetting weakness of the stylistics of fiction that it is partial, if not fragmentary: we find ourselves analysing a selection of linguistic features only, or analysing a small excerpt from a larger text. Attempting the analysis of a complete text is indeed essential if we are to illustrate properly the narratological theme introduced in the last chapter. Other approaches to fictional texts also gain from their integration within an overall treatment of a single work of fiction. We hope, therefore, that it will be seen as a fitting finale to the book to tackle here the analysis of a short story, using the techniques introduced in earlier chapters, and particularly the newer approaches introduced in Chapter 11.

How 'short' should such a short story be? Our answer is: very short indeed! For this purpose we have chosen 'The Bucket and the Rope', a story by T.F. Powys, first published in 1927 in a volume called *Fables*. It contains a mere 2739 words, plus its five-word title. To have chosen a longer story would have meant expanding this chapter to gigantic proportions – and, even so, it is long enough for most tastes. The brevity of the story means that we will be able to illustrate a range of cognitively-oriented approaches, and more importantly, show their interrelations with one another: narratology or 'story logic'; worlds structure (possible worlds, text worlds); point of view; and characterisation. At the same time, we will call on more traditional aspects of literary text exegesis (allusion, metaphor) as well as drawing on the techniques of textual analysis illustrated in earlier chapters, such as Chapter 3.

We said that the approaches we have taken from Chapter 11 are 'cognitively-oriented'. They do indeed illustrate the 'cognitive turn' of present-day stylistics (although we also look back for some structuralist models in the analysis of story). That is to say, these frameworks illustrate the nature of literary interpretation, conceiving it as a cognitive process of 'making sense', in the broadest sense, of a story and the way of telling it. Using the terms of Culpeper's (2001, p. 28) discussion of characterisation (*cf* section 11.2.3), this entails taking account of a combination of top-down and bottom-up interpretative processes. From the top down come cognitive 'givens' such as schemas, narrative frameworks or scripts, cognitive metaphors and prototype categories,[1] and the assumptions or expectations associated with these. From the bottom up come the observable linguistic features of the text; and the great challenge is to establish the connection between these two directions of analysis. For this purpose, one key tool in our explanatory equipment is inference (*cf* section 4.3.1), another is foregrounding – the recognition of salience against a background of 'the normal' (see sections 2.3 and 4.6) – which in this chapter can be tentatively extended from linguistic foregrounding to more abstract types of foregrounding, such as an unexpected turn in a narrative. We will make use of terms such as 'prototype', 'schema' and 'inference' (together with allied verbs and adjectives 'prototypical', 'schematic', 'inferencing', and so on). However, for reasons of space we often do not explain these cognitive processes and phenomena in full detail. The terms sometimes have to be regarded as shorthand tokens for a fuller explanation. Even with a very short story, a great deal of detail will have to be omitted or taken for granted.

Further, one approach introduced in Chapter 11 will unfortunately not be sufficiently exemplified in this chapter: the 'corpus linguistic turn' which we have placed alongside the 'cognitive turn' as one of the most significant recent research developments in stylistics. Choosing a very short story may be helpful for other kinds of stylistic analysis, but for corpus-based methods, the shorter the story, the less suitable it is. Corpus linguistic analysis thrives on large corpora such as the works of Henry James, where quantitative techniques can be reliably employed. Nevertheless, we will be able to make use of some insights and observations which come to the fore in corpus linguistics (e.g. collocational analysis, comparisons of frequency).

12.1 T.F. Powys

The author of 'The Bucket and the Rope', Theodore Francis Powys, could be unfamiliar to many readers and so some introductory information may be helpful. He was a brother of the better-known John Cowper Powys, the author of *The Glastonbury Romance*, an extract from which was examined in section 6.3. T.F. Powys was a prolific essayist, novelist and short-story writer, and 'The Bucket and the Rope' (first published in 1927) was included in a posthumous anthology of Powys's stories called *God's Eyes A-Twinkle* (1947) and also in *The Second Penguin Book of English Short Stories*, edited by Christopher Dolley (1973). Powys's stories are usually about simple country folk from an area not unlike Dorset, where he lived for much of his life. The stories are idiosyncratic in that they invoke a world where people can talk to the dead by visiting their graves, where God or Christ can arrive in a village and talk to the inhabitants, and where non-human animals and objects (the bucket and the rope in this case) can converse and show human-like intelligence. Thematically, the stories dwell on the basic human predicament, and often on the twin themes of love and death. As Charles Prentice puts it in the preface to *God's Eyes A-Twinkle*:

> Of all Powys's stories the *Fables* are farthest from everyday reality. Their conception leaves him free to depict the insignificance of man amid the huge disregarded company in which he lives – from seemingly dumb familiar objects to the hidden forces behind the mundane screen. Clearly, Good and Evil exist, though they change into each other bewilderingly; the good and honest life is good and honest; and humility and resignation are necessary to it. But no morals are drawn. Powys is no more a moralist than a philosopher – whatever moral and philosophical notions he may keep to himself.
>
> [*God's Eyes A-Twinkle*, p. xiii]

In the context of these remarks about man's insignificance it is interesting to note that the second title for the collection from which 'The Bucket and the Rope' came, *No Painted Plumage*, appears to be an allusion to Thomas Gray's 'Ode on the Spring', in which the insignificant fly is described, in contrast to birds and more colourful insects, as having 'no painted plumage'. This, incidentally, was an allusion which we did not recognise at first, but which we found by typing the phrase into the Google search engine.

12.2 'The Bucket and the Rope'

We now present the story, so that our readers can familiarise themselves with it and reach their own conclusions, before we discuss it. We have numbered the paragraphs of the story so that we can refer to them more easily in later discussion. We have not numbered each sentence, as that would be more distracting for our readers, and in any case, most of the paragraphs are short.

The Bucket and the Rope

A bucket once lay upon its side in a little shed, that was a short way down a by-lane, near to the village of Shelton. [1]

This bucket, a large one, had been kicked over by a man who had hanged himself up by the neck, by means of an odd piece of rope, that he had tied to a strong beam. [2]

The man's name, who had hanged himself was Mr Dendy, who rented a few pleasant fields that he used to plough happily, and, besides keeping a few good cows, he fattened some nice pigs. [3]

Every servant, be he never so humble, is interested in his master, whose habits of life, goings and comings, loves and hates, are watched and commented upon. Mr Dendy's movements as well as his behaviour had always been of great interest to the bucket and the rope; who, when together, which was often the case, for they lived in the same shed, would speak of all that Mr Dendy did, and endeavour to find out as best they might a reason for his actions. [4]

Both were interested in any kind of life that was not like themselves, such as mankind, because both were humble and did not consider, as so many do, that they or their own kind deserved the most notice. [5]

In order to study men, both the bucket and the rope decided to take Mr Dendy as an example of humanity, believing, as they well might, that the ways and notions of a simple countryman ought to be easier to understand than those of one more sly and cunning. They wished to study Mr Dendy in order to find out from his behaviour what other men were like; to learn from his doings how they did, to find out the causes of their sorrows and joys, so as to journey a little nearer to the Truth that is always so hard to discover. [6]

Now and again the two friends had been a little puzzled by Mr Dendy, who did not often act as they would have expected him to, for sometimes he would seem to be troubled, when, according to the bucket's ideas of cause and effect, there was no reason for him to be so. [7]

And now that Mr Dendy had hanged himself, pressing both of them into this last service, to forward his self-destruction, the bucket and the rope thought they would review the man's life, in the hope of finding one true reason at least for his final act. [8]

'Is it not a little curious if not altogether surprising,' observed the bucket, 'that we should have been put to so sad a use in helping our good master die? Perhaps you can remember as well as I the joyful day when we were first purchased, which happened to be the very day before Mr Dendy was married. [9]

'He married as you know, a woman, a creature created to ease a man of the heavy burden of his desire, a burden as troublesome to carry as a kicking ass.' [10]

'And who also,' observed the rope, 'was intended to cook and prepare a man's food, to rear his children and to clean his house.' [11]

'That should certainly be so,' said the other. [12]

'The day we were purchased,' continued the rope, 'happened to be one of those delightful May days when all things animate and inanimate, that exist under the sun, are entirely happy. [13]

'I was coiled up in the shop window of Mr Johnson, the ropemaker, a man whose shirt-sleeves were always turned up, so that his hairy arms made the children stare. The sun shone upon me, and in its pleasant warmth I soon fell asleep. I dreamed of my happy childhood, when I grew up in a large field, beside a million brothers and sisters who were all beautiful flowers. But I did not sleep for long, for as soon as the sun rose too high to shine into the window I awoke and looked out into the street. [14]

'Anyone with a proper desire for knowledge, if he has eyes, can always see something of interest in what goes on in a street. He has only to look and something will be sure to come near. [15]

'I began to watch the folk who moved along the pavement in front of the shop, and a few of them particularly attracted my notice. Two old women came by, whose feet seemed to stick to the stones at every step, while their tongues cackled and gabbled about the ill-conduct of their neighbours. [16]

'A grand military gentleman sauntered past, who saw his own reflection in every window that he went by, and became prouder than ever. A lady who followed him at a little distance wished to see herself too, but did not dare to look, because she feared that a servant girl who walked behind might notice what she did. [17]

'Presently there was a fine clatter of running feet; some schoolboys came by, pulling the caps from one another's heads, and then an alderman passed, who looked about him as if the town were all his own. [18]

'After him came two young and pleasing girls, who were ready for love; they watched coyly every young man in the street, and laughed in order to show what they longed for. [19]

'The clock in the church tower at the top of the town struck three, but no one seemed to give any heed to it, except a poor debtor, whose examination was to be at that very hour in the town hall, and who wished he had taken his wife's advice earlier, and drowned himself. [20]

'The clock had hardly finished striking when a young man, who had the joyful looks of a would-be bridegroom, together with a young girl entered the shop. I looked at her with admiration, and at him with pleasure. They seemed made for one another. Anyone could see that she had the sweetest of natures, that would be unlikely, for the fear of being cruel, to refuse anything a man might ask of her. The man was Mr Dendy, and she was to be his wife.' [21]

'Her arms had been opened to another before him,' murmured the bucket. [22]

'Only a grave could have prevented that' answered the rope; 'but allow me to continue: [23]

'Mr Dendy came forward to the window and looked at me, together with Mr Johnson. The girl looked elsewhere. Mr Johnson's hands, that were as hairy as his arms, took me up, uncoiled me, and stretched me out. Our master examined me for a little, satisfied that I was what he needed, and made the purchase. [24]

'Mr Dendy was about twenty-nine years old then, and the young girl about eighteen,' remarked the bucket. [25]

'So she was' said the rope, 'but it is curious to think now what she did next. While Mr Johnson and Mr Dendy were talking, she coiled and uncoiled me, and then, in her girlish amusement, for she looked at him lovingly, she made a running noose of me, slipped it over the master's head, and pulled it tight.' [26]

'Mr Johnson laughed, I suppose?' [27]

'Yes, but a little uneasily. While she toyed with me,' said the rope, 'I had a chance to look at her the more narrowly. She seemed just the creature to delight any man with her sweetness and eagerness for love. She had a yielding kindness, but no wickedness in her. She showed her good nature to a young man, the son of a lawyer, who happened to pass her in a by-street when Mr Dendy slipped into a small inn. The lawyer's son looked unhappy and she allowed him to kiss her, while Mr Dendy was out of the way.' [28]

'She had a little foot,' observed the bucket, 'and a winning gait, and had Mr Dendy peeped through the dingy bar-window, when he was having a merry jest with Farmer Pardy, he should have been glad to see that the lawyer's son thought her as nice as he did.' [29]

'A rope would have fancied so,' said the other dryly. [30]

'Mr Dendy had no sooner bought you,' said the bucket, 'than he went to the ironmonger's and purchased me. We were carried off together, and so we became acquainted, and that very evening I was made use of to collect the swill for the pigs; I remember even now the unpleasant smell of those rotten potatoes.' [31]

'It was not the stink of the sour garbage that made our master hang himself,' observed the rope thoughtfully, 'for he would be often whistling when he brought you in, full of the nastiest stuff. Neither could it have been the weight of you that troubled him, for he would ever carry you jauntily, as if the burden of a few gallons of swill was nothing to so powerful an arm as his.' [32]

'Oh no, he never minded carrying me,' said the bucket, 'for whatever the time of year was, whether the summer sun shone, or whether the dreary autumn rain fell, Mr Dendy would bear me along with the same sprightliness. He would perhaps tarry at a cottage gate, and have a merry word with the occupants, telling a droll story of country matters for the young girls to smile at, and bidding them to ask of his kind Betty what the fancies were that she had found the most useful in the getting of a husband.' [33]

'We could watch nearly all that he did,' remarked the rope, 'and he certainly appeared to be living a very happy life: the sweet country air, the plain and wholesome food that he ate, as well as his constant though not too tedious toil, gave him health and joy, and he was never in want of a shilling to spend when he needed one.' [34]

'Only once,' observed the bucket sadly, 'did I notice Mr Dendy act in a way that was not usual for a village man. He was bearing me, full, along a path from a small cottage where he bought swill. On each side of the path there were flowers, both white and yellow. Mr Dendy set me down, a rotten orange bobbed up on my surface. Mr Dendy rested by the path, plucked some of the flowers, and seemed to take delight in holding them in his hand.' [35]

'What did he do next?' asked the rope. [36]

'He carried the flowers home to his wife,' replied the bucket. . . . [37]

'The summer pleased Mr Dendy, and so did the winter,' said the rope. [38]

'In the winter we saw more of him, for we were used the more. During the winter the horses lay in, and straw had to be carried to them, and in the winter there were more pigs to be fattened. In the winter, too, a strong man feels his strength and his happiness more than in the summer. He learns to brave the keenest wind without a shudder, and cares nothing when the rain soaks him to the skin. No weather daunted Mr Dendy, and the more he bore with the storms outside the pleasanter was his parlour, with its cheerful light, and the warm presence of a wife who loved him.' [39]

'Why, then, did he hang himself?' asked the bucket. [40]

'The winter weather was certainly not to blame,' answered the rope, 'for I cannot think of those happy days without being sure that he enjoyed them. I was stouter then, and yet I think not, for I appear to be strong enough now to hold a pretty fair burden. Mr Dendy, who is carried by me, could carry a bundle then, he thought nothing of carrying as much straw with me as was enough for three men to bear. However large the bundle was, he would somehow get it upon his back, so that the straw upon either side of him would sweep the hedges in the lane, almost as though a whole stack was out a-walking.' [41]

'Yes, there was Mr Dendy!' exclaimed the bucket, 'a true and joyful countryman, doing his proper tasks. What could harm him? What could prevent him from living out his life contentedly and going down, as a

311

good man should, gently into the grave? Surely never was a poor man created who meant so well.' [42]

'Look at him now,' said the rope quietly; 'at first when he kicked you over I wondered if I should be strong enough to hold him. He struggled horribly, and I fancy that when he first felt me tighten round his throat he would have changed his mind. He tried to catch me to lessen the dreadful feeling of suffocation'. [43]

'You must have hurt him very much,' observed the bucket, 'for his face became quite black, and his eyes bulged out of his head. I wonder you did not let him fall, for in his death agony he kicked his legs and swung round, but you held him fast. Why did he do it?' [44]

'I believe the reason was,' replied the rope, 'that Mr Dendy did not like to see others happy.' [45]

'This is not easy to believe,' remarked the bucket, 'when one considers how happy he was himself.' [46]

'His wife made him so,' said the rope 'and feeling her success with him she naturally wished to make another happy too.' [47]

'What could be more proper?' said the bucket. [48]

'It was this summer,' continued the rope, 'and the master, having saved a few guineas, bought for himself a new Sunday suit "You look so well in it," his wife told him, "that you should go to church more often, for people will know how well you are getting on when they see you in your new clothes." Now, it was the time when Mr Dendy began to go to church of an evening that I noticed passing this shed the same young man who had given Betty a kiss in the by-street when Mr Dendy was drinking a glass in a little tavern. He still looked unhappy.' [49]

'A chance for Betty to turn his sorrow into joy!' laughed the bucket. [50]

'She wished to do so, and they met in this very shed, on a Sunday evening, when Mr Dendy was supposed to be gone to church.' [51]

'But had he gone?' asked the bucket. [52]

'No,' replied the rope. 'He had only put on the best clothes and walked out, as if to go. Instead of going to church, he came to this shed, took me up, and bound me round in a large bundle of straw. The bundle he placed against the wall of the shed, where there was a little chink, and, creeping under the straw to hide himself, he waited.' [53]

'For the pleasure of witnessing the kindness of his wife, I suppose,' said the bucket. [54]

'One would have thought so,' replied the rope, 'but the look upon Mr Dendy's face when he saw what was going on did not warrant such a supposition.' [55]

'Perhaps he thought,' reasoned the bucket, 'that Betty should have remained at home and warmed the rabbit pie for his supper; for the sermon preached by Mr Hayball always made him extremely hungry, and Betty was not to be expected to know that he was not at church. I have seen the pigs fed so often, and I know how hungry animals are, and, as food keeps man alive and prevents him from becoming a dead carcass, it is natural that a man should wish the woman that he keeps to prepare for him, even though she may prefer to be loving and kind to another man.' [56]

'You should have heard Mr Dendy,' said the rope; 'he gnashed his teeth and moaned horribly, and when his wife's friend seemed to be altogether forgetting his sorrow, being come, as the lyrical poet says, "Where comfort is –" Mr Dendy crept out of the bundle and hid in the lane, snarling like a bitten dog.' [57]

'His hunger, I suppose, had gone beyond the proper bounds,' suggested the bucket. [58]

'It is difficult' said the rope, after a few minutes' silence, as the body swung to and fro, 'for us to decide what could have troubled this good man. No one had robbed him. No one had beaten him or hurt him, and never once since they had been married had Betty refused his embraces.' [59]

'It must have been that nosegay,' exclaimed the bucket. [60]

12.3 Discussion of 'The Bucket and the Rope'

12.3.1 Provisional interpretative comments on the story

Before examining different aspects of the story and applying various techniques to them, we begin with a brief interpretation of what we think this rather enigmatic story is about.

In our view, the story is thematically concerned with *life and death, posi tive and negative*, and *appearance v. reality*. In it, the bucket and the rope try to work out why their owner, Mr Dendy, committed suicide (a negative factor) in spite of his being a naturally good and happy man (a positive factor). Mr Dendy used the bucket and the rope to kill himself, so they are directly involved, as well as interested students of humankind. But their schematic assumptions about how the world works, and should work, are different from ours. Although we are not told explicitly, we infer that Mr Dendy kills himself because he loves his wife and cannot bear it when he discovers her making love to the lawyer's son. But the bucket and the rope cannot see this. They are utilitarians, and so when they see Mr Dendy's wife satisfying both her husband and the lawyer's son sexually, they see this not as a problem, but as a good thing. However, the story is not just a comparison of two different visions of the same story. It also seems to suggest that although the bucket and the rope get it wrong, in mistaking the motives and feelings involved in the case, in another sense they get it right;

their attitude seems more 'logical' than that of Mr Dendy (and most readers of the story). In other words, the story 'deconstructs' or 'problematises' our standard assumptions about human love and sexual relations.

Another remarkable thing about the story relates to viewpoint and our attitude to what is described. It is about someone who has just committed suicide, but, because of the rather enigmatic and offhand way in which things are presented to us, instead of becoming involved emotionally with the man who killed himself, we are prompted to consider what happened in a more dispassionate way (which in turn helps us more easily to 'problematise' our own assumptions which the story draws on).

12.3.2 The title of the story: schemata and associations

A story's title can legitimately be considered part of the text, and part of what has to be interpreted. While this chapter was being written, a Google internet search for the phrase 'the bucket and the rope' resulted in 202 'hits', of which, after those for the title of Powys's story are removed, almost all are related in some way to wells and the schema of drawing water from wells. Some of the texts in which the phrase occurs are mathematical puzzles but the majority are stories, many of which are religious or related to mythology. The well, with its life-giving water, recurs most frequently in Christian and Muslim contexts in the Google set. This suggests that, for many, the phrase will be associated with life and possibly have religious associations as well. However, if we search for 'bucket' in the British National Corpus (BNC) we find an association between 'bucket' and the verb 'kick', as in 'kick the bucket', which is an colloquial idiom for dying. A Google search for 'kick the bucket' reveals 277,000 hits. We examined the first 50, of which 72 per cent were dictionary definitions of the phrase or straightforward 'die' uses.[2] In addition, the phrase 'the rope' has a strong association with death by hanging. Hence the title may well be perceived by readers as prefiguring the life/death theme, which is, of course, appropriate, given that the bucket and the rope are trying to work out why Mr Dendy has committed suicide, which he did by literally 'kicking the bucket'.

The other notable schematic connection for the title is with the fable genre. We have noted that 'The Bucket and the Rope' comes from a collection originally called *Fables*, and we may also recognise that the noun phrase structure 'the X and the Y' (as in 'the Hare and the Tortoise') is a common type of title for stories in Aesop's famous fables, with X and Y referring to animals or inanimate objects, and indeed this is also the case for the other stories in the *Fables/No Painted Plumage* collection. In many of Aesop's fables, as here, we meet animals and inanimate objects which talk, and thus enter into what Ryan (1991) calls a textual actual world (TAW) resembling our world in many ways (and so we can take many of our actual world assumptions along to it) but with an expanded inventory of characters. The title of the story, as well as the volume it first appeared in, thus sets us up to infer a 'moral' for the story, even if, in line with Prentice's comments in section 12.1, Powys does not tell us what the moral should be.

The last thing to note about the title is that it suggests that the story is about the bucket and the rope, in spite of the fact that we are likely to want to see it as being about the human beings in the story, and Mr Dendy in particular, because of our tendency to search for 'human significance' in texts (see Fairley 1988). We will return to these issues raised by the title below.

12.3.3 The story's discourse structure: narration, speech presentation and 'framing'

'The Bucket and the Rope' is a third-person narration in which the first eight paragraphs (420 words, or 15.3 per cent of the story) are entirely narration and the rest of the story is direct speech produced by the bucket and the rope, with no narrative intervention apart from the associated reporting clauses. These reporting clauses comprise only a further 132 words. If these are added to the first eight paragraphs of narration, we can see that only about 20 per cent of the story is narration and about 80 per cent of it is direct speech. At first sight, this helps to give the story a straightforward and simple air: the third-person narration (cf section 8.1.2b) is canonically associated with objective presentation of the 'facts of the story', and the direct speech mode creates the illusion that the narrator/author is 'interfering' with the speech presented (cf Figure 10.1 in section 10.1.3) in only minimal ways.

An examination of the relationship between the reporting and reported clauses confirms this straightforward and simple 'feel'. The conversation between the bucket and the rope has 41 direct speech turns, and all but two of these turns have an accompanying reporting clause, making it easy to attribute each turn to the relevant character. The reporting clauses themselves are also very straightforward. Only five of them contain anything other than a simple VS grammatical structure containing a verb followed by a simple determiner + noun reference to the relevant speaker (e.g. 'replied the rope'). Of these five, four contain a one-word manner adverb and one (the rope's last turn in the story) contains a twelve-word time reference: 'said the rope, after a few minutes' silence, as the body swung to and fro'. This clause, with its associated turn, is therefore foregrounded by its length as well as being prominent as the penultimate turn in the story. It seems to summarise the reasons for the bucket's and the rope's perplexity and brings us back to the realisation that the bucket and the rope are conducting their conversation across the body of the man who has used them to kill himself.

The story's rather clear division between the third-person narration and the dialogue between the bucket and the rope marks a distinction between the two main parts of the narrative: the 'framing' initial narration followed by the 'framed' direct speech dialogue. In the initial narration we are told that, in chronological terms, immediately before the beginning of the presentation of the story, the bucket and the rope have been used by Mr Dendy to commit suicide, and the bucket then suggests (in paragraph [9]) that this act is 'curious, if not altogether surprising'. Indeed, the narrator tells us that the bucket and the rope, who decide to review Mr Dendy's life in order to understand humankind better, are 'a little puzzled' [7] by a number of other things he has done in the past. The direct speech then contains descriptions of what the bucket and the rope saw, and their attempts to find a plausible (for them) hypothesis to explain Mr Dendy's suicide. The third-person past-tense narrative frame thus describes what is the fictional present and immediate past for the bucket and the rope, and in the direct speech dialogue (which also exists in their fictional present) they recall past occurrences they found to be significant and, later in the story (from [32] onwards), they compare suggestions on why Mr Dendy killed himself. Unlike most framing narratives, however, there is no real return to the narrative frame at the end of the story, apart from the final and apparently climactic minimal reporting clause, 'exclaimed the bucket' on which the story ends. In deictic shift theory terms (*cf* Galbraith (1995) and section 12.3.7 below), there is little opportunity for us to 'pop' back up to the deictic centre with which the story opens).

12.3.4 The story's 'structure'

The above description suggests that an account of the story/plot structure of 'The Bucket and the Rope' will need two parts, one related to the framing story and one to the framed story. Drawing on various narratological frameworks, we will outline and combine a set of different 'story structure' accounts below, but first, a few words of warning concerning analyses of story 'structure'. As reported in section 11.2.1, Herman (2002), among others, has shown that what he calls 'story logic' is not straightforwardly observable. Different readers may come up with alternative accounts, depending on the inferences that they make as they read the text, and there is also a question of how much specification of detail (see section 5.3) is found in a particular account of a story. In this respect, stories can be like textual summaries, which can be more or less detailed, depending on their interpretative purposes. Indeed, it is likely that literary analysts choose a 'structure' and level of detail when outlining what they see as the 'story logic' of a particular text so that they can relate it optimally to the interpretative account they are giving. What we provide below is merely an account which we find interpretatively plausible and for which we would want to argue on the basis of a range of evidence. There is, moreover, an interesting empirical question of whether different people's specifications of the structure of the story will be substantially different, leading to different interpretative consequences, or slightly different instantiations of the 'same' structure, rather like notational variants in formal accounts of grammar.

A fable is normally a story told chronologically, whereas this story is not. It will help, then, if we summarise the events of the 'The Bucket and the Rope' in chronological order (the *fabula* in Russian formalist terms), as far as we can discern it, in preparation for further analysis:

1. The day before his wedding, Mr Dendy buys the bucket and the rope to use on his smallholding.
2. Betty, the prospective Mrs Dendy, who is with Mr Dendy when he buys the rope, appears to be attracted to, and involved with, the lawyer's son when she is betrothed to Mr Dendy (who is eleven years older than her).
3. The bucket and the rope observe Mr Dendy over some years as he uses them. He appears to be 'a true and joyful countryman, doing his proper tasks', and from their perspective, the only thing that he does out of the ordinary is to pick a bunch of flowers which he gives to his wife.
4. Mr Dendy observes his wife and the lawyer's son making love in his barn while they think he is at church.
5. Mr Dendy kills himself, hanging himself by means of the bucket and the rope.
6. The bucket and the rope try to work out why Mr Dendy killed himself.
7. The bucket naively concludes that the bunch of flowers was the cause of Mr Dendy's suicide.

To begin our analysis, we will employ the structuralist account of Claude Brémond, allied with the possible worlds approach of Marie-Laure Ryan and Lévi-Strauss's interpretative structuralist analysis. The structuralist accounts of 'story logic' will need to be backed up by inferential analysis of the sort suggested by Herman (2002), as reported in section 11.2.1.

12.3.5 Structuralist and possible worlds accounts of literary narratives: Claude Brémond and Marie-Laure Ryan

Brémond (1973) suggests that stories go through one or more narrative cycles, from a state of narrative equilibrium through a process of mediation to a state of disequilibrium, and then, perhaps, back again, via a 'mediation' process to a state of equilibrium again, and so on (see also Figure 12.2 on p. 319):

$$\begin{array}{ccc}
\text{Equilibrium} & \rightarrow & \text{Mediation} \\
\uparrow & & \downarrow \\
\text{Mediation} & \leftarrow & \text{Disequilibrium}
\end{array}$$

Figure 12.1

If we apply this schema for the 'what happened' part of a story to the above summary of 'The Bucket and the Rope', we can perceive two inter-connected, but distinct, narrative cycles, depending on the viewpoint from which the events are perceived.

The framing narrative begins, from the bucket and the rope's point of view, with episode 5 in the list above, which is a disequilibrium (they are puzzled by Mr Dendy's suicide). The mediation takes place in 6, in their attempt to understand why he did it, and this attempt includes their recall of the earlier events described in 1–4. This re-ordering of the chronological order of the events (the *sjuzhet* in Russian formalist terms) helps us to understand how the story is presented in an exceptional sequence. In presentational order, the episodes of the story are as follows:

5. Mr Dendy kills himself, hanging himself by means of the bucket and the rope.
6. The bucket and the rope try to work out why Mr Dendy killed himself.
1. The day before his wedding, Mr Dendy bought the bucket and the rope to use on his smallholding.
2. Betty, the prospective Mrs Dendy, who is with Mr Dendy when he buys the rope, appears to be attracted to, and involved with, the lawyer's son when she is betrothed to Mr Dendy (who is eleven years older than her).
3. The bucket and the rope observe Mr Dendy over some years as he uses them. He appears to be 'a true and joyful countryman, doing his proper tasks', and from their perspective, the only thing that he does out of the ordinary is to pick a bunch of flowers which he gives to his wife.
4. Mr Dendy observes his wife and the lawyer's son making love in his barn while they think he is at church.
7. The bucket naively concludes that the bunch of flowers was the cause of Mr Dendy's suicide.

The final statement in both the chronological and presentational ordering is 7, an apparent state of equilibrium for the bucket, who makes the final remark. Given that the story ends at this point and we are not told that the rope dissents from this conclusion, we can assume for the present (but see section 12.3.7) that the rope's viewpoint is the same as the bucket's.

However, looking at the story from Mr Dendy's angle, the movement is in the opposite direction: from equilibrium to disequilibrium – that is, from the happy life he enjoys to the fact that he lives with a wife who is unfaithful to him, which he can 'resolve' only through suicide:

The bucket and the rope's narrative cycle	Mr Dendy's narrative cycle
Disequilibrium → Mediation	Equilibrium → Mediation
↓	↓
Equilibrium	Disequilibrium

Figure 12.2

If we apply Ryan's possible-worlds theory to the bucket and the rope's narrative cycle, we can see how her account of possible worlds helps to explain what drives the story forward. In her terms the initial disequilibrium in the bucket and the rope's narrative cycle relate to the fact that they know that their private knowledge world (K-world) conflicts with the textual actual world (TAW): they know that they do not know why Mr Dendy committed suicide. This is made clear in the last two pure narrative paragraphs [7] and [8], and also in the first part of the bucket's succeeding utterance, which opens the conversation between the bucket and the rope:

Now and again *the two friends had been a little puzzled by Mr Dendy*, who *did not often act as they would have expected him to*, for sometimes he *would seem to be troubled, when, according to the bucket's ideas of cause and effect, there was no reason for him to be so*. [7]

And now that Mr Dendy had hanged himself, pressing both of them into this last service, to forward his self-destruction, the bucket and the rope thought they would review the man's life, in the hope of finding one true reason at least for his final act. [8]

'*Is it not a little curious if not altogether surprising,*' observed the bucket, 'that we should have been put to so sad a use in helping our good master die? [. . .]' [9]

This lack of fit between the K-world and the TAW is indicated in the narrative by the italicised parts of the passages above, especially words like *puzzled, surprising, curious*. In terms of foregrounding, Mr Dendy's actions are deviant and hence noticeable by the standards of the bucket and the rope, whereas our own schemas and cause-and-effect relations are presumably much more in tune with Mr Dendy's. This TAW/K-world disequilibrium induces what Ryan calls a wish world (W-world) for the bucket and the rope: they want to make the TAW and their K-world consistent with one another. Their desire for this W-world, with the help of pragmatic inferencing via Grice's (1975) maxim of relation or Sperber and

Wilson's (1986) principle of relevance, pushes the conversation between the bucket and the rope forward, as they propose and reject in turn a series of possible explanations for Mr Dendy's behaviour:

(a) It was not the stink of the sour garbage [32].
(b) It was not the weight of the bucket [32], [33].
(c) It was not his life: he led a happy life, lived in 'the sweet country air', enjoyed his work and did not want for money [34].
(d) He picked a bunch of flowers and gave them to his wife [35]–[37] which the bucket recorded as 'not usual for a village man' (in this sense a foregrounded occurrence, but not taken up by the bucket or the rope as a reason for Mr Dendy's behaviour).
(e) It was not the weather [39], [41].
(f) He did not like to 'see others happy' [45] (the bucket rejects this suggestion by the rope).
(g) It was not his wife: she made him happy [47].
(h) Betty should have stayed at home to cook his dinner rather than make the lawyer's son happy [56] (this suggestion is apparently rejected as it is not taken up).
(i) 'His hunger, I suppose, had gone beyond the proper bounds [. . .]' [58] (again, this suggestion is apparently rejected as it is not taken up).
(j) 'It must have been that nosegay' [60] (this return to (d) appears to 'win out' as it is the suggestion which ends the story, but see section 12.3.9).

If we now use the Brémond narrative cycle to represent the framed story from Mr Dendy's point of view, rather than that of the bucket and the rope, note that (i) we are told of Mr Dendy's suicide as early as the narrative paragraph [3], (ii) we are given the rest of 'his' narrative cycle through the conversation of the bucket and the rope, and (iii) in order to see the elements of the cycle we have to infer them, because they are not explicitly stated by the bucket and the rope and their schemata for cause and effect is not the same as Mr Dendy's and ours would be. Figure 12.2 translates into Table 12.1 as follows.

Table 12.1

1. Disequilibrium	(a) Mr Dendy loves his wife but (b) she loves the lawyer's son.
2. Mediation	Mr Dendy wants (a) but not (b).
3. Equilibrium	He kills himself (thus resolving the 'paradox' by removing the first half of the opposition).

This particular narrative cycle is not straightforward to arrive at because (i) there are alternatives for describing the initial disequilibrium stage in particular, and (ii) it is not always possible to find statements in the text which state the propositions in the cycle as presented above, partly because we see the disequilibrium and mediation phases through the words of the bucket and the rope, who do not properly understand what is going on. As a consequence, we have to rely rather more on inferences based on our schematic assumptions about social life. Effectively, we are 'filling in' Brémond's rather abstract narrative cycle schema with particular content.

We are told that Mr Dendy married Betty in [9] and [10], but nowhere in the story is there a proposition which states that Mr Dendy loved her. Hence this needs to be inferred by the reader and argued for by the analyst. Schematically it is likely that Mr Dendy loved his wife, given that she was young (eleven years younger than him) and attractive, and that he chose to marry her. This assumption is later strengthened by the fact that the bucket presupposes that Betty loved Mr Dendy (in a relative clause at the end of [39]) and that in [59] the rope states that 'never once since they had been married had Betty refused his embraces'. The only thing which could count as a clear sign of Mr Dendy's love for his wife is the fact that he picks the bunch of flowers and gives them to her.

There are also issues in relation to the second of the coordinated propositions in the *disequilibrium* line above. We have used the verb 'love' partly to bring out lexically the opposition between the two propositions, and it is implicated that Betty loved the lawyer's son when she married Mr Dendy (*cf* [22] and [28]). But the opposition would still be there in schematic terms if 'loves his wife' in the first proposition was replaced by 'is married to Betty' and/or if 'loves' in the second proposition was replaced by 'has sex with'. This is because in our society (indeed most societies) love, marriage and sexual relations are very closely intertwined schematically.

The bucket's presupposition that Betty was 'loving and kind' to the lawyer's son just before Mr Dendy committed suicide [56] can easily be understood as a reference to sexual relations between them. The rope implicates strongly that Mr Dendy witnessed his wife *in flagrante delicto* with the lawyer's son [55], [57]. This implicated reference to the sexual act is foregrounded and strengthened by an allusion to a poem by Thomas Campion called 'Amaryllis':

[. . .] when his wife's friend seemed to be altogether forgetting his sorrow, being come, as the lyrical poet says, 'Where comfort is –' Mr Dendy crept out of the bundle and hid in the lane, snarling like a bitten dog. [57]

In Campion's poem *I care not for these ladies* (which we found using a Google search on 'come where comfort is'), Amaryllis is a country girl who is free with her favours compared with women who come from the town or higher social orders, and the refrain at the end of each of the three verses of the poem is 'But when we come where comfort is, she never will say no.' The response of Mr Dendy to what he sees seems schematically to confirm the sexual act interpretation.

The *mediation* proposition 2 above 'Mr Dendy wants (a) but not (b)' also cannot be found in the text, as the bucket and the rope do not see any problem in Betty giving her sexual favours both to her husband and the lawyer's son (indeed they see her satisfying both men as an advantage – *cf* [21], [28], [29], [47] and [54]). Again, schematic assumptions provide the otherwise missing link between the text and proposition 2: those who are married to (or are in love with or involved in long-term sexual relations with) another are disposed to want those relations to be exclusive for their partners.

What is the explanation for 'he kills himself' being the *equilibrium* line? There are two parts to this: (a) this proposition needs to be systematically relatable to the disequilibrium line which began the narrative cycle, and (b) as one of the two coordinated propositions in the disequilibrium line is removed, the application of logic means that the paradox is also removed.

In the next section we will try to be more explicit about the relationship between structure and understanding by relating it to Claude Lévi-Strauss's anthropological analyses of the structure of myths.

12.3.6 Linking structure and interpretation: Claude Lévi-Strauss

Lévi-Strauss argued in a series of publications (e.g. 1963, 1964, 1970) that the story structure of myths can be rearranged from the syntagmatic axis (the chronological order of the events of the story) into a paradigmatic set of four columns (A, B, C, D) in which the events can be seen to be related to one another through two thematic oppositions (A v. B and C v. D). He then suggests that myths can be *understood* as constituting narrative 'mediations' of sets of paradoxical beliefs which societies have, through the oppositions in the four paradigmatic columns. We do not have the space to go more fully into Lévi-Strauss's analyses here, but we do think that myths and fables are not far apart, and that it is insightful to resolve the events of stories into sets of binary oppositions. Many critics talk of particular literary texts as instantiating one or more pairs of thematic oppositions (e.g. life/death, nature/culture, appearance/reality), and Hendricks (1973b) has interestingly applied the Lévi-Straussian approach to a story by Ambrose Bierce, using a two-column thematic opposition, an approach we adopt below. It is proposed, then, that overall textual interpretation relates to the specific working out of one or more pairs of thematic oppositions, which is what we now attempt.

In Table 12.2, we take the two Brémond-style narrative cycles which we have argued for above, and juxtapose them in opposing columns. They

Table 12.2

Appearance: The bucket and the rope's view		Reality: Mr Dendy's view	
Equilibrium:	(a) Mr Dendy loves Mrs Dendy & (b) she loves the lawyer's son	*Disequilibrium:*	(a) Mr Dendy loves his wife & (b) she loves the lawyer's son
Mediation:	Mr Dendy acts in a way 'not usual for a village man' [35]: he picks a bunch of flowers and gives them to his wife	*Mediation:*	Mr Dendy wants (a) but not (b)
Disequilibrium:	Mr Dendy kills himself	*Equilibrium:*	Mr Dendy kills himself

represent two alternative views of the events of the story, which we can see as related on the one hand to *appearance* (the bucket and the rope's take on the events), and on the other hand to *reality* (Mr Dendy's view of events, which seems schematically close to ours – which is why we label them as 'reality'). We will try to construct an overall interpretation of the story by comparing these two 'thematic' columns.

If we first compare the initial row, where we have used '&' to represent logical conjunction (which can be realised by 'and' or 'but'), we can see that what is equilibrium for the bucket and the rope is disequilibrium for Mr Dendy. This reflects the fact that the combined propositions in the equilibrium line are opposed according to the social schemata we assume we share with Mr Dendy (we would most naturally use 'but' for '&' above), but not for the bucket and the rope (who would be happier with 'and'). This is because in the bucket and the rope's utilitarian view, unlike Mr Dendy's, it is natural to want to give pleasure to as many people as possible in all circumstances. The fact that the bucket and the rope share such a view can be seen in the following extracts, where they approve of Betty's actions towards the lawyer's son:

She had a yielding kindness, but no wickedness in her. She showed her good nature to a young man, the son of a lawyer [. . .]. The lawyer's son looked unhappy and she allowed him to kiss her, while Mr Dendy was out of the way.' [28]

[. . .] he should have been glad to see that the lawyer's son thought her as nice as he did.' [29]

'His wife made him [Mr Dendy] so [happy],' said the rope 'and feeling her success with him she naturally wished to make another happy too.' [47]

The same idea is expressed later, in paragraphs [49], [50], [53], [54] and [55]. The bucket and the rope approve of Betty's attitude towards the lawyer's son, but clearly do not understand Mr Dendy's despair – a more typically human reaction – when he finds out what is going on.

The mediation line is different in the two columns because the bucket and the rope think that it is the bunch of flowers that cause Mr Dendy to commit suicide, not his unhappiness about the affair between his wife and the lawyer's son, as we do. This, together with the different interpretations of the logical connector '&' in the first line, which we have already commented on, constitutes the difference between the appearance and reality views of the events in the TAW of 'the bucket and the rope'. But there is also an irony here, in that, although the bucket and the rope get it wrong, they also get it right by accident. When Mr Dendy picks the flowers, he does so to give them to his wife. Hence what is an inexplicable occurrence in the column for the bucket and the rope counts as an indication of the love Mr Dendy has for Mrs Dendy expressed in the first proposition of the first row of the *Reality* column, prompting his suicidal action.

Just as the first line of the above table is *equilibrium* for the bucket and the rope but *disequilibrium* for Mr Dendy, the last line, which presents Mr Dendy's suicide identically in both columns, shows opposite interpretations in the *appearance* and *reality* columns. But it is also worth noticing a slight oddity here in Mr Dendy's attitude. If accounts of domestic violence are to be believed, most people who find out about a spouse having an affair are likely to strike out, literally or metaphorically, at their spouse or their spouse's lover, not at themselves. So although Mr Dendy's attitude is mainly like the one we expect in schematic terms, it is not in this respect.

A comparison of the two columns with different ideological viewpoints raises the issue of which ideology is preferable, particularly when we remember the oddity of Mr Dendy taking his unhappiness out on himself, rather than his wife or her lover. The view of the bucket and the rope is perfectly logical in its own terms: Mr Dendy's self-destruction is an unusual form of behaviour, and this must be explained in relation to the only other unusual way he had behaved: his making and giving the posy to Betty. And in a sense this is the correct conclusion, as the nosegay appears to show his unusually deep feelings for his wife, which in turn explains his suicide. But the human view is also logical in its own terms. This same self-destruction, in the bottom line of Table 12.2, leaves intact proposition (b) of line 1: 'she loves the lawyer's son'. So Mr Dendy's deep feeling for this wife, as manifested in the posy-giving, leads to his sacrifice of himself, leaving Betty's love for the lawyer's son to enjoy.

As the bucket and the rope's direct speech is predominant in the text, the story arguably allows us to infer that there is no necessary reason to equate love or marriage with exclusive sexual relations, thus problematising (or mediating, in Lévi-Strauss's terms) two views which are richly paradoxical for many because they are held simultaneously.

12.3.7 Fictional worlds and viewpoint

In the previous section we have used Ryan's (1991) account of possible worlds in fiction, where she distinguished between the private world of the characters (K-worlds, W-worlds, and so on) and the TAW (textual actual world) – what in Chapter 5 we called 'the mock-reality'. In this section we concentrate on how we construct the TAW as we read, and how we arrive at a particular viewpoint. This story has a fable-like TAW because the set of human-like characters is extended to include the bucket and the rope (who can see, talk, reason, have views, and so on), but in all other respects appear to obey the natural and psychological laws of the real world. In this respect it obeys Ryan's (1991, pp. 48–60) principle of minimal departure of the TAW from the actual world (AW).

Below we will mainly use the 'text worlds' approach of Paul Werth and his followers in order to spell out aspects of the TAW. At the same time, we will rely on the relevant work of Emmott (1997), deictic shift theory, and more traditional stylistic work. Werth's text world analysis is preferred here to possible worlds and mental spaces theory, as Werth's approach has so far been applied to stories in more detail. To save space, however, we have to present our text world analysis in informal terms. Werth's style of analysis involves producing diagrams for each text world and sub-world, spelling out in considerable detail the various text-building elements of each (as indicated textually), and the relations among those worlds. We will concentrate on aspects of the story that can be related fairly directly to meaning and effect.

A. The opening of the story

As those who propose deictic shift analysis have pointed out, when we sit down to read we have our own deictic centre, based on ourselves and our space/time coordinates as we begin reading, but it does not take long before we have been 'pushed' (Galbraith 1995) mentally to a new deictic centre within the world we are reading about (and so on into the various sub-worlds of the story as it develops). Werth terms these worlds 'text worlds' (since not all worlds we read about are fictional) and points out that referential and deictic items in the text are crucial in defining the complex interrelated set of text worlds we 'create' as we read.

Our story begins with a third-person narration which locates it, in the first two sentences, in a shed somewhere near a village called Shelton containing a dead man hanging by a rope from a beam, with a bucket lying on its side underneath:

A bucket once lay upon its side in a little shed, that was a short way down a by-lane, near to the village of Shelton. [1]

This bucket, a large one, had been kicked over by a man who had hanged himself up by the neck, by means of an odd piece of rope, that he had tied to a strong beam. [2]

Figure 12.3 is a diagrammatic 'picture' of the scene created by these sentences:

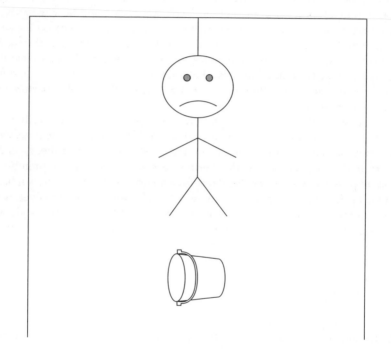

Figure 12.3

This picture is constructed mainly through noun phrases and prepositional phrases specifying objects, places and a human being ('a bucket', 'upon its side in a little shed that was a short way down a by-lane, near to the village of Shelton' ', 'a man who had hanged himself by the neck, by means of an odd piece of rope that he had tied to a strong beam'). The deictic shift theorists would say that these locational deictic expressions construct the deictic field within which the reader positions herself. By the time we have listed them all, there is little which is not quoted from the first two sentences, showing their key role in developing what Labov and Waletzky (1967) would call the orientation phase of the story, as well as the TAW in Ryan's terms. But there is also some inferencing work to be done, to integrate these textual details with schematic knowledge. We know, for example, that the man stood on the bucket before kicking it out from underneath himself. Death by hanging requires the feet to be clear of the ground, and the kicking away of the bucket is an obvious method of achieving this. Already we can see, as Werth and others have emphasised, the key role that inference plays in helping readers construct fictional worlds on the basis of textual information.

In terms of viewpoint, however, the TAW which we have now established is depicted rather idiosyncratically, focusing first of all on the bucket and its position, and not that of the man. The bucket is the subject and topic of the first two sentences, and the information about the suicide is presented in a defining relative clause postmodifying 'man' in the explanation of how the bucket came to be on its side, and is thus downgraded in informational terms (cf section 7.5.1). What is odd about this is that, in spite of the title, we still expect the story, like most stories, to be about people (cf Fairley 1988). But the information about Mr Dendy (which is very dramatic, after all) is not the topic of the sentence and is presented in a subordinate, backgrounding structure, as if it is not salient or important. In this description there is thus already a mismatch in our schematic assumptions about what should count as the figure and what should count as the ground (cf Stockwell 2002, Chapter 2). In terms of Figure 12.3, the textually foregrounded part of the picture is the bucket, not the hanging man, and so the very beginning of the story makes us concentrate not on the dead man, how awful the suicide was and what drove him to kill himself, but on the location and orientation of one of the instruments he used. All this conveys an idiosyncratic, almost ironic, slant on the contents of the TAW from the viewpoint of the third-person narrator, whose viewpoint we, as non-resisting readers (cf section 8.3), work to share.

Sentence/paragraph 3 continues this unusual, offhand approach to the suicide:

> The man's name, who had hanged himself was Mr Dendy, who rented a few pleasant fields that he used to plough happily, and, besides keeping a few good cows, he fattened some nice pigs. [3]

Its topic is 'the man's *name* who had hanged himself' (rather than the man himself), and the end-weighted information describes an apparently happy life, which thus gives no indication whatsoever of what drove him to suicide. Each aspect of the description given involves positive evaluative adjectives and adverbs: he had '*pleasant* fields' that he 'ploughed *happily*', '*good* cows' and he 'fattened *nice* pigs'. In this context even the verb 'fattened' is easily understood as being a positive thing (success in what a farmer is meant to do), even though it is not a straightforwardly evaluative term.

We might now expect some more direct information about the dead man, but in the rest of this initial section of third-person narrative we move instead to the shared mental world of the bucket and the rope, and their wish to understand Mr Dendy, their master, as part of their more general desire to 'study men' [6]. In this respect Werth's and Ryan's two approaches overlap. In Werth's terms this is a desire world, part of what he would see as a character-based attitudinal sub-world, and in Ryan's terms we have moved from the TAW to a W-world, which is also character-based. Our view of Mr Dendy is curiously distanced, as if the bucket and the rope have no concern for human suffering and emotion, but are motivated solely by intellectual curiosity.

B. The text-world structure of the rest of the story

The rest of the story, as we pointed out in section 12.3.3, is told through the direct speech of the bucket and the rope, and so we have to discern the reasons for Mr Dendy's suicide through the 'unreliable narration' provided within the direct speech. Within this direct speech we move in the first speech paragraph (which the bucket utters) from a verbal instantiation of the bucket and rope's joint desire world (with present and present perfect tenses and the interrogative form) to another character-accessible sub-world, a flashback via a generalised memory which the bucket shares with the rope:

> Perhaps you can remember as well as I the joyful day when we were first purchased, which happened to be the very day before Mr Dendy was married. [9]

The move from present to past tense and the time specification indicate a flashback, the place location of which is then specified in later paragraphs by definite reference. In text world terms, what happens from now on is complex, in the sense that we move fairly swiftly from one sub-world to another, sometimes at the same level, and sometimes at lower levels, embedded inside the flashback sub-world. And for some time the flashback sub-world and the other sub-worlds are not about Mr Dendy, thus frustrating further the reader's wish to find out why he killed himself. This is the text world equivalent of a 'shaggy dog story' as, in deictic shift theory terms (Galbraith 1995, Stockwell 2002, p. 47), we are 'pushed' down from one deictic centre to another and are, with very few exceptions, preventing from 'popping' back up to the TAW with which the story opens.

Below we present the text world structure in a rather simplified form, before discussing it in more detail. Each indentation in Figure 12.4 indicates that the sub-world referred to is embedded in the world immediately above it and, as before, the square-bracketed references indicates the relevant paragraphs of the story. The bucket and the rope are abbreviated as B and R respectively, to save space. We have only represented the worlds presented, showing which other worlds they are embedded in. We do not indicate sentence-by-sentence 'toggling' between an embedded world and the world it is embedded in (for example, where sentences relating straight-forwardly to the Flashback 1 level below are interspersed with some in-ferred minor character sub-worlds). Nevertheless, even with our somewhat simplified presentation, it can be seen that in text-world terms, this very short story turns out to be rather complex, with some sub-worlds being created for just a few words (e.g. those of the grand military gentleman and the lady in [17]):

Narrated text world (TAW in Ryan's terms): the scene in the shed [1–3]
    The bucket and the rope's (B&R's) desire sub-world (Ryan's wish-world) [4–8]
      B&R's shared discourse world (their direct speech) [9 onwards]
        Flashback 1 (R in the shop window and what it sees) [14–30]
          Flashback 2 (R remembers its childhood) [14]
          Inferred inner world of 'the grand military gentleman' [17]
          Inferred inner world of the 'lady' [17]
          Inferred inner world of the 'young and pleasing girls' [19]
          Inferred inner world of the 'poor debtor' [20]
          Inferred inner world of Betty [28]
        Flashback 3 (B remembers being purchased) [31]
        Flashback 4 (B being carried by Mr Dendy to collect swill) [31]
        R rejects the 'sour garbage' hypothesis world re the suicide [32]
        R rejects the 'heavy bucket' hypothesis world re the suicide [32]
        Flashback 5 (B being carried by Mr Dendy again) [33–34]
          Mr Dendy's discourse world [33]
        Flashback 6 (B remembers the nosegay incident) [35–39]
        Flashback 7 (R throttling Mr Dendy in his suicide) [43]
        R proposes the Mr Dendy's negative attitude hypothesis for the suicide [45] (which the bucket rejects [46] and the rope agrees [47])
        Flashback 8 (Betty's unfaithful behaviour) [49–58]
          Betty's discourse world [49]
          Betty's inner world [51]
        B's hypothesis about Mr Dendy's inner world (which is then rejected) [54–55]
          B's 'hungry man' hypothesis [56]
          B's nosegay hypothesis [60]

Figure 12.4

Apart from the overall text-world complexity of the story, we can see that by the time the bucket and rope begin to address what the reader is most interested in, their hypotheses concerning Mr Dendy's suicide, we are 32 paragraphs and 12 worlds into the story, many of the worlds being embed-ded four levels down from the initial TAW. In terms of Emmott's work on narrative comprehension (1997, pp. 103–132), the *dead* Mr Dendy is only 'primed' in the contextual frame of the scene in the shed (the TAW), but we have to monitor the rest of the text for matters relating to his suicide, as we move through the contextual frames associated with all the other text worlds created in the story. The world-structure of the story, like the way in which the scene is initially presented, thus goes strongly against our normal expectations. Given the overall brevity of the story, it is clear that, although many of these embedded worlds take up just a few words, they are nonetheless disruptive of our wish to understand why Mr Dendy killed himself.

Initially in Flashback 1 the rope is in a shop window, and can observe happenings in two directions, outside and inside the shop.[3] Paragraphs [16]–[21] describe what the rope saw outside the window, and we also move, presumably via the rope's inferencing abilities, inside the mental worlds of some of the people it observes. We are given brief pieces of knowledge about the attitudinal and desire worlds of a 'grand military gentleman', a lady, 'two young and pleasing girls' and a debtor, as well as being given external descriptions of other characters before, finally, the young Mr Dendy and his prospective wife are introduced externally in [21] ('The man was Mr Dendy, and she was to be his wife.').

Next, the bucket intervenes, with a flashback based on the initial flashback:

'Her arms had been opened to another before him,' murmured the bucket. [22]

The rope comments on this flashback and then resumes its own flashback narrative, concentrating on Mr Dendy and his fiancée, first outside the shop and then inside it.

All the time the reader, of course, is monitoring the text for information which is relatable to the initial narrative disequilibrium, Mr Dendy's suicide. The first conceivable possibility finally occurs in paragraph [26]:

'Mr Dendy was about twenty-nine years old then, and the young girl about eighteen,' remarked the bucket. [25]

'So she was' said the rope, 'but it is curious to think now what she did next. While Mr Johnson and Mr Dendy were talking, she coiled and uncoiled me, and then, in her girlish amusement, for she looked at him lovingly, she made a running noose of me, slipped it over the master's head, and pulled it tight.' [26]

The fact that his prospective wife makes the rope into a noose and puts it round Mr Dendy's neck cannot be related to his suicide in a direct way, but like the 'death' semantic prosody we perceived in the title phrases 'the bucket' and 'the rope' in section 12.3.2 (see also section 12.3.7 below), it can be seen as a possible prefiguring of what is to happen later in the chronological narrative. She has already been described in [21], via an attitudinal sub-world inferred by the rope, as having 'the sweetest of natures, that would be unlikely, for the fear of being cruel, to refuse anything a man might ask of her'. This, related to the bucket's secondary flashback in [22], suggests that Betty could well be like Amaryllis, the girl of easy virtue in Campion's poem (*cf* section 12.3.4). Moreover, in [28] she is described as letting the lawyer's son kiss her 'while Mr Dendy was out of the way'.

From [32] onwards we are presented with a series of hypothetical worlds giving possible explanations for Mr Dendy's motivation in killing himself, all of which are either not taken up or are explicitly rejected, until we get to the final hypothesis, concerning the nosegay, proposed by the bucket in an exclamatory utterance that appears to end the conversation, leading to the possibility that the rope has accepted the bucket's proposal. Whether we think that the rope has indeed accepted the bucket's suggestion is dependent to some degree on the character and general attitude of the rope, to which we will return in section 12.3.9 below.

C. *Other aspects of viewpoint: naming and discourse presentation*

We have seen how the topic-comment structure of the first three sentences of the story expressed a viewpoint in terms of interest which goes against what we would normally expect from a description of a man who has just committed suicide. Alongside this, there is a frustration of the reader's expectation, and a felt need (because of the disequilibrium) for an explanation of the suicide. We do not have the space to specify in detail the viewpoint-related factors in every paragraph, but it will be helpful to make some more comments about viewpoint in the story as a whole.

First, it is worth noting that in both the narrative and the direct speech of the bucket and the rope, the default expression used to refer to Mr Dendy is the 'title + last name' formulation we have just used. We never learn what his first name is. The narrator uses it seven times and the bucket and the rope 24 times. Even allowing for the more formal naming and address habits of 1927 (when the story was first published), this means that both the narrator and the bucket and the rope express a relatively distant, formal social relationship with the character, one which the reader is also likely to adopt, given the third-person narrator's (and hence, by conventional inference, the author's) stance (*cf* sections 8.3–8.5). There are some departures from this default expression, in addition to the standard pronominal forms *he*, *him*, etc. Before naming him, the narrator uses 'a man who had hanged himself by the neck' (twice) and 'the man' (three times), and the bucket and the rope use 'our master' three times and 'the master' twice, thus expressing their functional relation to Mr Dendy. This consistently distanced form of reference to the character helps to dissuade us from empathising with him, much as the strategy at the opening of the story does, leading us to consider Mr Dendy and his plight more dispassionately. All the other characters apart from Mr Dendy's wife are referred to with the 'title + last name' formulation or something even more distancing in type, and Betty's lover is kept even more distanced from us: he is never given a name (and we never enter his mental world), but is referred to as a 'young man' or in relation to another person in the story ('the lawyer's son', Betty's 'friend'), which distances him from us even further.

The narrator does not explicitly refer to Mr Dendy's wife (or indeed any of the other characters) at all. We learn everything about her through the direct speech of the bucket and the rope. Their favourite reference form for her is the first-name form 'Betty' which they use six times, and which expresses a familiarity towards her that they appear not to feel for their master. No doubt this can be partly attributed to her young age. But because 'Betty' is the only name given to the character, that reference form becomes the default, and indeed it feels most natural to us to refer to her as 'Betty' too, in spite of the fact that the third-person narrator never uses it. This seems to position us as closer to, and potentially more sympathetic towards, her than her husband, for whom 'Mr Dendy' is the only name available to us. The bucket and the rope also refer to Betty seven times as 'Mr Dendy's wife', thus expressing what they see as her most important relation to Mr Dendy, as well as using 'woman' and 'girl'.

We have already noted (section 12.3.3) that the story divides clearly into a narration section and a direct speech dialogue section, and that everything we learn about the events leading up to Mr Dendy's suicide, including his relations with all the other characters, are seen through the bucket and the rope's direct speech discourse world. It is this distancing, via discoursal embedding, which allows the possibility of the two interpretations of what the bucket and the rope tell us, leading to the appearance/reality theme and interpretation referred to earlier (sections 12.3.1 and 12.3.4). The speech of the bucket and the rope effectively becomes a shared embedded narration (they use 'we' to refer to themselves eight times as well as 'I' (29 times) and 'you' (12 times).

In addition to the dominant role of direct speech, there are some other points to make about discourse presentation in the story. Beginning with the first eight paragraphs of narration, we can see that the narrator establishes the wish world of the bucket and the rope partly through the presentation of their thoughts and mind states. Thought presentation analysis thus constitutes one of the ways in which we can provide evidence (in Werth's terms) for character-accessible sub-worlds. In the last half of the final sentence of [4], the first clause ('would speak of all that Mr Dendy did') is a narrator's presentation of a speech act (*cf* section 10.1.3) representing the bucket and rope's habitual speech act behaviour, and then the rest of the sentence slips into a form which is ambiguous between indirect speech and indirect thought presentation:

[. . .] [they would] endeavour to find out as best they might a reason for his actions. [4]

By way of contrast, the narrator tells us virtually nothing directly about Mr Dendy's thoughts. The only possible case of presentation of an internal view of Mr Dendy from the perspective of the third-person narrator occurs when we are told that he ploughed his fields 'happily' in sentence 3. This is extremely minimal internal narration (cf Semino and Short 2004, pp. 132–135). By paragraph [7], on the other hand, the bucket and the rope are making weak inferences about Mr Dendy's inner world:

> *Now and again the two friends had been a little puzzled by Mr Dendy,* who did not often act as they would have expected him to, *for sometimes he would seem to be troubled,* when, according to the bucket's ideas of cause and effect, there was no reason for him to be so. [7]

Here, the first clause is internal narration concerning the mind state of the bucket and the rope and the third clause shows Mr Dendy's internal mind state as inferred by the bucket and the rope (cf Semino and Short 2004, pp. 135–137), with appropriate hedging via the non-factive verb 'seem'. Given that the bucket and the rope cannot see into Mr Dendy's mind in the way that an omniscient third-person narrator could, we would expect the inferred thought presentation in the story to be minimal, and the absence of more direct forms of thought presentation for Mr Dendy means that even though he apparently kills himself for love, it is difficult for us to become emotionally involved with his plight. Indeed, in this respect Mr Dendy is treated rather like a minor character – for the mind states of a number of minor characters are also established through inferred narration of inner states, for example the 'grand military gentleman' in [17], who the rope tells us 'became prouder than ever'.

Within the bucket and the rope's direct speech there is not much embedded presentation of the speech or writing of the other characters, which is consistent with Powys's 'withdrawal of sympathy' tactic that we have just outlined. However, there is one example of embedded direct speech presentation (eDS – cf Semino and Short 2004, pp. 171–182), and one example of embedded direct writing presentation (eDW), both of which become foregrounded through internal deviation (cf section 2.6). The instance of eDS is in the first sentence of [49] 'You look so well in it [. . .]', when Betty encourages Mr Dendy to go to church so that she can carry on her secret affair with the lawyer's son. It thus highlights her duplicitous behaviour. The instance of eDW is the quotation from Thomas Campion's 'Amaryllis' in [57]. The quotation, as an allusion to the poem, prompts us to see a parallel between Betty and Amaryllis, who gives her favours so freely, underlining Betty's unfaithfulness to her husband. Hence we are likely to view Betty critically although in naming terms, as we have already seen, we are brought closer to her than to Mr Dendy.

12.3.8 Textual analysis in terms of lexis, grammar and meaning

The style of the story is rather simple and straightforward, as we would expect of a fable. But one general feature deserves comment – a tendency to archaism. We notice this in a number of words and expressions that strike the twenty-first-century reader, and would have struck even the reader of Powys's day, as somewhat quaint, old-fashioned and literary: for example, 'purchased' [13], 'the folk' [16] 'our master' [24], 'a winning gait' [28], 'a merry jest' [29], 'we became acquainted' [31], 'tarry', 'droll story', 'a-walking'. This is in keeping with the tone of a fable as a traditional story handing down folk wisdom. It is significant that this story contains no references that would enable us to place the events described historically. Except for the names 'Mr Dendy' and 'Betty', which tend to place it later than the Middle Ages, the story could have taken place during any century. The tendency to archaism underlines the timelessness of the story.

We now turn more generally to lexical patterning, and begin our obser-vations, paradoxically, with the last word of 'The Bucket and the Rope', 'nosegay', which is arguably also the most striking word in the story. It is foregrounded not just by its textual position but also by its rarity. We found no occurrences of 'nosegay(s)' in written British English corpora amount-ing to 2.8 million words of texts from the 1930–1991 period, and only eight occurrences in the 100-million-word British National Corpus, dating from the 1990s. This may suggest that this word is also fairly old-fashioned and may already have been so when Powys was writing. Indeed, the *Oxford English Dictionary* (*OED*) marks it as 'archaic'.

If we look at the semantic prosodies (*cf* Louw 1997) of 'nosegay' in these corpus entries we find that the word has opposing associations. As small bunches of flowers, nosegays are clearly pretty and sweet-smelling, and some text examples relate straightforwardly to this positive image, as do all of the entries for the word in the *OED*. But nosegays were also used historically to ward off evil smells (for example, during the plague and at funerals), and other text examples relate to this function. This 'Janus-faced' aspect of 'nosegay' relates interestingly to the life/death theme of the story and also to the appearance/reality theme discussed in section 12.3.4. The bucket and the rope see the nosegay in a negative light (possibly as causing Mr Dendy's death), whereas we see it initially as positive (when Mr Dendy offers it to his wife as a token of his affection) but then can also see it negat-ively as a 'sign' of that affection and therefore as a harbinger of his suicide.

Another case of lexical foregrounding is the collocation occurring when Betty is referred to as a cure for Mr Dendy's 'burden of his desire':

'He married as you know, a woman, a creature created to ease a man of the heavy *burden of his desire*, a burden as troublesome to carry as a kicking ass.' [10]

We will not comment on the bucket's sexist attitude, which is obvious enough, but instead examine the foregrounded effect of 'burden of desire' – an instantiation of what Lakoff and Turner (1989, pp. 25–26) call the 'life is a burden' or 'difficulty is a burden' metaphor. 'Desire' can be either positive (e.g. the desire to help others) or negative (e.g. the desire for power), and the BNC examples for 'desire for' reflect this split. But 'burden' has an obviously negative semantic prosody, thus forcing a negative semantic association for 'desire' here. The large majority of the BNC entries for 'burden(s) of' have a negative prosody and the examples below are taken from the first few entries. 'Burden of' is typically completed by heavy loads (e.g. '865 kilograms') or feelings or other objects and attitudes which are negative (e.g. 'guilt'). Hence in this story sexual desire is portrayed negatively, and it is interesting to note that the story emphasises the negative connotation of 'burden' elsewhere. 'Burden' is also associated with the 'kicking ass' simile which immediately follows 'burden of desire', locally reinforcing the 'difficulty is a burden' metaphor. In the story Betty is at first portrayed as good for Mr Dendy, and his desire to marry her seems at first to be a good thing. But the semantic prosody of 'burden of desire', like Betty's making a noose of the rope in the shop and slipping it over Mr Dendy's head, prefigures the change in her relation with Mr Dendy just before their marriage.

In addition to his use of particular foregrounded words and phrases, Powys displays a more general attention to lexical patterning in bringing out the themes of his story. We noted earlier (see pp. 327–8) how positive evaluative terms ('pleasant', 'happily', 'good', 'nice') accompany the mention of Mr Dendy when his dead body is first described hanging in the shed, contrasting with our normal reactions to suicide. This lexical pattern in the first three sentences could be a signal to alert the reader to other lexical patterns in the story, some of which could be related to the first one. The story has many positive words and phrases which relate to Mr Dendy (e.g. he would have 'a *merry* word with the occupants, telling a *droll* story of country matters *for the young girls to smile at*' [33] and the bucket refers to him as 'a *true and joyful* countryman, *doing his proper tasks*' [42]. Betty, initially, at least, also enjoys positive lexis (e.g. 'she had the *sweetest* of natures' [21] and 'she looked at him *lovingly*' [26].

But, more importantly, there are a lot of phrases and clauses (not included in the discussion above) which yoke the good and the bad together syntactically. Some are in simple contrastive constructions (*italics* = positive and **boldening** = negative):

335

> *loves* and **hates** [4]
> their **sorrows** and *joys* [6]

but as the story unfolds the good/bad relations become more complex, for example:

> He learns to *brave* the **keenest wind** <u>without a shudder,</u> and <u>cares nothing</u> when the **rain soaks him to the skin.** <u>No weather daunted</u> Mr Dendy, and **the more he bore with the storms** outside the *pleasanter was his parlour, with its cheerful light, and the warm presence of a wife who loved him.'* [39]

In the above examples, the underlined items cannot be classified straightforwardly on the basis of their lexical meaning. Three of the words involved, 'shudder', 'cares' and 'daunted' are arguably negative in associative terms, but they are involved in grammatical negation which reverses the overall semantic prosody. In the following example, pragmatic factors outweigh prototypical lexical assumptions in overall understanding:

> She had a yielding kindness, but no wickedness in her. [28]

'A yielding kindness' looks at first sight positive. But it is contrasted with 'no wickedness' here, which in turn involves a negation turning a negative prosody into a positive one. Hence, if 'yielding kindness' is being contrasted with a positive, it needs to be interpreted as having a negative prosody itself, and in context it clearly refers to the fact that, like Amaryllis, Betty seems not able to resist the attentions of men.

We have just seen that the lexical patterning in the story is easily interpreted as connected to the story's positive/negative and appearance/reality themes. The appearance/reality theme is also indicated by other lexical patterns. Not surprisingly, non-factive verbs of perception are quite prominent. For example, 'seem' occurs seven times in the story, 'thought' five times, 'appear' twice, 'look' (in its 'appear' meaning) five times, 'believe' twice, and 'fancy' twice; and the modal verbs 'can' and 'could' appear three and nine times respectively. Modal verbs connected with obligation and certainty are also reasonably prominent: 'should' appears nine times, along with one 'must' (in the final sentence, where the bucket's certainty is clearly unfounded), and one 'ought'. The modal adverb 'certainly' also appears three times.

Finally, there are also a number of expressions which indicate that various aspects of the behaviour of Mr Dendy are surprising or intriguing for the bucket and the rope:

(a) Mr Dendy's movements as well as his behaviour had always been of great *interest* to the bucket and the rope [4]

(b) Both were *interested* in any kind of life that was *not like themselves* [5]

(c) Now and again the two friends had been a little *puzzled* by Mr Dendy, who did *not* often act *as they would have expected* him to [...] [7]

(d) 'Is it not a little *curious* if not altogether *surprising*,' observed the bucket, 'that we should have been put to so sad a use in helping our good master die? [...]' [9]

(e) '[...] and a few of them particularly *attracted my notice* [...]' [16]

(f) '[...] it is *curious* to think now what she did next.' [26]

(g) 'Only once,' observed the bucket sadly, 'did I notice Mr Dendy act in a way that was *not usual for a village man.* [...]' [35]

Many of these expressions show the bucket and the rope noticing what they see as deviant behaviour and trying to understand it; but because they do not share human assumptions, they are not able to understand.

12.3.9 Characterisation

In the final section of this analysis we will look at characterisation in 'The Bucket and the Rope'. As already noted at the beginning of this chapter, Culpeper (2001, p. 28) points out the need to combine top-down (schemas etc.) and bottom-up (textual signals of various kinds) processing to arrive at an understanding of characters and characterisation (as indeed we have to do in relation to most aspects of textual understanding). In spite of its brevity, which gives little opportunity of character development or character change in the story, 'The Bucket and the Rope' illustrates well the top-down/bottom-up processing distinction.

Because we see little of Mr Dendy and Betty directly, there is not much opportunity for bottom-up processing in establishing what they are like. As we don't see them interact very much, we have to rely mainly on (i) what the bucket and the rope tell us about them (which, as we have seen, is unreliable), and (ii) schematic assumptions that we, as readers, bring to the text. Intriguingly, although we recognise that they are unreliable narrators, we tend not to reject what they say about the human characters unless it contradicts our schematic assumptions.

For the bucket and the rope, on the other hand, this top-down/bottom-up processing situation is reversed. We don't possess character schemata for talking buckets and ropes and how they might behave, and so we can only make bottom-up inferences. And apart from talking and thinking (which we mainly see through their talk), they don't actually carry out any actions. These inanimate objects apparently cannot move (*cf* Ryan's 1991, pp. 46–80 principle of minimal departure), even though they are able to talk and reason, and so we have to interpret their characters entirely on the basis of what they say.

Style in Fiction

A. Mr Dendy

We know from the omniscient third-person narrator that Mr Dendy is 'a simple countryman' [6], which invokes schemata in relation to country folk: that they are honest, naive, hard-working, have a traditional mindset (e.g. concerning sexual relations and marriage) and so on. We know that he is naturally happy and contented because the narrator says that he ploughed his fields 'happily' [3] and the bucket and the rope reinforce this view. The bucket says that he was 'a truly joyful countryman' [42], and that he whistles [32] and talks jokingly to others [33]. When the rope says that he carried the bucket 'jauntily, as if the burden of a few gallons of swill was nothing to so powerful an arm as his' [32], this confirms Mr Dendy's happy disposition and suggests via weak implicature that he is hard-working. He also puts up with all weathers with fortitude [33], [39]. Although he is mainly happy in the story he clearly becomes unhappy just before his suicide. But as we assume that he killed himself because of his wife's activities with the lawyer's son, we reject the rope's view that he killed himself because he 'did not like to see others happy' [45], which in any case is inconsistent with everything else we have been told about him. As Culpeper (2001, pp. 116–119), following Kelley (1972), points out, we can discount individual exceptional examples of behaviour as not contributing to character. For example, such behaviour may be affected by special contextual factors: if we see someone shouting angrily at someone who has assaulted him, we attribute that behaviour more to context than to character. This is especially true if the behaviour contrasts with habitual behaviour we have repeated evidence for, and so Mr Dendy's suicidal behaviour appears to be 'out of character'.

B. Betty

Our view of Betty is even more restricted than our view of Mr Dendy. We only learn about her through the direct speech of the bucket and the rope, much of which reinforces a conventional set of assumptions about attractive young women. She is sweet, loving and playful according to the following descriptions: 'in her girlish amusement, for she looked at him lovingly' [26]; 'she had the sweetest of natures' [21] and 'she seemed just the creature to delight any man with her sweetness' [28]. But at the same time, these positive qualities are mixed with others which are less positive – as we see from the rest of the constructions from which the above quotations come:

> She seemed just the creature to delight any man with her sweetness and *eagerness for love*. [21]

> [. . .] in her girlish amusement, for she looked at him lovingly, *she made a running noose of me, slipped it over the master's head, and pulled it tight*' [26]

Anyone could see that she had the sweetest of natures, *that would be unlikely, for the fear of being cruel, to refuse anything a man might ask of her.* [28]

And of course she does not pass up on the opportunity to turn the lawyer's son's 'sorrow into joy' [50]. Betty also appears to be manipulative, as her foregrounded direct speech indicates, when, somewhat ironically, she persuades her husband to go to church so that she can enjoy her clandestine affair [49]. Betty thus combines two contrasting stereotypes for fictional young women – sweetly attractive and dangerously attractive – and what we are told by the bucket and the rope reinforces these two partly contradictory stereotypes. We do not discount Betty's manipulative behaviour, perhaps because, as Culpeper (2001, p. 145), following Margolin (1983), points out, we tend to generalise from less evidence in fictional texts than in real life, because the knowledge base is complete and smaller – and indeed very small in a short story like this one.

C. The bucket and the rope
Are the bucket and the rope one character or two? They certainly have the same ideological assumptions and have the same difficulties in interpreting human behaviour, but they also exhibit some differences.

The rope talks much more than the bucket (1508 v. 675 words), but this difference is probably not character-related. We can discount it if we notice that around 700 of the rope's words relate to the description of the scene on the day when it was bought by Mr Dendy, when the bucket was not present. Hence this information, which is important for understanding the story, can be produced only by the rope. An examination of the turn-taking patterns in the conversation also reveals no big differences between the bucket and the rope. It is difficult to portray one as more powerful or talkative than the other, for example. There are no graphological indications of interruption and, because the two are talking to the same cooperative purpose, it is difficult to characterise particular turns as initiations or topic changes (in fact, their turns are often a combination of initiation and response).

That said, it could be argued, even though the data is limited, that the bucket is more emotional than the rope, and that the rope is more objective, careful and thoughtful than the bucket. The first piece of evidence for this character contrast is the set of hypotheses they consider to explain Mr Dendy's suicide. The rope seems to consider hypotheses and reject them. It tell us that it was 'not the stink of sour garbage' [32], not 'the weight of you [the bucket]', not his life [34], and not the weather [39], [41]. All of these instances except one are phrased using grammatical or semantic negation, and even the one actual suggestion that the rope produces is a negative one, that Mr Dendy 'did not like to see others happy'. The bucket, on the other hand, goes for positive explanations without much evidence in favour of them. It attributes the suicide (i) to the fact that Betty, failing to stay at home to cook Mr Dendy's dinner [56], made him too hungry [58], and (ii) to the nosegay (twice, in [35]–[37] and [60]). For a human observer, of course, these 'reasons' seem too trivial as explanations for suicide.

A little more evidence to support the contrast we have suggested can be found in the four reporting clauses which involve manner adverbs:

said the other [the rope] *dryly* [30]
observed the rope *thoughtfully* [32]
observed the bucket *sadly* [35]
said the rope *quietly* [43]

There are not enough instances to be certain of the pattern suggested, but each of the manner adverbs related to the rope suggest a thoughtful, distanced attitude whereas the one related to the bucket is a word expressing emotion. Although the numbers are again not large, an examination of the reporting verbs suggests a similar pattern:

Table 12.3

DS reporting clause verbs

Verb	Bucket	Rope
exclaimed	2	0
laughed	1	0
murmured	1	0
asked	2	1
remarked	2	1
observed	4	2
continued	0	2
said	4	8
answered	0	2
replied	1	2
reasoned	1	0
suggested	1	0
Total	19	18

The bucket's speech is described using the more emotional verbs 'exclaimed' and 'laughed' whereas the rope has no such verbs, and although only the bucket gets 'reasoned', the instance is arguably ironic, as it applies to the ridiculous suggestion that Mr Dendy committed suicide because he was hungry [56]. And although there are no graphological indications of interruption in the story it is worth noting here that the reporting clause verbs seem to position the bucket more as an initiator ('remarked' and 'observed' apply twice as much to the bucket's speech) and the rope as being interrupted and responding ('continued' and 'answered' are only used for the rope).

Although there is not enough data to be sure of the character difference described, it does seem as if the bucket is more impulsive and its judgment more questionable. Moreover, the rope's more cautious approach does suggest that it may not agree with the bucket's final conclusion about the nosegay, particularly as it does not pick up on the first version of the bucket's hypothesis in [35]–[37]. Thus the bucket's concluding 'solution' to the suicide puzzle remains poised on a point of ambiguity with respect to the individual attitudes of the bucket and the rope, as well as in relation to how the nosegay should be interpreted in terms of the 'appearance' and 'reality' views, as described in section 12.3.6.

12.4 Assessing the new techniques

We end this chapter by considering briefly the contributions of the analytical techniques we have used in addition to those we used in the first edition of *Style in Fiction*.

Although quantitative techniques of corpus linguistics did not prove useful here because of the size of the text, we did find one or two other corpus-analytic methods useful. First of all, in preparation for this chapter, we annotated the story for speech, writing and thought presentation using the Semino and Short (2004) model, and we used this data, and the patterns it revealed, as the basis for the points we have made about discourse presentation in the story. Second, electronic searching with Google helped us to pin down two foregrounded allusions that we did not recognise and, third, we also used corpus analysis (in the form of concordancing) to explore what Louw (1997) calls the semantic prosodies of particularly interesting words and phrases in the story. In these last two cases we had suspicions that 'something interesting was going on' and the computer-based techniques then enabled us to identify factors which were interpretatively useful. The general lesson here seems to be that computers will not solve all our problems, but careful and inventive use of corpus linguistic techniques can help interpretation, even on small texts, as well as identify style parameters in large texts or groups of texts.[4]

If used in a pragmatic, rather than an overly formal way, the combination of various narratological approaches provides a toolkit for interpreting the story logic of a text, and helped us in this case to explain the subtleties of a deceptively simple text. But how generalisable are these methods to other stories, and how far is such an analysis independently replicable? As always, there is a balance to be struck between a descriptive core of analysis, and an allowable variation among different critical responses.

The new approaches to fictional world construction and viewpoint were also revealing, but as with the story logic work, it is important that such work be grounded in textual and inferencing detail, which constitutes part of the demonstration in favour of a particular account of a text, and in turn helps others to evaluate the interpretative view proposed. At the time of writing this chapter, there is still a need to resolve the overlaps between the various 'worlds' accounts that could be adopted. It is arguable that the *mental spaces* approach might subsume the *possible worlds*, *text worlds* and *deictic shift* approaches. But such an all-encompassing framework could hide the analytical detail typical of stylistic analysis, which is so often revealing, both interpretatively and in terms of theory testing. Much more text-analytical work needs to be done in these areas before we can be sure of how to proceed and, as always, the devil will be in the analytical detail.

Although 'The Bucket and the Rope', just because it is so short, was unlikely to be very interesting in terms of characterisation, we did, none-theless, feel that applying Culpeper-style character analysis to it was revealing, both of the story and the methodology. The combination of top-down and bottom-up processing analysis usefully allows one to pro-vide detailed textual evidence which can be quite straightforwardly related to critical concerns.

Much work remains to be done in all of these new 'cognitive' stylistic approaches, especially in trying to apply them in detail to a range of inter-esting texts, before we can be sure which models, or combinations of models, are best for our purposes. However, this outcome will only be achieved, in our view, if we try to be as rigorous as possible in relating the linguistic details of texts to stylistic theories, critical concerns and the inter-pretative effects of the texts themselves.

Notes

1. These constructs of cognitive linguistics can be followed up in Ungerer and Schmid (forthcoming).
2. The only versions of the phrase which did not mean 'to die', using informal language, were one reference to an artwork, one to a bucket full of good things and eleven references to a pop song for which the phrase had been used as a title, and which was an animal rights attack on the KFC 'bucket' of chicken portions.
3. There is a theoretical issue concerning whether the flashback is within the desire world (the bucket and the rope are talking about what they remember in order to achieve their wish world) or at the same narrative level and sequential to it. Another issue is what exactly counts as belonging to which sub-world. In the following paragraphs, the rope remembers dreaming of its childhood, so Flash-back 2 is a brief flashback within a flashback. But in [15] we have a generalisation

which is both relatable to the desire sub-world referred to above and also to the main flashback sub-world, as it gives, in generalised form, an explanation of why the rope saw what it did. This is problematic for text world analysis, as a generic statement can apply simultaneously to a number of text words or sub-worlds.

4. We suggest that stylisticians and corpus linguists could usefully cooperate to develop software which could be used more effectively in stylistics and corpus linguistics more generally. This kind of cooperation is potentially useful for both kinds of research.

Passages and topics
for further study

The following pages provide material which can be used for follow-up work on each chapter. In some cases, we refer students to extracts quoted elsewhere in the book; in other cases, we provide additional passages for practical analysis. Ideally, the study of each passage should be preceded by a reading of it in its context in the work from which it is taken.

Chapter 1: Style and choice

1A: The dualist view (sections 1.3–1.4) that it is possible to translate or paraphrase a literary work can be tested by comparing two translations into English of a novel or story written in a foreign language. Compare the following two translations of a passage from Kafka's *The Trial*. Note in detail the differences between one version and the other, and consider how far they can be regarded as paraphrases of one another. What differences of meaning and differences of effect do you observe? Which of the two versions (leaving aside faithfulness to the original) do you prefer? Why?

> Someone must have been telling lies about Joseph K., for without having done anything wrong he was arrested one fine morning. His landlady's cook, who always brought him his breakfast at eight o'clock, failed to appear on this occasion. That had never happened before. K. waited for a little while longer, watching from his pillow the old lady opposite, who seemed to be peering at him with curiosity unusual even for her, but then, feeling both put out and hungry, he rang the bell. At once there was a knock at the door and a man entered whom he had never seen before in the house. He was slim and yet well knit, he wore a closely fitting black suit, which was furnished with all sorts of pleats, pockets, buckles, and buttons, as well as a belt, like a tourist's outfit, and in consequence looked eminently practical, though one could not quite tell what actual

purpose it served. 'Who are you?' asked K., half raising himself in bed. But the man ignored the question, as though his appearance needed no explanation, and merely said: 'Did you ring?' 'Anna is to bring me my breakfast,' said K., and then with silent intensity studied the fellow, trying to make out who he could be. The man did not submit to this scrutiny for very long, but turned to the door and opened it slightly so as to report to someone who was evidently standing just behind it: 'He says Anna is to bring him his breakfast.' A short guffaw from the next room came in answer; one could not tell from the sound whether it was produced by several individuals or merely by one. Although the strange man could not have learned anything from it that he did not know already, he now said to K., as if passing on a statement: 'It can't be done.'

[Franz Kafka, *The Trial*, Chapter 1, translated by Willa and Edwin Muir]

Someone must have been spreading lies about Josef K. for without having done anything wrong he was arrested one morning. His landlady's cook, who brought him his breakfast every morning at about eight o'clock, did not come on that particular day. This had never happened before. K. waited a little while, watching from his pillow the old woman who lived opposite and who was observing him with a quite uncharacteristic curiosity; but then, feeling both hungry and disturbed, he rang. At once there was a knock at the door and a man he had never seen in the flat before came in. He was slim and yet strongly built; he wore a well-fitting black suit which was like a travelling outfit in that it had various pleats, pockets, buckles, buttons and a belt, and as a result (although one could not quite see what it was for) it seemed eminently practical.

'Who are you?' K. asked, immediately sitting up a little in bed. But the man ignored the question, as if the fact of his appearance simply had to be accepted, and merely said: 'You rang?'

'Anna is supposed to bring me my breakfast,' K. said, endeavouring, silently at first and by careful scrutiny, to work out who the man actually was. But he did not submit to K.'s gaze for long, turning instead to the door which he opened slightly and saying to someone else who was obviously just on the other side of the door:

'He wants Anna to bring him his breakfast.'

There was a brief burst of laughter from the next room, but it was not clear from the sound whether there might not be more than one person there. Although the unknown visitor could not have learnt anything from the laughter that he did not know before, he now said to K., as if making an announcement:

'It's not possible.'

[Franz Kafka, *The Trial*, Chapter 1, translated by
Douglas Scott and Chris Waller]

1B: Anthony Burgess's 'alternative version' of the opening of Joyce's *Portrait* (pp. 27–28) is paralleled by a similar version which he provides of the opening of Joyce's *Ulysses*. Below we give part of Burgess's 'reworking' of Joyce, preceded by Joyce's original. Examine the two versions, and discuss the differences in style between them. What does Burgess add and omit? How far does he stick to the vocabulary and syntax of the original? Discuss the technique and effect of Joyce's original in the light of Burgess's 'reworking'.

He came over to the gunrest and, thrusting a hand into Stephen's upper pocket, said:
— Lend us a loan of your noserag to wipe my razor.
Stephen suffered him to pull out and hold up on show by its corner a dirty crumpled handkerchief. Buck Mulligan wiped the razorblade neatly. Then, gazing over the handkerchief, he said:
— The bard's noserag. A new art colour for our Irish poets: snot-green. You can almost taste it, can't you?
He mounted to the parapet again and gazed out over Dublin bay, his fair oakpale hair stirring slightly.
— God, he said quietly. Isn't the sea what Algy calls it: a grey sweet mother? The snotgreen sea. The scrotumtightening sea. *Epi oinopa ponton.* Ah, Dedalus, the Greeks. I must teach you. You must read them in the original. *Thalatta! Thalatta!* She is our great sweet mother. Come and look.
Stephen stood up and went over to the parapet. Leaning on it he looked down on the water and on the mailboat clearing the harbour mouth of Kingstown.
— Our mighty mother, Buck Mulligan said.
He turned abruptly his great searching eyes from the sea to Stephen's face.
— The aunt thinks you killed your mother, he said. That's why she won't let me have anything to do with you.
— Someone killed her, Stephen said gloomily.
[James Joyce, *Ulysses*, Penguin edn, 1978, pp. 10–11]

After a time Mulligan inserted a plump hand into the upper pocket of Stephen's black suit and said, 'Lend me your noserag to wipe my razor.' He held it up and said at length: 'It's covered in mucus.'
'Green mucus,' said Stephen. 'Green for Ireland.'
Mulligan moved his plump form to the parapet to look out intently at the bay.
'It's the colour of the sea too, I guess,' he said. 'Look at the sea. When you get near the sea it makes your guts tighten, did you know that? The wine-dark sea is what the Greeks called it. Come and look at it.'
Stephen went over to look at the sea. He leaned coldly on the parapet next to his friend's plump form and looked down at the water. The

mailboat was just leaving Kingstown harbour. Neither of them thought that in their lifetimes it would change its name to Dun Laoghaire (pronounced Dunleary), following the withdrawal of English domination from the Irish scene.

'Somebody once called it our mighty mother,' said Mulligan. 'A poet, I guess.'

He turned his large observant eyes from looking at the sea and turned them to look at the face of his friend.

'My aunt thinks you killed your mother,' he said at last. 'She doesn't want us to be, you know, friends.'

'Somebody killed her,' said Stephen.

[Anthony Burgess, *Joysprick*, 1973, p. 14]

1c: Examine the passage from Golding's *The Inheritors* (section 1.5; p. 26): list examples of (a) intransitive verbs; (b) adverbials of time and place; (c) non-human subjects; (d) simple past tense verbs. Where, if at all, does the passage deviate from these typical choices?

Retell the events of this passage as if you were what Burgess (section 1.4) calls a 'Class 1 novelist', giving a common-sense *homo sapiens* view of them. What aspects of the original (e.g. vocabulary, syntax) remain unchanged in your version? In what respects have you made the story clearer? Are there any places where you have had to guess what is going on in the original story?

1d: The following is a longer extract from the beginning of Peake's *Gormenghast* than those quoted in sections 1.4 and 4.6. Examine the various ways in which it deviates from normal expectations regarding the use of the English language; i.e. ways in which language is *foregrounded* (sections 1.4, 3.2C). How do you make sense of these foregrounded features? How do they contribute to your interpretation of the passage? (For further explanation of foregrounding, read Chapters 3 and 4 of G.N. LEECH, *A Linguistic Guide to English Poetry*.)

Titus is seven. His confines, Gormenghast. Suckled on shadows; weaned, as it were, on webs of ritual: for his ears, echoes, for his eyes, a labyrinth of stone: and yet within his body something other – other than this umbrageous legacy. For first and ever foremost he is *child*.

A ritual, more compelling than ever man devised, is fighting anchored darkness. A ritual of the blood; of the jumping blood. These quicks of sentience owe nothing to his forbears, but to those feckless hosts, a trillion deep, of the globe's childhood.

The gift of the bright blood. Of blood that laughs when the tenets mutter 'Weep'. Of blood that mourns when the sere laws croak 'Rejoice!' O little revolution in great shades!

Titus the seventy-seventh. Heir to a crumbling summit: to a sea of net-tles: to an empire of red rust: to rituals' footprints ankle-deep in stone.
Gormenghast.
Withdrawn and ruinous it broods in umbra: the immemorial masonry: the towers, the tracts. Is all corroding? No. Through an avenue of spires a zephyr floats; a bird whistles; a freshet bears away from a choked river. Deep in a fist of stone a doll's hand wriggles, warm rebellious on the frozen palm. A shadow shifts its length. A spider stirs . . .
And darkness winds between the characters.

[Mervyn Peake, *Gormenghast*, Chapter 1]

Chapter 2: Style, text and frequency

2A: Make a table similar to Table 2.1 (section 2.4) comparing passages [1], [2] and [7] in this chapter; but instead of comparing frequency of con-nectives, compare (a) sentence length (in terms of words per sentence); (b) word length (in terms of syllables per word); and (c) word length (in terms of morphemes per word). How far do these simple measures of com-plexity correlate with one another? Do the figures merely confirm your expectations, or do they tell you something you didn't anticipate? Relate your findings to the literary function of each passage.

2B: Using the passages from *Dombey and Son* (section 2.7), identify instances of these features in each of the passages [3], [4], [5] and [7]: (a) parallelism, especially paired constructions; (b) anaphora and other lexical repetitions; (c) alliteration and other phonological patterns; (d) parenthetical construc-tions; (e) *-ing* forms of the verb; (f) personification; (g) other metaphors and similes. Relate your findings to the different narrative function of each extract. Does the comparison provide some means of identifying an under-lying 'Dickensian' style common to each passage? Are there other features of language which seem to mark the characteristic style of Dickens as exemplified in these passages? Discuss the difficulty of quantifying these features of style.

2C: Here is a further passage from *Dombey and Son*, part of the chapter (Chapter 5) describing Paul's christening ceremony. Compare it with pas-sages [3], [4], [5] and [7] in respect of the features discussed in 2B above. Which of the Dickensian 'substyles' illustrated in these passages does it most resemble?

Arrived at the church steps, they were received by a portentous beadle. Mr Dombey dismounting first to help the ladies out, and standing near him at the church door, looked like another beadle. A beadle less gorgeous but more dreadful; the beadle of private life; the beadle of our business and our bosoms.

Miss Tox's hand trembled as she slipped it through Mr Dombey's arm, and felt herself escorted up the steps, preceded by a cocked hat and a Babylonian collar. It seemed for a moment like that other solemn institution, 'Wilt thou have this man, Lucretia?' 'Yes, I will.'

'Please to bring the child in quick out of the air there,' whispered the beadle, holding open the inner door of the church.

Little Paul might have asked with Hamlet 'into my grave?' So chill and earthy was the place. The tall shrouded pulpit and reading desk; the dreary perspective of empty pews stretching away under the galleries, and empty benches mounting to the roof and lost in the shadow of the great grim organ; the dusty matting and cold stone slabs; the grisly free seats in the aisles; and the damp corner by the bell-rope, where the black trestles used for funerals were stowed away, along with some shovels and baskets, and a coil or two of deadly-looking rope; the strange, unusual, uncomfortable smell, and the cadaverous light; were all in unison. It was a cold and dismal scene.

'There's a wedding just on, Sir,' said the beadle, 'but it'll be over directly, if you'll walk into the westry here.'

Before he turned again to lead the way, he gave Mr Dombey a bow and a half smile of recognition, importing that he (the beadle) remembered to have had the pleasure of attending on him when he buried his wife, and hoped he had enjoyed himself since.

The wedding looked dismal as they passed in front of the altar. The bride was too old and the bridegroom too young, and a superannuated beau with one eye and an eyeglass stuck in its blank companion, was giving away the lady, while the friends were shivering. In the vestry the fire was smoking; and an over-aged and over-worked and underpaid attorney's clerk, 'making a search', was running his forefinger down the parchment pages of an immense register (one of a long series of similar volumes) gorged with burials. Over the fireplace was a ground-plan of the vaults underneath the church; and Mr Chick, skimming the literary portion of it aloud, by way of enlivening the company, read the reference to Mrs Dombey's tomb in full, before he could stop himself.

After another cold interval, a wheezy little pew-opener afflicted with an asthma, appropriate to the churchyard, if not to the church, summoned them to the font – a rigid marble basin which seemed to have been playing a churchyard game at cup and ball with its matter of fact pedestal, and to have been just that moment caught on the top of it. Here they waited some little time while the marriage party enrolled themselves; and meanwhile the wheezy little pew-opener – partly in consequence of her infirmity, and partly that the marriage party might not forget her – went about the building coughing like a grampus.

Presently the clerk (the only cheerful-looking object there, and *he* was an undertaker) came up with a jug of warm water, and said something, as he poured it into the font, about taking the chill off; which millions of gallons boiling hot could not have done for the occasion. Then the clergyman, an amiable and mild-looking young curate, but obviously afraid of the baby, appeared like the principal character in a ghost-story, 'a tall figure all in white;' at sight of whom Paul rent the air with his cries, and never left off again till he was taken out black in the face.

[Charles Dickens, *Dombey and Son*, Chapter 5]

Chapter 3: A method of analysis and some examples

The following are four passages which may be analysed according to the technique explained in sections 3.1–3.2 and exemplified in sections 3.3–3.5:

3A: In the garden the birds that had sung erratically and spasmodically in the dawn on that tree, on that bush, now sang together in chorus, shrill and sharp; now together, as if conscious of companionship, now alone as if to the pale blue sky. They swerved, all in one flight, when the black cat moved among the bushes, when the cook threw cinders on the ash heap and startled them. Fear was in their song, and apprehension of pain, and joy to be snatched quickly now at this instant. Also they sang emulously in the clear morning air, swerving high over the elm tree, singing together as they chased each other, escaping, pursuing, pecking each other as they turned high in the air. And then tiring of pursuit and flight, lovelily they came descending, delicately declining, dropped down and sat silent on the tree, on the wall, with their bright eyes glancing, and their heads turned this way, that way; aware, awake; intensely conscious of one thing, one object in particular.

Perhaps it was a snail shell, rising in the grass like a grey cathedral, a swelling building burnt with dark rings and shadowed green by the grass. Or perhaps they saw the splendour of the flowers making a light of flowing purple over the beds, through which dark tunnels of purple shade were driven between the stalks. Or they fixed their gaze on the small bright apple leaves, dancing yet withheld, stiffly sparkling among the pink-tipped blossoms. Or they saw the rain drop on the hedge, pendent but not falling, with a whole house bent in it, and towering elms; or, gazing straight at the sun, their eyes became gold beads.

[Virginia Woolf, *The Waves*, Penguin edn 1964, pp. 62–63]

3B: They worked together, coming and going, in a rhythm, which carried their feet and their bodies in tune. She stooped, she lifted the burden of sheaves, she turned her face to the dimness where he was, and went with her burden over the stubble. She hesitated, set down her sheaves, there was a swish and hiss of mingling oats, he was drawing near, and she must turn again. And there was the flaring moon laying bare her bosom again, making her drift and ebb like a wave.

He worked steadily, engrossed, threading backwards and forwards like a shuttle across the strip of cleared stubble, weaving the long line of riding shocks, nearer and nearer to the shadowy trees, threading his sheaves with hers.

And always, she was gone before he came. As he came, she drew away, as he drew away, she came. Were they never to meet? Gradually a low, deep-sounding will in him vibrated to her, tried to set her in accord, tried to bring her gradually to him, to a meeting, till they should be together, till they should meet as the sheaves that swished together.

And the work went on. The moon grew brighter, clearer, the corn glistened. He bent over the prostrate bundles, there was a hiss as the sheaves left the ground, a trailing of heavy bodies against him, a dazzle of moonlight on his eyes. And then he was setting the corn together at the stook. And she was coming near.

He waited for her, he fumbled at the stook. She came. But she stood back till he drew away. He saw her in shadow, a dark column, and spoke to her, and she answered. She saw the moonlight flash question on his face. But there was a space between them, and he went away, the work carried them, rhythmic.

Why was there always a space between them, why were they apart? Why, as she came up from under the moon, would she halt and stand off from him? Why was he held away from her? His will drummed persistently, darkly, it drowned everything else.

[D.H. Lawrence, *The Rainbow*, Chapter 4]

3c: At least once a fortnight a corps of caterers came down with several hundred feet of canvas and enough coloured lights to make a Christmas tree of Gatsby's enormous garden. On buffet tables, garnished with glistening hors-d'oeuvres, spiced baked hams crowded against salads of harlequin designs and pastry pigs and turkeys bewitched to a dark gold. In the main hall a bar with a real brass rail was set up, and stocked with gins and liquors and with cordials so long forgotten that most of his female guests were too young to know one from another.

By seven o'clock the orchestra has arrived, no thin five-piece affair, but a whole pitful of oboes and trombones and saxophones and viols and cornets and piccolos, and low and high drums. The last swimmers have come in from the beach now and are dressing upstairs; the cars from New York are parked five deep in the drive, and already the halls and salons and verandas are gaudy with primary colours, and hair bobbed in strange new ways, and shawls beyond the dreams of Castile. The bar is in full swing, and floating rounds of cocktails permeate the garden outside, until the air is alive with chatter and laughter, and casual innu-endo and introductions forgotten on the spot, and enthusiastic meetings between women who never knew each other's names.

The lights grow brighter as the earth lurches away from the sun, and now the orchestra is playing yellow cocktail music, and the opera of voices pitches a key higher. Laughter is easier minute by minute, spilled with prodigality, tipped out at a cheerful word. The groups change more swiftly, swell with new arrivals, dissolve and form in the same breath; already there are wanderers, confident girls who weave here and there among the stouter and more stable, become for a sharp, joyous moment the centre of a group, and then, excited with triumph, glide on through the sea-change of faces and voices and colour under the constantly chang-ing light.

Suddenly one of these gypsies, in trembling opal, seizes a cocktail out of the air, dumps it down for courage and, moving her hands like Frisco, dances out alone on the canvas platform. A momentary hush; the orchestra leader varies his rhythm obligingly for her, and there is a burst of chatter as the erroneous news goes around that she is Gilda Gray's understudy from the Follies. The party has begun.

[F. Scott Fitzgerald, *The Great Gatsby*, Chapter 3]

3D: Fog everywhere. Fog up the river, where it flows among green aits and meadows; fog down the river, where it rolls defiled among the tiers of shipping and the waterside pollutions of a great (and dirty) city. Fog on the Essex marshes, fog on the Kentish heights. Fog creeping into the cabooses of collier-brigs; fog lying out on the yards and hovering in the rigging of great ships; fog drooping on the gunwales of barges and small boats. Fog in the eyes and throats of ancient Greenwich pensioners, wheez-ing by the firesides of their wards; fog in the stem and bowl of the afternoon pipe of the wrathful skipper, down in his close cabin; fog cruelly pinching the toes and fingers of his shivering little 'prentice boy on deck. Chance people on the bridges peeping over the parapets into a nether sky of fog, with fog all round them, as if they were up in a balloon and hanging in the misty clouds.

Gas looming through the fog in divers places in the streets, much as the sun may, from the spongey fields, be seen to loom by husbandman and ploughboy. Most of the shops lighted two hours before their time – as the gas seems to know, for it has a haggard and unwilling look.

The raw afternoon is rawest, and the dense fog is densest, and the muddy streets are muddiest near that leaden-headed old obstruction, appropriate ornament for the threshold of a leaden-headed old corpora-tion, Temple Bar. And hard by Temple Bar, in Lincoln's Inn Hall, at the very heart of the fog, sits the Lord High Chancellor in his High Court of Chancery.   [Charles Dickens, *Bleak House*, Chapter 1]

Chapter 4: Levels of style

4A: (i) Identify *stylistic variants* (sections 4.3–4.4) of the following sentence (sentence 6) from the passage from Conrad's *The Secret Agent* quoted on pp. 190–1:
His wife had gone raving mad – murdering mad. Possible variants:

(a) Graphological variants:
His wife had gone raving mad, murdering mad.
His wife had gone raving mad. *Murdering* mad.
His wife had gone raving mad, murdering mad!
(b) Syntactic variants:
His wife had gone raving, murdering mad.
His wife had gone murdering mad – raving mad.
His wife, she'd gone raving, murdering mad.
(c) Semantic variants:
Mrs Verloc had become a raving, murdering mad woman.
The conjugal companion of Mr Verloc had suddenly become ravingly, murderingly insane.
'Winnie's gone raving mad – murdering mad', he thought.
[Mr Verloc calls his wife 'Winnie' in the novel.]

What differences in style, meaning and effect do the variants produce?

4A: (ii) Examine the following sentence of the passage quoted in Exercise 10A, pp. 375–7. Construct possible variants and discuss the differences in style and meaning which result:

But her long fair hair was girlish: and girlish, and touched with the wonder of mortal beauty, her face.

4B: For further study of authors' revisions, consider the following alternative versions from Henry James's *The Portrait of a Lady*, those marked (a) being from the 1881 edition of the novel, and those marked (b) from the text which resulted from a revision some 25 years later:

(i) Caspar Goodwood had never corresponded to her idea of a delightful person, and she supposed that this was why
(a) he was so unsatisfactory.
(b) he left her so harshly critical.

(ii) [Lord Warburton has just proposed marriage to Isabel, and has received an offputting reply.]

He held out his hand, and she gave him hers a moment – a moment long enough

  (a) for him to bend his head and kiss it. Then, shaking his hunting-whip with little quick strokes, he walked rapidly away. He was evidently very nervous.

  (b) for him to bend his handsome bared head and kiss it. Then, still agitating, in his mastered emotion, his implement of the chase, he walked rapidly away. He was evidently much upset.

(iii) [referring to the proposal above]

But what disturbed her, in the sense that it struck her with wonderment, was this very fact that it cost her so little

  (a) to refuse a great opportunity.

  (b) to refuse a magnificent 'chance'.

(iv) (a) Isabel, on this occasion, took little share in the conversation.

  (b) Isabel took on this occasion little part in the talk.

 (v) (a) His utterance was like the tinkling of glass . . .

  (b) His utterance was the vibration of glass . . .

[These examples are taken from Wallace Hildick, *Word For Word*, London 1965, pp. 146–150]

4c: Examine the fourth and fifth paragraphs of the passage quoted in 10A (pp. 364–5) from the point of view of foregrounded features.

Chapter 5: Language and the fictional world

5a: Reconsider the passages given in 2c, 3b and 3d above from the point of view of symbolic specification of detail (section 5.3). For example, in the passage describing Paul's christening (2c) many details contribute to the ironic juxtaposition of babyhood (christening) and death (funerals); an irony, which gains force, in retrospect, from Paul's early death. Examine how the choice of language contributes to the elaboration of symbolic detail.

5b: Realism in dialogue (section 5.4). Compare the two passages of dialogue below, in terms of their representation of (a) dialect and idiolect; (b) the characteristics of real conversation. In what ways have their authors 'idealised' for artistic purposes what happens in real dialogue?

Jem turned out the living-room lights and pressed his nose to a window screen. Aunt Alexandra protested. 'Just for a second, Aunty, let's see who it is,' he said.

Dill and I took another window. A crowd of men was standing around
Atticus. They all seemed to be talking at once.

'... movin' him to the county jail tomorrow,' Mr Tate was saying, 'I
don't look for any trouble, but I can't guarantee there won't be any...'

'Don't be foolish, Heck,' Atticus said. 'This is Maycomb.'

'... said I was just uneasy.'

'Heck, we've gotten one postponement of this case just to make
sure there's nothing to be uneasy about. This is Saturday,' Atticus said.
'Trial'll probably be Monday. You can keep him one night, can't you?
I don't think anybody in Maycomb'll begrudge me a client, with times
this hard.'

There was a murmur of glee that died suddenly when Mr Link Deas
said, 'Nobody around here's up to anything, it's that Old Sarum bunch
I'm worried about... can't you get a — what is it, Heck?'

'Change of venue,' said Mr Tate. 'Not much point in that, now is it?'

Atticus said something inaudible. I turned to Jem, who waved me to
silence.

'– besides,' Atticus was saying, 'You're not scared of that crowd, are
you?'

'... know how they do when they get shinnied up.'

[Harper Lee, *To Kill A Mocking Bird*, Chapter 15]
*(The foregoing narrative is set in the southern states of the USA. Atticus,
a lawyer, has undertaken to defend a Negro accused of rape.)*

'You know,' said Ginger, 'it was awful luck meeting you two to-day. I
was getting awfully fed up with London. It's so damn slow. I came back
meaning to have a good time, you know, paint the place a bit red, and all
that. Well, the other day I was reading the paper, and there was a bit that
said that the posh place to go to dance nowadays was the Casanova
Hotel in Bloomsbury. Well, it seemed a bit rum to me – place I'd never
heard of, you know – but, still, I'd been away for some time and places
change and all that, so I put on my bib and tucker and toddled off,
hoping for a bit of innocent amusement. Well, I mean to say, you never
saw such a place. There were only about three people dancing, so I said,
"Where's the bar?" And they said, "Bar!" And I said, "You know, for a
drink," And they said, well, they could probably make me some coffee.
And I said, "No, not coffee." And then they said they hadn't got a licence
for what they called alcohol. Well, I mean to say, if that's the best London
can do, give me Colombo. I wonder who writes things like that in the
papers?'

'As a matter of fact, *I* do.'

'I say no, do you? You must be frightfully brainy. Did you write all
that about the green bowlers?'

'Yes.'

'Well, I mean to say, whoever heard of a green bowler, I mean. . . . I tell you what, you know, I believe it was all a leg pull. You know, I think that's damn funny. Why, a whole lot of poor mutts may have gone and bought green bowlers.'

[Evelyn Waugh, *Vile Bodies*, Chapter 7]
(The foregoing narrative is about the 'smart set' of pleasure-seeking youth in the London of the 1920s.)

5c: The rendering of the fiction (section 5.5). Choose a short story, and analyse how the author presents the narrative in terms of fictional point of view (section 5.5.1), fictional sequencing (section 5.5.2) and descriptive focus (section 5.5.3). We recommend for this purpose Hemingway's *The Short Happy Life of Francis Macomber*, or Joyce's *The Dead*.

Chapter 6: Mind style

6A: Each of the following two passages describes a struggle. Compare the ways in which the authors portray the struggle in terms of participant relations (section 6.1):

She took Lennie's hand and put it on her head. 'Feel right aroun' there an' see how soft it is.'

Lennie's big fingers fell to stroking her hair.

'Don't you muss it up,' she said.

Lennie said, 'Oh! That's nice,' and he stroked harder. 'Oh, that's nice.'

'Look out, now, you'll muss it.' And then she cried angrily, 'You stop it now, you'll mess it all up.' She jerked her head sideways and Lennie's fingers closed on her hair and hung on. 'Let go,' she cried. 'You let go.'

Lennie was in a panic. His face was contorted. She screamed then, and Lennie's other hand closed over her mouth and nose. 'Please don't,' he begged. 'Oh Please don't do that. George'll be mad.'

She struggled violently under his hands. Her feet battered on the hay and she writhed to be free; and from under Lennie's hand came a muffled screaming. Lennie began to cry with fright. 'Oh! Please don't do none of that,' he begged. 'George gonna say I done a bad thing. He ain't gonna let me tend no rabbits.' He moved his hand a little and her hoarse cry came out. Then Lennie grew angry. 'Now don't,' he said, 'I don't want you to yell. You gonna get me in trouble jus' like George says you will. Now don't you do that.' And she continued to struggle, and her eyes were wild with terror. He shook her then, and he was angry with her. 'Don't you go yellin',' he said, and he shook her; and her body flopped like a fish. And then she was still, for Lennie had broken her neck. [John Steinbeck, *Of Mice And Men*, Chapter 5]

Something brushed against the back of the shelter. Piggy kept still for a moment, then he had his asthma. He arched his back and crashed among the leaves with his legs. Ralph rolled away from him.

Then there was a vicious snarling in the mouth of the shelter and the plunge and thump of living things. Someone tripped over Ralph and Piggy's corner became a complication of snarls and crashes and flying limbs. Ralph hit out; then he and what seemed like a dozen others were rolling over and over, hitting, biting, scratching. He was torn and jolted, found fingers in his mouth and bit them. A fist withdrew and came back like a piston, so that the whole shelter exploded into light. Ralph twisted sideways on top of a writhing body and felt hot breath on his cheek. He began to pound the mouth below him, using his clenched fist as a hammer; he hit with more and more passionate hysteria as the face became slippery. A knee jerked up between his legs and he fell sideways, busying himself with his pain, and the fight rolled over him. Then the shelter collapsed with smothering finality; and the anonymous shapes fought their way out and through. Dark figures drew themselves out of the wreckage and flitted away, till the screams of the littluns and Piggy's gasps were once more audible.

[William Golding, *The Lord of the Flies*, Chapter 10]

6B: Analyse the style of the following passage, giving particular attention to mind style.

JACKSON. Alt. 294 ft. Pop. (A.D. 1950) 201,092.

Located by an expedition of three Commissioners selected appointed and dispatched for that single purpose, on a high bluff above Pearl River at the approximate geographical centre of the State, to be not a market nor industrial town, nor even as a place for men to live, but to be a capital, the Capital of a Commonwealth;

In the beginning was already decreed this rounded knob, this gilded pustule, already before and beyond the steamy chiaroscuro, untimed unseasoned winterless miasma not any one of water or earth or life yet all of each, inextricable and indivisible; that one seethe one spawn one mother-womb, one furious tumescence, father-mother-one, one vast incubant ejaculation already fissionating in one boiling moil of litter from the celestial experimental Work Bench; that one spawning crawl and creep printing with three-toed mastodonic tracks the steamy-green swaddling clothes of the coal and the oil, above which the pea-brained reptilian heads curved the heavy leather-flapped air;

Then the ice, but still this knob, this pimple-dome, this buried half-ball hemisphere; the earth lurched, heaving darkward the long continental flank, dragging upward beneath the polar cap that furious equatorial womb, the shutter-lid of cold severing off into blank and heedless void one last sound, one cry, one puny myriad indictment already fading and then no more, the blind and tongueless earth spinning on, looping the long recordless astral orbit, frozen, tideless, yet still was there this tiny gleam, this spark, this gilded crumb of man's eternal aspiration, this golden dome preordained and impregnable, this minuscule foetus-glint tougher than ice and harder than freeze; the earth lurched again, sloughing; the ice with infinitesimal speed, scouring out the valleys, scoring the hills, and vanished; the earth tilted further to recede the sea rim by necklace-rim of crustacean husks in recessional contour lines like the concentric whorls within the sawn stump telling the tree's age, bearing south by recessional south toward that mute and beckoning gleam the confluent continental swale, baring to light and air the broad blank mid-continental page for the first scratch of orderly recording – a laboratory-factory covering what would be twenty states, established and ordained for the purpose of manufacturing one: the ordered unhurried whirl of seasons, of rain and snow and freeze and thaw and sun and drouth to aerate and slack the soil, the conflux of a hundred rivers into one vast father of rivers carrying the rich dirt, the rich garnering, south and south, carving the bluffs to bear the long march of the river towns, flooding the Mississippi lowlands, spawning the rich alluvial dirt layer by vernal layer, raising inch by foot by year by century the surface of the earth which in time (not distant now, measured against that long signatureless chronicle) would tremble to the passing of trains like when the cat crosses the suspension bridge; . . . [William Faulkner, *Requiem For a Nun*, Act 2]

Chapter 7: The rhetoric of text

7A: Analyse the style of the following passage, giving particular attention to the iconic (section 7.7) factor in syntactic and phonological patterns, and the cohesion of the text (section 7.8):

Nothing moved in the parlour till Mrs Verloc raised her head slowly and looked at the clock with inquiring mistrust. She had become aware of a ticking sound in the room. It grew upon her ear, while she remembered clearly that the clock on the wall was silent, had no audible tick. What did it mean by beginning to tick so loudly all of a sudden? Its face indicated ten minutes to nine. Mrs Verloc cared nothing for time, and the ticking went on. She concluded it could not be the clock, and her sullen gaze moved along the walls, wavered, and became vague, while she strained her hearing to locate the sound. Tic, tic, tic.

After listening for some time Mrs Verloc lowered her gaze deliberately on her husband's body. Its attitude of repose was so homelike and famil-iar that she could do so without feeling embarrassed by any pronounced novelty in the phenomena of her home life. Mr Verloc was taking his habitual ease. He looked comfortable.

By the position of the body the face of Mr Verloc was not visible to Mrs Verloc, his widow. Her fine, sleepy eyes, travelling downward on the track of the sound, became contemplative on meeting a flat object of bone which protruded a little beyond the edge of the sofa. It was the handle of the domestic carving knife with nothing strange about it but its position at right angles to Mr Verloc's waistcoat and the fact that something dripped from it. Dark drops fell on the floor-cloth one after another, with a sound of ticking growing fast and furious like the pulse of an insane clock. At its highest speed this ticking changed into a continuous sound of trickling. Mrs Verloc watched that transformation with shadows of anxiety coming and going on her face. It was a trickle, dark, swift, thin. . . . Blood!

[Joseph Conrad, *The Secret Agent*, Chapter 11]

7B: The following is an extract from Norman Mailer's *Armies of the Night* directly preceding the extract already quoted (see p. 187). Considering both extracts as a single passage, analyse the style of the passage, giving particular attention to iconicity and cohesion (sections 7.7–7.8):

That flat breast of the hill at the foot of the monument had that agreeable curve one finds on an athletic field graded for drainage. Here, the curve was more pronounced, but the effect was similar: the groups and couples walking down from Washington Monument toward the round pool and the long reflecting pool which led to Lincoln Memorial, were revealed by degrees – one saw their hats bobbing on the horizon of the ridge before you saw their faces; perhaps this contributed to a high sense of focus; the eye studied the act of walking as if one were looking at the gait of a troop of horses; some of the same pleasure was there: the people seemed to be prancing. It was similar to the way men and women are caught in the films of very good directors; the eye watching the film knows it has not been properly employed before. These people were animated; the act of stepping along seemed to loosen little springs in their joints, the action was rollicking, something was grave. Perhaps this etching of focus had to do with no more than the physical fact that Mailer, approaching somewhat lower on the swell of the hill, was therefore watching with his eyes on a line with those rollicking feet. That could not however be all of it. A thin high breath of pleasure, like a child's anticipation of the first rocket to be fired on Fourth of July, hung over the sweet grass of the hill on Washington Monument. They were prancing past this hill, they were streaming to battle. Going to battle! He realized that he had not taken in precisely this thin high sensuous breath of pleasure in close to twenty-four years, not since the first time he had gone into combat, and found to his surprise that the walk toward the fire fight was one of the more agreeable – if stricken – moments of his life. Later, in the skirmish itself it was less agreeable – he had perspired so profusely he had hardly been able to see through his sweat – much later, months later, combat was disagreeable; it managed to consist of large doses of fatigue, the intestinal agitations of the tropics, endless promenades through mud, and general apathy toward whether one lived or not. But the first breath had left a feather on his memory; it was in the wind now; he realized that an odd, yes a *zany* part of him had been expecting quietly and confidently for years, that before he was done, he would lead an army. (The lives of Leon Trotsky and Ernest Hemingway had done nothing to dispel this expectation.)

[Norman Mailer, *The Armies of the Night*, Book 1, Part 3, Chapter 2]

7c: Re-examine passages 3B and 3c from the point of view of iconicity.

Chapter 8: Discourse and the discourse situation

8A: Using the diagram (Figure 8.5) on p. 216, explain the peculiar discourse structure of the following extract from Kurt Vonnegut's *Breakfast of Champions*:

I thought it would be a good idea to let him have a good look at me, and so attempted to flick on the dome light. I turned on the windshield washers instead. I turned them off again. My view of the lights of the County Hospital was garbled by beads of water. I pulled at another switch, and it came away in my hand. It was a cigarette lighter. So I had no choice but to continue to speak from darkness.

'Mr Trout,' I said, 'I am a novelist, and I created you for use in my books.'

'Pardon me?' he said.

'I'm your Creator,' I said. 'You're in the middle of a book right now – close to the end of it, actually.'

'Um,' he said.

'Are there any questions you'd like to ask?'

'Pardon me?' he said.

'Feel free to ask anything you want – about the past, about the future,' I said. 'There's a Nobel Prize in your future.'

'A what?' he said.

'A Nobel Prize in medicine.'

'Huh,' he said. It was a noncommittal sound.

'I've also arranged for you to have a reputable publisher from now on. No more beaver books for you.'

'Um,' he said.

'If I were in your spot, I would certainly have lots of questions,' I said.

'Do you have a gun?' he said.

I laughed there in the dark, tried to turn on the light again, activated the windshield washer again. 'I don't need a gun to control you, Mr Trout. All I have to do is write down something about you, and that's it.'

[Kurt Vonnegut, Jr, *Breakfast of Champions*, Cape 1974, pp. 291–292]

8B: Show how features of style contribute to the irony of the following passage:

This is America – a town of a few thousand, in a region of wheat and corn and dairies and little groves.

The town is, in our tale, called 'Gopher Prairie, Minnesota'. But its Main Street is the continuation of Main Streets everywhere. The story would be the same in Ohio or Montana, in Kansas or Kentucky or Illinois, and not very differently would it be told Up York State or in the Carolina hills.

Main Street is the climax of civilization. That this Ford car might stand in front of the Bon Ton Store, Hannibal invaded Rome and Erasmus wrote in Oxford cloisters. What Ole Jenson the grocer says to Ezra Stowbody the banker is the new law for London, Prague, and the unprofitable isles of the sea; whatsoever Ezra does not know and sanction,that thing is heresy, worthless for knowing and wicked to consider.

Our railway station is the final aspiration of architecture. Sam Clark's annual hardware turnover is the envy of the four counties which constitute God's Country. In the sensitive art of the Rosebud Movie Palace there is a Message, and humor strictly moral.

Such is our comfortable tradition and sure faith. Would he not betray himself an alien cynic who should otherwise portray Main Street, or distress the citizens by speculating whether there may not be other faiths?

[Sinclair Lewis, *Main Street*, prologue]

8C: In the following sentence from Dickens's *Little Dorrit*, show how the textual rhetoric, especially the sequencing of impressions, contributes to ironic impact (see the discussion of the Somerset Maugham example (p. 224):

Mrs Sparkler, who was not unfeeling, had received them [the tidings of her father's death] with a violent outburst of grief, which had lasted twelve hours; after which she had arisen to see about her mourning, and to take every precaution that could ensure its being as becoming as Mrs Merdle's.

8D: Examine the *tone* of Gulliver's description of the Yahoos in section 5.5.3 (p. 144). What is the source and nature of the irony, and how does it find expression through lexical choice?

Chapter 9: Conversation in the novel

9A: Using the conversational analysis outlined in Chapter 9, compare the following two dialogues:

'Henry, can I get down?'

He remained staring at David. 'Why?'

'I want to read my book.'

'You're a fucking little ninny.'

'Please.'

'Bugger off then.'

He had not looked at her. The Mouse came back with the third bottle, and the Freak looked nervously up at her, as if her permission was needed as well. There was a little nod, then David felt his thigh being briefly squeezed. The Freak's hand had reached along beneath the table, apparently to give him courage. She stood up and went down the room and up the stairs. Breasley pushed the bottle towards David. It was not a politeness, but a challenge.

'Not for me, thanks. I've had enough.'

'Cognac? Calvados?'

'No thanks.'

The old man poured himself another full glass of wine.

'This pot stuff?' He nodded sideways down the room.

'That's the book she wants to read.'

The Mouse said quietly, 'She's given it up. You know that perfectly well.'

He took a mouthful of the wine.

'Thought all you young whiz-kids indulged.'

David said lightly, 'Not personally.'

'Interferes with the slide-rule stuff, does it?'

'I imagine. But I'm not a mathematician.'

'What do you call it then?'

The Mouse waited, eyes down. Evidently she could not help him now, except as a silent witness. It was not worth pretending one did not know what that 'it' meant. David met the old man's stare.

'Mr Breasley, most of us feel abstraction has become a meaningless term. Since our conception of reality has changed so much this last fifty years.'

[John Fowles, *The Ebony Tower*]

(The painter, Breasley, lives with two young women he calls the Mouse and the Freak. David has come to interview him in connection with a book he is writing on him.)

Guy did not as usual come up the steps immediately; he paused, and Doris at once surmised that the boy had gone down to meet him in order to tell him of the morning's incident. She shrugged her shoulders. The boy evidently wanted to get his story in first. But she was astonished when Guy came in. His face was ashy.

'Guy, what on earth's the matter?'

He flushed a sudden hot red.

'Nothing. Why?'

She was so taken aback that she let him pass into his room without a word of what she had meant to speak of at once. It took him longer than usual to have his bath and change his clothes and luncheon was served when he came in.

'Guy,' she said, as they sat down, 'that woman we saw the other day was here again this morning.'

'So I've heard,' he answered.

'The boys were treating her brutally. I had to stop them. You must really speak to them about it.'

Though the Malay understood every word she said, he made no sign that he heard. He handed her the toast.

'She's been told not to come here. I gave instructions that if she showed herself again she was to be turned out.'

'Were they obliged to be so rough?'

'She refused to go. I don't think they were any rougher than they could help.'

'It was horrible to see a woman treated like that. She had a baby in her arms.'

'Hardly a baby. It's three years old.'

'How d'you know?'

'I know all about her. She hasn't the least right to come here pestering everybody.'

'What does she want?'

'She wants to do exactly what she did. She wants to make a disturbance.'

For a little while Doris did not speak. She was surprised at her husband's tone. He spoke tersely. He spoke as though all this were no concern of hers. She thought him a little unkind. He was nervous and irritable.

'I doubt if we shall be able to play tennis this afternoon,' he said. 'It looks to me as though we were going to have a storm.'

[W. Somerset Maugham, *The Force of Circumstance*]

9B: Analyse in pragmatic terms (with reference to speech acts and implicatures) the conversation quoted in exercise 8A. How well does it account for the meaning of the speaker's utterances? Can you think of any ways of extending or modifying pragmatic analysis in order to account for unexplained conversational meanings you perceive in this passage or those in 9A?

Chapter 10: Speech and thought presentation

10A: Analyse the style of the following passage, giving particular attention to speech and thought presentation:

There was a long rivulet in the strand and, as he waded slowly up its course, he wondered at the endless drift of seaweed. Emerald and black and russet and olive, it moved beneath the current, swaying and turning. The water of the rivulet was dark with endless drift and mirrored the high-drifting clouds. The clouds were drifting above him silently and silently the sea-tangle was drifting below him and the grey warm air was still and a new wild life was singing in his veins.

Where was his boyhood now? Where was the soul that had hung back from her destiny, to brood alone upon the shame of her wounds and in her house of squalor and subterfuge to queen it in faded cerements and in wreaths that withered at the touch? Or where was he?

He was alone. He was unheeded, happy and near to the wild heart of life. He was alone and young and wilful and wild-hearted, alone amid a waste of wild air and brackish waters and the sea-harvest of shells and tangle and veiled grey sunlight and gayclad lightclad figures of children and girls and voices childish and girlish in the air.

A girl stood before him in midstream, alone and still, gazing out to sea. She seemed like one whom magic had changed into the likeness of a strange and beautiful seabird. Her long slender bare legs were delicate as a crane's and pure save where an emerald trail of seaweed had fashioned itself as a sign upon the flesh. Her thighs, fuller and soft-hued as ivory, were bared almost to the hips, where the white fringes of her drawers were like feathering of soft white down. Her slate-blue skirts were kilted boldly about her waist and dovetailed behind her. Her bosom was as a bird's, soft and slight, slight and soft as the breast of some dark-plumaged dove. But her long fair hair was girlish: and girlish, and touched with the wonder of mortal beauty, her face.

She was alone and still, gazing out to sea; and when she felt his presence and the worship of his eyes her eyes turned to him in quiet sufferance of his gaze, without shame or wantonness. Long, long she suffered his gaze and then quietly withdrew her eyes from his and bent them towards the stream, gently stirring the water with her foot hither and thither. The first faint noise of gently moving water broke the silence, low and faint and whispering, faint as the bells of sleep; hither and thither, hither and thither; and a faint flame trembled on her cheek.

– Heavenly God! cried Stephen's soul, in an outburst of profane joy.

He turned away from her suddenly and set off across the strand. His cheeks were aflame; his body was aglow; his limbs were trembling. On and on and on and on he strode, far out over the sands, singing wildly to the sea, crying to greet the advent of the life that had cried to him.

Her image had passed into his soul for ever and no word had broken the holy silence of his ecstasy. Her eyes had called him and his soul had leaped at the call. To live, to err, to fall, to triumph, to recreate life out of life! A wild angel had appeared to him, the angel of mortal youth and beauty, an envoy from the fair courts of life, to throw open before him in an instant of ecstasy the gates of all the ways of error and glory. On and on and on and on!

[James Joyce, *A Portrait of the Artist as a Young Man*, Chapter 4]

10B: Identify categories of speech and thought presentation in the following passages, and discuss their literary function:

But though she did not speak, Katharine had an uneasy sense that silence on her part was selfishness. It was selfish of her to continue, as she wished to do, a discussion of subjects not remotely connected with any human beings. She roused herself to consider their exact position upon the turbulent map of the emotions. Oh yes – it was a question whether Ralph Denham should live in the country and write a book; it was getting late; they must waste no more time; Cassandra arrived to-night for dinner; she flinched and roused herself, and discovered that she ought to be holding something in her hands. But they were empty. She held them out with an exclamation.

'I've left my bag somewhere – where?' The gardens had no points of the compass, so far as she was concerned. She had been walking for the most part on grass – that was all she knew. Even the road to the Orchid House had now split itself into three. But there was no bag in the Orchid House. It must, therefore, have been left upon the seat. They retraced their steps in the preoccupied manner of people who have to think about something that is lost. What did this bag look like? What did it contain?

'A purse – a ticket – some letters, papers,' Katharine counted, becoming more agitated as she recalled the list. Denham went on quickly in advance of her, and she heard him shout that he had found it before she reached the seat. In order to make sure that all was safe she spread the contents on her knee. It was a queer collection, Denham thought, gazing with the deepest interest. Loose gold coins were tangled in a narrow strip of lace; there were letters which somehow suggested the extreme of intimacy; there were two or three keys, and lists of commissions against which crosses were set at intervals. But she did not seem satisfied until she had made sure of a certain paper so folded that Denham could not judge what it contained. In her relief and gratitude she began at once to say that she had been thinking over what Denham had told her of his plans.

He cut her short. 'Don't let's discuss that dreary business.'

[Virginia Woolf, *Night and Day*, Chapter 25]

Here arises a feature of the Circumlocution Office, not previously mentioned in the present record. When that admirable Department got into trouble, and was, by some infuriated member of Parliament, whom the smaller Barnacles almost suspected of labouring under diabolic possession, attacked, on the merits of no individual case, but as an Institution wholly abominable and Bedlamite; then the noble or right honourable Barnacle who represented it in the House, would smite that member and cleave him asunder, with a statement of the quantity of business (for the prevention of business) done by the Circumlocution Office. Then would that noble or right honourable Barnacle hold in his hand a paper containing a few figures, to which, with the permission of the House, he would entreat its attention. Then would the inferior Barnacles exclaim, obeying orders, 'Hear, Hear, Hear!' and 'Read!' Then would the noble or right honourable Barnacle perceive, sir, from this little document, which he thought might carry conviction even to the perversest mind (Derisive laughter and cheering from the Barnacle fry), that within the short compass of the last financial half-year, this much-maligned Department (Cheers) had written and received fifteen thousand letters (Loud cheers), twenty-four thousand minutes (Louder cheers), and thirty-two thousand five hundred and seventeen memoranda (Vehement cheering). Nay, an ingenious gentleman connected with the Department, and himself a valuable public servant, had done him the favour to make a curious calculation of the amount of stationery consumed in it during the same period. It formed a part of this same short document; and he derived from it the remarkable fact, that the sheets of foolscap paper it had devoted to the public service would pave the footways on both sides of Oxford Street from end to end, and leave nearly a quarter of a mile to spare for the park (Immense cheering and laughter); while of tape – red tape – it had used enough to stretch, in graceful festoons, from Hyde Park Corner to the General Post-Office. Then, amidst a burst of official exultation, would the noble or right honourable Barnacle sit down, leaving the mutilated fragments of the Member on the field.

[Charles Dickens, *Little Dorrit*, Book 2, Chapter 8]

How could he have thought so evil of the world when succour was at hand all the time? And now he had reached the summit. Ah, Yvonne, sweetheart, forgive me! Strong hands lifted him. Opening his eyes, he looked down, expecting to see, below him, the magnificent jungle, the heights, Pico de Orizabe, Malinche, Cofre de Perote, like those peaks of his life conquered one after another before this greatest ascent of all had been successfully, if unconventionally, completed. But there was nothing there: no peaks, no life, no climb. Nor was this summit a summit exactly: it had no substance, no firm base. It was crumbling too, whatever it was, collapsing, while he was falling, falling into the volcano, he must have climbed it after all, though now there was this noise of foisting lava in his ears, horribly, it was in eruption, yet no, it wasn't the volcano, the world itself was bursting, bursting into black spouts of villages catapulted into space, with himself falling through it all, through the inconceivable pandemonium of a million tanks, through the blazing of ten million burning bodies, falling, into a forest, falling –

Suddenly he screamed, and it was as though this scream were being tossed from one tree to another, as its echoes returned, then, as though the trees themselves were crowding nearer, huddled together, closing over him, pitying . . .

Somebody threw a dead dog after him down the ravine.

[Malcolm Lowry, *Under the Volcano*, Chapter 12]

Chapter 11: Stylistics and fiction 25 years on
Chapter 12: 'The Bucket and the Rope'

As Chapter 11 is a review of developments in stylistics since 1981, we do not suggest any exercises for that chapter alone. However, we do make some suggestions in relation to the approaches explained in Chapter 11 and applied in Chapter 12, using the passages quoted previously in this section of the book. You will probably need to make yourself more familiar with these approaches than the discussions in Chapters 11 and 12 allow. Consequently, following up on some of the references in those chapters or in the Further Reading section in this book will constitute useful groundwork preliminary to analysis.

12A: Draw a series of pictures of the scenes described in passage 3c, noting as you do so the words and phrases in the passage which relate to what you draw. One picture for each paragraph will be a useful starting point. Then attempt a Werthian text-world analysis. Sections 1.2 and 2.5 of Werth (1999) will be helpful in the first of these tasks, and reading Chapters 7 and 8 will be helpful preparation for the second task.

12B: Read Chapter 6 of Ryan (1991) and use it to provide a possible worlds analysis of one of the two passages in **9A**. You may also find it helpful to consult Chapter 3 of Verdonk and Weber (1995) and/or section 12.4 of Short (1996), which provide, respectively, more traditional stylistic analyses of these passages.

12C: Using Semino and Short (2004, pp. 9–16, 26–39 and 41–64) as a guide, annotate passage **10B** in detail for speech and thought presentation, being careful to note any ambiguities. Then consider your annotation in terms of possible worlds analysis.

12D: Using Brémond's narrative-cycle approach (you may find it helpful to consult Bal 1997 [1985], pp. 188–193), analyse in detail the passage from Steinbeck's *Of Mice and Men* in **6A**. It will be helpful to remember that judgments of what counts as an equilibrium or disequilibrium may vary according to viewpoint (e.g. that of the reader or individual characters).

Further reading*

These pages are intended to help the student to follow up topics dealt with in this book in more depth and detail. We have completely rewritten them, taking account particularly of new work that has appeared since the first edition of *Style in Fiction* (1981).

A. General: style etc.

The following publications are useful for finding one's bearings in the general field of stylistics, without any particular reference to prose fiction. Wales's *Dictionary* is an essential and humane companion for the student of stylistics, and Asher (1994), Frawley (2003) and Brown (2006) are multi-volume encyclopedias including entries on various areas within stylistics. Carter (1982) gives a flavour of early established stylistics, Carter and Simpson (1989) give a flavour of the 'discourse turn'. Fowler (1996 [1986]) and Short (1996) integrate these two phases. The more recent 'cognitive turn' is represented separately in section G, 'Cognitive stylistics, including metaphor' below. Goodman and O'Halloran (see section O, 'Particular topics: characterisation, creativity etc.) is also worth consulting for general matters.

ASHER, R.E., ed. (1994) *The Encyclopedia of Language and Linguistics*, Oxford, Pergamon Press.
ATTRIDGE, D. (1996 [1987]) 'Closing statement: linguistics and poetics in retrospect', in in WEBER, J.J. (below in this section), 10–35.
BEX, T., BURKE, M. and STOCKWELL, P., eds (2000) *Contextualised Stylistics*, Amsterdam and Atlanta, GA, Rodopi.
BROWN, K., ed. (2006) *Encyclopedia of Language and Linguistics*, Amsterdam and London, Elsevier.

---

* Place of publication includes London unless otherwise indicated.

Style in Fiction

CARTER, R.A., ed. (1982) *Language and Literature: an introductory reader in stylistics*, Allen and Unwin.

CARTER, R.A. and SIMPSON, P., eds (1989) *Language, Discourse and Literature*, Unwin Hyman.

CARTER, R.A. and STOCKWELL, P., eds (2007) *The Language and Literature Reader*, Routledge.

CLUYSENAAR, A. (1976) *Introduction to Literary Stylistics*, Batsford.

FOWLER, R. (1996 [1986]) *Linguistic Criticism*, Oxford, Oxford University Press.

FRAWLEY, W.J., ed. (2003) *International Encyclopedia of Linguistics*, New York, Oxford University Press.

HASAN, R. (1989) *Language, Linguistics and Verbal Art*, Oxford, Oxford University Press.

SHORT, M. (1996) *Exploring the Language of Poems, Plays and Prose*, Longman.

TOOLAN, M., ed. (1992) *Language, Text and Context: essays in stylistics*, Routledge.

WALES, K. (2001 [1989]) *A Dictionary of Stylistics*, Longman.

WEBER, J-J., ed. (1996) *The Stylistics Reader: from Roman Jakobson to the present*, Arnold.

B. The novel and style in prose writing

The following set of readings is targeted more on prose fiction, including contributions from both more literary and more linguistic viewpoints.

FLUDERNIK, M. (1996) 'Linguistics and literature: prospects and horizons in the study of prose', *Journal of Pragmatics* **26**, 5, 583–611.

FOWLER, R. (1977) *Linguistics and the Novel*, Methuen.

LODGE, D. (1976) *Language of Fiction*, Routledge and Kegan Paul.

NASH, W. (1990) *Language in Popular Fiction*, Routledge.

TOOLAN, M. (1990) *The Stylistics of Fiction*, Routledge.

TOOLAN, M. (2001 [1988]) *Narrative: A Critical Linguistic Introduction*, Routledge.

VERDONK, P. and WEBER, J-J., eds (1995) *Twentieth-Century Fiction: from text to context*, Routledge.

C. Foregrounding, differentness, etc.

Foregrounding, discussed especially in Chapters 1 (section 1.4) and 4 (section 4.6) of this book, is one way of looking at what is 'special' or 'different' about literary language. The studies in this section concern themselves with various approaches to this 'differentness'.

370

ATTRIDGE, D. (1988) *Peculiar Language: Literature as Difference from the Renaissance to James Joyce*, Ithaca, NY, Cornell University Press.

ATTRIDGE, D. (2004) *The Singularity of Literature*, Routledge.

COOK, G. (1994) *Discourse and Literature: The Interplay of Form and Mind*, Oxford, Oxford University Press.

DOUTHWAITE, J. (2000) *Towards a Linguistic Theory of Foregrounding*, Alessandria, Edizioni dell'Orso.

LOPES, J.-M. (1995) *Foregrounded Description in Prose Fiction: five cross-cultural studies*, Toronto, Toronto University Press.

VAN PEER, W. (1986) *Stylistics and Psychology: investigations of foregrounding*, London, Croom Helm. (Although it deals with poetry rather than prose, this is an important study of foregrounding in general.)

D. Text worlds, fictional worlds and the like

In Chapter 5 of this book, the nature of the 'fictional world' or 'mock-reality' of novels and short stories is explored. In the following books, this topic is investigated in greater depth from stylistic, textlinguistic and narratological viewpoints.

BRIDGEMAN, T. (1998) *Negotiating the New in the French Novel: building contexts for fictional worlds*, Routledge.

RONEN, R. (1994) *Possible Worlds in Literary Theory*, Cambridge, Cambridge University Press.

RYAN, M-L. (1991) *Possible Worlds, Artificial Intelligence, and Narrative Theory*, Bloomington, IN, Indiana University Press.

SEMINO, E. (1997) *Language and World Creation in Poems and Other Texts*, Longman.

WERTH, P. (1999) *Text Worlds: representing conceptual space in discourse*, Longman.

E. Narrative, narratology

Narratology, the theoretical investigation of narratives and narrations, has burgeoned in the past 25 years, becoming closely interrelated with issues in cognitive linguistics and the language of fiction, especially in relation to story/plot, viewpoint and characterisation. The publications listed below explore this field, which has been growing in importance (see section 11.2.1 on story/plot). Ronen (1994) and Ryan (1991) in the previous section and some of the works referred to in the point of view and focalisation section (H) and the presentation of speech and thought section (L) are also relevant.

ABBOTT, H.P. (2002) *The Cambridge Introduction to Narrative*, Cambridge, Cambridge University Press.

BAL, M. (1997 [1985]) *Narratology: Introduction to the theory of narrative*, New York, University of Toronto Press.

BORTOLUSSI, M. and DIXON, P. (2003) *Psychonarratology: foundations for the empirical study of literary response*, Cambridge, Cambridge University Press.

CHATMAN, S. (1978) *Story and Discourse Narrative Structure in Fiction and Film*, Ithaca, NY, Cornell University Press.

CHATMAN, S. (1990) *Coming to Terms: the rhetoric of narrative in fiction and in film*, Ithaca, NY, Cornell University Press.

COBLEY, P. (2001) *Narrative*, Routledge.

DE REUCK, J. (1993) 'Ways of worldmaking: a study of narrative transmission in Henry James's *The Aspern Papers*', *Journal of Literary Studies* **9**, 3/4, 355–370.

DOLEŽEL, L. (1998) *Heterocosmica: fiction and possible worlds*, Baltimore, MD, Johns Hopkins University Press.

FLUDERNIK, M. (1996) *Towards a 'Natural' Narratology*, Routledge.

GENETTE, G. (1988) *Narrative Discourse Revisited*, trans. J.E. Lewin, Ithaca, NY, Cornell University Press.

HERMAN, D. (2001) 'Narrative theory and the cognitive sciences', *Narrative Inquiry* **11**, 1, 1–34.

HERMAN, D. (2002) *Story Logic: problems and possibilities of narrative*, Lincoln, NE: University of Nebraska Press.

HERMAN, D., ed. (2003) *Narrative Theory and the Cognitive Sciences*, Centre for the Study of Language and Information (CSLI), Stanford, California.

RIMMON-KENAN, S. (2002 [1983]) *Narrative Fiction: contemporary poetics*, Routledge.

F. Mind style

The following are useful explorations of mind style (the topic of Chapter 6) with reference to particular authors and works:

BANKS, D. (1992) 'Men, women and transitivity in *To the Lighthouse* and *A Farewell to Arms*' in: TOSSER, Y. and P. GALLIOU, eds, *Mirroirs de la Femme dans la Littérature d'Expression Anglaise*, Brest, Groupe de Recherche sur le Roman et la Nouvelle de Langue Anglaise, Université de Bretagne Occidentale.

BOCKTING, I. (1995) *Character and Personality in the Novels of William Faulkner*, Lanham, MD, University Press of America.

HALLIDAY, M.A.K. (1996 [1971]) 'Linguistic function and literary style: an inquiry into the language of William Golding's *The Inheritors*', in WEBER, J.J. (under A. General: Style etc., above), pp. 56–86.

SEMINO, E. (2002) 'A cognitive stylistic approach to mind style in narrative fiction', in SEMINO and CULPEPER (under G. Cognitive Stylistics, below), pp. 95–122.

SEMINO, E. and SWINDLEHURST, K. (1996) 'Metaphor and mind style, in *One Flew Over the Cuckoo's Nest'*, *Style* **30**, 1, 143–166.

G. Cognitive stylistics, including metaphor

Another field that has achieved great significance in the past 25 years is cognitive linguistics, which in turn has led to the development of cognitive stylistics (see section 11.1). The following publications show how the mental models and operations involved in the interpretation of texts can be studied in depth, using Fauconnier's mental spaces and blending theory, and newer, fuller understandings of metaphor. Fauconnier's book is cited below, although it is not concerned with stylistics as such.

DANCYGIER, B. (2005) 'Blending and narrative viewpoint: Jonathan Raban's travels through mental spaces', *Language and Literature* **14**, 2, 99–127.

EMMOTT, C. (1997) *Narrative Comprehension: a discourse perspective*, Oxford, Oxford University Press.

FAUCONNIER, G. (1985 [1997]) *Mental Spaces*, Cambridge, MA, MIT Press. [Second edition published by Cambridge University Press, New York.]

FAUCONNIER, G. and TURNER, M. (2002) *The Way We Think: conceptual blending and the mind's hidden complexities*, New York, Basic Books.

GAVINS, J. and STEEN, G., eds (2003) *Cognitive Poetics in Practice*, Routledge.

GIBBS, R.W. (1994) *The Poetics of Mind*, Cambridge, Cambridge University Press.

LAKOFF, G. and TURNER, M. (1989) *More than Cool Reason: a field guide to poetic metaphor*, Chicago, Chicago University Press.

LANGUAGE AND LITERATURE (2006) **15**(1) *Special Issue: Blending*.

SEMINO, E. (1992) 'Schema theory and the analysis of text worlds in poetry', *Language and Literature* **4**(2), 79–108.

SEMINO, E. and CULPEPER, J., eds (2002) *Cognitive Stylistics: language and cognition in text analysis*, Amsterdam and Philadelphia, John Benjamins.

SIMON-VANDENBERGEN, A.-M. (1993) 'Speech, music and dehumanisation in George Orwell's *Nineteen Eighty-Four*: a linguistic study of metaphors', *Language and Literature* **2**(3), 157–182.

STEEN, G. (1989) *Understanding Metaphor in Literature: an empirical approach*, Longman.

STOCKWELL, P. (2002) *Cognitive Poetics: an introduction*, London, Routledge.

TURNER, M. (1996) *The Literary Mind*, Oxford, Oxford University Press.

ZWAAN, R.A. (1993) *Aspects of Literary Comprehension: a cognitive approach*, Amsterdam and Philadelphia, Benjamins.

H. Point of view, focalisation, and the like

The broad concept of point of view (or viewpoint), discussed in Chapters 5 and 8 of this book, leads us into a more socially-oriented exploration of fictional style. Starting with Wayne Booth's seminal work, the following list shows how more recent publications have explored new angles and approaches, such as those associated with focalisation. This area has been explored in considerable depth by narratologists as well as stylisticians, as reflected in the list below. Many of the books in the Narratology section above also contain chapters on point of view, and the notion of mind style (see Section F above) can arguably be subsumed under viewpoint.

BOOTH, W. (1961 [1983]) *The Rhetoric of Fiction*, Chicago, Chicago University Press.

CHATMAN, S. and VAN PEER, W. (2001) *New Perspectives on Narrative Perspective*, Albany, State University of New York Press.

EHRLICH, S. (1990) *Point of View: a linguistic analysis of literary style*, Routledge.

LANSER, S. (1981) *The Narrative Act: point of view in prose fiction*, Princeton, NJ, Princeton University Press.

MARGOLIN, U. (1996) 'Telling our story: on "we" literary narratives', *Language and Literature* 5(2), 115–133.

MCINTYRE, D. (2006) *Point of View in Plays: a cognitive stylistic approach to viewpoint in drama and other text-types*, Amsterdam and Philadelphia, John Benjamins.

NELLES, W. (1990) 'Getting focalization into focus', *Poetics Today* 11(2), 365–382.

SASAKI, T. (1994) 'Towards a systematic description of narrative "point of view": an examination of Chatman's theory with an analysis of *The Blind Man* by D.H. Lawrence', *Language and Literature* 3(2), 125–138.

SHORT, M., CULPEPER, J. and SEMINO, E. Language and context: Jane Gardam's *Bilgewater*, in BEX, T., BURKE, M. and STOCKWELL, P., eds (2000) *Contextualised Stylistics*, Amsterdam and Atlanta, GA, Rodopi.

SIMPSON, P. (1993) *Language, Ideology and Point of View*, Routledge.

I. Text and discourse orientation: including critical discourse analysis

Taking the social orientation further, this section shows how developments in the domain of discourse analysis have shed new light on literature. One particular field, that of critical discourse analysis (CDA, see section 11.1), has attracted a great deal of attention in the last twenty-five years, harnessing the analysis of such ideological issues as power, identity and gender to the interpretation of fictional texts. The articles by Fairclough and Widdowson below are a small sample of polemic papers illustrating how the 'critical' stance of CDA has itself evoked criticism and debate.

BIRCH, D. (1991) *The Language of Drama: critical theory and practice*, Macmillan.

CARTER, R. (1996) *English as Language: discourse, stylistics and the curriculum*, Routledge.

CARTER, R. and SIMPSON, P., eds (1995 [1989]) *Language, Discourse and Literature: an introductory reader in discourse stylistics*, Routledge. (Quite a lot on prose, conversation in fiction, etc.)

FAIRCLOUGH, N. (1996) 'A reply to Henry Widdowson's "Discourse analysis: a critical view"', *Language and Literature* 5(1), 49–56.

FAIRCLOUGH, N. (2001 [1992]) *Language and Power*, Harlow, Pearson Education.

FAIRCLOUGH, N. (2003) *Analysing Discourse: textual analysis for social research*, Longman.

FOWLER, R. (1981) *Literature as Social Discourse: the practice of linguistic criticism*, Batsford.

FOWLER, R. (1991) *Language in the News: Discourse and Ideology in the press*, Routledge.

HUNSTON, S. and THOMPSON, G., eds (2000) *Evaluation in Text: authorial stance and the construction of discourse*, Oxford, Oxford University Press.

MILLS, S. (1995) *Feminist Stylistics*, Routledge.

O'HALLORAN, K. (2004) *Critical Discourse Analysis and Language Cognition*, Edinburgh, Edinburgh University Press.

WEBER, J.J. (1992) *Critical Analysis of Fiction: essays in discourse stylistics*, Amsterdam, Rodopi. (Deals with a range of fictional classics.)

WIDDOWSON, H.G. (1996) Discourse analysis: a critical view, *Language and Literature* 4(3), 157–172.

WIDDOWSON, H.G. (1998) 'The theory and practice of critical discourse analysis', *Applied Linguistics* 19(1), 136–151.

J. Pragmatics and literature

Pragmatics is another sub-discipline of linguistics that has burgeoned in the last 25 years. In Chapters 8 and 9 of this book we tried to show how some tools of pragmatics – speech acts, conversational implicature, politeness theory – could be applied to fictional works. But progress has been made since then, and can be followed up in a number of publications. The list below includes some works from a field called 'literary pragmatics' (e.g. Sell 2000), but not all those who use pragmatic analysis for literature would consider themselves to be part of a literary pragmatics 'school'.

Style in Fiction

HICKEY, L., ed. (1989) *The Pragmatics of Style*, London, Routledge.

PILKINGTON, A. (2000) *Poetics Effects: a relevance theory perspective*, Amsterdam, Benjamins.

PRATT, M.L. (1977) *Toward a Speech Act Theory of Literary Discourse*, Bloomington, IN, Indiana University Press.

SELL, R.D., ed. (1991) *Literary Pragmatics*, Routledge.

SELL, R.D. (2000) *Literature as Communication. The Foundations of Mediating Criticism*, Benjamins. (Interesting glossary on literary pragmatics, etc.)

VERDONK, P. (1995) 'Words, words, words: a pragmatic and socio-cognitive view of lexical repetition', in Verdonk and Weber (under B: The novel and style in prose writing above), pp. 7–31.

K. Speech, voices and dialogue

In an obvious sense, 'speech' in novels refers to the fictional speech put into the mouths of characters, as already explored in this book in Chapters 5 (section 5.4), 9 and 12. This area of study has been explored further through more specialised publications such as Chapman (1994) below, and through the investigation of style in drama, represented in other publications listed. In an extended sense, terms such as 'dialogue' (especially its adjective 'dialogic') and 'voices' have been applied to the 'conversation' between different narrators, characters, genre styles, and so on, which often make a work of fiction a complex of interacting authorial and narratorial presences. A seminal figure here is the Russian philosopher and literary scholar Mikhail Bakhtin, who, like other Soviet-era scholars, was belatedly 'discovered' by the West, and has posthumously influenced stylistic thinking. Although we did not expressly refer to this 'polyphonic' aspect of the language of fiction, arguably much of Chapters 9 and 10 deal with it implicitly, particularly in the concluding section of Chapter 10.

BAKHTIN, M. (1981) *The Dialogic Imagination*, ed. M. Holquist, and trans. C. Emerson and M. Holquist, Austin, University of Texas Press.

BUCK, R.A. and AUSTIN, T.R. (1995) 'Dialogue and power in E.M. Forster's *Howards End*', in Verdonk and Weber (under B: The novel and style in prose writing above), pp. 63–77.

BURTON, D. (1980) *Dialogue and Discourse*, Routledge and Kegan Paul.

CHAPMAN, R. (1994) *Forms of Speech in Victorian Fiction*, Longman.

CULPEPER, J., SHORT, M. and VERDONK, P., eds (1998) *Exploring the Language of Drama: from text to context*, Routledge.

DENTITH, S. (1995) *Bakhtinian Thought: an introductory reader*, Routledge.

HERMAN, V. (1995) *Dramatic Discourse: dialogue as interaction in plays*, Routledge.

THOMAS, B.E. (1997) ' "It's good to talk"? An analysis of a telephone conversation from Evelyn Waugh's *Vile Bodies*', *Language and Literature* **6**(2), 105–119.

TOOLAN, M. (1985) 'Analysing fictional dialogue', *Language and Communication* **5**(3), 193–206.

L. Presentation of speech and thought

The following publications are a sample of the extensive work on speech and thought representation that has been continuing as a strong theme in the stylistics of fiction.

BRAY, J. (2003) *The Epistolary Novel: representations of consciousness*, Routledge.

COOPER, A. (1994) ' "Folk-speech" and "book English": re-presentation of dialect in Hardy's novels', *Language and Literature* **3**(1), 21–41.

FLUDERNIK, M. (1993) *The Fictions of Language and the Languages of Fiction: the linguistic representation of speech and consciousness*, Routledge.

PAGE, N. (1973) *Speech in the English Novel*, Longman.

PALMER, A. (2004) *Fictional Minds*, Lincoln, NE, University of Nebraska Press.

SEMINO, E. and SHORT, M. (2004) *Corpus Stylistics: Speech, Writing and Thought Presentation in a Corpus of English Writing*, Routledge.

SHORT, M., SEMINO, E. and WYNNE, M. (2002) 'Revisiting the notion of faithfulness in discourse presentation using a corpus approach', *Language and Literature* **11**(4), 325–356.

M. Computational, quantitative and corpus methods

For obvious reasons, the computer today is a much more powerful tool for the study of literary style than it was in 1980. For example, there is now a community of 'corpus stylisticians' working with large collections of texts on computer, giving a much more solidly empirical basis to the study of style as discussed in Chapters 2 and 3. The short list below shows something of the range of topics and techniques covered. Semino and Short (2004), referred to in the last section, also use a corpus-based approach, but based on hand-annotation rather than automatic annotation using specially developed software. Biber *et al.* (1998) and Kennedy are useful introductions to corpus linguistics.

BIBER, D., CONRAD, S. and REPPEN, R. (1998) *Corpus Linguistics: investigating language structure and use*, Cambridge, Cambridge University Press.

FINCH, A.M. (1995) 'The imagery of a myth: computer-assisted research on literature', *Style* **19**(4), 511–521. (Followed by a comment by L. Milic.)

HARDY, D.E. (2003) *Narrating Knowledge in Flannery O'Connor's Fiction*, Colombia, University of South Carolina Press.

HOOVER, D. (1999) *Language and Style in* The Inheritors, Lanham, MD, University Press of America.

HORI, M. (2004) *Investigating Dickens' Style: a collocational analysis*, Basingstoke, Palgrave.

KENNEDY, G. (1998) *An Introduction to Corpus Linguistics*, Longman.

MILIC, L.T. (1967) *A Quantitative Approach to the Style of Jonathan Swift*, The Hague, Mouton.

MILIC, L.T. and SLANE, S. (1994) 'Quantitative aspects of genre in the Century of Prose corpus' *Style* **28**(1), 309–340.

STUBBS, M. (2005) Conrad in the computer: examples of quantitative stylistic methods, *Language and Literature*, **14**(1), 5–24.

N. Style of particular authors

One way in which the stylistics of fiction has advanced is in detailed studies of individual authors' work, as illustrated by the following titles. Hardy (2003), Hoover (1999) and Hori (2004), referred to in the above section, are also studies of individual authors. Corpus stylistics works well on large data sets like groups of novels.

ATTRIDGE, D. (2000) *Joyce Effects: on language, theory and history*, Cambridge, Cambridge University Press.

BUCK, R.A. and AUSTIN, T.R. (1995) 'Dialogue and power in E.M. Forster's *Howards End*', in Verdonk and Weber (under B: The novel and style in prose writing above), pp. 63–77.

CHATMAN, S. (1972) *The Later Style of Henry James*, Oxford, Blackwell.

FOWLER, R. (1995) *The Language of George Orwell*, Basingstoke, Macmillan.

PAGE, N. (1972) *The Language of Jane Austen*, Oxford, Blackwell.

PAXMAN, D. (2003) 'Metaphor and knowledge in George Eliot's *Middlemarch*', *Metaphor and Symbol* **18**(2), 107–124.

STOKES, M. (1991) *The Language of Jane Austen*, London, Macmillan.

WALES, K. (1992) *The Language of James Joyce*, Basingstoke, Macmillan.

WATT, I. (1969 [1960]) 'The first paragraph of *The Ambassadors*: an explication', reprinted in LOVE, G.A. and PAYNE, M. (1969) *Contemporary Essays on Style*, Glenview, IL, Scott Foresman, pp. 266–283.

O. Particular topics: characterisation, creativity, etc.

One cannot always assign new work in stylistics and poetics to neat categories. Perhaps one sign of the vitality of stylistics is its potential to spark off interest in areas which are of less central concern for many readers, but which have the potential to illuminate literary style in new ways. The following is a 'mixed bag' of publications inviting the engagement of the reader in a variety of specific ways:

ALLEN, G. (2000) *Intertextuality*, Routledge.
BELLARD-THOMSON, C. (1992) *The Literary Stylistics of French*, Manchester, Manchester University Press.
CARTER, R. (2004) *Language and Creativity*, Routledge.
CULPEPER, J. (2001) *Language and Characterisation: people in plays and other texts*, Longman.
GOODMAN, S. AND O'HALLORAN, K. (2006) *The Art of English: literary creativity*, Basingstoke, Palgrave Macmillan.
FISCHER, O. and NANNY, M., eds (2001) *The Motivated Sign: iconicity in language and literature 2*, Amsterdam, John Benjamins.
NASH, W. (1998) *Language and the Creative Illusion*, Longman.
STOCKWELL, P. (2000) *The Poetics of Science Fiction*, Longman.

P. Pedagogical stylistics, including textbooks for students

In the study of language-in-literature, pedagogy has always had a high priority, whether in the teaching of native-speaker or second-language students of English. The following list includes introductory textbooks for students, as well as publications expounding pedagogical issues and methods. *Language and Style* is a web-based introductory stylistics course which is freely available, and *Language and Literature* **15**(3) describes pedagogical investigations based on it. Carter (1982), listed under section A above, is also relevant here.

CARTER, R. and LONG, M.N. (1987) *The Web of Words: exploring literature through language* (Student and Teacher books), Cambridge University Press.
CARTER, R. and MCRAE, J. (1996) *Language, Literature and the Learner: creative classroom practice*, Longman.
HUGHES, R. (1996) *English in Speech and Writing: investigating language and literature*, Routledge.
LANGUAGE AND LITERATURE (2006) **15**(3) *Special Issue: The* Language and Style *Pedagogical Investigations*.
LANGUAGE AND STYLE (www.lancs.ac.uk/fass/projects/stylistics/start.htm).
SANGER, K. (1998) *The Language of Fiction*, Routledge.
SHORT, M. (1983 [1982]) 'Stylistics and the teaching of literature: with an example from Joyce's *Portrait of the Artist as a Young Man*', in Brumfit, C.J. ed., *Teaching Literature Overseas: language-based approaches*, ELT Document 115, Pergamon Press and the British Council.

SHORT, M. (1986) 'Literature and language teaching and the nature of language' in D'HAEN, T., ed., *Linguistics and the Study of Literature*, Amsterdam, Rodopi, pp. 152–186.

SHORT, M. (1993) 'Stylistics upside down: using stylistics in the teaching of language and literature' *Textus* **6**, 3–30 [Reprinted in CARTER, R. and MCRAE, J. (1996) above].

SHORT, M. ed. (1989) *Reading, Analysing and Teaching Literature*, Longman.

SIMPSON, P. (1992) 'Teaching stylistics: cohesion and narrative structure in a short story by Ernest Hemingway', *Language and Literature* **1**(1), 47–67.

SIMPSON, P. (1997) *Language through Literature*, Routledge.

SIMPSON, P. (2004) *Stylistics: a resource book for students*, Routledge.

STYLE (2003) **37**(1) *Special Issue: Pedagogy of Style and Stylistics*.

TOOLAN, M. (1998) *Language in Literature: an introduction to stylistics*, Arnold.

WIDDOWSON, H. (1975) *Stylistics and the Teaching of Literature*, Longman.

WIDDOWSON, H. (1992) *Practical Stylistics* Oxford, Oxford University Press.

Q. Relevant publications strictly outside the domain of stylistics and style in fiction

As a postscript, we mention the following, as resources useful for the student approaching fiction from a linguistic viewpoint:

CARTER, R. and NASH, W. (1990) *Seeing through Language: a guide to styles of English writing*, Oxford, Blackwell.

DAVIES, D. (2005) *Varieties of Modern English*, Longman.

GREENBAUM, S. and QUIRK, R. (1990) *A Student's Grammar of the English Language*, Longman.

LEECH, G. (1969) *A Linguistic Guide to English Poetry*, Longman.

NASH, W. (1992) *An Uncommon Tongue*, Routledge.

PILKINGTON, A. (2000) *Poetic Effects: a relevance theory perspective*, Amsterdam, John Benjamins.

Bibliography*

ASTON, G. and BURNARD, L. (1998) *The BNC Handbook: exploring the British National Corpus with SARA*, Edinburgh, Edinburgh University Press.

AUSTIN, J.L. (1962) *How To Do Things With Words*, Oxford, Clarendon Press.

BACH, E. and HARMS, R. (1968) *Universals in Linguistic Theory*, New York, Holt, Rinehart & Winston.

BAILEY, R.W. (1969) 'Statistics and style: a historical survey' in DOLEŽEL, L. and BAILEY, R.W. (1969), 217–236.

BAL, M. (1997 [1985]) *Narratology: introduction to the theory of narrative*, New York, University of Toronto Press.

BALLY, C. (1951) *Traité de Stylistique Française*, 3rd edn, Paris, Klincksieck.

BANFIELD, A. (1973) 'Narrative style and the grammar of direct and indirect speech', *Foundations of Language*, **10**, 1–39.

BANN, S. and BOWLT, J.E., eds and trans. (1973) *Russian Formalism: a collection of articles and texts in translation*, Edinburgh, Scottish Academic Press.

BARTHES, R. (1957) *Mythologies*, Paris, Seuil.

BARTHES, R. (1967) *Writing Degree Zero*, trans. A. Lavers and C. Smith, Cape.

BARTHES, R. (1971) 'Style and its image' in CHATMAN, S. (1971a), 3–15.

BARTHES, R. (1977 [1966]) 'Introduction to the structural analysis of narratives' (translation of Barthes 1966), in BARTHES, R. (1977) *Image-Music-Text*, Fontana, 79–124.

BARZUN, J. (1975) *Simple and Direct*, New York, Harper & Row.

BATESON, F.W. and SHAKEVITCH, B. (1962) 'Katherine Mansfield's *The Fly*: a critical exercise', *Essays in Criticism*, **12**, 39–53.

BAUGH, A.C. and CABLE, T. (2002) *A History of the English Language*, 2nd edn, Routledge & Kegan Paul.

BERKOWITZ, L., ed. (1969) *Advances in Experimental Social Psychology*, Vol. 4, New York, Academic Press.

BEX, T., BURKE, M. and STOCKWELL, P., eds (2000) *Contextualised Stylistics*, Amsterdam and Atlanta, GA, Rodopi.

---

* Place of publication includes London unless otherwise indicated.

Style in Fiction

ce

BIBER, D. (1988) *Variation Across Speech and Writing*, Cambridge, Cambridge University Press.

BIBER, D., CONRAD, S. and REPPEN, R. (1998) *Corpus Linguistics: investigating language structure and use*, Cambridge, Cambridge University Press.

BIBER, D., JOHANSSON, S., LEECH, G., CONRAD, S. and FINEGAN, E. (1999) *Longman Grammar of Spoken and Written English*, Longman.

BIRCH, D. (1989) *Language, Literature and Critical Practice*, Routledge.

BIRCH, D. (1991) *The Language of Drama*, Macmillan.

BLOCH, B. (1953) 'Linguistic structure and linguistic analysis' in HILL, A.A., ed., *Report of the Fourth Annual Round Table Meeting on Linguistics and Language Study*, Washington DC, Georgetown University Press.

BLOOMFIELD, L. (1935) *Language*, UK edn, Allen & Unwin.

BOCKTING, I. (1995) *Character and Personality in the Novels of William Faulkner*, Lanham, MD, University Press of America.

BOLINGER, D. (1975) *Aspects of Language*, New York, Harcourt.

BOLINGER, D. (1977) *Meaning and Form*, Longman.

BOLINGER, D. (1980) *Language – the Loaded Weapon*, Longman.

BONHEIM, H. (1982) *The Narrative Modes*, Cambridge, D.S. Brewer.

BONHEIM, H. (1990) *Literary Systematics*, D.S. Brewer.

BOOTH, W.C. (1961) *The Rhetoric of Fiction*, Chicago, Chicago University Press.

BORTOLUSSI, M. and DIXON, P. (2003) *Psychonarratology: foundations for the empirical study of literary response*, Cambridge, Cambridge University Press.

BRADFORD, R. (1993) *A Linguistic History of English Poetry*, Routledge.

BRADFORD, R. (1997) *Stylistics*, Routledge.

BRADLEY, A.C. (1904) *Shakespearean Tragedy*, Macmillan.

BRÉMOND, C. (1973) *Logique du Récit*, Paris, du Seuil.

BROOK, G.L. (1958) *A History of the English Language*, Deutsch.

BROOK, G.L. (1970) *The Language of Dickens*, Deutsch.

BROWN, P., and LEVINSON, S. (1987) *Politeness: Some Universals of Language Use*, Cambridge, Cambridge University Press.

BRUMFIT, C.J. and CARTER, R.A. (1986) *Literature and Language Teaching*, Oxford, Oxford University Press.

BURGESS, A. (1973) *Joysprick: an introduction to the language of James Joyce*, Deutsch.

BURTON, D. (1980) *Dialogue and Discourse: a sociolinguistic approach to modern drama dialogue and naturally occurring conversation*, Kegan Paul.

CARTER, R.A., ed. (1982) *Language and Literature*, Allen & Unwin.

CARTER, R.A. and MCRAE, J. (1996) *Language, Literature and the Learner: creative classroom practice*, Longman.

CARTER, R.A. and SIMPSON, P., eds (1989) *Language, Discourse and Literature*, Unwin Hyman.

CASSIRER, E. (1944) *An Essay on Man*, New Haven, CN, Yale University Press.

CHAFE, W. (1970) *Meaning and the Structure of Language*, Chicago, University of Chicago Press.

382

Bibliography

CHATMAN, S. (1969) 'New ways of analysing narrative structures', *Language and Style*, **2**, 3–36.

CHATMAN, S., ed. (1971a) *Literary Style: a symposium*, Oxford University Press.

CHATMAN, S. (1971b) 'The semantics of style', in KRISTEVA, J. *et al.* eds (1971), 399–422.

CHATMAN, S. (1972) *The Later Style of Henry James*, Oxford, Blackwell.

CHATMAN, S. (1978) *Story and Discourse Narrative Structure in Fiction and Film*, Ithaca, NY, Cornell University Press.

CHOMSKY, N. (1957) *Syntactic Structures*, The Hague, Mouton.

CHOMSKY, N. (1972) *Studies on Semantics in Generative Grammar*, The Hague, Mouton.

CHOMSKY, N. (1976) *Reflections on Language*, Maurice Temple Smith.

CLARK, H.H. and CLARK, E.V. (1977) *Psychology and Language*, New York, Harcourt Brace Jovanovich.

CLUYSENAAR, A. (1976) *Introduction to Literary Stylistics*, Batsford.

COLE, P. and MORGAN, J., eds (1975) *Syntax and Semantics*, III: *Speech Acts*, New York, Academic Press.

COOK, G. (1992) *Discourse of Advertising*, Routledge.

COOK, G. (1994) *Discourse and Literature: the interplay of form and mind*, Oxford, Oxford University Press.

CORBETT, E.P.J. (1969) 'A method of analyzing prose style with a demonstration analysis of Swift's *A Modest Proposal*', in LOVE, G.A. and PAYNE, M. (1969), 81–98.

COULTHARD, M. (1977) *An Introduction to Discourse Analysis*, Longman.

CULLER, J. (1975) *Structuralist Poetics*, Routledge & Kegan Paul.

CULPEPER, J. (2001) *Language and Characterisation: people in plays and other texts*, Longman.

CULPEPER, J. (2002) 'A cognitive stylistic approach to characterisation', in SEMINO, E. and CULPEPER, J. (2002), 251–278.

CULPEPER, J., SHORT, M. and VERDONK, P., eds (1998) *Exploring the Language of Drama: from text to context*, Routledge.

CUTLER, A. (1976) 'Beyond parsing and lexical look-up: an enriched description of auditory sentence comprehension', in WALKER, E. and WALES, R., eds (1976), 133–150.

DANCYGIER, B. (2005) 'Blending and narrative viewpoint: Jonathan Raban's travels through mental spaces', *Language and Literature*, **14** (2), 99–127.

DEW, D. and JENSEN, P. (1977) *Phonetic Processing: the Dynamics of Speech*, Columbus, Ohio, Merrill.

DOLEŽEL, L. and BAILEY, R.W. (1969) *Statistics and Style*, New York, Elsevier.

DOUTHWAITE, J. (2000) *Towards a Linguistic Theory of Foregrounding*, Turin, Edizioni dell'Orso.

DRY, H.A. (1981) 'Sentence aspect and the movement of narrative time', *Text*, **1** (3), 233–240.

DRY, H.A. (1983) 'The movement of narrative time', *Journal of Literary Semantics*, **12** (2), 19–53.

DUCHAN, J.F., BRUDER, G.A. and HEWITT, L.E., eds (1995) *Deixis in Narrative: a cognitive science perspective*, Hillsdale, NJ, Lawrence Erlbaum.

ECO, U. (1990) *The Limits of Interpretation*, Bloomington, IN, Indiana University Press.

ELLEGÅRD, A. (1978) *The Syntactic Structure of English Texts: a computer-based study of four kinds of text in the Brown University Corpus*, Gothenburg Studies in English, 43.

EMMOTT, C. (1997) *Narrative Comprehension: a discourse perspective*, Oxford, Oxford University Press.

EMMOTT, C., SANFORD, A.J. and MORROW, L.I. (2006) 'Capturing the attention of readers? Stylistic and psychological perspectives on the use and effect of text fragmentation in narratives', *Journal of Literary Semantics*, **35** (1), 1–30.

EMPSON, W. (1953) *Seven Types of Ambiguity*, 3rd edn, Chatto.

ENKVIST, N.E. (1964) 'On defining style', in ENKVIST, N.E., SPENCER, J. and GREGORY, M.J. (1964), 1–56.

ENKVIST, N.E. (1973) *Linguistic Stylistics*, The Hague and Paris, Mouton.

ENKVIST, N.E., SPENCER, J. and GREGORY, M.J. (1964) *Linguistics and Style*, Oxford University Press.

EPSTEIN, E.L. (1975) 'The self-reflexive artefact: the function of mimesis in an approach to a theory of value for literature', in FOWLER, R. (1975), 40–78.

EPSTEIN, E.L. (1978) *Language and Style*, Methuen.

ERLICH, V. (1969) *Russian Formalism: history, doctrine*, 3rd edn, The Hague, Mouton.

ERVIN-TRIPP, S.M. (1969) 'Sociolinguistics', in BERKOWITZ, L. (1969), 93–107.

FAIRCLOUGH, N. (1989) *Language and Power*, Longman.

FAIRCLOUGH, N. (1995) *Critical Discourse Analysis: the critical study of language*, Longman.

FAIRCLOUGH, N. (1996) 'A reply to Henry Widdowson's "Discourse analysis: a critical view"', *Language and Literature*, **5** (1), 49–56.

FAIRCLOUGH, N. (2000) *New Labour, New Language?*, Routledge.

FAIRCLOUGH, N. (2003) *Analysing Discourse: textual analysis for social research*, Longman.

FAIRLEY, I.R. (1988) 'The reader's need for conventions: when a mushroom is not a mushroom', in VAN PEER, W., ed. (1988), 292–316.

FAUCONNIER, G. (1985) *Mental Spaces: aspects of meaning construction in natural language*, Cambridge, MA, MIT Press.

FAUCONNIER, G. and TURNER, M. (2002) *The Way we Think: conceptual blending and the mind's hidden complexities*, New York, Basic Books.

FILLMORE, C.J. (1968) 'The case for case', in BACH, E. and HARMS, R., eds (1968), 1–88.

FISH, S.E. (1970) 'Literature and the reader: affective stylistics', *New Literary History*, **2**, 123–62.

FISH, S. (1996 [1973]) 'What is stylistics and why are they saying such terrible things about it?', in WEBER, J.-J. (1996), 94–116.

FLUDERNIK, M. (1993) *The Fictions of Language and the Languages of Fiction*, Routledge.

FLUDERNIK, M. (1996) *Towards a 'Natural' Narratology*, Routledge.

FORSTER, E.M. (1974 [1927]) *Aspects of the Novel*, Arnold.

FOWLER, R., ed. (1966) *Essays on Style and Language*, Routledge & Kegan Paul.

FOWLER, R. (1971) *The Languages of Literature*, Routledge & Kegan Paul.

FOWLER, R. (1975) *Style and Structure in Literature: essays in the new stylistics*, Oxford, Blackwell.

FOWLER, R. (1977) *Linguistics and the Novel*, Methuen.

FOWLER, R. (1991) *Language in the News: discourse and ideology in the press*, Routledge.

FOWLER, R. (1996 [1986]) *Linguistic Criticism*, 2nd edn, Oxford, Oxford University Press.

FOWLER, R. and MERCER, P. (1971) 'Criticism and the language of literature: some traditions and trends in Great Britain', in FOWLER, R. (1971), 101–123.

FOWLER, R., HODGE, R., KRESS, G. and TREW, T. (1979) *Language and Control*, Routledge & Kegan Paul.

FREEBORN, D. (1996) *Style: text analysis and linguistic criticism*, Macmillan.

FREEMAN, D.C. (1970) *Linguistics and Literary Style*, New York, Holt, Rinehart & Winston.

FREEMAN, D.C., ed. (1981) *Essays in Modern Stylistics*, Methuen.

FREEMAN, D.C. (forthcoming) *Shakespearean Metaphor: a cognitive approach*.

FREEMAN, M.H. (2005) 'The poem as complex blend: conceptual mappings of metaphor in Sylvia Plath's "The Applicant"', *Language and Literature*, **14** (1), 25–44.

FRYE, N. (1957) *The Anatomy of Criticism*, Princeton, NJ, Princeton University Press.

GALBRAITH, M. (1995) 'Deictic shift theory and the poetics of involvement in narrative', in DUCHAN, J.F., BRUDER, G.A. and HEWITT, I.E. (eds) (1995), 19–59.

GARVIN, P.L., ed. and trans. (1958) *A Prague School Reader on Esthetics, Literary Structure and Style*, Washington, DC, American University Language Centre.

GAVINS, J. (2003) 'Too much blague? An exploration of the text worlds of Donald Barthelme's *Snow White*', in GAVINS, J. and STEEN, G. (2003), 129–144.

GAVINS, J. and STEEN, G., eds (2003) *Cognitive Poetics in Practice*, Routledge.

GERRIG, R. (1993) *Experiencing Narrative Worlds: on the psychological activities of reading*, Yale, Yale University Press.

GHISELIN, B. (1952) *The Creative Process: a Symposium*, New York, New American Library.

GIGLIOLI, P.P. (1975) *Language and Social Context*, Harmondsworth, Penguin.

GIMSON, A.C. (1980) *An Introduction to the Pronunciation of English*, 3rd edn, Edward Arnold.

GOLDENVEIZER, A.B., ed. (1923) *Talks with Tolstoy*, trans. S. Kotelicinsky and V. Woolf, Richmond, L. and V. Woolf.

GREENBAUM, S. and QUIRK, R. (1990) *A Student's Grammar of The English Language*, Longman.

GREENBERG, J.H., ed. (1963a) 'Some universals of grammar with particular reference to the order of meaningful elements', in GREENBERG, J. (1963b), 58–90.

GREENBERG, J.H., ed. (1963b) *Universals of Language*, 2nd edn, Cambridge, MA, MIT Press.

GREGORY, M. (1965) 'Old Bailey speech in *A Tale of Two Cities*', *Review of English Literature*, **6**, 42–55.

GRICE, H.P. (1975) 'Logic and conversation', in COLE, P. and MORGAN, J., eds (1975), pp. 41–58.

GUTWINSKI, W. (1976) *Cohesion in Literary Texts*, The Hague, Mouton.

HAKEMULDER, J. (2000) *The Moral Laboratory: experiments examining the effects of reading literature on social perception and moral self-concept*, Philadelphia, Benjamins.

HALLIDAY, M.A.K. (1967) 'Notes on transitivity and theme in English: Part I', *Journal of Linguistics*, **3**, 37–81.

HALLIDAY, M.A.K. (1968) 'Notes on transitivity and theme in English: Part II', *Journal of Linguistics*, **3**, 199–244.

HALLIDAY, M.A.K. (1971) 'Linguistic function and literary style: an inquiry into William Golding's *The Inheritors*', in CHATMAN, S. (1971a), 330–365.

HALLIDAY, M.A.K. (1973) *Explorations in the Functions of Language*, Edward Arnold.

HALLIDAY, M.A.K. and HASAN, R. (1976) *Cohesion in English*, Longman.

HALLIDAY, M.A.K. and MATTHIESSEN, C. (2004) *An Introduction to Functional Grammar*, Arnold.

HARDY, D.E. (2003) *Narrating Knowledge in Flannery O'Connor's Fiction*, Colombia, University of South Carolina Press.

HARDY, D.E. (2005) 'Technology and stylistics: the web connection', in CALDAS-COULTHARD, C.R. and TOOLAN, M., eds (2005) *The Writer's Craft, the Culture's Technology*, Amsterdam and New York, Rodopi, 195–208.

HASAN, R. (1989) *Linguistics, Language and Verbal Art*, Oxford, Oxford University Press.

HAWKES, T. (1972) *Metaphor*, Methuen.

HAWKES, T. (1977) *Structuralism and Semiotics*, Methuen.

HENDRICKS, W.O. (1972) 'The structural study of narration', *Poetics*, **3**, 100–123 (also reprinted in HENDRICKS 1973b, 152–174).

HENDRICKS, W.O. (1973a) 'Methodology of structural analysis', *Semiotica*, **7**, 163–186 (also reprinted in HENDRICKS 1973b, 175–195).

HENDRICKS, W.O. (1973b) *Essays on Semiolinguistics and Verbal Art*, The Hague, Mouton.

HERMAN, D. (2002) *Story Logic: problems and possibilities of narrative*, Lincoln and London, University of Nebraska Press.

HERMAN, D., ed. (2003) *Narrative Theory and the Cognitive Sciences*, Stanford, CA, Center for the Study of Language and Information.

HERMAN, V. (1995) *Dramatic Discourse: dialogue as interaction in plays*, Routledge.

HIDALGO DOWNING, L. (2000) *Negation, Text Worlds and Discourse: the pragmatics of fiction*, Stanford, CA, Ablex.

HILDICK, W. (1965) *Word for Word: a study of authors' alterations with exercises*, Faber.

HOCKETT, C.F. (1958) *A Course in Modern Linguistics*, New York, Macmillan.

HOEY, M. (1983) *On the Surface of Discourse*, George Allen and Unwin.

HOEY, M. (1991) *Patterns of Lexis in Text*, Oxford, Oxford University Press.

HOOVER, D. (1999) *Language and Style in* The Inheritors, Lanham, MD, University Press of America.

HORI, M. (2004) *Investigating Dickens' Style*, Basingstoke and New York, Palgrave Macmillan.

HOUGH, G. (1969) *Style and Stylistics*, Routledge & Kegan Paul.

IHWE, J.F. (1976) 'The Philosophy of Literary Criticism Reconsidered', *Poetics*, 5, 339–372.

ISER, W. (1974) *The Implied Reader: patterns of communication in prose fiction from Bunyan to Beckett*, Baltimore, MD, Johns Hopkins University Press.

ISER, W. (1978) *The Act of Reading: a theory of aesthetic response*, Longman.

JAKOBSON, R. (1961) 'Closing statement: linguistics and poetics', in SEBEOK, T.A. (1961), 350–377.

JEFFRIES, L. (1993) *The Language of Twentieth Century Poetry*, Macmillan.

JONES, C. (1968) 'Varieties of speech presentation in Conrad's *The Secret Agent*', *Lingua*, 20, 162–176.

JONES, D. (1977) *Everyman's English Pronouncing Dictionary*, rev. and ed. by GIMSON, A.C., Dent.

KACHRU, B.B. and STAHLKE, F.W. (1972) *Current Trends in Stylistics*, Edmonton, Alberta, and Champaign, IL, Champaign Linguistic Research Inc.

KELLY, H.H. (1972) 'The processes of causal attribution', *American Psychologist*, 28, 107–28.

KENNEDY, C. (1976) 'Systemic grammar and its use in literary analysis', *Journal of the Midlands Association of Linguistic Studies*, new series 1, 17–36.

KINTSCH, W. and VAN DIJK, T. (1983) *Strategies of Discourse Comprehension*, New York, Academic Press.

KNIGHTS, L.C. (1963 [1946]) 'How many children had Lady Macbeth?', in *Explorations: essays in criticism mainly on the literature of the seventeenth century*, Chatto, 1–39.

KOESTLER, A. (1964) *The Act of Creation*, Hutchinson.

KRISTEVA, J., REY-DEBOVE, J. and UMIKER, D.J. eds (1971) *Essays in Semiotics*, The Hague, Mouton.

KUČERA, H. and FRANCIS, W.N. (1967) *Computational Analysis of Present-day American English*, Providence, Brown University Press.

LABOV, W. (1972) *Language in the Inner City*, Philadelphia, University of Pennsylvania Press.

LABOV, W. (1995) 'Speech actions and reactions in personal narrative', *Georgetown University Round Table on Languages and Linguistics*, 219–247.

LABOV, W. and WALETSKY, J. (1967) 'Narrative analysis: oral versions of personal experience', in HELMS, J., ed. *Essays on the Verbal and Visual Arts*, Seattle, WA, University of Washington Press, 12–44.

LAKOFF, G. and JOHNSON, M. (1980) *Metaphors we Live by*, Chicago, University of Chicago Press.

LAKOFF, G. and TURNER, M. (1989) *More than Cool Reason: a field guide to poetic metaphor*, Chicago, University of Chicago Press.

LASCELLES, M. (1965) *Jane Austen and Her Art*, 2nd edn, Oxford University Press.

LAWRENCE, C. (1978) 'Speech representation in the seventeenth-century legal deposition with special reference to Pott's *Wonderfull Discoverie of Witches in the Countie of Lancaster*', unpublished MA project, University of Lancaster.

LEASKA, M.A. (1970) *Virginia Woolf's Lighthouse: a study in critical method*, Hogarth Press.

LEE, B. (1966) 'The new criticism and the language of poetry' in FOWLER, R. (1966), 29–52.

LEECH, G. (1965) ' "This Bread I Break": language and interpretation', *Review of English Literature*, **6** (2), 66–75; reprinted in FREEMAN, D.C., ed. (1970), 119–128.

LEECH, G. (1969) *A Linguistic Guide to English Poetry*, Longman.

LEECH, G. (1974) *Semantics*, Harmondsworth, Penguin.

LEECH, G. (1977a) *Language and Tact*, Linguistic Agency, University of Trier, Series A, paper 46.

LEECH, G. (1977b) 'Literary criticism and linguistic description', *Dutch Quarterly Review of Anglo-American Letters*, **7** (1), 2–22.

LEECH, G. (1980) *Explorations in Semantics and Pragmatics*, Amsterdam, John Benjamins.

LEECH, G. (1983) *Principles of Pragmatics*, Longman.

LEECH, G. and SHORT, M.H. (1981) *Style in Fiction*, Longman.

LEECH, G. and SVARTVIK, J. (2002 [1975]) *A Communicative Grammar of English*, 3rd edn, Longman.

LÉVI-STRAUSS, C. (1963) 'The structural study of myth', in LÉVI-STRAUSS, C., *Structural Anthropology*, New York and London, Basic Books, 206–231.

LÉVI-STRAUSS, C. (1964) *Structural Anthropology*, trans. C. Jacobsen and B. Grundfest Schoepf, Basic Books.

LÉVI-STRAUSS, C. (1970) *The Raw and the Cooked*, trans. J. and D. Weightman, Jonathan Cape.

LEVIN, H. (1966) *The Gates of Horn*, New York, Oxford University Press.

LEVIN, S.R. (1965) 'Internal and external deviation in poetry', *Word*, **21**, 225–237.

LODGE, D. (1966) *Language of Fiction*, Routledge & Kegan Paul.

LODGE, D. (1970) 'Hemingway's clean, well-lighted, puzzling place', *Essays in Criticism*, **21**, 33–56; reprinted in LODGE, D. (1971), 184–202.

LODGE, D. (1971) *The Novelist at the Crossroads*, Routledge & Kegan Paul.

LOUW, W. (1993) 'Irony in the text or insincerity in the writer?: the diagnostic potential of semantic prosodies', in BAKER, M., FRANCIS, G. and TOGNINI-BONELLI, E. eds, *Text and Technology: in honour of John Sinclair*, Amsterdam and Philadelphia, John Benjamins, 157–176.

LOUW, W. (1997) 'The role of corpora in critical literary appreciation', in WICHMANN, A. *et al.*, eds, *Teaching and Language Corpora*, Longman, 240–252.

LOUWERSE, M. and VAN PEER, W. (2002) *Thematics: interdisciplinary studies*, Amsterdam and Philadelphia, John Benjamins.

LOVE, G.A. and PAYNE, M. (1969) *Contemporary Essays on Style*, Glenview, IL, Scott Foresman.

LYONS, J. (1970) *Chomsky*, Fontana.

LYONS, J. (1977) *Semantics*, 2 vols, Cambridge University Press.

MACKAY, R. (1996) 'Mything the point: a critique of objective stylistics', *Language and Communication*, **16** (1), 81–93.

MACKAY, R. (1999) 'There goes the other foot: a reply to Short *et al.*', *Language and Literature*, **8** (1), 59–66.

MARCHAND, H. (1969) *The Categories and Types of Present-Day English Word-Formation*, 2nd edn, Munich, C.H. Beck.

MARGOLIN, U. (1983) 'Characterization in narrative: some theoretical prolegomena', Neophilologus, **67**, 1–14.

MARGOLIN, U. (1989) 'Structuralist approaches to character in narrative: the state of the art', *Semiotica*, **75** (1/2), 1–24.

MARGOLIN, U. (1990) 'The what, the when and the how of being a character in a literary narrative', *Style*, **24** (3), 453–468.

MARGOLIN, U. (1996) 'Telling our story: on "we" literary narratives', *Language and Literature*, **5** (2), 115–133.

MATEJKA, L. and POMORSKA, K., eds (1971) *Readings in Russian Poetics: formalist and structuralist views*, Cambridge, MA, MIT Press.

MCDOWELL, A. (1973) 'Fielding's rendering of speech in *Joseph Andrews* and *Tom Jones*', *Language and Style*, **6**, 83–96.

MCENERY, T. and WILSON, A. (2001 [1996]) *Corpus Linguistics*, 2nd edn Edinburgh, Edinburgh University Press.

MCHALE, B. (1978) 'Free indirect discourse: a survey of recent accounts', *Poetics and Theory of Literature*, **3**, 235–287.

MEYER, B.J.F. (1975) *The Organisation of Prose and Its Effects on Meaning,* Amsterdam, North-Holland.

MILIC, L.T. (1967) *A Quantitative Approach to the Style of Jonathan Swift,* The Hague, Mouton & Co.

MUKAŘOVSKÝ, J. (1958) 'Standard language and poetic language', in GARVIN, P.L. (1958), 17–30; reprinted in FREEMAN, D.C. (1970), 40–56.

NASH, W. (1982) 'On a passage from Lawrence's "Odour of Chrysanthemums"', in CARTER, R. (1982), 101–120.

NÜNNING, A. (1993) 'Renaissance eines anthropomorphisierten passepartouts oder nachruf auf ein literaturkritisches phaenomenon? Überlegungen und alternativen zum konzept des implied author', *Deutsche Vierteljahrsschrift,* **67** (1), 1–25.

OHMANN, R. (1964) 'Generative grammars and the concept of literary style', *Word,* **20**, 423–439; reprinted in FREEMAN, D.C. (1970), 258–278.

OHMANN, R. (1966) 'Literature as sentences', *College English,* **27**, 261–267; reprinted in LOVE, G.A. and PAYNE, M. (1969), 149–157.

OHMANN, R. (1971a) 'Speech, action and style', in CHATMAN, S. (1971a), 241–254.

OHMANN, R. (1971b) 'Speech acts and the definition of literature', *Philosophy and Rhetoric,* **4**, 1–19.

OHMANN, R. (1972) 'Instrumental style: notes on the theory of speech as action', in KACHRU, B.B. and STAHLKE, F.W. (1972), 115–142.

PAGE, N. (1972) *The Language of Jane Austen,* Oxford University Press.

PAGE, N. (1973) *Speech in the English Novel,* Longman.

PAVEL, T.G. (1985) *The Poetics of Plot: the case of Renaissance drama,* Manchester, Manchester University Press.

PAVEL, T.G. (1986) *Fictional Worlds,* Cambridge, MA, Harvard University Press.

PERSON, R.F. (1999) *Structure and Meaning in Conversation and Literature,* Lanham, MD, University Press of America.

PFISTER, M. (1988) *The Theory and Analysis of Drama,* Cambridge, Cambridge University Press.

PRATT, M.L. (1977) *Toward a Speech Act Theory of Literary Discourse,* Bloomington, IN, Indiana University Press.

PRINCE, G. (1973) *A Grammar of Stories,* The Hague, Mouton.

PRINCE, G. (1982) *Narratology: the form and functioning of narrative,* Berlin, Mouton.

PROPP, V. (1968 [1928]) *Morphology of the Folktale,* trans. L. Scott, Austin, TX, University of Texas Press.

QUIRK, R. (1959) *Charles Dickens and Appropriate Language,* Durham, University of Durham Press.

QUIRK, R. (1968) *Essays on English Language, Medieval and Modern,* Longman.

QUIRK, R. (1974) *The Linguist and the English Language,* Edward Arnold.

QUIRK, R., SVARTVIK, J., DUCKWORTH, A.P., RUSIECTI, J.P.L. and COLIN, A.J.T. (1968) 'Studies in the correspondence of prosodic to grammatical features in English', in QUIRK, R. (1968), 120–135.

QUIRK, R., GREENBAUM, S., LEECH, G. and SVARTVIK, J. (1985) *A Comprehensive Grammar of the English Language*, Longman.

RANSOM, J.C. (1938a) 'Poetry: a note on ontology', in RANSOM, J.C. (1938b), 111–142.

RANSOM, J.C. (1938b) *The World's Body*, New York, C. Scribner's Sons.

RICHARDS, I.A. (1929) *Practical Criticism: a study of literary judgment*, Routledge.

RICOUER, P. (1983) *Temps et Récit I*, Paris, Seuil.

RIFFATERRE, M. (1971) *Essais de Stylistique Structural*, trans. D. Delas, Paris, Flammarion.

RIMMON-KENAN, S. (2002 [1983]) *Narrative Fiction: contemporary poetics*, Routledge.

RINGBOM, H., ed. (1975) *Style and Text: studies presented to Nils Erik Enkvist*, Stockholm, Språkforlaget Skriptor AB and Åbo Akademi.

ROEH, I. and NIR, R. (1990) 'Speech presentation in the Israel radio news: ideological constraints and rhetorical strategies', *Text*, **10** (3), 225–244.

RONEN, R. (1994) *Possible Worlds in Literary Theory*, Cambridge, Cambridge University Press.

RUMELHART, D.E. (1995) 'Notes on a schema for stories', in BOBROW, D.G. and COLLINS, A., *Representation and Understanding: studies in cognitive science*, New York, San Francisco and London, Academic Press, 211–236.

RYAN, M-L. (1991) *Possible Worlds, Artificial Intelligence, and Narrative Theory*, Bloomington, IN, Indiana University Press.

SAUSSURE, F. DE (1959) *Course in General Linguistics*, trans. W. Baskin, New York, McGraw-Hill.

SEARLE, J.R. (1969) *Speech Acts*, Cambridge University Press.

SEARLE, J.R. (1975a) 'What is a speech act?' in GIGLIOLI, P.P., ed. (1975), 136–154.

SEARLE, J.R. (1975b) 'The logical status of fictional discourse', *New Literary History*, **6**, 319–332.

SEBEOK, T.A., ed. (1961) *Style in Language*, Cambridge, MA, MIT Press.

SEMINO, E. (1997) *Language and World Creation in Poems and Other Texts*, Longman.

SEMINO, E. (2002) 'A cognitive approach to mind style in narrative fiction', in SEMINO, E. and CULPEPER, J. (2002), 95–122.

SEMINO, E. (2006) 'Blending and characters' mental functioning in Virginia Woolf's "Lappin and Lapinova"', *Language and Literature*, **15** (1), 55–72.

SEMINO, E. and CULPEPER, J. (2002) *Cognitive Stylistics: language and cognition in text analysis*, Amsterdam and Philadelphia, John Benjamins.

SEMINO, E. and SHORT, M. (2004) *Corpus Stylistics: speech, writing and thought presentation in a corpus of English writing*, Routledge.

SEMINO, E. and SWINDLEHURST, K. (1996) 'Metaphor and mind style in Ken Kesey's *One Flew Over the Cuckoo's Nest*', *Style*, **30** (1), 143–166.

SEMINO, E., SHORT, M. and CULPEPER, J. (1997) 'Using a computer corpus to test a model of speech and thought presentation', *Poetics*, **25**, 17–43.

391

SEMINO, E., SHORT, M. and WYNNE, M. (1999) 'Hypothetical words and thoughts in contemporary British narratives', *Narrative*, **7** (3), 307–334.

SHORT, M. (1989) *Reading, Analysing and Teaching Literature*, Longman.

SHORT, M. (1996) *Exploring the Language of Poems, Plays and Prose*, Longman.

SHORT, M. (1999) 'Graphological deviation, style variation and point of view in *Marabou Story Nightmares* by Irvine Welsh', *Journal of Literary Studies/ Tydskrif vir Literatuurwetenskap*, **15** (3/4), 305–323.

SHORT, M. (2003) 'A corpus-based approach to speech, thought and writing presentation', in WILSON, A., RAYSON, P. and MCENERY, T., eds, *Corpus Linguistics by the Lune: a festschrift for Geoffrey Leech*, Frankfurt/Main, Peter Lang, 242–271.

SHORT, M. and SEMINO, E. (forthcoming) 'Stylistics and evaluation', in VAN PEER, W., ed., *The Quality of Literature: studies in literary evaluation*, John Benjamins.

SHORT, M. and VAN PEER, W. (1999) 'A reply to Mackay', *Language and Literature*, **8** (3), 270–275.

SHORT, M., CULPEPER, J. and SEMINO, E. (2000) 'Language and context: Jane Gardam's *Bilgewater*', in BEX, T., BURKE, M. and STOCKWELL, P. (2000), 110–131.

SHORT, M., FREEMAN, D.C., VAN PEER, W. and SIMPSON, P. (1998) 'Stylistics, criticism and mythrepresentation again: squaring the circle with Ray Mackay's subjective solution for all problems', *Language and Literature*, **7** (1), 39–50.

SHORT, M., SEMINO, E. and CULPEPER, J. (1996) 'Using a corpus for stylistics research: speech and thought presentation', in THOMAS, J. and SHORT, M.H. (1996), 110–131.

SHORT, M., SEMINO, E. and WYNNE, M. (1999) 'Reading reports: discourse presentation in a corpus of narratives, with special reference to news reports', in DILLER, H-J. and STRATMANN, E. O-G., eds, *English via Various Media*, Heidelberg, Winter, 39–65.

SHORT, M., SEMINO, E. and WYNNE, M. (2002) 'Revisiting the notion of faithfulness in discourse report/(re)presentation using a corpus approach', *Language and Literature*, **11** (4), 325–355.

SIBLEY, F. (1968) 'Objectivity and aesthetics', *Proceedings of the Aristotelian Society*, Supp. **42**, 31–54.

SIMPSON, P. (1988) 'Access through application', *Parlance*, **1** (2), 3–28.

SIMPSON, P. (1993) *Language, Ideology and Point of View*, Routledge.

SIMPSON, P. (1997) *Language through Literature: an introduction*, Routledge.

SIMPSON, P. (2003) *Stylistics: a resource book for students*, Routledge.

SIMPSON, P. (2004) *On the Discourse of Satire: towards a stylistic model of satirical humour*, Amsterdam and Philadelphia, John Benjamins.

SINCLAIR, J. MCH. (1972) 'Lines about lines', in KACHRU, B.B. and STAHLKE, H.F. (1972), 251–261.

SINCLAIR, J. MCH. (1975) 'The linguistic basis of style', in RINGBOM, H. *et al.*, eds (1975), 75–89.

SINCLAIR, J. MCH. and COULTHARD, M. (1975) *Towards an Analysis of Discourse*, Oxford University Press.

SINCLAIR, J. (2004) *Trust the Text: language, corpus and discourse*, Routledge.

SPERBER, D. and WILSON, D. (1986) *Relevance: communication and cognition*, Oxford, Blackwell.

SPITZER, L. (1948) *Linguistics and Literary History*, Princeton, NJ, Princeton University Press.

STANZEL, F. (1984) *A Theory of Narrative*, trans. C. Goedsche, Cambridge, Cambridge University Press.

STOCKWELL, P. (2000) *The Poetics of Science Fiction*, Longman.

STOCKWELL, P. (2002) *Cognitive Poetics*, Routledge.

STUBBS, M. (2005) 'Conrad in the computer: examples of quantitative stylistic methods', *Language and Literature*, **14** (1), 5–24.

TAAVITSAINEN, I. (1999) 'Personality and styles of affect in *The Canterbury Tales*', in LESTER, G., ed. (1999) *Chaucer in Perspective: Middle English essays in honour of Norman Blake*, Sheffield, Sheffield Academic Press, 218–234.

THOMAS, J.A. and SHORT, M. (1996) *Using Corpora for Language Research*, Longman.

THOMPSON, G. (1996) 'Voices in the text: discourse perspectives on language reports', *Applied Linguistics* **17** (4), 501–530.

THORNE, J.P. (1965) 'Stylistics and generative grammars', *Journal of Linguistics*, **1**, 49–59.

TODOROV, T. (1969) *Grammaire du Décaméron*, The Hague, Mouton.

TOOLAN, M. (1990) *The Stylistics of Fiction*, Routledge.

TOOLAN, M. (1992) *Language, Text and Context: essays in stylistics*, Routledge.

TOOLAN, M. (1996 [1990]) 'Stylistics and its discontents: getting off the Fish hook', in WEBER, J.-J. (1996), 117–135.

TOOLAN, M. (1997) *Language in Literature: an introduction to stylistics*, Arnold.

TOOLAN, M. (2001 [1988]) *Narrative: a critical linguistic introduction*, Routledge.

TURNER, M. (1996) *The Literary Mind*, Oxford, Oxford University Press.

TSUR, R. (1992) *Toward a Theory of Cognitive Poetics*, Amsterdam, North Holland Press.

TSUR, R. (2003) *On the Shore of Nothingness: a study in cognitive poetics*, Exeter and Charlottesville, VA, Imprint Academic.

TURNER, M. (1996) *The Literary Mind: the origins of language and thought*, Oxford, Oxford University Press.

ULLMANN, S. (1957) *Style in the French Novel*, Oxford University Press.

ULLMANN, S. (1973) *Meaning and Style*, Oxford, Blackwell.

UNGERER, F. and SCHMID, H-J. (forthcoming [1996]) *An Introduction to Cognitive Linguistics*, 2nd edn, Longman.

USPENSKY, B. (1973) *A Poetics of Composition*, trans. V. Zavarin and S. Wittig, Berkeley, CA, University of California Press.

VAN DIJK, T. (1977) *Text and Context: explorations in the semantics and pragmatics of discourse*, Longman.

Style in Fiction

VAN DIJK, T. (1981) *Studies in the Pragmatics of Discourse*, The Hague, Mouton.

VAN PEER, W. (1986) *Stylistics and Psychology: investigations of foregrounding*, Croom Helm.

VAN PEER, W. (1988) *The Taming of the Text*, Routledge.

VAN PEER, W. and CHATMAN, S., eds (2001) *New Perspectives on Narrative Perspective*, Albany, NY, SUNY Press.

VERDONK, P., ed. (1993) *Twentieth Century Poetry: from text to context*, Routledge.

VERDONK, P. and WEBER, J.-J., eds (1995) *Twentieth Century Prose: from text to context*, Routledge.

WALES, K. (2000 [1989]) *A Dictionary of Stylistics*, 2nd edn, Longman.

WALKER, E. and WALES, R., eds (1976) *New Approaches to Language Mechanisms*, Amsterdam, North-Holland.

WATT, I. (1960) 'The first paragraph of *The Ambassadors*: an explication', *Essays in Criticism*, **10**, 250–74; reprinted in LOVE, G.A. and PAYNE, M. (1969), 266–283.

WEBER, J-J. (1992) *Critical Analysis of Fiction: essays in discourse stylistics*, Amsterdam, Rodopi.

WEBER, J-J., ed. (1996) *The Stylistics Reader: from Roman Jakobson to the present*, Arnold.

WEINSHEIMER, J. (1979) 'Theory of character: Emma', *Poetics Today*, **1**, 185–211.

WERTH, P. (1999) *Text Worlds: representing conceptual space in discourse*, Longman.

WHORF, B.L. (1956) *Language, Thought and Reality*, ed. CARROLL, J.B., New York, MIT Press.

WIDDOWSON, H.G. (1975) *Stylistics and the Teaching of Literature*, Longman.

WIDDOWSON, H.G. (1995a) *Practical Stylistics*, Oxford, Oxford University Press.

WIDDOWSON, H.G. (1995b) 'Discourse analysis: a critical view', *Language and Literature*, **4** (3), 157–172.

WIDDOWSON, H.G. (1996) 'Reply to Fairclough: discourse and interpretation: conjectures and refutations', *Language and Literature*, **5** (3), 57–69.

WIDDOWSON, H.G. (2000) 'On the limitations of linguistics applied', *Applied Linguistics*, **21** (1), 3–25.

WIMSATT, W.K. (1941) *The Prose Style of Samuel Johnson*, Yale Studies in English, 94, New Haven and London, Yale University Press.

WODAK, R. and MEYER, M. (2001) *Methods of Critical Discourse Analysis*, Sage.

WOLD, A.H. (1978) *Decoding Oral Language*, Academic Press.

YNGVE, V. (1961) 'The depth hypothesis' in *Structure of Language and its Mathematical Aspects, Proceedings of Symposia in Applied Mathematics*, **12**, 130–138.

YORK, R.A. (1986) *The Poem as Utterance*, Methuen.

ZWAAN, R. (1993) *Aspects of Literary Comprehension*, Amsterdam, Benjamins.

Index of works discussed

General index

action theory, 291, 292, 293, 295, 296
addressee, 185, 206–9, 211–12, 214–15, 217, 222, 231, 300
addresser, 185–6, 206–7, 213, 215, 218, 222, 231, 300
aesthetic terms, 38
alliteration, 14–15, 23, 71, 104, 220
Amis, Kingsley, *Lucky Jim*, 133
anaphora, 47, 51, 63, 84
anticipatory constituent, 181–5
anticipatory structures, 62, 65, 81
assonance, 71–2, 220
Austen, Jane, 38, 42–3, 226, 253, 266
  Emma, 44, 219–20, 222–3, 248
  Mansfield Park, 134–5, 208, 253
  Persuasion, 261–2, 268, 272
  Pride and Prejudice, 233–6, 243, 253
  Sense and Sensibility, 219–20
Austin, J.L., 233

Bailey, R.W., 32n
Bally, C., 15
Banfield, A., 281n
Barthes, R., 15, 139, 149n, 290, 291
Barzun, J., 205n
Bateson, F.W., 287
Beckett, Samuel, *Watt*, 202–4
Bennett, Arnold, *Clayhanger*, 140–1, 273
blending theory, 286, 291, 295
Bloch, B., 34–6
Bolinger, D., 33n, 188
Booth, W.C., 149n, 208–9, 222, 272, 300
Brémond, Claude, 317–22
Bronte, Charlotte, 135
  Jane Eyre, 212–13

Bronte, Emily, *Wuthering Heights*, 135, 210–11, 238
Brown University Corpus, 57n, 94n
Bunyan, John, *The Pilgrim's Progress*, 201
Burgess, Anthony, 22–4, 28
  A Clockwork Orange, 213
Butler, Samuel, *The Way of All Flesh*, 107–8, 223

Camus, Albert, *The Outsider*, 15
Cassirer, Ernst, 126
category, 52–3, 55, 60–6, 88
  lexical, 61–2
  grammatical, 62–3
Chafe, W., 117n
character, characterisation, 289, 296–8
Chatman, S., 32n, 58n, 167n
chi–square test, 94n
Chomsky, N., 33n, 39
Christie, Agatha, *Destination Unknown*, 237–8
Clark, H.H., and Clark, E.V., 117n, 205n
climax, principle of, 179–81, 205n
Cluysenaar, A., 190
cognitive metaphor theory, 285
cognitive turn, 286, 306
cognitive stylistics, 286, 291, 298
cognitive linguistics, 291
  approaches, 305–6, 342
cohesion, 64, 66, 72, 76, 85–6, 196–204, 205n
collocation, 36, 76, 84, 151–2, 224, 285, 286, 334
conceptualization, 29–30

Style in Fiction